4/18/13
$39.95

Renegades, Rebels and Rogues Under the Tsars

PETER JULICHER

McFarland & Company, Inc., Publishers
Jefferson, North Carolina, and London

LIBRARY OF CONGRESS CATALOGUING-IN-PUBLICATION DATA

Julicher, Peter, 1946–
    Renegades, rebels and rogues under the tsars / Peter Julicher.
    p.   cm.
    Includes bibliographical references and index.

    ISBN-13: 978-0-7864-1612-7
    (softcover : 50# alkaline paper) ∞

    1. Russia — Politics and government.   2. Political rights —
Russia.   I. Title.
DK61.J85   2003
947'.009'9 — dc21   2003012494

British Library cataloguing data are available

On the cover: Detail from *Morning of the Streltsy Execution,* Vasily Surikov,
oil on canvas 86" × 149", *1881*

Manufactured in the United States of America

McFarland & Company, Inc., Publishers
  Box 611, Jefferson, North Carolina 28640
  www.mcfarlandpub.com

ACKNOWLEDGMENTS

Research for this book began in the late 1980s when I was developing an elective course in Russian and Soviet Studies at Cranbrook Kingswood School in Bloomfield Hills, Michigan. Although interest for this kind of course was high, there was a dearth of suitable reading material for those with little or no background in Russian history. Moreover, I was hoping to identify a theme that would allow me to explain the country's difficulty in developing the democratic traditions necessary for a modern state. To this end, I decided to write a narrative about how Russians, individually and collectively, resisted and eventually destroyed autocratic rule under the tsars.

This project would not have gotten off the ground had it not been for the guidance and support of my former teacher and mentor at Temple University, Professor Emeritus Roderick E. McGrew. Years after I had left the university, his encouragement and guidance eventually led to our collaboration on this book, which he was kind enough to proofread and critique. It was also a pleasant surprise to learn that other scholars working at the university level would be so generous with their help and advice. Among these were Valerie Kivelson at the University of Michigan, who examined my work and offered many useful suggestions, Chester Dunning at Texas A&M, who alerted me to valuable new sources, and David Macey at Middlebury College, who helped me find critical information when I thought I had searched everywhere.

I also benefited from the generous support of the Cranbrook Kingswood School administration and a number of colleagues whose creativity and dedication to service has truly created an extraordinary learning atmosphere at our school. Foremost among these was James Woodruff, whose erudition and academic example both inspired and sustained me. His willingness to proofread the manuscript involved a lot of work with no reward except the eternal gratitude and friendship of the author. Also helping to proofread at times were Eric Linder, Herb Snitz, Bob Cowie, and Maria Caswell. Finally, I must thank Rich Lamb for introducing me to computers and Greg Miller for helping me to make use of the latest technology to complete this project.

It has been my great fortune to travel to the Soviet Union and Russia many times since 1977 to meet talented and generous people who helped me in ways both practical and academic. One of these was my late brother-in-law, Rudolf Duganov, who introduced me to the intricacies of the Lenin Library in Moscow and whose insights and sense of humor about Russian literature and history enriched me greatly. Another indispensable resource has been a multi-talented artist, craftsman and friend, Nikolai Ejkin, who shared his incredible knowledge of Moscow as we raced around the city, usually late at night, in his Soviet-era army jeep. I also enjoyed the support of an alert and resourceful sister-in law, Natalya Sheftelyevich, who helped me identify and locate many useful illustrations. Finally, I must thank my dear wife, Olga, above all for her patience but also for her encouragement and many useful suggestions. Her uncanny intuition about things Soviet and Russian did much to promote the success of this endeavor.

CONTENTS

A NOTE ABOUT RUSSIAN NAMES, WORDS, AND DATES

All Russians have a first name and a patronymic or middle name, which is derived from their father's first name. However, the feminine forms of names usually end in the letter "a." Thus, the tsar Boris Feodorovich Godunov's son was called Feodor Borisovich Godunov and his daughter was called Xenia Borisovna Godunova. The transliteration of these names has many variations, but I have tried to adhere to a system which I believe will be easiest for the reader. In addition, I have anglicized the first names of all the men and women who actually ruled. Thus, Tsar Mikhail becomes Michael, Alexei become Alexis, Piotr becomes Peter, and so on. Russian words used in the narrative can also be a problem for the reader; those that I believe are not familiar to the reader I have italicized and defined. However, the following Russian titles will not be italicized: tsar (male ruler), tsaritsa (female ruler or wife of the tsar), tsarevich (heir to the throne), and tsarevna (daughter of the tsar). In some cases, I have rendered the plural of these words in Russian, such as the word *oprichnik* (a member of Ivan the Terrible's elite special police), which in the plural becomes *oprichniki*. However, in most cases I have anglicized the plural, such as in the word Bol'shevik (a member of the majority faction of the Social Democratic Labor Party) which in the plural becomes Bol'sheviks. Finally, the use of the apostrophe in many Russian words shall be to indicate the presence of the Russian 'soft sign,' or *miaki znak*, for which there is no exact equivalent in English. Its function is to soften the pronunciation of the preceding consonant.

Another source of confusion that requires explanation is the calendar. Until the time of Peter the Great, the Russians had always counted time from the beginning of the world. Thus, the year 1700 in western Europe was the year 7,208 for people living in old Muscovy. However, in that year, Tsar Peter decreed that his subjects adopt the Julian calendar even though it was eleven days behind the more accurate Gregorian calendar. By the 20th century, dates in Russia had fallen thirteen days behind when the Bol'sheviks came to power in 1918 and imposed the Gregorian calendar. To avoid confusion, I have cited dates according to both the Julian and Gregorian calendars throughout most of the book. Thus, the date for the Bol'shevik Revolution will appear as October 25 (November 7), 1917.

European Russia (courtesy of Professor Chester Dunning, Texas A&M University)

INTRODUCTION

The collapse of the Romanov Dynasty in the spring of 1917 was an ominous event for the allied armies fighting the Central Powers in World War I. For two and one-half years, the Russians had waged war on the eastern front, mostly against Germany and Austria, and suffered appallingly in the process. Still, their courage and endurance had sufficiently occupied the enemy to prevent a German victory in the west. But with the abdication of Tsar Nicholas II on March 15, the Russian army seemed on the verge of disintegration. A provisional government was hastily formed, but its authority was challenged by the creation of the more radical Soviet of Workers' and Soldiers' Deputies. These bodies occupied separate wings of the Tauride Palace in Petrograd (renamed from St. Petersburg at the beginning of the war), and both claimed to rule in the name of the people. The provisional government, mostly made up of mostly liberal members of the now defunct State *Duma*, called for elections to a constituent assembly and victory over the Central Powers. The Soviet, dominated by the Menshevik or minority faction of the Marxist Social Democratic Party, demanded an end to the war and a thorough reorganization of the economic and social order.

The chaos engendered by war and revolution intensified with the return of Vladimir Lenin to Petrograd after years of self-imposed exile. As the leader of the Bolshevik or majority faction of the Social Democrats, he had been surprised by the tsar's overthrow but was helped to return by the Germans, who rightly calculated that he would work to end the war. But Lenin had other plans as well, seeking to promote a socialist revolution in Russia that would ultimately engulf the entire world. To this end, he called for "peace, bread and land," and "all power to the Soviets," which

1

the Bolsheviks sought to dominate. At first, events worked in his favor. In June, a Russian offensive in the west failed miserably, prompting troops to desert by the thousands. This was followed by Bolshevik-instigated riots in July by soldiers, sailors, and workers who plundered the capital and terrified the population. The Provisional Government suppressed the insurgents and arrested those responsible. Lenin, who feared that the uprising might have been premature, was forced to flee to Finland. The following month, however, the commander of all Russian forces, General Lavr Kornilov, disgusted by the general lawlessness and confusion in Petrograd, ordered his troops to the capital to establish a military dictatorship. He thought he had the support of the Provisional Government's new prime minister, Alexander Kerensky, but the latter ordered his arrest.

This episode greatly strengthened the Bolsheviks as soldiers and workers in the capital flocked to their banner. Thus, by early fall, Lenin, who was still in Finland, began to urge his comrades to overthrow the Provisional Government. Many were hesitant, but Lenin's will finally prevailed. On the evening of November 6, the Winter Palace was surrounded by armed Bolsheviks, who occupied government offices, telegraphs, railway stations, and city bridges. There was little resistance, and the government's ministers surrendered the following evening; only Kerensky escaped. In the days that followed, the Bolsheviks easily succeeded in imposing their authority on other parts of the country. Only in Moscow was there serious resistance, but this was suppressed within a week.

Lenin immediately took steps to increase the Bolsheviks' popular support. He called for an end to the war and the nationalization of land, with the understanding that the peasants were to keep what they held. He also allowed the previously planned elections to the Constituent Assembly to proceed, although he was dismayed when the Bolsheviks won only twenty-four percent of the seats. When the new body convened in January, Lenin dispersed it by force. By now, he had established the Soviet (or Council) of People's Commissars and had begun the task of constructing the new socialist order. Among the consequences of this new order were the outlawing of private ownership of the means of production, the expropriation of all private bank accounts, enforced separation of church and state, renunciation of foreign debts, and the establishment of the *Cheka* or secret police. All this was crowned by a policy of official hostility toward the West that was to last more than seven decades, interrupted only by the popular front against fascism in the 1930s and the second world war.

Nearly forgotten during this time were the members of the imperial family: the ex-tsar Nicholas II, his wife Alexandra, and their five children. Initially they had been placed under house arrest at Tsarskoe Selo, their residence outside Petrograd, and many moderates had hoped that they could be safely sent into exile, possibly to England. But the Petrograd Soviet was adamantly opposed to their leaving, and many wanted to try the tsar for crimes against the people. That summer, the atmosphere in the capital became so hostile that it was decided to move them to the town of Tobolsk in western Siberia. This afforded the family a measure of tranquillity for a while, but the overthrow of the Provisional Government in November brought renewed demands that Nicholas stand trial. To this end, the prisoners were moved closer to Moscow to the city of Yekaterinberg, just east of the Ural Mountains, in the spring of 1918. They resided in the former governor's mansion while they waited for their fate to be decided.

By now, however, the country was mired in a civil war pitting the Bolshevik Red Army against the White Army, which sought to overthrow the new socialist regime. That summer, when the Whites moved toward Yekaterinberg to rescue the imperial family, a decision was made to execute Nicholas and his family. In the early morning hours of July 17, the family and its four servants were awakened, ordered to dress, and taken to the basement. They were told that cars would soon arrive to take them to a safer location. Moments later, however, they were executed by a firing squad. Their remains were mutilated, burned and buried, several miles away in a location that was to remain secret for nearly sixty years.

Nicholas was not the first tsar to die at the hands of his subjects. Over the previous 370 years, three others had suffered the same fate. Indeed, even those who had managed to die peacefully had frequently been harassed and threatened during their reigns by all kinds of troublemakers, whose goals and motivations were often quite varied. Some of these individuals were opposed to aspects of the social order or to the introduction of foreign influences. Others were driven by the prospect of personal gain or religious fanaticism. In the case of Nicholas' executioners, the motive was more fundamental: his enemies (and even many of his supporters) opposed the absolute nature of his rule and his refusal to accept any limitations on his power. But Russia's last tsar fervently believed, as had his predecessors, that he was divinely ordained by God to rule. Thus, any opposition to his will was treason and was to be savagely suppressed.

To understand how this policy of absolutism and suppression came to be, one must understand some of the more important episodes and themes that have defined Russian history. In the tenth century, there had been an important Slavic princedom centered in the city of Kiev in what is now Ukraine. This state, Kiev Rus, which flourished for about 150 years, began to decline in the 12th century and was eventually plundered and destroyed by the Mongols in the year 1240. Subsequently, the khans of the Golden Horde (as the northwestern part of the huge Mongol empire came to be known) dominated Kiev Rus for the next 240 years. They imposed a stiff annual tribute on the many individual princedoms and isolated them from the progressive winds of the Renaissance, but the Russians found unity in their Orthodox faith and in the growing power of the state of Muscovy, on which the Mongols relied to collect and deliver their tribute. By the end of the fifteenth century, the Muscovite Grand Prince was strong enough to defy the Mongols and eventually expel them from the land.

As the Muscovite state began to reestablish systematic contact with Europe during the reign of Grand Prince Ivan III (1440-1505), she became painfully conscious of her own military and cultural inferiority. Consequently, many Muscovites were inclined to welcome western traders and travelers, hoping to learn from them. But the more conservative elements, and the Church in particular, resisted these contacts, fearful that foreign ideas would mar the spiritual purity of the country's Byzantine cultural and religious heritage. Thus, Russian Orthodoxy, which had been a civilizing force in Kiev Rus and during the period of the Mongol domination, now became a serious impediment to progress. Its obsession with ritual and tradition encouraged a mentality of suspicion and hostility to virtually all innovation and change.

In some instances, the tsars felt obliged to make use of their autocratic prerogatives to force changes they deemed necessary to enhance the power and security of the state. However, their desire to achieve progress on their own terms led to serious contradictions. For example, to remedy Russia's military vulnerability, they encouraged the growth of serfdom so that its military servitors could avail themselves of a source of free labor on their estates, but the persistence of serfdom and the social order that supported it impeded the growth of an entrepreneurial middle class. It was precisely this middle class in the West that was to be so important to economic growth, technological progress, and the gradual development of democratic government and a civil society. The tsars may well have suspected they could not achieve westernization without encouraging some movement toward democracy.

Indeed, this tendency that began with the early Russian tsars to impose change from above created deep and lasting antagonisms. Protest and resistance was often so violent and extreme that the tsars were provoked to react savagely. In time, this developed into an almost conditioned reflex which future rulers, including those in the communist period, would not be able to overcome. The result was the creation of a virtual breeding ground for determined renegades and rebels, as well as a few clever rogues, who, time and time again, rose to challenge and even deny the authority of the sovereign by threatening his tsardom (and sometimes his person), and, in many instances, succeeded in usurping his power and thwarting his initiatives.

In America and other western countries, with the evolution of democratic procedures, principled dissidents could hope to have a positive impact on the system without resorting to destructive or criminal behavior. For example, the men and women who became abolitionists, muckrakers, feminists, civil rights activists, environmentalists, etc., all suffered harassment and vilification by the government whose policies they sought to change. Yet these dissident groups all succeeded in making their message heard and in bringing about some positive change. Also, many of those who led these groups achieved a fair amount of official respectability in the process.

In Russian history, such cases are non-existent. Individuals who criticized or challenged the system were invariably treated like enemies as their activities and warnings were forcibly suppressed. In Russia, men and women trying to change government policy could not hope to do so by offering loyal opposition in accordance with the dictates of their conscience. Indeed, as most were well aware, their only hope was to overthrow the system. Ironically, many of those who tried to do so were aided by the government itself, which adopted measures that were so irrational and self-defeating that they only encouraged more opposition. To demonstrate this paradox, I have described the activities of the most important dissidents and agitators, from the reign of the first crowned tsar, Ivan the Terrible, to the fall of the Romanov dynasty in 1917 under Nicholas II. I believe that this survey is important because it describes themes and patterns of dissent and reaction that continued throughout the communist period.

As the title of the book suggests, some of these fascinating individuals were serious activists intent on achieving political and economic change. Others were opportunistic scoundrels and adventurers mainly interested in their own selfish ends. Taken together, their stories enable us to explore a theme in Russian history that largely explains why a civil society did not begin to take root in that country until the end of the twentieth century. Thus, I have gone beyond the personal idiosyncrasies of individual activists to explore the causes that provoked them and the consequences they engendered. In particular, I demonstrate that the tsars, time and time again, were goaded into reacting and overreacting in ways that compounded their own problems and those of Russia and that many of these problems endured into the communist era.

1. RENEGADE PRINCE

Late at night on the last day of April in 1564, Andrei Mikhailovich Kurbsky, Prince of Smolensk and Yarolslavl', committed treason. He abandoned his post as military governor of the Lithuanian town of Dorpat,[1] and, with twelve other noblemen of his court, rode southwestward to the town of Wolmar. There he was welcomed by three other Russian defectors: Artemy, abbot of the Trinity Monastery,[2] and two former artillery captains, Timofey Teterin and Mark Sarykhozin. These men had also deserted their sovereign, Tsar Ivan IV of Muscovy,[3] better known to history as Ivan the Terrible, and had entered the service of Sigismund II Augustus, King of Poland and Grand Prince of Lithuania. Like them, Kurbsky would serve the Polish king, who was struggling to prevent Russian Muscovite armies from gaining territory in the Baltic area of Livonia. Ultimately, however, the prince probably hoped to do much more. Indeed, it is likely that his real goal was to remove Ivan as tsar and either kill him or force him into exile.

That such a high ranking prince would take up arms against his own country was, to most Orthodox Russians, a serious crime and a grave affront to their Church. For the war in Livonia was, in large part, also a war of religion. Tsar Ivan, having initiated the struggle, was not merely an invader but a crusading prince, defending the Eastern Orthodox faith against the encroachments of the infidel Roman Catholics of Poland and Lithuania. Kurbsky fully shared the tsar's antipathy for the Catholics, but he had become alarmed at Ivan's reckless disregard for the rights of the Muscovite nobility of which Kurbsky himself was a prominent member. In recent years, the tsar had began to act against many of Muscovy's leading nobles, including his own *boyars*.[4] These were proud landed aristocrats who had been appointed to this rank by the tsar himself for extraordinary service. By tradition, the *boyars* were to assist the sovereign in ruling the Muscovite state, but Ivan sought to change all this. Not only did he begin to curtail their rights and ignore their counsel, but he imprisoned or executed many of them on questionable charges. He also enriched his own coffers by confiscating their estates and possessions while expanding his own power as tsar and autocrat far beyond what precedent had ever allowed.

Historians usually trace the origin of Ivan's hostility to the abuse he suffered during his childhood. When his father, Grand Prince Vasily Ivanovich, died in 1533, a regency was established by Ivan's mother to run the country. Her mysterious death five years later, possibly by poison, left the eight-year-old Ivan at the mercy of two competing *boyar* families, the Shuiskys and the Belskys. In their determination to keep him weak and subservient, they isolated and abused him. They also murdered each other, raided the treasury and purged anyone else who threatened their interests. One such victim was Metropolitan Iosef (Joseph), who burst into Ivan's bedroom in the dead of night with the Shuiskys in hot pursuit. The prelate had hoped to find refuge with the young grand prince, but was caught, beaten, and incarcerated in a monastery. Such episodes left their mark on the boy, who then became subject to bouts of hysteria and paranoia for the rest of his life. It was also during this early period that Ivan developed a fondness for sadistic amusements. These included throwing small animals from high Kremlin towers to watch them splatter on the ground below and slashing ordinary Muscovites with his whip as he rode on horseback through the streets.

Born in 1528, Prince Kurbsky was two years older than the tsar and may have been acquainted with him as an adolescent. In any case, the two eventually became friends, and, not long after Ivan's elevation to the rank of tsar[5] in January of 1547, the prince began to play an increasingly prominent role in public affairs. Possibly, he was among those who had been called upon for support during the horrible fire of Moscow that broke out on June 21 of that year. With much of the city destroyed, the young tsar and his relatives were forced to flee the Kremlin for Vorobevo, a small village in the Sparrow Hills overlooking the Moscow River. Soon a rumor was circulated that the fire was started by Ivan's maternal grandmother, Anna Glinskaya, who was alleged to have employed witchcraft to that end. To refute these charges, Ivan's uncle, Yuri Glinsky, returned to the Kremlin only to be beaten to death by an angry crowd. Three days later, another mob marched out to the Sparrow Hills to find more Glinskys and threatened the tsar to force him to reveal their whereabouts. Ivan held firm and

Ivan the Terrible by Victor M. Vasnetsov (1848–1926). Tretiakovsky Gallery. Tsar Ivan IV often brooded about the disloyalty of his subjects and the need to sweep treason from the land. L.P. Bushchik, *Illustrirovanaya Istoriya SSSR*, XVvv, Proveshcheniye, 1970.

had some of the ringleaders arrested. Still, he was deeply shaken by the incident.

In the aftermath of the tragedy, Ivan fell under the influence of a priest from Novgorod named Sylvester, who declared that the blaze was punishment for the young tsar's sins. The indictment so tormented Ivan that he resolved to take dramatic steps to rule in accordance with divine will. To this end, he ignored the *boyar duma,* whose members he didn't trust, and formed a new group of advisers called the chosen council. Its members included Sylvester, a minor nobleman named Alexei Adashev, and the metropolitan of Moscow, Makari. This cabinet soon embarked on a number of important reforms, including the creation of the *Zemsky Sobor,* or Assembly of the Land, to which Ivan appointed members of the nobility, gentry, clergy, and merchants. At first, the sole responsibility was to approve the tsar's initiatives and to offer respectful advice. Later, it became involved in Russian politics and actually elected two tsars. In any case, Ivan took this body very seriously from the start. At its opening session in the throne room of the Palace of Facets on February 27, 1549, he apologized for the mistakes of his youth, urged the boyars to mend their ways, and promised to rule according to God's will.

Other reforms enacted during Ivan's so called "good period" rule included the summoning of three Church councils during which a number of local Russian saints were canonized and stern measures were taken to raise the moral and educational level of the clergy. A new law code was promulgated to reinforce central authority and to promote the interests of the service gentry. Administrative departments, or *prikazy,* were introduced for specific functions of state such as foreign affairs, justice, taxation, etc., and the long practiced system of local government known as *kormlenie* was abolished, thus ending the exploitation of provincial areas by appointed administrators, or *namestniki,* who had been allowed to pocket taxes collected in excess of what the central government demanded. (These were replaced by military governors, or *voevodas,* and by elected magistrates and tax collectors.) Finally, the military was reorganized and invigorated. Some three thousand soldiers called *strel'tsy,* so named because they used muskets, were assigned to serve as the tsar's personal bodyguards. Ivan and his advisers also improved and expanded the artillery and introduced the first engineering troops.

Kurbsky's role in all these changes is not precisely known. To be sure, his position at court as *stol'nik,* or groom-in-waiting, put him near the center of power, but the record does not include him as having been an active participant in these matters. His most important service to the tsar was as a military commander. In 1549, he was assigned to lead a force to capture the Tatar khanate of Kazan on the Volga River. The Tatars[6] had long tormented the rulers of Muscovite Russia by raiding and plundering settlements and selling their captives into slavery. Ivan resolved to end these incursions and, by all accounts, received valuable aid from Prince Kurbsky, who was one of the leaders in the final storming of the city in October, 1552. The prince was gravely wounded in this endeavor but recovered sufficiently to lead a punitive expedition against the Tatars the following year.

An even more important turning point in Kurbsky's career came in 1553, just months after the great victory at Kazan. Ivan had fallen deathly ill and was convinced he would soon die. Hoping to ensure a smooth transfer of power, he summoned the leading boyars and noblemen to his bedside to swear allegiance to his infant son, Dmitri.[7] To his utter consternation, many refused to do so. A few, in fact, openly expressed the desire that the crown be offered to Prince Vladimir of Staritsa, the tsar's cousin. Kurbsky, however, remained steadfast and swore to support the child. This seemed to prompt others to do the same. Eventually, the tsar recovered, and the question became moot, but Ivan never forgot what happened. In the future, he would show fierce resentment to those boyars who had resisted him and would rely on the prince more and more.

In the summer of 1556, Ivan elevated Andrei Kurbsky to the rank of *boyar* and is believed to have also offered him a seat on the prestigious chosen council.[8] Thus, the prince had now risen as high as he could ever hope to as a servant of the tsar. With the threat of an invasion, however, by the Crimean Tatars growing in the south, he was soon sent thither to check their advance. His successes in the numerous border clashes that followed won him more fame but did not eliminate the Tatars as a potent enemy. Kurbsky therefore allied himself with other influential advisers in the chosen council, including Sylvester and a minor nobleman named Alexei Adashev, and urged the tsar to send an army to the Crimea to destroy the khanate once and for all. Ivan, however, for quite some time had been developing other plans, and in January 1558, ordered an all-out attack in Livonia.[9]

To be sure, the tsar's quest to win territory in what is now Lithuania, Latvia, and Estonia was not without good reason. Having only recently opened commercial relations with England, there was a clear need to acquire a seaport on the Baltic Sea in order to exploit this initiative to the fullest. Too, Livonia was much closer to Moscow than the Crimea, which made military operations in this area from a logistical standpoint much more feasible. Of course, such a campaign would also entail risks as some of his advisers warned. For although the armies of the Livonian Order were not formidable, there was the distinct possibility that other powers like Poland or Sweden would intervene to prevent Russia's westward expansion. But the tsar, eager to test the efficacy of his military reforms undertaken at the beginning of his reign, was not to be dissuaded.[10]

The Russian invasion of Livonia initially went very well. With Prince Kurbsky in an important command, town after town fell to Ivan's forces, and by the end of the year, the Russian army was poised to attack Riga. The Livonians, frantic to gain time and find allies, applied to King Christian III of Denmark, who, in May of 1559, succeeded in negotiating a six-month truce with the tsar. In retrospect, it seems amazing that Ivan agreed to stop fighting just when so much progress was being made, but it is likely that some of his advisers convinced him that he could prevail both in the north and in the south. In any case, the tsar sent an army to the Crimea during the armistice under the command of Adashev's brother, Daniel. This campaign, however, soon bogged down and ultimately achieved nothing. In the meantime, the Livonians concluded a defensive treaty with Poland and, in October 1559, went on the offensive against the Russian forces in the Baltic.

This disturbing turn of events stunned and angered the tsar, who had been on a pilgrimage with his wife and two sons at the town of Mozhaisk, about one hundred miles to the west of Moscow. His advisors in the Kremlin, in near panic, urged him to return immediately, but the onset of the rainy season, coupled with Anastasia's poor health, made the going very slow. Thus, the trip, short as it was, took much longer than expected, and it was only with the greatest of difficulty that the tsar and his entourage reached the capital in early December. By that time, however, the tsaritsa had fallen seriously ill. Her condition worsened steadily over the following months, and she died in August of 1560.

Anastasia's death seems to have genuinely affected the tsar and seems to have been a major turning point in his reign. Suspecting that she had been poisoned, he began to look for scapegoats and soon focused on Sylvester and Adashev. Neither could be in Moscow to respond to the charges Ivan leveled against them. Sylvester had retired to a monastery far to the north in the Beloozero[11] region, and Adashev had been banished to a military unit in Livonia. Thus the two were tried in absentia, declared guilty, and duly punished. Sylvester was deported farther north to the Solovetsky Monastery on the White Sea, and Adashev was imprisoned in the town of Dorpat where he died in December of 1560. By some accounts, he was poisoned on orders from the tsar.

By coincidence, Kurbsky, in the spring of 1560, had also been sent to Dorpat to lead another campaign against the Livonian Order. Fortunately for him, things went relatively well, and he continued to enjoy Ivan's good favor. Still, he was dismayed by the tsar's treatment of Sylvester and Adashev and his persecution of their friends and relatives. In fact, the prince's own association with the two former advisers put him in some danger, which was made immeasurably more acute when he lost a major battle at Nevel in August of 1562. Ivan was particularly incensed by the fact that Kurbsky had commanded a much larger force than the one opposing him. Still, the prince was not immediately punished. The tsar, in his own inscrutable way, would sometimes delay his reaction even when severely provoked. Indeed, Kurbsky was allowed to gain partial redemption six months later by participating in the victory at Polotsk in what is now Belarus on the Western Dvina River. But not long after that, the tsar and his general fell into an angry quarrel near the town of Veliki Luki, about 250 miles west of Moscow, which resulted in the latter being sent again to Dorpat to assume another, less prestigious military assignment. To the prince, mindful of Adashev's fate, this demotion had a distinctly sinister quality, and he soon began to fear for his life. This led to secret negotiations with the King of Poland who eventually offered him asylum.

Kurbsky's drastic step was in all probability not done solely to avoid punishment or execution. There were larger issues at stake, such as the steady erosion of the rights and privileges of the nobility, which had actually begun during the 15th century during the reign of the tsar's grandfather, Grand Prince Ivan III (the Great). It was he who diminished the status of his nobles, first by denying them the right to serve other princes, and then by altering the traditional system of land tenure. Henceforth, land grants were made mainly to those who performed service to the state. Nobles who displeased the sovereign might have their estates confiscated. The new system was driven in large part by military necessity, but whereas Ivan the Great and his son and successor, Grand Prince Vasily III, had generally been judicious in its application, Ivan the Terrible had become increasingly arbitrary and unpredictable.

Thus, not long after his arrival in Lithuania, Kurbsky, as most historians assert, began a correspondence with the tsar that is remarkable for its disrespect, anger, and acrimony. The first letter was written in Russian Church Slavonic and dated May of 1564. It fiercely sets the tone as the prince justifies his defection and denounces Ivan for ignoring his advisers, persecuting the innocent and violating the traditional rights of the boyars: "And why have you conceived against your well-wishers and against those who lay down their lives for you unheard-of torments and persecutions and death, falsely accusing the Orthodox of treachery and magic and other abuses, and endeavoring with zeal to turn light into darkness and to call sweet bitter?"[12] Ivan's answer, allegedly written two months later, is sixteen times as long as Kurbsky's original and totals 28,000 words. In it, he fairly explodes with sarcasm and indignation, berating the prince for his treason and cowardice, and insisting that, as tsar, he ruled by God's will alone: "If you are truly just and pious, why do you not permit your-self to accept suffering from me, your froward master, and so to inherit the crown of life?"[13] Ivan was also able to employ personal insult with dev-astating effect: "But what is it, you dog, that you write and for what do you grieve having committed such evil? What will your council, stinking worse than dung, resemble?"[14]

Over the next fifteen years, Kurbsky is supposed to have written four more times and Ivan once. Although the subsequent letters essentially repeat the same charges and accusations, they seem to add important details about this period and the reign of Ivan the Terrible. However, in 1971, Professor Edward Keenan of Harvard University pronounced the entire correspondence a forgery, asserting that the letters and other works attrib-uted to the prince[15] were actually composed by others after his death. There is at least some reason to suspect that this may indeed have been the case. For one, according to court records compiled during Kurbsky's stay in Lithuania, it seems that, although able to read, the prince could not write.[16] Thus, he could not have corresponded with the tsar or writ-ten anything else of sophistication. Defenders of the authenticity of the correspondence have dismissed this fact as irrelevant, asserting that, in any case, the letters were probably dictated to scribes. However, the ear-liest extant "copy" of the first letter was composed no earlier than the late 1590s, and there is no evidence that an original of this particular letter once existed and was then lost.[17]

At the center of the controversy is the text of Kurbsky's first letter, which is supposed to have been written less than a month after his defec-tion. Some historians allege that it includes certain phrases that may have been copied from later sources. If true, the entire correspondence must be considered a forgery.[18] But this raises the questions: who would want to perpetrate such a fraud, and why? The answers can only be guessed at, but those who deny the authenticity of the correspondence believe that it was carried out by politically sophisticated individuals, mostly in the 17th cen-tury, who wished to remain anonymous as they argued the nature of the tsar's power and the duty of his subjects to submit to his will.[19]

Virtually all of Ivan's biographers, however, have rejected this argu-ment. While they admit that many aspects of the correspondence are puz-zling, they do not accept that it was all an elaborate hoax.[20] In fact, one Russian scholar, Boris Morozov, who has spent much of his academic life studying the manuscripts, argues that most of the textual clues indicate that the letters do indeed belong to the late 16th century.[21] Moreover, he rejects Keenan's hypothesis that 16th century Muscovite society was sharply divided between ecclesiastical and lay spheres that were entirely distinct. He further argues that it was not unusual for men of high-birth to be able to read and write and even to dabble in the composition of music. Thus, he accepts the correspondence as an important resource for understanding the reign of Ivan the Terrible.

Whatever the truth about the origin and significance of the correspondence, it does not detract from Kurbsky's status as an important dissident, whose defection to the King of Poland angered and embarrassed the tsar. Indeed, the record suggests that his treachery did much to stimulate the paranoid fantasies in Ivan that subsequently prompted his strangest and most hideous behavior. By the mid 1560s, the tsar had began to see treason everywhere and believed a mob uprising in Moscow was imminent. In December of 1564, he abandoned the Kremlin while the war in Livonia still raged, taking with him his treasury and personal belongings. Accompanied by a detachment of cavalry in full battle array, he took up residence in the town of Alexandrov,[22] sixty miles northeast of Moscow. He then sent an angry letter to Metropolitan Afanasii denouncing the treasonous activities of the boyars, churchmen and other high officials. He threatened to abdicate unless he be allowed to divide his tsardom into two realms: one to be called the *zemshchina* and the other the *oprichnina*. The former was to be administered by the *boyar duma* in the traditional manner, and the latter was to be ruled absolutely by the tsar himself. Though the territories to be encompassed by the *oprichnina* were substantial and included many of the best lands, Ivan's terms were accepted.

In the *oprichnina*, the tsar gave full vent to his autocratic impulses and established a model for despotism that would haunt Russia for hundreds of years. He organized a new court at Alexandrov along the lines of a monastery with himself as abbot. His followers, mostly low born and chosen mainly for their ruthlessness, became his disciples and monks. The regime they followed was bizarre and sadistic. Prayer and fasting alternated with orgiastic feasting which was then followed by the ritual torture of political prisoners. The latter languished in cells beneath the monastery, having been brought to Alexandrov for the sole purpose of being tormented by Ivan and his henchmen.[23]

At other times these same monks served as *oprichniki*, or members of Ivan's personal bodyguard. They dressed in black and patrolled the country with a broom and a dog's head attached to the saddle. The meaning of these symbols soon became clear to all. The *oprichniki* were to attack

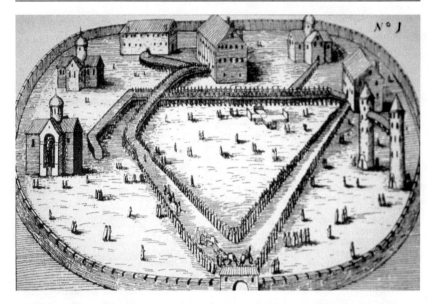

Not long after Prince Kurbsky's defection to Lithuania, Tsar Ivan abandoned the Kremlin and established a new residence at Alexandrov or Alexandrovskaya Sloboda. There he and his select followers engaged in a bizarre routine that alternated between prayer and religious ritual and the torture and murder of Ivan's political enemies. L.P. Bushchik, *Illustrirovanaya Istoriya SSSR, SV–vv.* Moksva, Proveshcheniye, 1970.

treason ruthlessly and sweep it from the land. The savagery that followed the unleashing of these thugs defies description. There were murders and executions by every possible means, from hanging and beheading to impalement and submersion in boiling water. Many of these were staged as public ceremonies in which Ivan would ask the crowd if the culprit really deserved death. The answer was invariably yes. In any case, the tsar is said to have taken great pleasure in devising new ways to exterminate his enemies, and even high-ranking churchmen were not exempt from his abuse.

Such indeed was the fate of a priest named Filipp, who had been Abbot of the Solovetsky Monastery, located on an island in the White Sea. Ivan had at first been impressed by this scholarly man, whose noble birth and privileged status had not prevented him from voluntarily choosing a life of ascetic meditation. In July of 1566, Ivan named him to the post of metropolitan of Moscow, confident that he would concern himself only with spiritual matters. But Filipp possessed qualities the tsar had not foreseen. These included a tenacious determination to act according to conscience and raw courage in the face of physical danger. From the very beginning, not only did Filipp have the temerity to urge Ivan to abolish the *oprichnina*, but he also implored him to rule and behave in a more Christian manner. Ivan was infuriated by the old man's presumption and began to loath and despise him.

But the new metropolitan refused to stifle his indignation to suit the tsar and reprimanded him publicly when he thought it appropriate. On March 22, 1568, during Sunday mass in the Cathedral of the Assumption, Ivan entered the church with a group of his *oprichniki* and demanded to be blessed. Not only did Filipp refuse, but he loudly berated Ivan for his evil ways. A similar scene occurred a few mouths later during a special service at the Novodevichy Monastery[24] two miles south of the Kremlin. There the metropolitan again loudly rebuked the tsar, this time for allowing one of his *oprichniki* to enter the cathedral wearing a skullcap. Ivan seethed at this affront, but still he did not act. Instead, he ordered evidence to be gathered so that Filipp could be found guilty of some crime. Filipp's long-expected punishment came on St. Michael's Day, November 8, 1568. At Ivan's instigation, armed *oprichniki* burst into the cathedral during mass and seized him. Then, as they stripped him of his vestments, Alexei Basmanov, one of the tsar's more unscrupulous favorites, loudly announced to the terrified congregation that the metropolitan had been found guilty of sorcery. The *oprichniki* then roughly led Filipp from the cathedral in chains and eventually banished him to the Monastery of Otroch near the city of Tver.

The tsar, however, who seemed to be both disturbed and intrigued by the former metropolitan's ability to confront and defy him, could not let the matter rest. About a year later, he sent one his most notorious henchmen, Maliuta Skuratov,[25] to Filip's monastery cell to demand his blessing for a punitive expedition he was planning against Novgorod.[26] But Filip staunchly refused and is alleged to have replied: "I give my blessing only to good men undertaking good works. For a long time I have been waiting for death. Let the sovereign's will be accomplished."[27] At that moment the *oprichnik* leaped on the old man and strangled him.

Historians have generally written scathingly about Ivan's excesses and sadism in dealing with challenges to his authority, even as they concede that he lived in a violent age. However, in his attack on Novgorod in January of 1570, the tsar stunned much of Europe as he committed what is probably his most infamous atrocity. Convinced that the city's ruling elite had entered into treasonous negotiations with Lithuania, Ivan ordered the *oprichnina* to attack and pillage the entire population over a period of some six weeks. Contemporary accounts describe the horror inflicted on the weak and the innocent. The tsar then went on to commit another such outrage at Pskov[28] in February, where he arrested local church leaders and confiscated much of the city's wealth. However, this time the population was mostly spared because of the intervention of an ascetic holy man, or Fool in Christ, named Nikola, whom Ivan visited in his monastery cell. The old man, who was frail, emaciated, and dressed in rags, was not much impressed by his august visitor. Having heard of the massacre at Novgorod, he sternly warned the tsar not to harm the innocent in Pskov. Amazingly, Ivan accepted this rebuke and withdrew from the city.

However, appeals to the sovereign's religious sensibilities did not always bring about the desired result. When one of his most trusted servants, Ivan Viskovaty, petitioned the tsar to stop the violence and to remember his responsibility to God, the latter became enraged and resolved to exterminate his domestic enemies once and for all. Accordingly, on July 25, 1570, he arranged for a grand public execution of some 300 of those he suspected of disloyalty. Typically, at the last moment, he pardoned 184 of those who were least guilty in his judgment and focused his wrath on those who remained. What followed was an orgy of violence so gruesome that many contemporaries were unable to watch. Among the first to die was Viskovaty, who was publicly accused of conspiring with the King of Poland, the Sultan of Turkey, and the Khan of the Crimea. When a group of *oprichniki* urged him to beg the tsar for forgiveness, he shouted: "To hell with you and your tyrant!"[29] whereupon he was hacked to death. The next victim was the treasurer Nikita Funikov, whose only crime was that he was a friend of Viskovaty. He was boiled to death in a vat of scalding water. The carnage, which went on for hours, was followed by more executions in the weeks and months to come. Only when the Crimean Tatars attacked and burned Moscow in November of the following year did Ivan realize the extent to which he had rendered the country incapable of defending itself. He then disbanded the *oprichnina* only to order the execution of many of the *oprichniki* for failing to defend Russia.

No doubt Ivan would also have liked to execute Andrei Kurbsky, whose enthusiasm in taking up arms against his former sovereign must have stung deeply, but the prince, though well rewarded by the King of Poland in properties and titles, had sorrows of his own. Perhaps his main source of anguish was the abandonment of his wife and son in 1564 and the knowledge that he had little hope of seeing either ever again. When his Russian wife died in 1569, Kurbsky remarried the following year but found himself trapped in a union that made him miserable and sullied his name. After an acrimonious divorce, he married more successfully in 1579, but by now he was plagued by poor health, debt, and endless litigation. Some of the latter resulted from his divorce, but other suits involved accusations of dishonesty in various business transactions.[30] His reputation was further tarnished by his unsuccessful military campaigns that gave his adopted countrymen little reason to respect him as a commander or value his counsel with regard to Russia. Thus, when Andrei Kurbsky died in 1583, after nearly two decades of self-imposed exile, few mourned his passing.

The tsar survived the renegade prince by about a year, but, to judge from certain 20th century scientific findings, the final period of his reign must have been filled with much physical pain. In 1963, Ivan's tomb in the Cathedral of the Archangel had to be opened and repaired to arrest damage to the crypt caused by seeping groundwater. Soviet authorities used this occasion to perform a forensic examination on the tsar's remains, which revealed not only that he was congenitally deformed, with one clavicle and shoulder blade considerably larger than the other, but that he also suffered from a painful form of arthritis known as *ankylosing spondylitis*. This condition, which leaves growths at the points of insertion of major arm and leg muscles, fused the vertebrae of his spine into a single rod. One may question whether he could have been fully ambulatory during his final years. Moreover, a chemical analysis of his bones indicates that he had been treated with various mercurials which are known to produce bizarre behavioral alterations. In the face of such physical evidence, one wonders how he could possibly have carried out the strenuous administrative and ceremonial functions that as tsar he was called upon to perform.[31]

Interestingly, the facts suggest that much of the time he may not have wanted to. In 1574, Ivan, for reasons unknown, suddenly renounced his throne in favor of a Tatar prince named Simeon Bekbulatovich. Pretending to pay him homage, the tsar left the Kremlin and retired to the Arbat section of Moscow where he lived as an ordinary *boyar*. This charade continued for about a year, when he abruptly returned to the Kremlin, took back his crown, and ordered another invasion of Livonia. In what would be his final military initiative, he scored some stunning victories and nearly won the war. A successful Polish-Lithuanian counteroffensive, however, quickly eliminated all that had been gained, and the tsar had to apply to the pope in order to arrange a cease-fire. The peace treaty that was signed in 1582 actually left the Russians worse off than they had been in 1558.[32]

Ivan's personal life during this period likewise brought him little satisfaction. In the summer of 1580, he married Maria Nagaya, his seventh and last wife. This event was actually celebrated as a double wedding in which his younger, semi-retarded son, Feodor Ivanovich, married Irina

Godunova, the sister of a prominent adviser. Superficially, the tsar seemed to enjoy this occasion, and many hoped it to be an omen for better times to come. Such optimism seemed justified the following year when his new wife gave birth to a healthy baby boy, whom he named Dmitri. Unfortunately, this happy event had already been eclipsed by a sudden and hideous tragedy. In November of 1581, the tsar accidentally killed his twenty-six year old son, Ivan Ivanovich, following a domestic argument. By most accounts, the father, in a rage, hit the tsarevich on the side of the head with his iron scepter. The young man bled to death three days later. The tsar, having now killed the heir to the throne, was overcome with grief and could not be consoled. He tried in vain to appease his conscience by giving money to monasteries to pray for the souls of the thousands of victims who had died during his rampages.

During his final two years, Ivan once again thought of renouncing the throne and entering a monastery. At the same time, fearing a *boyar* coup, he considered moving to England, but these fantasies were never acted upon as he endured his last days in physical pain and mental torment. By 1584, with his body swollen and putrefying, he was unable to concentrate on affairs of state and often distracted himself by admiring the gold, precious stones and jewels in his treasury, but any respite he might have enjoyed could only have been temporary. Consumed by anxiety and guilt and unable to sleep at night, he wandered the Kremlin palaces, talking to himself incoherently. He also consulted astrologers and soothsayers hoping to learn the exact date of his death. The end finally came on March 18, 1584, while he was playing a game of chess with one of his boyars. He was only fifty-three years old.

Ivan's funeral was conducted according to tradition. The corpse was washed, tonsured and dressed in a coarse woolen habit. An embroidered apron depicting the Crucifixion was then laid over his chest. The metropolitan read prayers over the body and gave him the name Brother Ionas (Jonas) to signify his spiritual entry into a community of monks. For two days his body lay in an open coffin to be viewed by the people. Finally, he was interred in the Cathedral of the Archangel beside his son, Ivan Ivanovich. His tomb was sealed off by bricks and eventually enclosed by a bronze sepulcher, upon which were inscribed his name and titles.

Memory of the terrible tsar did not soon fade. For the next three centuries, his very name evoked a sense of power and majesty accompanied by fear and respect. Thus, in the final years of tsarism, the empress Alexandra could urge her weak and indecisive husband, Nicholas II, to be more like Tsar Ivan, and even among the communists there were those who sought to inspire reverence for the absolute nature of his despotism. Josef

Stalin, during the early days of World War II, ordered Soviet film director Sergei Eisenstein to make a two-part movie about Russia's first tsar. Eisenstein succeeded brilliantly in the first part and was awarded a Stalin prize. However, in the second, which depicted the excesses of the *oprichnina*, he was denied official approval. To explain his objections, Stalin summoned both the director and his leading actor, Nikolai Cherkassov, to the Kremlin for a late night meeting in February 1947. It was not the fact that such excesses were graphically presented, but rather that Ivan himself was seen to show remorse for his cruelty and even to pray for the souls of his victims. Stalin was of the opinion that the tsar had to deal savagely with his enemies even if the innocent were also forced to suffer. It is a judgment that few modern leaders would openly accept, although, as the following chapters will illustrate, most of the Soviet dictator's tsarist predecessors rarely hesitated to use the most brutal force whenever they thought it necessary.

Selected Bibliography

One of the best sources for background about the Muscovite state is Crummey's *The Formation of Muscovy, 1304–1613*. Many useful biographies háve been publishing in English about Ivan the Terrible. Among the best are Payne and Romanoff's *Ivan the Terrible* and Bobrecht's *Fearful Majesty: The Life and Reign of Ivan the Terrible*. These works also contain much useful information about Prince Kurbsky and his correspondence with the tsar, although neither addresses Edward Keenan's hypothesis that the letters were forgeries. To better understand his arguments, read Keenan's *The Kurbskii-Grozni Apocrypha* and Crummey's "Kurbskii-Groznyi Controversy" in the *Modern Encyclopedia of Russian and Soviet History*.

Bobrecht, Benson. *Fearful Majesty: The Life and Reign of Ivan the Terrible*. New York: G.P. Putnam's Sons, 1987.

Carr, Francis. *Ivan the Terrible*. Totowa, N.J.: Barnes and Noble Books, 1981.

Crummey, Robert O. *The Formation of Muscovy 1304–1613*. New York: Longman, 1987.

_____. "Kurbskii-Groznyi Controversy." *Modern Encyclopedia of Russian and Soviet History*, ed., Joseph L. Wieczynski, 54 vols. With suppl. Gulf Breeze, Fla., 1976–90.

Graham, Hugh F. "Adashev, Aleksei Fedorovich." *Modern Encyclopedia of Russian and Soviet History*, ed., Joseph L. Wieczynski, 54 vols. With suppl. Gulf Breeze, Fla., 1976–90.

_____. "Filaret." *Modern Encyclopedia of Russian and Soviet History*, ed., Joseph L. Wieczynski, 54 vols. With suppl. Gulf Breeze, Fla., 1976-90.

_____. "Sil'vester." *Modern Encyclopedia of Russian and Soviet History*, ed., Joseph L. Wieczynski, 54 vols. With suppl. Gulf Breeze, Fla., 1976-90.

_____. "Viskovati, Ivan Mikhailovich." *Modern Encyclopedia of Russian and Soviet History*, ed., Joseph L. Wieczynski, 54 vols. With suppl. Gulf Breeze, Fla., 1976-90.

Halpren, Charles. "A Heretical View of Sixteenth-Century Muscovy. Edward L. Keenan: The Kurbskii-Grozny Apochrypha." *Jahrbücher für Geschichte Osteuropas*. Wiesbaden, Germany: Franz Steiner Verlag, 1974. Vol. 22, 161-186.

_____. "Keenan's Heresy Revisited." *Jahrbücher für Geschichte Osteuropas*. Wiesbaden, Germany: Franz Steiner Verlag, 1980. Vol. 28, 481-499.

Keenan, Edward L. *The Kurbskii-Grozni Apocrypha*. Cambridge, Mass.: Harvard University Press, 1971.

_____. "Vita: Ivan Vasilevich: Terrible Czar (1530-1584). *Harvard Magazine*, Jan.-Feb. 1978, p. 49.

Payne, Robert, and Romanoff, Nikita. *Ivan the Terrible*. New York: T.Y. Crowell, 1975.

Skrynnikov, Ruslan G. *Ivan Grozny*. Moscow: Nauka, 1981.

Troyat, Henri. *Ivan the Terrible*, trans. by Joan Pinkham. New York: E.P. Dutton, 1982.

Zenkovsky, Serge A. "Ivan IV (Ivan Vasil'evich)" *Modern Encyclopedia of Russian and Soviet History*, ed., Joseph L. Wieczynski, 54 vols. With suppl. Gulf Breeze, Fla., 1976-90.

2. The Great Pretender

The town of Uglich (pronounced OOglich), lying roughly 120 miles to the northeast of Moscow on the Volga River, had been a quiet backwater for most of its history. Distinguished only by its favorable location on the river and the attractiveness of its churches, it had been remote from most of the turbulent events that had shaped Russia during the 16th century. To the new Tsar Feodor and his advisors, however, it was an excellent place to send Maria Nagaya and her son, Dmitri, the widow and son of Ivan the Terrible, to keep them from becoming involved in plots against the new regime. Under more settled circumstances, such a precaution might have been unnecessary, since the boy, just two years old in 1584, had been born to the tsar's seventh wife. The fact was significant because the Church did not recognize any marriage beyond a third, hence, Dmitri was not eligible to become tsar. In a Russia recovering from the tyranny and wars of the previous decades, however, circumstances were anything but settled. Not only did the mother believe her son to be the legitimate tsarevich, but she considered their exile a grave injustice. She also had relatives and friends who were prepared to go to almost any length to promote her interests.

Feodor Ivanovich[1] was twenty-seven when he ascended to the throne. Although his titles tsar and *veliky gosudar* (great sovereign) suggested power and majesty, the new ruler was actually the object of pity. Mildly retarded and in poor health, Feodor Ivanovich could often be seem wandering around the Kremlin with a fixed grin on his face. Unable to concentrate on matters of state, he was mostly occupied with religious ritual and was particularly fascinated by the ringing of church bells. Under the circumstances, it was clear that a regency would have to be established. At first, this consisted of a seven-member council-of-state of powerful *boyars*.[2] However, this arrangement lasted little more than two years until an ambitious minor nobleman named Boris Godunov, who was also the tsar's brother-in-law, became recognized as sole regent.

With Feodor reigning and Boris ruling, political stability, if not prosperity, returned to Russia in a manner that might have justified considerable optimism about the future. There was, however, a problem: Feodor was expected neither to live long nor to sire an heir. With no candidate qualified by blood to succeed him, a dynastic crisis and possible civil war loomed. This caused some to view the availability of the child Dmitri in Uglich as an attractive alternative to the turmoil expected after Feodor's death. It also gave Boris Godunov, whose imperial ambitions were well-known, good reason to wish that the young boy would somehow cease to be among the living. As it turned out, Dmitri was not destined to live long. On the morning of May 15, 1591, Maria Nagaya heard screams from the courtyard of her palace and rushed outside to discover the dead body of her son with a gaping wound in his throat. The child had been playing *tychka* with four other boys, a game that involves flipping a knife in the air so that the blade lands in the ground. According to the three nannies also present, Dmitri suffered an epileptic seizure and stabbed himself in the throat. But Maria, hysterical in grief and anger, ignored this explanation and began to beat one of the women with a large stick as she accused the woman's son, Osip Volokhov, of murdering Dmitri.

The tocsin was sounded as the child's corpse was carried into the nearby Church of the Savior. As curious townspeople began to arrive, Maria, prodded by her conniving older brother, Mikhail, altered her story. She now insisted that two other boys had also participated in the murder, despite the fact that neither had been present at the time. One of them was the son of a very unpopular government official named Mikhail Bitiagovsky, who had been sent to Uglich a year earlier by Boris Godunov as the town's chief magistrate. It was his job to supervise tax collection and the drafting of soldiers for the army. He had also been assigned the chore of paying the resentful Nagoys their periodic government allowance, and probably to spy on them as well. Biatiagovsky, who had heard the tocsin and had gone to the church was soon confronted by an angry crowd. He appealed for calm and promised a full investigation, but his efforts were offset by the inflammatory rhetoric of Mikhail and Grigori Nagoy, both of whom were now drunk. So effectively did they goad the crowd that a riot ensued in which a number of government offices and private homes were ransacked. In the process, fifteen people were killed, including Mikhail Bitiagovsky and Osip Volokhov. The bodies were thrown into the moat surrounding the fortress.

Boris Godunov reacted swiftly to the Uglich tragedy and immediately appointed a government commission headed by Prince Vasily Shuisky to determine the facts. The investigators arrived in the evening of May 18, guarded by a detachment of *strel'tsy*. Over the next eleven days, they interviewed 140 people and compiled a report that is still on file in the Kremlin archives. The recorded depositions vary considerably in their versions of what happened, but those taken from eyewitnesses describe Dmitri's death as having been caused by a self-inflicted knife wound as he suffered a seizure.[3] The same report also indicted the Nagoys for trying to exploit the tragedy for the purpose of discrediting the government, but this came as no surprise. Indeed, Maria's relatives had often made threatening and seditious statements about the rulers in the Kremlin and were known to have consulted mystics hoping to learn how long the tsar would live. Moreover, their resentfulness had influenced young Dmitri, imbuing him with a fierce sense of entitlement. A German visitor once recalled how the young prince had his playmates make snow figures of his "enemies" in Moscow in order to perform mock executions. He promised to do the real thing when he became tsar.

Surprisingly, Maria and her relatives were dealt with quite leniently. Not a single member of the Nagoy family was executed even though at least some were clearly guilty of inciting the murder of a government agent and of treachery elsewhere. On May 24, while the investigating committee was still at work, mysterious fires broke out in Moscow. Later it was learned that one of Maria's cousins, Afanasy Nagoy, had hired arsonists to incite rebellion in the capital and other cities. Still, the threat was easily dealt with, and the punishments imposed, although mild by the standards of the previous tsar, seemed sufficient to end the Nagoys as a political force. Maria was sent to a convent in Beloozero, and several of the male members of the family were imprisoned in faraway places. The townsmen who had participated in the violence were sent to Siberia.

Concern about the Uglich affair faded quickly as a new crisis emerged in Muscovy. The country had been at war with Sweden in the Baltic since January of 1590, trying to regain territories that had been lost in the previous decade. The Russian army had scored some important successes that seemed very much in jeopardy when it was learned that a huge force of Crimean Tatars, led by Khan Kaza Girei, was approaching Moscow from the south. As the Tatars drew near, panic gripped the capital. Many remembered a previous attack by the same enemy twenty years earlier that had left Moscow a gutted and smoldering mess. Now, in July of 1591, with the bulk of the army still engaged by the Swedes in Livonia, it seemed only a miracle could prevent another disaster.

According to legend, the pious Tsar Feodor himself tried to provide one by ordering a sacred icon, Our Lady of the Don,[4] taken to an area just south of the Kremlin where it was believed the main attack would occur. On the eve of battle, it is said that the khan dreamt that he and his men were encamped in a dark forest. Disturbed by chants in the distance, he was stunned to see the icon appear in the sky and drift to a spot directly over his tent. Suddenly, thousands of burning arrows began to issue from the image, falling upon his men. At this point, the khan is said to have awakened in terror and ordered a retreat.

In fact, the Tatars did retreat on the appointed day, and much of the credit must go to Boris Godunov. It has never been claimed that the regent was a military genius, but he does seem to have worked effectively with the army and a five-man council of war in organizing the defense of the capital. At his suggestion, cannon were judiciously placed on the recently completed White Stone Wall,[5] which surrounded the inner city, and special fortifications were prepared for an area just south of the Kremlin known as Zamoskvorechie.[6] It was here, at a sharp bend in the Moscow River, that the Tatars had focused their attacks so often in the past. Once the fighting had begun, Boris ordered bonfires lit on all the Kremlin towers and commanded his soldiers to fire their muskets randomly into the air. Others were told to blow trumpets and beat drums in order to create the impression that reinforcements were arriving from the north. Finally, a huge mobile wooden castle armed with light field cannon was wheeled onto the field. (Possibly this was something like an early form of tank.) The Tatars were thoroughly confused and thrown into a disorganized retreat. The victory was soon followed by others over the Swedes, and in May of 1595, a "treaty of eternal peace" was signed in which Russia's claim to the Baltic and her control of the Neva River were formally recognized. This was probably the high point of the Godunov regency.

However, it all came to an end on January 7, 1598, with the death of Tsar Feodor, and the dynasty that had ruled Muscovy for three hundred years ceased to exist. With the long-awaited crisis now at hand, the *Zemsky Sobor* met in the Kremlin to choose a successor. The patriarch, Iov (Job), became acting regent and presided over its deliberations. Boris Godunov and his sister, the tsaritsa Irina, retired to the Novodevichy Monastery on the outskirts of Moscow. He claimed not to be interested in gaining the throne but allowed demonstrations to be organized in his behalf. The assembly considered a number of candidates, including Feodor Romanov, who was related to Ivan the Terrible's beloved first wife, but Godunov's many years as de facto ruler in Tsar Feodor's government gave him significant advantages. Not only did the patriarch himself owe his rank and status within the Eastern Orthodox Church to Boris' vision and negotiating skills,[7] but the gentry, too, had benefited by his policies.[8] Thus, on February 20, following a vote of the *Zemsky Sobor*, a procession of citizens marched to Novodevichy to persuade Boris to become their new tsar. At first he refused, feigning modesty, but, when the same crowd returned the following day, he submitted to the will of the people.

Boris' coronation took place on September 1, 1598, and was lavishly celebrated. Favors were distributed to people of all ranks, and, somewhat later, as a special act of piety, the new tsar ordered the completion of the huge bell tower of Ivan the Great,[9] which soon rose to become the highest point in the Kremlin. Still, there was indignation: the Godunovs were nearly devoid of royal blood, and Boris' rise to power had been achieved mainly by his service in Tsar Ivan's *oprichnina*, the very apparatus by which so many noble families had been savagely persecuted. Now that he was tsar, he keenly appreciated the need to curry favor with the leading Muscovite aristocrats and solemnly promised to rule justly and to execute no one. Still, dissatisfaction among the boyars persisted. Many had opposed Boris' election from the beginning and were particularly incensed by his intention to establish a new dynasty with his son, Feodor, as heir. But, the new tsar was determined to have his way and had his brother and head of his security police, Semen Godunov, draw up a kind of loyalty oath. The signers had to agree to refrain from a number of specific activities. These included any fraternization with Simeon Bekbulatovich, who had acted as tsar for one year during the reign of Ivan the Terrible. The man was now old and blind, but he apparently had some support among the nobility.

It was about this time that rumors first began to be circulated about the miraculous survival of Tsarevich Dmitri. According to one, Boris had indeed attempted to have the child assassinated by his agents in Uglich, but they murdered the wrong child. The real Dmitri was in hiding and would eventually come to claim his throne. Boris strongly suspected *boyar* complicity in circulating these stories, but proceeded carefully. He eventually took action against a certain Bogdan Yakovlevich Bel'sky, who had been a member of Tsar Feodor's regency. In 1599, he gave him a military assignment to get him out of Moscow, sending him far to the south to supervise the construction of a new fort named Tsarev-Borisov. Having completed the task, Bel'sky began to boast that although Godunov might be tsar in Moscow, he (Bel'sky) was tsar in the new fort. Boris was so offended by his impertinence that he devised a special punishment: He ordered a Scottish surgeon to yank out Bel'sky's beard hair by hair. Not only did the procedure cause pain, but it was an insult to the prince's masculinity and demeaned him in the eyes of the Orthodox Church.[10]

Boris also kept a wary eye on the Romanovs, whose treachery he feared much more. When some of their household slaves informed Semen Godunov that certain members of the family were planning to kill the tsar by sorcery and poison, the matter promptly went to trial. In June of 1601, all were found guilty and punished by exile. One of the convicted, Feodor Romanov, was also forcibly shorn as a monk in order to make him ineligible ever to become tsar. In fact, the effort proved futile: two decades later, this same man son's would be tsar and be the most powerful man in Muscovy. It also made Boris' enemies even more devious and determined and deprived him of much cooperation and support that he would soon need to confront a crisis that would challenge the new dynasty's very existence.

Unusually rainy weather that summer, followed by a severe frost in August, caused a crop failure that was nothing short of catastrophic. Within months, starvation throughout much of the realm had become of such intensity that people ate tree bark, grass, dead animals, and even human flesh. Jacques Margaret, a French soldier and statesman who served the tsar, wrote a book in which he described how four women, abandoned by their husbands, had strangled a peasant delivering wood to one of their homes. They proceeded to eat his horse and might have eaten him had they not been discovered. Later, it was learned that he had been their fourth victim. According to Margaret, incidents of this nature were by no means rare.[11]

Godunov reacted to this crisis with characteristic energy and determination. He authorized a massive system of relief and fed the destitute from palace granaries. He also opened the treasury to provide for the poor and attacked unemployment by creating an extensive building program in Moscow. Even the plight of serfs and slaves in the countryside aroused his concern. In 1601, he issued an *ukase*[12] that partially restored the right of the former to seek better working conditions in the period around St. George's Day. Another such ukase in 1602 provided special certificates of emancipation to homeless slaves who had been forced off their estates by landowners unable or unwilling to feed them.

But Boris' best efforts were overwhelmed by sheer numbers. Thousands left their fields in the countryside for Moscow, only to find that there was not enough charity to go around. In some areas, desperation gave way to violence. In September of 1603, a certain Cossack[13] renegade in the Ukraine named Khlopko Kosolap led an army of fugitive slaves all the way to Moscow where they were finally checked by troops under the experienced military commander, Ivan Basmanov. Khlopko was captured and hanged, although many of his followers escaped. As the famine continued, wild rumors about the Tsarevich Dmitri's imminent reappearance grew louder and more insistent. The stories were not entirely unfounded. Indeed, a young man claiming to be Dmitri had appeared in Poland some months earlier and had attracted a sizable following. The tsar, weary and depressed from combating the famine, was alarmed by this development and fell into doubt. In the spring of 1604, he summoned Maria Nagaya from her convent to question her about her son's death. Her ambiguous testimony, however, was not reassuring. He subsequently interrogated Vasily Shuisky, who, it will be remembered, had headed the investigation of Dmitri's death in 1591. The prince stated categorically that the child had died and was buried. If this were true, however, who was this other Dmitri in Poland?

An answer was soon forthcoming. Semen Godunov and the security police had investigated the matter and identified the man as the son of a minor Russian nobleman named Yuri Otrepiev from the town of Galich. He was known to have had worked for the estate of Prince Boris Cherkasski, who had been banished for treason in 1601 along with the Romanovs. The young man himself, though implicated, had managed to escape punishment by becoming a monk and assuming the name Grigori. Subsequently, he had wandered from cloister to cloister, eventually winding up in the Chudov Monastery located in the Moscow Kremlin. Grigori's highly developed literary skills and quick mind soon impressed his superiors, and he was offered a position assisting the patriarch. This supposedly allowed him to learn details about the tsarevich and the Uglich tragedy. Armed with this information, and inspired by a plan, he eventually made his way to an estate in what was then eastern Poland called Brahin.[14] There he entered the service of a powerful Polish magnate named Adam Wisnowiecki.[15]

Grigori initially took a position as a lowly household servant for the prince, but soon revealed himself to be Dmitri, the son of Ivan the Terrible, and the heir to the throne of Russia. He also declared his determination to some day return to Moscow and rule according to his God-given right and pleaded for the prince to help him. Wisnowiecki was both surprised and intrigued by this intense young man, despite the fact that his short stature and crude appearance did not much resemble royalty. But the prince had good reason to hate Boris Godunov, whose armies had occasionally plundered his lands, and he calculated that the tsar's removal would be most welcome in Poland. Thus, sensing that the young man's cause could be exploited, he informed the Polish king of his find and took steps to provide for the "tsarevich's" safety. Accordingly, he bade his brother, Konstantin, to accompany Dmitri (as he shall henceforth be called) to the estate of Jerzy Mniszech at Sambor, which was deemed a more secure location.

There the tsarevich generally made a good impression by behaving like an aristocrat in exile. He also fell in love with, and proposed marriage to, Mniszech's ambitious daughter, Marina. She, however, was rather less smitten than he, and she made her answer conditional upon his becoming tsar. Jesuits serving at the prince's court immediately took an interest in this fervent young man. Eager for any excuse to lead a Roman Catholic crusade against Orthodox heresy, they imagined they could use Dmitri for their own ends. Accordingly, they urged him to accept their faith and groomed him to meet other influential Polish magnates, whose support he would need.

A project soon began to materialize. At the end of January 1604, the tsarevich traveled to Krakow to meet more nobles, and, on March 15 (25), was received by King Sigismund III. The meeting was private, but it is known that Dmitri pleaded for Polish help to win back his throne from the usurper and child-murderer, Boris Godunov. Sigismund listened with interest but did not commit himself; he had only recently concluded a twenty-two-year truce with the Kremlin, and he was not keen to begin hostilities without a clear prospect of success. Still, he agreed to supply Dmitri with a modest stipend and urged his nobles to offer what help they could.

Jerzy Mniszech, who expected to grow rich should the venture succeed, was anxious to comply. So were the Jesuits at the Polish court and a number of noblemen and other adventurers. Preparations proceeded so enthusiastically all summer that, by the end of August, Dmitri's army was ready to move. Thus, from the town of Sambor in what is now Ukraine, the tsarevich took command of an army of about two thousand Poles and Ukrainians. He would soon be joined by another two thousand Cossacks from the Don River, who believed that they were helping the true tsar claim his rightful throne.

Dmitri's army crossed into Russia on October 16 (26), 1604, and, against minimal resistance, scored victories at Moravsk and Chernigov. Serious fighting, however, did take place in December at Novgorod-Seversk, about three hundred miles southwest of Moscow. There the Russian defenders, led by a favorite of Tsar Boris, Piotr Basmanov, not only withstood a brief siege but with the arrival of reinforcements, dared to go on the offensive with the arrival of reinforcements. Since the pretender's forces had also been strengthened, they were able to counterattack and decisively rout the Russians. This victory, however, was marred by an incredibly confusing aftermath. As thousands of Cossacks arrived to support his cause, Dmitri's army began to disintegrate because he had no money to pay the men. The resulting turmoil so discouraged his followers that many of them, including his future father-in-law, Jerzy Mniszech, abandoned him in disgust.

Not surprisingly, disaster awaited the pretender's weakened forces when he engaged Prince Vasily Shuisky's troops at Dobrynichi, in January 1605. The Russians easily swept the rebel army from the field and nearly captured Dmitri himself. The latter had ineptly led a cavalry charge during the battle and was thoroughly routed. Humiliated, the tsarevich fled to the town of Rylsk and later to Putivl', where he watched his army further unravel. At one point, he, too, tried to flee, but was prevented from doing so by local citizens who threatened to turn him over to Tsar Boris if he did not remain steadfast.

By the spring of 1605, Dmitri's prospects were clearly on the wane and might have been extinguished altogether if Shuisky had pursued the rebels after Dobrynichi. Instead, the prince decided to take vengeance on the residents of the Komaritsky district in Ukraine, where support for the tsarevich had been particularly strong. There, men, women, and children were cruelly put to death in great numbers; some were hung by their feet in trees and shot. Such savagery was frighteningly reminiscent of the worst excesses of Ivan the Terrible and served only to solidify hatred for the Godunov regime.

Indeed, Boris himself seemed to sense this hatred, and despite his improved military situation, he became depressed, isolated, and increasingly detached from affairs of state. He consulted soothsayers and holy people in a desperate attempt to find spiritual peace. He was also in bad health, although it was not thought to have been serious until the evening of April 13 (24). On that occasion, Boris ate a large meal and suddenly became deathly ill. His doctors were summoned, but they were powerless to help him. Just before expiring, his entire body began to tremble as blood streamed from his mouth, ears and nose.[16]

To the pretender, and those who supported him, Boris' sudden death must have seemed like a miracle. As new supporters flocked to his cause, Dmitri remained in Putivl' and reorganized his forces against an enemy that no longer seemed formidable. The new tsar, Feodor Borisovich Godunov, just sixteen when the throne passed to him, was overwhelmed by the hostility and chaos he had inherited. He had hoped to rely on Piotr Basmanov to defend the regime, but when the latter declared for Dmitri on April 27 (May 7), all was lost.

His triumph all but assured, the pretender left Putivl' on May 25 (June 4) for Kromy, and from there for Tula. Early in June, he sent two messengers to Red Square with a proclamation for the people of Moscow. From the *Lobnoe Mesto*,[17] near the Church of St. Basil the Blessed,[18] a pardon was offered for all who had acted against Dmitri in ignorance of his true identity. The emissaries also denounced the Godunovs, promising that they would soon be brought to justice. Then Vasily Shuisky, who was present in the crowd, stepped forward to speak. He reversed his original testimony made fourteen years earlier with regard to Dmitri's death at Uglich. He now announced that the tsarevich had survived and that another child had been murdered instead.

This revelation so excited the crowd that it began to surge toward the Kremlin. The imperial guards were easily brushed aside as the angry mob charged through the gates and toward the tsar's palace. The Godunovs were alerted and braced for the worst. Young Feodor sat at the tsar's place of honor in the throne room and waited. His mother, Maria, and sister, Xenia, hoping to protect him, ventured out into the square near the Cathedral of the Annunciation[19] holding sacred icons. Their brave front, however, was in vain as brazen thugs seized them, smashed the icons, and tore the jewelry off their clothing. Others broke into the palace and savagely flung the tsar from his throne. The three Godunovs were then arrested and confined in the stables of Tsar Boris' old Kremlin residence.

For one week the deposed tsar, his mother, and his sister were kept in confinement to await their doom. On June 10 (20), Princes Vasily Golitsyn and Vasily Masalsky were sent to Moscow to execute the prisoners. Assisted by at least five others, the deed was accomplished in short order. Tsaritsa Maria fainted in horror as the executioners prepared to strangle her with a rope. The son, however, resisted fiercely. The executioners wrestled with him for some time before smothering him with a pillow. Xenia, who was widely admired for her beauty and gentle nature, was spared only to endure a more humiliating fate. By some accounts, she was held until Dmitri's triumphant arrival on June 20 (30) and forced to become his mistress. If the pretender did enjoy her for a while, he did not forget about his planned marriage to Marina Mniszech. In any case, she was eventually banished to a convent.

Dmitri had barely been in Moscow three days when he made his first mistake. Upon learning that Vasily Shuisky had been trying to incite the people against him, the new tsar ordered his arrest and put him on trial. The prince was sentenced to be beheaded in Red Square, but, just as the executioner was about to deliver the blow, Dmitri sent a messenger out from the Kremlin to announce that Shuisky's punishment had been changed to exile. Why he did this is not clear, but even that sentence was quickly commuted, whereupon the prince was returned to the capital to dissemble gratitude as he resumed his treachery.

A formal coronation took place on July 21 (31) in the Cathedral of the

The French soldier of fortune Jacques Margaret described Tsar Dmitri as "a prince who loved honor and made great account of it." However, his willingness to tolerate Poles and Catholics in his entourage led to this undoing. *Skazaniye sovremmenikov o Dmitrii Samozvantse*, tom I, chast' vtoraya, St. Petersburg, 1859.

Assumption, as the dynasty of Ivan the Terrible was miraculously returned to power. The Poles in attendance probably smiled as they watched Dmitri waddle stiffly in his gem-studded robes during the solemn procession to don the imperial crown. Most of them had never believed that he was anything but a rogue-opportunist, although they may well have appreciated his flair for the dramatic. Three days earlier, he had participated in a scene worthy of Shakespeare when he was reunited with his "mother," Maria Nagaya. He had summoned the old woman from her monastery to recognize and embrace him after a separation of fourteen years.

The new tsar, however, was not play-acting once he began to rule. He took his responsibilities seriously, and soon began to think and plan on a grand scale. One of his more ambitious projects concerned a religious crusade against Turkey. To this end, he reorganized the military, participated enthusiastically in training exercises (with himself in the starring role), and oversaw the stockpiling of arms and ammunition. He also took a keen interest in domestic affairs and was determined to be a champion of the people. To win their affection, he held public audiences on Wednesdays and Saturdays and welcomed their petitions. He also tried to recodify Muscovite law, eliminate bribery in the courts, and lower taxes. In his endeavor to please everyone, however, some of his initiatives flirted with contradiction. To support the gentry, he confirmed an earlier law that gave landowners five years to recover fugitive peasants. To protect the latter, however, he decreed that those who had fled by necessity during the famine could not be reclaimed.

Dmitri seems to have meant well, but, through ignorance, insensitivity, and bad advice, he antagonized at least some of his Russian subjects at every turn. His most conspicuous shortcoming was that he simply didn't act like a tsar. He could often be seen wandering around town in Polish dress, unaccompanied by his proper imperial retinue. Many were also annoyed by his casual deportment on solemn occasions and by his apparent lack of religious conviction. He rarely attended church, ignored fasts, and allowed the hated Catholics to open a chapel in Moscow. Despite all this, Dmitri's progressive policies won him much popularity among the common people who truly believed he was the "good tsar" they had all been waiting for. Unfortunately, he failed to appreciate the extent to which he had offended the nobility, who fumed about his preference for foreign advisers and his plan to model the *boyar duma* after the Polish Senate.

Their antagonism for the new tsar reached a critical mass on the occasion of his marriage to Marina Mniszech. Ironically, many of Dmitri's most well-meaning advisers had pressed for an elaborate celebration because they believed it would provide a stimulus for the tsar to promote

Marina was married to Tsar Dmitri only eight days before his brutal assassination. Later she married a second false Dmitri hoping to regain power. *Skazaniye sovremmenikov o Dmitrii Samozvantse*, tom II, chast' vtoraya, St. Petersburg, 1859.

Catholicism in Russia. In fact, it did exactly the opposite. The wedding, which was to be performed in the sacred Cathedral of the Assumption in May of 1606, drew an unprecedented number of Poles to Moscow. Many were housed in private dwellings in Kitaigorod[20] to the dismay of the local inhabitants. The visitors made themselves obnoxious by acting like conquerors and by barring ordinary Russians from visiting the Kremlin during the festivities.

A boyar-led conspiracy that had been brewing for some time was set in motion on May 17 (27), just nine days after the grand wedding. Some time after midnight, soldiers from Novgorod were ordered to occupy all the Kremlin gates. At about 4 A.M., the tocsin was sounded, summoning the populace to Red Square. Prince Vasily Shuisky and some other boyars appeared at the head of an armed force. He warned the people not to allow the Poles into the Kremlin, claiming that they intended to murder the tsar. The ruse worked to perfection as the conspirators themselves entered the fortress to assault the lightly guarded tsar's palace. Piotr Basmanov, who had become one of Dmitri's most trusted advisers, tried to fend off the attackers but was killed almost immediately. The tsar was slow to appreciate what was happening but managed briefly to escape by jumping out an upper floor palace window. However, he either seriously sprained or broke his leg in the fall and lay for a while on the ground unconscious. He was hidden temporarily by some loyal Ukrainian musketeers, but Shuisky and the others soon discovered his whereabouts and closed in.

The conspirators then had the satisfaction of watching Dmitri plead for his life as he writhed in agony from his injuries. At some point, someone fired a shot into his chest, which prompted others to beat and stab the lifeless body. The dead tsar was then stripped naked and dragged to Maria Nagaya's residence in the Terem Palace.[21] The old woman cursed and spat upon the man she had only recently embraced as her son. Finally, the corpse was deposited just outside the Trinity Gate where it lay in the mud for several days. People entering and leaving the Kremlin were encouraged to mock and further mutilate Dmitri's remains.

The pretender was buried without ceremony in a field outside Moscow. Soon, however, a new rumor surfaced that the tsar had miraculously survived yet another attempt to assassinate him. The body was dug up and burned, and the ashes were stuffed into several different cannons before being fired in the direction of Poland. This precaution was taken in deference to Dmitri's reputation as a sorcerer. Many feared that, even now, he could unite what remained of his body and rise from the dead.

Selected Bibliography

The classic study of this period is Sergei Platonov's *The Time of Troubles*, which, although dated, is still worth reading. However, his scholarship has been enhanced by Chester Dunning in *Russia's First Civil War*. Not only has the author rigorously reinvestigated a number of questions and controversies regarding this period, but his portraits of Tsar Boris Godunov and Tsar Vasily Shuisky are fully developed and most useful. For those desiring a shorter, more concise account, Robert O. Crummey's *The Formation of Muscovy 1304–1613* is excellent. Another helpful source is Ruslan G. Skrynnikov's *The Time of Troubles: Russia in Crisis* although many interpretations have been challenged by Dunning. An excellent biography of the pretender is Philip Barbour's *Dimitri, Called the Pretender, Tsar and Great Prince of All Russia 1605–1606*.

Barbour, Philip. *Dmitri, Called the Pretender, Tsar and Great Prince of All Russia. 1605–1606.* Boston: Houghton Mifflin, 1966.

Dunning, Chester S.L. *Russia's First Civil War.* University Park: Pennsylvania State University Press, 2001.

_____. "Shuiskii, Vasilii Ivanovich." *Modern Encyclopedia of Russian and Soviet History*, ed., Joseph L. Wieczynski, 54 vols. With suppl. Gulf Breeze, Florida: Academic International Press, 1976–90.

Graham, Hugh F. "Fedor Ivanovich." *Modern Encyclopedia of Russian and Soviet History*, ed. Joseph L. Wieczynski, 54 vols. With suppl. Gulf Breeze, Florida: Academic International Press, 1976–90.

Graham, Stephen. *Boris Godunov.* Ann Arbor, Michigan: Archon Books, 1970.

Margaret, Jacques. *The Russian Empire and Grand Duchy of Muscovy.* Trans. and ed. by Chester S. L. Dunning. Pittsburgh: University of Pittsburgh Press, 1983.

Orchard, G. Edward. "Filaret." *Modern Encyclopedia of Russian and Soviet History*, ed. Joseph L. Wieczynski, 54 vols. With suppl. Gulf Breeze, Florida: Academic International Press, 1976–90.

Rowland, Daniel B. "Mniszek, Marina." *Modern Encyclopedia of Russian and Soviet History*, ed. Joseph L. Wieczynski, 54 vols. With suppl. Gulf Breeze, Florida: Academic International Press, 1976–90.

Skrynnikov, Ruslan G. *Boris Godunov.* The Russian Series, v. 35. Moscow: Nauka, 1988.

_____. *Samozvansty v Rossii v Nachale XVII veka-Grigorii Otrep'ev.* Novosibirsk: Nauka, 1987.

_____. *The Time of Troubles: Russia in Crisis.* Ed. and trans. Hugh Graham. Gulf Breeze, Florida: Academic International Press, 1988.

Vernadsky, George. *A History of Russia. Vol. 5.* New Haven: Yale University Press, 1963.

Wieczynski, Joseph L. "Uglich Affair." *Modern Encyclopedia of Russian and Soviet History*, ed. Joseph L. Wieczynski, 54 vols. With suppl. Gulf Breeze, Florida: Academic International Press, 1976–90.

3. BOYARS, COSSACKS, AND MORE PRETENDERS

The calm that settled on the Kremlin after the pretender's assassination gave rise to an eerie uncertainty: no one knew who would now be tsar. The conspirators had destroyed one dynasty and now had to establish another. To be sure, there was no shortage of candidates, but after two days of secret negotiations, the man who emerged was none other than the chief conspirator himself, Vasily Ivanovich Shuisky.[1] In some ways, this should have been an appropriate choice, since the prince was from one of the oldest and most noble families in the land. At fifty-four years of age, he was experienced, having proven his intelligence and ability in a number of official and unofficial capacities. However, as tsar, his years on the throne would bring the country to the verge of calamity and disintegration.

Shuisky's problems were at least in part caused by his extremely negative public image. Not only had he proven himself to be a devious, double-dealing liar, but he was also perceived, as a man wholly without majesty or charisma. A contemporary, Prince I.M. Katyrev-Rostovsky, described him thus:

> Tsar Vasily was short of stature, physically very unattractive, and had eyes that were dull, as if he were blind. He was rather cultured, and his reasoning was sound and pointed. He cared only for those who brought him gossip and rumors about people, and he used to receive such persons with a joyful face, and with sweet pleasure, did he listen to them. He was given to sorcery and cared little for the military.[2]

Tsar Vasily was crowned on June 1 (10), 1606, in accordance with tradition but without any special pomp. Sensing dissatisfaction, he made a number of concessions to strengthen his position. Among other things, he promised not to impose the death penalty on noblemen without trial by the boyar court, not to listen to unsubstantiated denunciations, and not to arbitrarily confiscate the possessions from noble families found guilty of crimes. He cooperated with some high-ranking boyars to secure the election of a suitable patriarch,[3] and ordered the relics of the Tsarevich Dmitri brought from Uglich for reinterment in the Kremlin's Cathedral of the Archangel.[4] This latter gesture had both a theatrical and a practical purpose. Shuisky met the casket when it reached Moscow and marched behind it so that all could see, once and for all, that the youngest son of Ivan the Terrible really had died and was finally being buried for good.

Few believed it, of course, and soon the ghost that Shuisky himself had helped to invent was exploited by two other schemers who did not wish the new tsar well. One was a minor nobleman named Prince Grigori Shakhovskoy, who had supported Tsar Dmitri and prospered during his rule. Shuisky, however, sensed this man's enmity and got rid of him by making him military governor of Putivl'. He had similar suspicions about another malcontent prince, Andrei Teliatevsky, whom he sent to Chernigov to become military governor, but both Shakhovskoy and Teliatevsky resented their exile and resolved to oust the new tsar and his high-born supporters. Thus, almost immediately after Shuisky's elevation, they collaborated in spreading rumors about Tsar Dmitri's miraculous survival and were pleased to learn that there were still people willing to flock to his banner. One was a certain Ivan Isaevich Bolotnikov, who years before had served Prince Teliatevsky as a military retainer. Now, in the summer of 1606, he suddenly appeared at the head of a large army preparing to march on the Kremlin.

Bolotnikov must be considered one of the boldest adventurers in Russian history. Having run away as a young man to join the Don Cossacks, he had fallen into captivity while fighting the Tatars. They in turn sold him to the Turks to become a galley slave. He escaped some years later by jumping overboard during a sea battle, was rescued by a German ship, taken to Venice, and released to begin the long journey home. Traveling through the town of Sambor in Poland, he became acquainted with Mikhail Molchanov, a friend of Shakhovskoy and a participant in the murder of the boy-tsar, Feodor Godunov. Molchanov, a minor nobleman who had fond memories of the pretender's short rule, thoroughly hated Vasily Shuisky and was now prepared to impersonate Dmitri himself if it would help oust the *boyar* tsar.[5]

A former serf who ran away to join the Don Cossacks, Ivan Bolotnikov was a charismatic and gifted military leader. He attracted followers from all classes to fight against the *boyar* tsar Vasily Shuisky. G.N. Gorelov (1880–1966). *Istoria Russkogo Iskusstvo.*

Bolotnikov may have been illiterate and politically naive, but his physical presence was imposing. Molchanov sensed the young Cossack could be useful and, giving him a saber, a fur coat, and a small amount of money, sent him to join Shakhovskoy and the rebel army in Putivl'. In fact, it wasn't much of an army, but rather a mixture of various malcontented groups including peasants, runaway slaves, middle and lower class gentry, and Don and Terek Cossacks. The one thing they all had in common was that their economic plight had become increasingly desperate over the last year. They were destitute, angry, and eager for action. Bolotnikov understood their frustrations and soon won their confidence. Shakhovskoy was also impressed and appointed him commander of the army.

The former galley slave organized the revolt in remarkably short order. By August 1606, the rebels probably numbered more than 50,000 men and were ready to march on Moscow. Bolotnikov divided this force into two large columns, one to be led by himself and the other by a service nobleman from Tula named Istoma Pashkov. Operating independently and traveling by different routes, the two groups rumbled toward the capital, plundering towns and wreaking havoc along the way. As Bolotnikov's column approached Kaluga in late September, the tsar sent his brother, Ivan

Shuisky, to confront the rebels. The battle that ensued was both bloody and decisive. The government troops at first fought ferociously, but then broke and ran. The rebels gave chase, continuing north through Serpukhov against only minimal opposition.

In October, however, Bolotnikov's force was checked at the Pakhra River twelve miles south of the Kremlin by Tsar Vasily's young nephew, Mikhail Skopin-Shuisky, who would soon prove to be the most gifted commander in the Muscovite army. For three weeks, he stoutly resisted the rebel advance and prevented their two columns from linking up. Pashkov, meanwhile, having traveled a more easterly route, was encountering stiff resistance at Kolomna, although his column eventually overwhelmed the defenders and destroyed the town. This was followed by another rebel victory at Troitskoe, whereupon Pashkov and his men established an encampment at the village of Kolomskoe,[6] just a few miles from the Kremlin. The battle of Moscow was set to begin.

Things had begun to look very bad for Tsar Vasily. Not only was his army plagued by desertion, but much of the populace was openly hostile. Still, the tsar worked feverishly to find new recruits for the army. He subsequently divided his force into smaller units suitable for guerrilla war-

In a battle that took place near Moscow in November of 1606, rebel soldiers struggle to push their cannon into position. Bolotnikov on horseback is visible in the background with his arm raised to greet a detachment of Cossacks who had just joined the rebels. E.E. Lissner (dates unknown). L.P. Bushchik, *Ilustrirovanaya Istoriya SSSR*, XV–XVII vv. Moskva, Proveshcheniye, 1970.

fare and, anticipating that the main attack would come along the Moscow River, built up his defenses on the southern end of the city. Then, in mid–November, just when a rebel victory seemed inevitable, a large number of landowners from Riazan led by a certain Prokofii Liapunov went over to the government side. This was followed by another wave of defections in December led by Istoma Pashkov. The siege was finally ended when a Muscovite force commanded by Skopin-Shuisky drove the rebels off and forced Bolotnikov to flee to Kaluga.

The disintegration of the rebel army must have seemed like a miracle to the defenders in the Kremlin, but in retrospect it was probably inevitable. Bolotnikov's followers were a disparate lot, united only by a common determination to oust an evil tsar. The gentry members of this force had become increasingly concerned about the chaos that might follow their victory. They began to fear the peasants and serfs whose economic and social demands threatened them as landowners, but credit must also be given to Shuisky's resourcefulness. At a critical moment, he was able to exploit dissension in the enemy's ranks by a clever ruse. He instructed townsmen loyal to him to go to the rebel camp and promise to surrender if Tsar Dmitri would come to Moscow and appear before them. Incredibly, Bolotnikov fell for this trick and sent messengers to Putivl' urging the non-existent (true) tsar to return posthaste. In the meantime, Shuisky authorized his representatives to make lavish promises to the gentry members of the rebel army, and he won many of them over.

The victory caused much rejoicing among Shuisky's supporters in Moscow, but the crisis was far from over. Not only was Bolotnikov still at large, but a new pretender had appeared in the south. He called himself the Tsarevich Piotr (Peter) and claimed to be the son of Tsar Feodor, although none ever existed. In fact, he was a certain Ileika Gorchakov from Murom, a cobbler's son who had once worked as a shop assistant in Nizhni-Novgorod and later as a cook on a Volga merchant vessel. At some point, he jumped ship during a port call at Astrakhan and joined a group of Terek Cossacks. He later sold himself into slavery to a service nobleman, possibly to ride out a difficult economic situation, but soon he rejoined the Cossacks. At some point during the summer of 1606, he began to claim that he was Tsar Feodor's only surviving son and thus the rightful heir to the throne.

This new pretender was not an attractive personality, and in better times would probably have been ignored, but widespread economic misery, coupled with the depth of the boyar tsar's unpopularity, helped keep alive the hope that a "good tsar" would soon appear to liberate the people from their oppressors.[7] For this, Tsarevich Piotr fit the bill perfectly. He was notorious for his hatred of the landowning nobility, and soon developed a following of some 300 Cossacks, slaves, and *strel'tsy*. Moreover, the plundering raids he led in Astrakhan and along the Volga did more than win booty; they seemed to punish those who had abused the poor and the weak. When Shakhovskoy heard of this man, he was inspired. Possibly in the belief that Bolotnikov's earlier effort had failed for lack of a unifying symbol, the prince invited the "tsarevich" to come to Putivl' to enlist him in the revolt against Shuisky. He also concocted a new fable: the infant daughter of Tsar Feodor, born in 1596, had actually been a boy. Moreover, this boy had survived and grown into a man named Piotr, who would soon be joining forces with Bolotnikov in Tula to prepare a campaign to oust the boyar usurper, Vasily Shuisky.

Bolotnikov, however, was trapped in Kaluga by Muscovite troops. It took six months and a determined rebel effort to raise the government siege so that the Cossack could escape to join Tsarevich Piotr. But once free he soon had to contend with an even more potent Muscovite force. By June of 1607, Tsar Vasily had assembled about 150,000 troops and had appointed Skopin-Shuisky to lead an attack on Tula. Bolotnikov and his former master, Prince Teliatevsky, made several futile and costly attempts to check the Muscovite army's advance as it marched south. Ultimately, the rebels were forced to retreat and were soon trapped behind Tula's fortified walls, outnumbered five to one.

If we are to believe the testimony of a certain nobleman named Ivan Funikov,[8] who spent nineteen weeks in rebel captivity, the defenders were soon reduced to the foulest misery. They were forced to eat dogs and rats as their numbers dwindled steadily from disease and exhaustion. Nevertheless, Bolotnikov's leadership was inspired and resourceful, and the rebels were able to frustrate all attempts by government troops to subdue the town. By fall, Shuisky became desperate as he watched his own troops tire of the siege and begin to desert. Finally, at the suggestion of a certain petty nobleman from the town of Murom, Ivan Krovkov, the tsar ordered the Upa River to be dammed up in order to flood the city. The results were spectacular. The defenders lost many of their supplies due to the high water and were soon forced to get around on rafts and small boats. This eventually led to negotiations and, in October, a government offer of amnesty in return for surrender.

Shuisky, true to form, had no intention of honoring his word, and he personally interrogated both the Tsarevich Piotr and Bolotnikov as they stood before him in chains. Eyewitness accounts of this confrontation describe Bolotnikov's behavior admiringly. When Shuisky demanded to know if he, Bolotnikov, "was the bandit and traitor who rose against his

sovereign," the Cossack acknowledged that he had indeed pledged to serve
a man who called himself the true Dmitri while in Poland. However, he
justified his behavior, claiming that he had sincerely believed he was serving a just cause. Now that he was at the tsar's mercy, he promised that if
offered clemency, he would serve the tsar "as truly as I have served until
now him who has forsaken me."[9] But Shuisky was unmoved and sent the
two to Moscow for torture and trial. Tsarevich Piotr was found guilty of
treason, and hanged at the Danilov Monastery[10] on the outskirts of Moscow. Bolotnikov was convicted of the same charge and sentenced to exile
at Kargopol in the far north. One year later, he was blinded and drowned.[11]

This time the tsar's triumph seemed complete but was again short-
lived. Even before the rebels at Tula had laid down their arms, another False
Dmitri had appeared in the Polish city of Starodub in May of 1607. Almost
nothing is known for certain about him, including his real name. According to one account, he had originally presented himself as Andrei Nagoy,
a relative of Ivan the Terrible's last wife, as a messenger of hope. He claimed
the true Dmitri was abroad but would arrive in Starodub any day to begin
a campaign to win back his throne. Later, when the good tsar failed to
appear, he claimed that he was Dmitri and that he had hidden his identity
for fear of assassination.[12]

This new False Dmitri had no outstanding personal qualities, but his
name attracted support from all over. He had hoped to attack the tsar's
forces and rescue Bolotnikov's army at Tula, but the rebels had surrendered before he could act. Thus, the pretender was forced to endure the
winter at Orel, about two hundred miles to the southwest of Moscow. In
the spring of 1608, his army approached the capital and thrashed a government force led by the tsar's brother, Dmitri Shuisky. Still, the rebels
were not strong enough to penetrate the city's defenses, and in June they
occupied a hill near the confluence of a small brook and the Moscow River
called Tushino. As the rebel encampment grew, it was soon transformed
into a disorganized, muddy, foul-smelling slum, with tents and straw-roof
huts strewn haphazardly over the hillside. It was here, some eight miles
west of the Kremlin, that the second False Dmitri's army remained for the
better part of two years.[13]

In September 1608, the pretender's position was symbolically
strengthened by the arrival of Marina Mniszech and her father at Tushino,
both of whom had been held in captivity since May of 1606.[14] Marina, who
apparently had hoped that her husband had somehow survived, was urged
by her father to accept this new False Dmitri.[15] Ultimately, the daughter
did acquiesce, but, to those who remembered her previously, her presence
now in the rebel camp was not entirely welcome. She was physically

unattractive with a high forehead and a long nose, and she was notoriously haughty and imperious. Even her supporters found her arrogant and insensitive. As tsaritsa, she had scorned the Orthodox faith and paraded her Catholicism, oblivious to the insult such behavior offered religious Muscovites. Later she would become infamous for her willingness to sleep with ordinary soldiers, even though she now insisted on the formality of a secret marriage ceremony to this new Dmitri in order to avoid sin in the eyes of the Roman Catholic Church.

The struggle between Shuisky and the second False Dmitri soon reduced Muscovy to a state of virtual anarchy. Normal government activity ceased as boyars, gentry, and merchants shamelessly exploited the situation by pledging their support to first one and then the other tsar in return for lucrative appointment and material gain.[16] As the fighting intensified, Tsar Vasily found himself on the defensive as Dmitri's army operated in the countryside. The rebels had hoped to capture various strategic points around the capital and starve it into submission. Among these was the massive Trinity Monastery, some forty miles to the north. A siege that began there in the fall of 1608 was to last fifteen months, with the defenders fighting tenaciously against superior numbers.

In time, however, Shuisky's cause was aided by the barbarous behavior of Dmitri's troops, who were living off the land around Moscow by robbing peasants and lesser gentry. This drove many rural inhabitants into the tsar's camp as they resisted the rebel plunderers. In anger and scorn, they began to refer to Dmitri as the "Thief of Tushino,"[17] and their tenacity in defending what was theirs breathed new life into Shuisky's cause. However, the tsar was eager to have a decisive victory and decided to seek military help from Sweden. In November, he sent Prince Mikhail Skopin-Shuisky to Novgorod to explore this possibility. After many months of difficult negotiations, the Russians agreed to abandon their claims to Livonia in exchange for a multinational mercenary army led by the Swedish general Jacob De la Gardie.

In the short run, this expedient seemed to work. In May of 1609, the mercenaries scored a triumph over a rebel force at Tver, but then a large part of the new army began to desert for lack of pay. Indeed, De la Gardie himself returned to Novgorod with many of his men. This left Skopin with only a small detachment of Swedes in addition to his original force. Undaunted, the young commander turned east toward the Volga where he managed to recruit some local militia units and won a victory over a rebel force in August. When De la Gardie rejoined him the following month, their combined forces broke the rebel siege of the Trinity Monastery in January, 1610. This triumph made Skopin a national hero yet aroused the jealousy not only of the tsar but also of his brothers, who saw the commander as a future rival for the throne.[18]

With his forces everywhere on the defensive, the Thief abandoned his wife and fled to Kaluga on December 27, 1609. Once again, however, the tsar was denied respite because some months earlier the King of Poland had laid siege to Smolensk. Shuisky had tried to prevent this by negotiating the armistice the previous July, but Sigismund reneged when he learned the tsar had solicited support from Sweden.[19] Moreover, many of Dmitri's former followers at Tushino decided to join him. On February 4 (14), 1610, a group of them signed a document by which they agreed to accept Sigismund's son, Wladyslaw, as tsar of Russia. The latter, however, had to convert to Orthodoxy and promise not to confiscate lands belonging to the Church, boyars, or other high officials.

Tsar Vasily was by no means prepared to tolerate these developments, and sent the seemingly indefatigable Skopin-Shuisky to prepare a campaign to break the siege of Smolensk. Tragedy intervened, however, when the young commander died from an undetermined illness on April 23 (May 3). The tsar then gave the same assignment to his hapless younger brother, Dmitri, who promptly led the army to disaster. The defeat that the Russians suffered in June at Klushino was total and sealed the fate of the tsar. A popular uprising on July 7 (17), 1610 forced Tsar Vasily to abdicate, and he was subsequently taken to a monastery and shorn as a monk.

In the past five years, Russia had had four tsars. With no obvious candidate to replace Shuisky, a regency of seven boyars was set up, headed by Feodor Mstislavsky. These men were supposed to run the country until provincial representatives could meet to elect a new tsar. However, this posed a serious dilemma. Not only did the regents need to be certain that the new sovereign would protect their status and privileges, but such a man also had to be acceptable to enough of the population to end the civil war. They soon became convinced that the only solution was to find a foreign candidate. To this end, they opened negotiations with the Polish military commander, Stanislav Zolkiewsky, and ultimately agreed to invite the heir to the Polish throne, Prince Wladyslaw, to become tsar.[20]

The boyar regency concluded an agreement with the Poles on August 17 (27) and awaited the arrival of the new Tsar Wladyslaw, but the boy never came. Sigismund had no intention of sending his son to Moscow to occupy the throne that he himself coveted. The council of seven were slow to catch on to this, however, and in a supreme act of folly one month later, they allowed a detachment of Polish soldiers to occupy the Kremlin. Their commander, Zolkiewski, had prudently arranged for this to occur at night so as not to provoke any opposition from patriotic Muscovites. He then relinquished his command to Colonel Alexander Gosiewsky and returned to Poland with a number of important prisoners including the former tsar, Vasily Ivanovich Shuisky, and a future patriarch, Filaret Romanov.

Many of those who hoped to resist Polish rule were prepared to support the second False Dmitri, now in Kaluga. He had been rejoined by Marina Mniszech and a certain Cossack *ataman*[21] named Ivan Martynovich Zarutsky,[22] a man whose background and leadership skills much resembled Bolotnikov's. Indeed, Zarutsky might have been called upon to lead a campaign against Moscow in the pretender's name, but it was not to be. On the morning of December 11 (17), 1610, the captain of Dmitri's personal guard, Piotr Urusov, decided to avenge the death of a fellow Tatar for which he believed the Thief responsible. He shot the pretender at point blank range as he rode in his sleigh along a country road, severed the victim's head, and left the body in the snow.

The second pretender's death had stunned his followers and left them without the symbol they needed. No one was more distraught over this development than the ambitious Marina Mniszech, who was now eight months pregnant. When she learned of her husband's murder, she ran out of her residence in Kaluga screaming and tearing at her hair. She then ripped open her blouse and exposed her breasts, demanding to be killed like her husband. Given her unpopularity at camp, there may have been those who wished to oblige her. But Marina's grief subsided as her determination to gain power reasserted itself. She soon married the Cossack Zarutsky, and in January 1611, gave birth to a boy, naming him Ivan Dmitrievich. Not surprisingly, she claimed that as Tsar Dmitri's son, the infant was the rightful heir to the Muscovite throne.

The country's infatuation with pretenders, however, was by no means sated. Not long after the death of the second False Dmitri, a third appeared hundreds of miles to the northeast in the town of Ivangorod. As in the case with the previous impostor, his identity is uncertain, although many historians refer to him as either Matiuska or Sidorka. He is believed to have been a church deacon in Moscow and later became a petty trader in Novgorod. He was apparently none too successful at the latter occupation and was ultimately forced to beg in the streets. By all accounts, he was a thoroughly pathetic creature, and his decision to impersonate Dmitri Ivanovich may well have been an act of desperation. He did not attract much of a following at first but persisted, possibly because he sensed people were confused enough to at least wonder if he were telling the truth.

To attract followers, Matiuska concocted a story that was fantastic even by medieval Russian standards. Referring to the tragedy at Uglich in 1591, he claimed to have been merely wounded, having survived with the help of patriotic Russians who had nursed him back to health. Then, following his assassination and cremation in Moscow, God had restored him to life and had resurrected him again after his recent shooting and beheading near Kaluga. Of course, all but the most gullible knew this was nonsense, but, for more than a year, many supported him for cynical reasons. Such was the case with a group of Cossack leaders who were meeting in Moscow in March of 1612. The participants were well aware Matiuska was a fake, but they elected to support him as tsar once the Kremlin was liberated. However, the following month, this third False Dmitri was invited to Moscow only to make himself so obnoxious that he barely escaped assassination. He ended up on display in the city streets chained to a post.

Neither Zarutsky or Marina seemed to have taken this latest impostor very seriously. In fact, even before his decline, they had attached themselves to a liberation movement headed by a prominent landowner from Riazan named Prokopi Liapunov. But Zarutsky was aware that almost no one in this new army was prepared to support the infant's claim to the throne, and he soon began to consider other options. He even negotiated with the Poles during this period hoping to gain a lucrative position in return for his military expertise and support. Nothing ever came of these overtures, however, and Zarutsky remained with Liapunov's followers, clearly prepared to switch sides should the right deal present itself.

In the meantime, the Poles intensified the siege of Smolensk, which was yet another violation of the agreement signed in August of 1610. This caused many more prominent Russians to become active in the resistance. Among these was the Patriarch Hermogen in Moscow, who now spoke out forcefully against King Sigismund's treachery. The aged patriarch had previously supported the candidacy of Prince Wladyslaw in the sincere belief that the young man, once properly converted to Orthodoxy, would restore order and unity to the land. The king's refusal to honor this agreement enraged him, and he began to write letters and manifestos to the people urging them to fight the aggressor. The Poles tried to intimidate him and finally imprisoned him in the Kremlin's Chudov Monastery, but the old man's defiance could not be broken. His example helped other Russians solidify and focus their anger.

The Polish commander in the Kremlin, Alexander Gosiewsky, sensed this growing hostility among the population and took vigorous steps to counter it. As his own forces prepared for a possible siege, he ordered all Muscovites off the street after dark and tried forcibly to disarm them by establishing checkpoints around the city to collect sabers, pistols, axes, and knives. Despite the fact that violators were frequently executed, compliance proved impossible to achieve. People merely became more careful, avoided roadblocks, and stored weapons and gunpowder at hidden locations. At the same time, Russian soldiers who had organized in other cities and towns began secretly to filter into Moscow. In most cases, they were protected by patriotic citizens, who sensed that an uprising was imminent.

In 1611, Easter, that most joyous of Russian holidays, fell on March 10 (17), but its arrival did little to lift the foul and vengeful mood of the capital. The Poles had wanted to ban the traditional religious procession in Red Square, fearing that it would attract large crowds and possibly lead to violence. But the boyar regency, in a rare display of patriotic backbone, insisted that it take place. The weather was bitterly cold, but the traditional rituals and ceremonies were observed. The patriarch, Hermogen, released from incarceration for this occasion, led the procession on a horse that was supposed to represent a donkey. He was preceded by twenty splendidly attired nobles who lined his path with fine cloth. Following behind was a sleigh bearing an artificial tree, on which were hung artificial apples, and accompanied by a choir of boys singing psalms. Bells rang all over Moscow as people blessed and kissed each other exclaiming, "Christ is risen! Truly He is risen!"

The great holiday passed without incident, but two days later, as the advance guard of the national army moved into the outskirts of Moscow, the Poles grew fearful since they had not completed their defensive preparations. Foolishly, they tried to enlist some Russian carters to help move cannon to the towers of the walls of Kitai-Gorod. The latter resisted, and a fight broke out in Red Square that quickly spread and intensified. This was accompanied by a raging fire that gutted much of the inner city. The Muscovites, who were initially unarmed, suffered more than a thousand casualties. The Poles, however, were not able to finish what they had started. Late in the day when they tried to occupy a part of town known as Beli-Gorod, they were driven back by angry townsmen, who had armed and organized themselves.

During the battle, the boyar regency and most of the high nobility had aided the enemy against their own countrymen. One exception, however, was Prince Dmitri Pozharsky, a former *voevoda* of Zaraisk, whose residence was located north of the Kremlin on Sretenka Street. Upon hearing alarm bells in Kitai-Gorod, he assumed command of a detachment of *strel'tsy* and led them into fierce hand-to-hand combat with the Poles and their mercenaries. The prince paid dearly for his valor, however, and fell during the fighting with a saber slash to the head. For a time, he lay near death, but he was rescued by his men who treated the wound and transported him to the Trinity Monastery.

Thus with Pozharsky convalescing away from the capital, the national army was preparing to oust the Poles from the Kremlin. During the summer of 1611, three leaders had emerged: Liapunov, Ivan Zarutsky, and Dmitri Trubetskoy. They had agreed to wield joint executive power in military and civilian affairs, but they could not agree on who should become tsar after the Poles were expelled. The Cossacks seemed to favor Marina's son, but Liapunov urged that a prince be invited from Sweden. Eventually, he persuaded some others in the new government to send a delegation to Novgorod to open negotiations. This initiative, however, was resented by many, especially the Cossacks, who were angry that Liapunov had tried to impose discipline on them.[23] As the disharmony in the national army became obvious, the Poles decided to exploit it. They composed a letter urging an anti-Cossack crusade in Russia and forged Liapunov's signature. The latter was confronted but fiercely denied that he had written anything of the kind. The Cossacks refused to believe him and hacked him to death with their swords. This event greatly weakened the effectiveness of the first national army as it prepared to liberate Moscow. Zarutsky and Trubetskoy did attempt operations of a sort, but they lasted only a few months and accomplished very little. Complicating the situation now was the fall of Smolensk to the Poles on June 3 (13) and the fall of Novgorod to the Swedes on July 6 (16). In the latter instance, the people had formally agreed to recognize the king of Sweden as their protector, although this seems to have been done without much enthusiasm. Despite the agreement, the Novgorodians were unable to prevent the Swedes from occupying other Baltic territories.

By the fall of 1611, the Muscovite state seemed very close to extinction, but at the urging of certain prominent church leaders, including Patriarch Hermogen,[24] a new attempt to free the land from foreign control began in the Nizhni-Novgorod[25] area. The man who became the leader of this movement was a remarkable butcher named Kuzma Minin. Born in the city of Balakhna to a family of merchants, he had long been known for his patriotism and interest in civic affairs. In September, he had been elected *starosta*[26] of the local land assembly and soon thereafter began to collect donations for a new national army. Minin actually convinced the local authorities of the necessity for passing a property tax that amounted to one-fifth of each citizen's wealth. Later, this tax was applied to monasteries and large estates, which previously had been exempt.

Of course, what the country really needed was leadership. Thus, with no tsar in the Kremlin, Minin himself pressed a wounded veteran of the Moscow Easter uprising, Prince Dmitri Pozharsky, to take command the new national army which had begun to form. It was not an obvious choice.

The prince was not particularly high-born and had attained only the modest rank of *stol'nik.*[27] Nor was he eager to accept such a responsibility, since his health was poor and he had recently begun to suffer from fits of epilepsy, but the butcher was persistent and traveled to Pozharsky's estate in Mureevo to plead his case in person. Other influential townsmen did the same. The prince finally relented, but he insisted that Minin be appointed treasurer and assist him in organizing and supplying the army.

Ultimately, the civic high-mindedness of Minin and Pozharsky proved infectious as people responded not only to the need to expel the invader, but also to elect a new tsar. In the spring of 1612, elections were held for a new *Zemsky Sobor* in cities and towns all across Russia. The military preparations, however, did not go as well. Serious difficulties emerged from the distrust and enmity that many Russians felt for the Cossack units under Ivan Zarutsky. Some Church officials, desperate for unity, had urged cooperation, but the ataman's well-known Polish sympathies and his desire to place Marina's child on the throne made this impossible. The break finally came when Zarutsky, who felt threatened by the formation of the new Russian national army, tried to blunt its effectiveness by sending a detachment to occupy Yaroslavl', a key city in the north. Pozharsky, however, had anticipated such a move, and got there first. He made Yaroslavl' his headquarters as he planned the liberation of Moscow.

Zarutsky's next move was to enter into secret negotiations with the Polish *hetman*[28] and military commander, Jan Chodkiewicz, whose army was rapidly approaching Moscow from the west to provide support for the Polish forces still in the Kremlin. When this act of treachery failed to bear fruit, Zarutsky, Marina, and her son fled to Kostroma, accompanied by an armed force of twenty-five hundred. Trubetskoy subsequently joined forces with Minin and Pozharsky in Yaroslavl', and in August 1612, the second national army of liberation finally began to move toward Moscow.

Liberation now was just a matter of time, although to many people it may have already seemed too late. The capital's most sacred cathedrals had been desecrated, its civil structures gutted, and the Kremlin treasures plundered. Red Square had become a squalid and desolate wasteland covered with rubble and trash. Neglect and decay were everywhere as trade and commerce struggled to survive. Lack of food was a persistent problem for all. Even in the best of times, most Muscovites subsisted on little more than bread, groats, turnips, and cabbage.[29] But now, with agricultural production minimal, it was common to see people wandering about crazed with hunger, scavenging everywhere to find nourishment.

The decisive battle between the Poles and the Russians occurred on August 22 (September 1), near Novodevichy Monastery, and raged back and forth for three days with the outcome much in doubt. The turning point came when Kuzma Minin led a counterattack in which the Cossacks, who had previously refused to fight, now joined. The Poles under Hetman Chodkiewicz were forced to withdraw. This left the Polish garrison in the Kremlin isolated and without hope of reinforcement. Their inevitable surrender occurred on October 22 (November 1), 1612.

The liberation of the Kremlin was a joyous event for townsmen weary of war and turmoil, but it did not end the crisis that threatened the existence of the Muscovite state. Indeed, the Poles viewed their recent defeat and expulsion as temporary and almost immediately began to plan another offensive. The Swedes, who still occupied Novgorod, also hoped to gain territory at Russia's expense. Thus for the military commanders who reoccupied the citadel in the final months of 1612, defense and rebuilding were primary concerns. Of no less importance, however, was the need to choose a new tsar. To this end the *Zemsky Sobor*, elected some nine months earlier, was convened in January 1613, in the Kremlin's Cathedral of the Assumption.[30]

There were a number of prominent candidates to consider, including Prince Karl Philip of Sweden; the Cossack leader, Dmitri Trubetskoy; and a sixteen-year-old named Michael Romanov, who was distantly related to Ivan the Terrible's first wife. The deliberations continued for more than a month. Complete unanimity was never achieved, but eventually a compromise was worked out. On February 21 (March 3), 1613, Michael Feodorovich Romanov was elected tsar of Russia. The new ruler's most attractive qualities were that he was native-born, young, and utterly inexperienced. Most seemed to want a weak sovereign who would not be too demanding or assertive.

All that remained now was to inform the young man of his election, but no one quite knew where he was. During much of the Polish occupation, the boy and his mother, Marfa, had been trapped in the Kremlin. Once the Poles had been expelled, the two escaped and were thought to be hiding somewhere in the Yaroslavl' region. A delegation of important men, including the boyar Feodor Sheremetev, the Archbishop Feodorit, and the monk Avraamy Palitsyn, was appointed by the *Zemsky Sobor* to find young Michael and escort him to Moscow. The group set out on March 2, and, twelve days later, located the tsar-elect at the Ipatiev Monastery in Kostroma.

The "good news" they bore, however, was not well-received. In fact, both the boy and his mother tearfully and angrily rejected the throne outright. Their reaction was understandable. The four previous tsars had all been engulfed by tragedy, and there seemed little reason to believe that things would now be different. But the men who journeyed from Moscow could not accept this answer. Solemnly and persuasively, they swore before God that, as tsar, Michael would be protected by the whole land. Mother and son finally relented, but they were actually in more danger than they suspected. A detachment of Polish soldiers, having learned of the young man's election, was determined to find and assassinate him before he could ascend the throne. To this end, they enlisted a peasant named Ivan Susanin from the village of Domnino, who promised to take them to the new tsar. But Susanin only pretended to cooperate and actually led the soldiers into a tractless forest. When the Poles caught on to his ruse, they killed him.[31]

It took six weeks for the imperial party to make it back to Moscow, and not until July 11 (21) was Michael crowned, one day before his seventeenth birthday. The scars of war and enemy occupation in the Kremlin were still visible, but the mood was festive. Every attempt was being made to revive the country's sacred traditions, which had all but perished in the turmoil of the recent past. On the appointed day, participating nobles and officials gathered in the Palace of Facets[32] to await the new tsar, who arrived at about two o'clock. A solemn procession then began to move toward the Cathedral of the Assumption, only a few yards across Cathedral Square. The thirty-three bells in the tower of Ivan the Great pealed furiously as the dignitaries filed into the most sacred church in the land. Prominent among the participants was Michael's uncle, Ivan Romanov, who carried the crown of Vladimir Monomakh;[33] Dmitri Trubetskoy, who carried the imperial scepter; and Dmitri Pozharsky, who bore the diamond-studded golden orb. Most prominent among those not invited to participate was Kuzma Minin,[34] whose low birth barred him from a place of honor despite his heroism during the struggle to liberate Moscow.

The new tsar, who had come to Moscow with such reluctance, probably did not much enjoy the cheering crowds that filled the Kremlin that day. Weighed down by the heavy ceremonial robes, he slowly made his way into the Cathedral preceded by a priest sprinkling holy water before him. Once inside, he stood among the four large columns that support the domed roof with its gilded cupolas. The cathedral, which was filled to capacity, was permeated with the smell of incense. Every eye was focused on the small, frightened young man, standing stiffly before the magnificent iconostasis. Around him loomed imposing frescoed images of saints and Russian heroes in bright colors, illuminated by flickering candles and natural sunlight from narrow windows set high in the church's walls. Higher still, in the central cupola, majestically presiding over it all, the severe image of Christ the Savior gazed down.

At the appointed moment, the metropolitan, Efrem,[35] stepped forward and solemnly asked God's blessing for the new tsar. Michael himself then spoke briefly about the misfortunes of the previous fifteen years, expressing the hope that peace and unity would now return to the Russian land. The metropolitan placed the crown of Monomakh on Michael's head, blessed him, and gave him Holy Communion. The tsar took up the orb and scepter, symbols of imperial power, and turned to join the procession leaving the cathedral.

As the new tsar marched among the nobles who would serve in his new government, he might have wondered whom he could really trust. Some had been chosen by his mother, and included close relatives like Boris and Mikhail Saltykov. These men almost certainly could be expected to remain loyal, if only out of self-interest, but there were others who had opposed his candidacy from the beginning and who did not expect him to last long. One of these was Feodor Mstislavsky, who at one time had sought the throne himself and subsequently had tried to secure it for Prince Wladyslaw. This same man now cheered Tsar Michael showering him with gold coins as he left the cathedral.

Although the new government was threatened on all sides, little doubt remained that the lingering challenge posed by the Cossack Zarutsky, his wife Marina Mniszech, and her young son, Ivan Dmitrievich, would be among the first to be dealt with. The Polish woman's insistence that her son was the rightful tsar had no firm support anywhere, but the three were still thought to be a source of potential trouble for the new regime. As early as May of 1613, troops led by Prince Odoevsky in the name of the Provisional Government had defeated Zarutsky's force near Voronezh and drove him south to Astrakhan. There he briefly became a vassal of the Shah of Persia, and planned to lead an army up the Volga. He expected to attract peasants and Cossacks along the way and imagined that he would eventually be strong enough to attack Moscow.

But Zarutsky's ambitions could not be realized, mainly because the majority of Cossacks were inclined to support the newly crowned tsar in Moscow. Even in Astrakhan, where resistance to the Kremlin was a time-honored tradition, Zarutsky and Marina encountered indifference which gradually solidified into hostility. They soon felt compelled to withdraw into the city's kremlin for safety, becoming virtual prisoners. Later they fled and sought refuge among the Yaik Cossacks, who at first defended the family but later turned against them. In June of 1614, the three were handed over to a detachment of *strel'tsy*, and sent to Moscow for trial.

Tsar Michael was urged by the boyar duma to deal harshly with these troublemakers, and he did. Marina, who was sentenced to life imprisonment, was sent to Kolomna where she did not live long. Undoubtedly, her end was hastened by her grief at the execution of her small son, Ivan Dmitrievich. The child, who was not yet four, could not possibly have understood the crimes that others had committed in his name. Still, he was seen as a potential threat and was unceremoniously hanged at Serpukhov gates just outside Moscow. Zarutsky's role was seen as much more sinister, and he was condemned to death by impalement. Much to the satisfaction of his captors, he died writhing in agony. In resorting to such vindictiveness, however, little did the Romanovs suspect that they were nurturing a tradition that would eventually attend the dynasty's own tragic end.

Selected Bibliography

One of the most confusing and controversial periods in Russian history, the Time of Troubles, is best treated in Chester Dunning's thoroughly researched and well-explained *Russia's First Civil War*. This book is also to be recommended for its excellent maps and illustrations. A shorter version of this period may be found in Robert Crummey's *The Formation of Muscovy 1304–1613*. Paul Avrich describes the Bolotnikov rebellion in interesting detail in *Russian Rebels*. There is no separate biography in English for Vasily Shuisky, but Chester Dunning's treatment of this controversial tsar ("Shuisky, Vasilii Ivanovich") in the *Modern Encyclopedia of Russian and Soviet History*, (ed., Joseph L. Wieczynski, 54 vols., with suppl., Gulf Breeze, FL, 1976–90) covers the most the most essential elements of his life and reign.

Avrich, Paul. *Russian Rebels*. New York: W.W. Norton, 1972.

Crummey, Robert O. *The Formation of Muscovy 1304–1613*. New York: Longman, 1987.

Dunning, Chester S.L. *Russia's First Civil War*. University Park: Pennsylvania State University Press, 2001.

_____. "Shuiskii, Vasilii Ivanovich." *Modern Encyclopedia of Russian and Soviet History*, ed. Joseph L. Wieczynski, 54 vols. With suppl. Gulf Breeze, Florida: Academic International Press, 1976–1990.

Orchard, G. Edward. "Zarutsky, Ivan Martynovich." *Modern Encyclopedia of Russian and Soviet History*, ed. Joseph L. Wieczynski, 54 vols. With suppl. Gulf Breeze, Florida: Academic International Press, 1976–1990.

Roweland, Daniel B. "Pozharsky, Dmitri Mikhailovich." *Modern Encyclopedia of Russian and Soviet History*, ed. Joseph L. Wieczynski, 54 vols. With suppl. Gulf Breeze, Florida: Academic International Press, 1976–1990..

_____. "Mniszek, Marina." *Modern Encyclopedia of Russian and Soviet History*, ed.

Joseph L. Wieczynski, 54 vols. With suppl. Gulf Breeze, Florida: Academic International Press, 1976–1990.

Skrynnikov, Ruslan G. *Sviatityeli i Vlasti*. Lenizdat, Leningrad, 1990.

_____. *The Time of Troubles: Russia in Crisis*. Ed. and trans. Hugh Graham. Gulf Breeze, Florida: Academic International Press, 1988.

Vernadsky, George. *A History of Russia. Vol. 5, The Tsardom of Moscow*. New Haven: Yale University Press, 1963.

Wiita, John. "Bolotnikov, Ivan Isaevich." *Modern Encyclopedia of Russian and Soviet History*, ed. Joseph L. Wieczynski, 54 vols. With suppl. Gulf Breeze, Florida: Academic International Press, 1976–90.

Zenkovsy, Sergei A. ed. *Medieval Russia's Epics, Chronicles and Tales*. New York: E.P. Dutton, 1974.

4. Mobs, Mutinies, and the Church Schism

Tsar Michael was in almost every way uniquely unqualified to be an autocrat. He was barely literate, a slow thinker, weak-willed and in poor health. Still, the task of restoring the Muscovite state was of such urgency that a spirit of cooperation prevailed during his first years in power. This goodwill was accompanied by a modest economic revival, aided by a substantial loan from the Stroganov family to pay the army while peace treaties with Sweden and Poland were being concluded. At the same time, the new dynasty was struggling to establish legitimacy at home and to win respect abroad. To these ends, eleven new departments, or *prikazy*, were created in the first six years of Michael's reign. These included an Apothecary Department to minister to the tsar's many ailments, a Brigand Department to deal with a growing crime rate, and a Masonry Department to rebuild the crumbling walls of the Kremlin and other damaged structures. The old fortress actually took on a new look in the 1620s as the Spassky, or Savior's Tower, was enlarged and fitted with a huge clock visible to all from Red Square.

Firm leadership for the new dynasty was provided by the tsar's father, sixty-six-year-old Patriarch Filaret, who in 1619 was returned to Moscow from Polish captivity. In many ways the opposite of his meek and retiring son, he quickly took charge of both the Church and the government. Not only did he exile or punish those who displeased him, but he created his own four-man privy council, mostly ignoring the boyar Duma and the *Zemsky Sobor*. Filaret's normally sound judgment, however, was impaired by his hatred of the Poles and his desire to regain the city of Smolensk. To these ends in 1632, he tried to use King Sigismund III's death to gain a military alliance with Sweden. Urging the Swedish king Gustavus Adolphus to join Muscovy in an attack on their common enemy, he promised to support his ally's claim to the Polish crown. Gustavus' death in battle, however, effectively ended the alliance. Meanwhile, the Muscovite army, having failed to capture Smolensk, was thrown on the defensive when the Crimean Tatars invaded from the south and the Poles counterattacked in the west. Thus, when Filaret died in October of 1633, there was little desire in Moscow to continue the struggle.

The peace that was concluded reflected the full extent of Muscovy's defeat. Not only did the tsar have to accept Poland's continued occupation of Smolensk and other towns that had been lost during the Time of Troubles, he had to agree to an indemnity of 20,000 rubles. Moreover, there was anger and indignation in the capital against the Russian commander, Mikhail Borisovich Shein, who was blamed for the army's poor showing. He was put on trial and eventually executed. Steps were subsequently taken to strengthen the southern border against Tatar raids, but such measures ultimately did little to enhance the reputation of the Muscovite state in the European community. This became painfully evident in 1644 when Michael was unable to entice the Danish prince, Waldemar, to marry his daughter. It was another embarrassing failure for the tsar, who was now suffering acutely from a number of ailments including lameness and dropsy. In July of 1645, he was stricken in church while celebrating his name day. He died hours later, survived by his three daughters and a sixteen-year-old boy named Alexis.

Despite his youth, the ascendance of Tsar Alexis to the throne was in many ways reassuring. Not only was he in good health, physically imposing, and well-educated, he actually enjoyed participating in the endless ceremonies and rituals that had so exhausted his father. Too, the new tsar was aided by many of the same advisers who had served Tsar Michael. One of these was his own brother-in-law and former tutor, Boris Morozov, who, if not entirely popular with most Muscovites, was at least recognized for his ability and experience. Unfortunately, many of these advisers, Morozov included, were arrogant, corrupt, and determined to pursue policies that benefited the ruling elite at the expense of everyone else. This created a reservoir of resentment that resulted in a nasty confrontation on June 1 (11), 1648.

It began as the tsar was returning to Moscow from his annual pilgrimage at the Trinity Monastery. As his carriage passed through the Sretenka Gate at the outskirts of the city, a large crowd was gathered there to greet him and offer the traditional symbols of welcome, bread and salt.

The mood was friendly and cheerful until a few malcontents tried to press a petition on him to complain about a corrupt public official named Leonti Pleshcheev, but Alexis refused to accept the document. As the tsar's *strel'tsy* guard began pushing people back, the imperial retinue abruptly started moving again toward the Kremlin, but the petitioners would not disband and, a short time later, tried to impose the same document on the tsaritsa when her carriage passed. Again it was rejected, but this time there was violence, injuries, and arrests.

The episode had been unpleasant but brief and probably would have been forgotten had it not been for a similar confrontation the following day. The tsar was again detained by a crowd, this time as he was leaving a church service on Sretenka Street in Belyi-Gorod. There was shouting and more complaints about "those who suck out our blood and torture us without cause." Brazenly, the petitioners followed Alexis back to the Kremlin and forced their way through the gates behind his carriage. They surged into Cathedral Square[1] and began to mass before the imperial palace, demanding the release of those arrested the day before and the execution of Leonti Pleshcheev.

Tsar Alexis, just nineteen years old, was terrified by the mob. Having occupied the throne less than three years, he had never faced such a challenge to his authority, and his inexperience as a ruler was woefully apparent. When he found he could not restore order himself, he summoned Boris Morozov, who addressed the rabble in bold language. When this had no effect, Morozov ordered the tsar's *strel'tsy* bodyguard to open fire. To his horror, they refused. Seeing this, the mob began to attack government officials and plunder the homes of the wealthy. Among the latter was Morozov's own Kremlin residence. Not only did the insurgents smash sacred icons and kill at least one servant, but they threatened Morozov's wife, who was ultimately spared only because she was the tsaritsa's sister. The rampage went on until the tsar surrendered Pleshcheev to the mob. The young sovereign watched helplessly as the bureaucrat was beaten to death and his body mutilated.

The violence continued the next day. Fires broke out all over the city as angry voices demanded that more officials be punished for their transgressions. One of those to be sacrificed was Piotr Trakhaniotov, whose crimes as head of a provincial regional chancellory had offended gentry and townsmen alike. He was beheaded before a jeering crowd on June 5 (15). Death was also urged for Boris Morozov, but the tsar could not bear to lose his most trusted advisor. He tearfully pleaded to be allowed to retain this man but was finally compelled to banish him to a monastery at Beloozero in the far north.[2] Fortunately, by this time the violence had

The Salt Mutiny of June 1648 featured a furious assault on the Kremlin by an angry mob. Tsar Alexis was so terrified by the violence that he introduced a new law code the following year. Among other things, the *Ulozhenie* of 1649 provided the legal basis for both serfdom and autocracy. E.E. Lissner (dates unknown). L.P. Bushchik, *Illustrirovanaya Istoriya SSSR, XV–XVII vv.* Moskva, Prosveshcheniye, 1970.

largely subsided, its end having been hastened by the appearance of a gentry militia force under the command of Prince Iakov (Jacob) Cherkassy. Only then was order fully restored.

In retrospect, the causes of the rebellion are not hard to identify. The tsar's refusal to accept the petition on June 1 (11) provided the spark,[3] but there were deeper grievances as well. Morozov's fiscal initiatives were among the most provocative. As the tsar's chief adviser on financial affairs, he had endeavored to save money by laying off government workers and reducing the salaries of others, including the *strel'tsy*. The merchants were angered when he made the sale of tobacco and salt government monopolies, and there was bitter resentment over his intrusive new census designed to generate more revenue, coupled with a stunning rise in the salt tax by four-hundred percent. Ultimately, it was this final initiative and the offensive manner in which it was levied that brought matters to a head. The poorest Muscovites gave up salt altogether, which resulted in large amounts of it turning to brine in government warehouses. Many people, frustrated by such needless waste, tried to petition the tsar, but Morozov and his officials saw to it that their efforts got nowhere. Thus, this tax and the rebellion it engendered brought on at least one important unintended consequence: a new law code designed to prevent any such future upheavals.

Recovering from his panic, Alexis assigned five men to compile what is known in Russian as the *Ulozhenie*. This compilation of laws and principles, when it was completed in January 1649, consisted of twenty-five chapters and 967 articles. Not surprisingly, it placed great emphasis on law and order and the security of the tsar's person. Chapter II, entitled "the Sovereign's Honor and How to Guard his Health," prescribed the death penalty for virtually every transgression imaginable including "malicious thoughts" (although it is not clear how authorities intended to identify these). Punishments for lesser crimes were also severe: tobacco law violators were to have their noses slit, counterfeiters were be forced to swallow molten lead, and thieves were subject to hand amputation. Finally, the new code also indirectly legalized serfdom, not by open proclamation, but by extending indefinitely the recovery period for runaway serfs. The semi-enslavement of a large portion of the peasant population became a source of seething antagonism that the ruling elite would not be able to arrest.

The *Ulozhenie* is generally considered one of the more notable accomplishments of Alexis' reign in large part because many of its provisions remained in effect until well into the 19th century. But it was also this document that provided the legal foundation for autocracy in Russia. Future tsars would allude to the *Ulozhenie* as they defended with ever greater tenacity their power and near divine status. Still, the new law code did not in itself bring about the peace and tranquility that Alexis desired. The following year, a fierce rebellion erupted in the famine-plagued area around Pskov and Novgorod incited by townsmen and poor farmers to prevent grain from being shipped to Sweden as part of a trade agreement. The government's reaction was typically heavy-handed as regular army units were sent to restore order. There seems to have been no thought of ending the strife by sending food to feed the hungry.

To be sure, the compulsion to use force whenever possible came naturally to the Muscovite ruling elite, possibly because most of the time it seemed to work. In at least one area, however, it proved quite useless. In the mid–1650s, when a dispute concerning rituals and liturgy developed within the Church, Alexis faced resistance from men and women whose convictions went far beyond their own physical well-being or any other material considerations. Indeed, the government's attempt to gain submission through coercion or bribery only engendered increased defiance,

Patriarch Nikon was determined to impose conformity on the Church and to assert his authority in affairs of state. However, his arrogance and self-righteousness offended Tsar Alexis, who eventually convened a church council to have him removed from power. *Zhit'e Protopopa Avvakum*, Moskva, Academia, 1934.

a fact the tsar and his advisers found mystifying. The religious schism that developed in the second half of the seventeenth century proved to be both long lasting and profound. Ultimately, it diminished the stature of the Church, divided the country, and created a whole new class of dissidents against the tsar.

Ironically, the great schism was caused by an attempt to unify and revitalize Russian Orthodoxy. When the aged and passive patriarch, Iosef (Joseph), died in April of 1652, Alexis named Nikon, the vigorous metropolitan of Novgorod, to replace him. The new patriarch was an imposing figure. He stood six-feet-six-inches tall and was well known for his intense spirituality and uncompromising devotion to principle. He was also courageous in the face of danger. During the Pskov-Novgorod riots of 1650, while other city officials cowered in fear, Nikon had boldly confronted the rebels and helped to restore order. The young tsar was impressed. Here was a man who seemed prepared not only to lead the Russian Church, but also to assume a more prominent position among the other patriarchs in the Eastern Orthodox world.

In many ways, the new patriarch resembled Tsar Alexis' grandfather, Patriarch Filaret, who had been accorded the title *veliki gosudar* or "great sovereign"[4] and was recognized as the *de facto* ruler of Muscovy until his death in 1633. Like Filaret, Nikon believed his position as spiritual leader of the Church was superior to that of the tsar; thus, he insisted that the tsar and boyars swear obedience to him in all ecclesiastical matters. He also demanded that certain offending clauses of the *Ulozhenie* be suspended.[5] Finally, Nikon announced to the tsar that it would be his intention to serve as patriarch for three years. Only then would he decide whether the support he was receiving from the young sovereign warranted his continuing in office.

The tsar readily accepted these conditions and the new patriarch went to work. One of his earliest initiatives was to reduce the consumption of alcohol by limiting the number of licensed taverns and wine shops and by banning sales on Sundays and other fast days. He also prevailed upon Tsar Alexis to force non-baptized foreigners to move outside the city,[6] and he began a campaign to eliminate all non-Orthodox religious works of art. To accomplish the latter, he sent his agents to search the homes of Muscovites known to have cosmopolitan tastes. Religious paintings not done in the Byzantine style were confiscated and, in some cases, publicly smashed in the Cathedral of the Assumption.

Nikon's majestic view of his power and responsibilities did not come entirely from within. He had been encouraged to think in a grand manner while he was still a bishop by Patriarch Paisos of Antioch. The latter had visited Moscow in January of 1649 seeking financial support for Christians living in virtual captivity under the Muslim Turks. Paisos spoke passionately of the Russian Church's historic mission as the only eastern rite church free of Islamic or Catholic rule. However, he also expressed displeasure about certain differences in the Russians' liturgy and ritual, which he believed were essential to correct spirituality. Nikon not only came to agree with the patriarch's point of view, but would eventually far exceed his determination in correcting these differences. To this end, he was soon in collaboration with a certain Greek scholar named Arsenios to prepare his flock for the necessary reforms. By 1653, this had resulted in a new corrected psalter and changes in liturgy and ritual. Henceforth, the sign of the cross would be made with three fingers rather than two, the spelling of the name Jesus would be corrected, the manner of genuflecting in church would be modified according to the Greek, processional marches would follow an easterly rather than a westerly direction, and "alleluia" would be sung three times rather than twice during the service.

The reforms that Paisos hoped to promote were encouraged by events in Ukraine and parts of Belorussia. In 1648, a certain Ukrainian Cossack named Bogdan Khmel'nitsky[7] had led the Orthodox population in rebellion against Polish rule. The issues were complex but involved the favoritism shown to a small percentage of the Cossacks living in these lands who had been recruited into Polish military service. These were entered in a register, which entitled them to tax immunities, and were free from any obligation to serve landlords in Poland or Lithuania. However, the mass of Ukrainian Cossacks were deliberately denied this status, since the king not only wanted to tax them, but also convert them from Orthodoxy to Roman Catholicism. After some initial victories, however, the Cossacks lost their momentum as the Poles fought back. In 1651, Khmel'nitsky turned to the Kremlin, offering to submit the territories under his control to a Muscovite protectorate in return for military aid. Both the tsar and the patriarch were attracted to the offer, since the lands in question had once been part of the old Kievan empire and thus, in their opinion, rightly belonged to Muscovy. Still, there was good reason to be cautious. Alexis undoubtedly remembered the last conflict with Poland two decades earlier in which the Muscovites had been soundly thrashed. Military reforms had since been undertaken, but there was doubt as to whether they had been extensive enough to ensure a different outcome. For his part, Nikon's concerns were more complicated. He knew well that the rituals and liturgy practiced in the territories controlled by Poland were more purely Greek than those practiced in Muscovy. Thus, should the tsar succeed in absorbing these lands, it would be the patriarch's task to bring his own flock into conformity with the rest of the Orthodox world.

In the end, the decision to intervene on behalf of the Ukrainian Cossacks was based not only on the desire to win land, but also on the allure of a religious crusade against the Catholics. Added to this was Alexis' need to test his mettle as a military commander. Not that he intended to personally lead soldiers into battle, but he was eager to involve himself in the planning of military strategy, training, and logistics. By May of 1654, all was ready as he appeared at the head of the Sovereign's Regiment in Red Square attired in vestments studded with pearls and bearing his orb and scepter to receive the patriarch's blessing. The Muscovite army's main objective was Smolensk,[8] three hundred miles to the southwest on the Dnieper River. With the troops poised to move out, the tsar mounted a carriage with gold trim and crimson upholstery and specially guarded by twenty-four hussars. Leading the regiment was a rider carrying Alexis' personal ensign depicting a golden eagle against a black-and-white striped background bearing the motto "Fear God and Obey the Tsar."

But Alexis was leaving a capital agitated over Nikon's reforms and the Church's increasingly dominant role in society. The first resistance had appeared nearly a year earlier in the Moscow Printing Office when a number of workers, including an influential cleric named Ivan Nasedka, resigned to protest the new psalter. The patriarch had promptly dismissed the dissidents and placed the Printing Office under his jurisdiction. But protests were also voiced by a group called the Zealots of Piety,[9] whose spirituality and devotion could not be ignored. These men, who included Bishop Pavel of Kolomna, Longin of Murom, Ivan Neronov, and the Archpriest Avvakum, truly believed these changes violated the very essence of their faith. Alarmed, they banded together and made a fervent, albeit futile, appeal to the tsar. Nikon eventually had them all imprisoned or exiled, but he did not succeed in stifling their dissent. In time, their followers grew dramatically in number and became known as Old Believers, or *staroobriadtsy*.[10]

As the patriarch continued to press for acceptance of his reforms that summer, those inclined to look for signs of God's judgment on this matter were confused by a mixed message. The tsar's army was generally victorious in the west, but Moscow itself was attacked by a plague so virulent that people were dying faster than they could be buried. By early fall, public order in the capital had virtually disintegrated amid rioting and looting. Dogs and pigs roamed the streets to scavenge among the corpses, sometimes attacking the living. The six *strel'tsy* regiments whose responsibility it was to keep order perished almost to the man. When the tsar heard of the emergency, he implored Nikon to accompany the imperial family to a safe location far from Moscow. The move was clearly necessary, but provoked much hostility toward the patriarch from those who believed he had abandoned his flock. Others were glad to see him go, but only because they were convinced that his reforms were poisoning their faith. This latter conviction seemed more compelling than ever on August 12 (22), when a solar eclipse darkened parts of Muscovy, terrifying the populace. Nikon blamed this omen on the clauses in the Law Code of 1649 that he believed had unfairly restricted the Church. To regain divine favor, he sent two holy icons to Moscow and a letter in which he urged the suffering to seek relief through spirituality and prayer. The gesture seemed feeble to most, but the tsar never wavered in his support of his spiritual father. In February of 1655, after the plague had subsided, he returned to the capital to thank Nikon for his service. He also reaffirmed the title of great sovereign that he had bestowed on him earlier.

However, the pressure of the previous few years seemed to have taken its toll on the patriarch, whose behavior was becoming increasingly arrogant, arbitrary, and even bizarre. He began to dress in expensive, jewel-studded vestments of Greek design and embarked on a costly building program that featured a sumptuous new patriarchal palace in the Kremlin and two other monasteries not far from Moscow. He also lengthened the mass, added music imported from Kiev, spied on his own priests, and verbally abused errant boyars in public. On one occasion, he managed to shock even Alexis. During mass on the first Sunday of Lent, Nikon was lecturing the worshippers about the need to make the sign of the cross in the Greek manner (i.e., with three fingers). Then as he became increasingly agitated, he started to rant about the popularity of "Frankish" icons[11] in Moscow, many of which his agents had confiscated and delivered to the cathedral. To the horror of everyone, he began smashing them to bits after announcing the home in which each had been found. He finally ordered the fragments burned on the spot but was prevented from doing so by the tsar, who gently suggested that the pieces be buried instead.

As complaints about the patriarch mounted during the summer of 1655, Alexis was absorbed by an increasingly complicated military situation in the west. For the most part, the campaign had gone quite well. Smolensk had been taken the previous year, and a final victory over the Poles seemed within reach; in July, however, Sweden suddenly entered the conflict occupying Warsaw and Kracow. The move had been prompted by the newly crowned king's desire to prevent further Muscovite expansion and to win territory from Poland. Alexis countered this initiative in October by taking Lvov, in what is now western Ukraine. However, with the onset of winter, the tsar left the army to return to Moscow to decide on his next move. Some advisers urged him to negotiate, but Alexis deferred to the patriarch who insisted on a military solution. Thus, war was declared on Sweden in May of 1656 only to have the army become mired in a frustrating stalemate that lasted several years. The peace that was finally arranged in 1661 was profoundly disappointing, since it forced the tsar to abandon much of what had been previously gained.

Alexis ultimately blamed Nikon for this unhappy turn of events, but the enmity that developed between them was fueled by other factors as well. For one, the tsar was no longer the timid, inexperienced adolescent in awe of his mentor. The three years he had spent campaigning with the army had done much to increase his independence and self-confidence. As he began to take his royal prerogatives more seriously, he was increasingly offended by the patriarch's condescending manner and interference in affairs of state.

Historians often refer to Tsar Alexis as "*tishaishii*" meaning gentle, thoughtful, and most quiet. For the most part, the epithet was apt. He spent many hours in church each day, read widely, and is the first tsar known to have composed letters in his own hand. He was also admired for giving alms to the poor and visiting jails to improve conditions for the inmates, but the tsar also had an explosive temper that was backed up by a powerful physique. Once, at a particularly tense moment during the war against Poland, he was angered by some immoderate boasting by his own father-in-law, Ilya Miloslavsky, a man notorious for his loud mouth and general incompetence. When the old man pleaded to be given a command so he could win a great victory and capture the Polish King, Alexis exploded in fury, knocked him to the ground, and began kicking him in the side as he yanked on his beard.

To be sure, the tsar was more circumspect in dealing with Nikon, whose position he was bound to respect. Still, as the patriarch's behavior continued to offend, Alexis' resentment grew. The turning point came in 1657 when the two clashed publicly about a successor to the vacant metropolitan's seat at Kiev and also resumed a previous dispute about provisions in the Law Code of 1649. The quarrel escalated when the tsar snubbed his former mentor by failing to invite him to a state banquet honoring the King of Teimuraz from Georgia. When the patriarch sent a representative to the tsar's palace to inquire about the reason, the emissary was not only rebuffed, but beaten. Another insult was offered just days later when Alexis officially revoked Nikon's title of *great sovereign* and then declined to attend two very important religious events at which the patriarch officiated. Deeply offended, Nikon decided to make a dramatic gesture. After writing the tsar a letter in which he explained his grievances, he abandoned the Kremlin and moved to the New Jerusalem Monastery forty miles to the west of Moscow.

Although the tsar took the patriarch's departure as his resignation, the latter continued to demand that important policy decisions go through him. Alexis tried to ignore this and appointed the metropolitan Piturim on an interim basis to handle routine ceremonial and administrative matters. He also ordered that Nikon's name no longer be mentioned during services, countermanded many of his decisions, and transferred several patriarchal estates to the government. However, when Nikon still did not resign, the tsar tried to find incriminating evidence by spying on him and having his papers in the Kremlin searched. None of these measures, however, achieved the desired result.

Exasperated, Alexis summoned a church council to deal with this unprecedented situation. In February 1660, testimony was taken from at least two individuals who claimed that Nikon had indeed announced his decision to abdicate. This seemed to provide the necessary legal basis to remove Nikon, since canon law held that, when any bishop resigned his office without good reason, a replacement had to be found within six months. It all fell through, however, when a protest was raised by a monk from Kiev named Epifani Slavinetsky, who insisted that Nikon had not actually resigned. Thus foiled, Alexis subsequently tried a different approach: he wrote a conciliatory letter to Nikon meekly asking to be allowed to ordain a new patriarch for the good of the Church. Nikon agreed, but only on condition that all church laws be duly observed and that he be allowed to come to Moscow to participate in the proceedings. The tsar seemed prepared to accept these conditions, but the boyars prevailed on him to decline. They feared that if Nikon were allowed to return to the capital, he would somehow manipulate the situation to his advantage.

Meanwhile, the tsar was distracted by other difficulties. Among these was the financial strain of supporting a large standing army because of the unresolved military conflict in the west. With many areas of Muscovy suffering from famine, a tax increase was out of the question, so Alexis decided to replenish the treasury by printing copper coins to be of equal value with those of silver. In resorting to this dubious expedient, he decreed that foreign trade would continue to be conducted in gold or silver while all government salaries and debts would be paid in copper. The immediate result was runaway inflation. Those possessing only copper coins were forced to pay as much as three hundred percent more to buy what they needed. Moreover, gangs of counterfeiters were able to exploit the situation while the government appeared to do nothing. All this came to a head on the morning of July 25 (August 4), 1662, when agitators appeared around Moscow holding signs that described certain government officials as thieves and speculators. When the police tried to remove them, a huge mob formed and marched to the tsar's summer residence at Kolomenskoe where the sovereign was celebrating the birth of a daughter with his family. The situation was reminiscent of June 1648, but this time Alexis was not intimidated and walked out to meet the troublemakers. Amid the shouting and complaining, however, a few grabbed at his robes demanding immediate redress to their grievances. The tsar heard them out, promised a full investigation, but firmly ordered the intruders leave his estate. They did, but many returned a short time later as part of a larger group to resume the protest. By this time, however, a detachment of *strel'tsy* had arrived from Moscow. Their attack on the crowd was so savage that seven thousand perished in the ensuing slaughter. Many of those who survived were rounded up and subjected to partial dismemberment, branding, and exile.

Shaken and angry, the tsar once again turned to the problem of removing Nikon. He now decided that his best hope was to develop a persuasive argument to convince the other patriarchs that such action was not only legal, but necessary. To this end, he assigned a Greek scholar and cleric named Paisios Ligarides[12] to collaborate with a prominent boyar, Semen Streshnev, to compose two sets of questions with answers, presumably to serve as a kind of catechism for Alexis to make his case. The first set dealt with certain offensive aspects of the patriarch's general behavior and the second his specific encroachments on the tsar's authority. A third set of questions was compiled somewhat later *without answers,* and sent to the other patriarchs so that they could express their views. All this was done in anticipation of a special Church Sobor or council that was set to try Nikon by the end of 1666.

In the meantime, Alexis thought he had found a new ally in his struggle against the patriarch. At some point in 1660, he had decided that Avvakum, who had been banished to Siberia in 1653 for his opposition to Church reform, might be willing to denounce Nikon. He ordered the dissident's return to Moscow, but due to slow communications and the enormous distances involved, the archpriest did not arrive until 1664. During his long absence, however, his status among Old Believers and others had grown greatly. The tsar calculated that he might finally succeed in getting rid of Nikon if Avvakum would denounce the man responsible for sending him into exile. Of course, it was also hoped that the archpriest would accept the Church reforms that he had previously rejected, which could also result in ending the schism.

The tsar, however, seemed not to have understood this extraordinary man who was prepared to endure anything to protect the true faith. Years later, Avvakum wrote an autobiography[13] in which he describes important incidents and events of his life before and during exile. The reader is struck not only by his literary skill, but by the enormous power of his spirit:

> There came to my village dancing bears with drums and lutes, and I, miserable sinner, was zealous in Christ's service, and I drove them out and I broke the buffoon's mask and the drums, on a common outside the village, one against many, and two great bears I took away — one I clubbed senseless, but he revived, and the other I let go into the open country. And after that Vasily Petrovich Sheremetiev, who was sailing up the Volga to Kazan to take over the governorship, took me on board, and he sternly reprimanded me and ordered me to bless his son who had a shaven face. And when I saw that image of shame I would not bless him, but condemned him from the Scriptures. So my lord waxed terribly wroth and ordered that I should be flung into the Volga and, having inflicted many hurts, they cast me aside, but in later years their rough handling turned to friendliness, for we were reconciled with one another in the antechamber of the tsar, and my youngest brother was my lady's confessor. Thus does God fashion the lives of his people.[14]

Later, after he had been sent into exile, he was appointed chaplain of an expedition to explore a remote area near Lake Baikal. For the next six years, the archpriest and his family endured almost unbelievable suffering and privation caused by the exhausting travel and the harsh climate. During this time, two of his children died, and his own life was menaced by the expedition's commander, Afanasy Pashkov, who frequently punished him with beatings and imprisonment because of his continuing opposition to Church reform.

> And after that they brought me to the fortress of Bratsky, and flung me into a dungeon, and gave me straw to lie upon, And there I lay till Advent, in a freezing tower; these are the seasons when winter reigns, but God kept me warm, and that without garments. Like a poor dog I lay on the straw; and sometimes they fed me, and sometimes they did not; there were many mice and I would strike at them with my biretta — the fools had not given me a a stick; I lay all the time on my belly, my back covered with sores, and of fleas and lice there was abundance.[15]

Alexis rejoiced at Avvakum's arrival and accorded him the warmest of welcomes. He offered the archpriest money, presents, and almost any position he wanted if he would denounce Nikon and accept the reforms. Initially, Avvakum seems to have been tempted, but his resolve stiffened when he heard the new mass with the changes in ritual and liturgy. Thoroughly appalled, he wrote the tsar no fewer than five letters pleading that he return to the true faith. With a heavy heart, Alexis ordered his rearrest and incarceration.

With the tsar once again at a dead end, he decided to heed the advice of the other Orthodox patriarchs and to try once again for reconciliation. The prospects did not seem good, since Nikon had seen the document that had been prepared against him a year earlier by Ligarides and Streshnev and was in an unusually defiant mood. Nevertheless, in December of 1664, Alexis contacted the patriarch through the boyar, Nikita Ziuzin, who asked him to come to the Cathedral of the Assumption *alone* on December 18 to attend matins and to meet with the tsar. Nikon agreed but arrived with a large retinue. Alexis, who had hoped to keep the meeting secret, was aghast and ordered him to return immediately to his monastery. Nikon obeyed, but, as if in spite, took the patriarchal crozier with him. Alexis sent horsemen to overtake the disgraced prelate and retrieve the sacred symbol of Church power.[16]

There the matter rested until December 1666, when the long anticipated Church council met in the Kremlin's palace banquet hall. Nikon was summoned before Alexis, the patriarchs of Alexandria and Antioch, and a number of other Russian and Greek churchmen to account for his actions. Absent were the patriarchs from Constantinople and Jerusalem, who had made it clear that they did not support the case against the Russian patriarch. Throughout the trial, the tsar himself conducted the prosecution while the accused sat in haughty disdain. Even as a defendant, his presence was intimidating, and few dared to speak out against him during the next ten days. Still, the outcome was never in doubt because there was no one to speak in Nikon's behalf. He was found guilty of abandoning his duties and dishonoring the tsar. As punishment he was reduced in rank to a simple monk and exiled to the Ferapontov Monastery at Beloozero for the rest of his life.[17]

The Church Sobor, which remained in session until June, marks a major turning point in the reign of Tsar Alexis. Not only did it accomplish the removal of Nikon from his post, but it also took steps to discourage any future patriarch from aspiring to so much power. To this end, it officially recognized the sovereign as supreme in both the temporal and spiritual realms and put limits on the Church's power to acquire and dispose of property. (The latter was an abuse that was generally thought to have become particularly flagrant during Nikon's tenure.) Finally, and most importantly, the new liturgy and rituals of the Russian Church were at long last made official and mandatory. Anyone resisting these dictates would be subject to excommunication.

The pronouncements of the Church Sobor, however, did not much impress Avvakum. His resistance to the changes became, if anything, even more extreme despite the tsar's continuing efforts to win his cooperation. Ultimately, the recalcitrant archpriest was banished to the Arctic town of Pustozersk on the Pechora River. There he was imprisoned in a deep hole for twelve years and subjected to various forms of physical and psychological abuse. Still, his opposition remained steadfast, and even the execution of his wife and two youngest sons, all of whom were buried alive, did not weaken his resolve.[18] Incredibly, Avvakum survived the tsar by several years only to meet a horrible end in April of 1682.[19] After Alexis' death in 1676, he wrote the new tsar, Feodor III, a letter declaring that his father was being tormented in hell for approving Nikon's reforms. For this the archpriest was condemned to be burned at the stake in the town square in Pustozersk. Far from discouraging the Old Believers, however, Avvakum's martyrdom seems to have filled them with terrible resolve. Now convinced that the end of the world was near, thousands of schismatics withdrew to remote areas to practice their faith. The government's persistence in hunting them served only to drive them to the ultimate sacrifice. For some, this meant setting fire to their own churches while locked inside; for others, it meant a fight to the end. Such was the case when a detachment of *strel'tsy* arrived at the Solovetsky Monastery[20] on the White Sea in 1668 to force compliance with the reforms. The monks, armed with cannon, fought like demons and held out for nearly eight years. However, Muscovite troops were finally able to penetrate the fortress and annihilate the survivors when a defector revealed a poorly repaired breach in the outer wall.

Alexis' final years on the throne were difficult ones. Along with the inevitable physical afflictions of advancing age, he was confronted by a huge Cossack revolt (to be described in the next chapter) which took years to suppress. He was also much aggrieved in March of 1669 by the death of his beloved wife, the tsaritsa Maria, and the heir to the throne, Alexis Alexeevich, just nine months later.[21] With the future of the dynasty now in jeopardy, the tsar was encouraged to marry again and soon developed an affection for a nineteen-year-old woman named Natalya Naryshkina,[22] the future mother of Peter the Great, who happened to reside in the home of his chief minister, Artemon Matveev. Alexis was enchanted with her from the beginning and planned a festive wedding to be held in January of 1672. The celebration was lavish, but the occasion was not enjoyed by all. Among those who disapproved of the union were the entire Miloslavsky clan (Maria's relatives), who resented being replaced by the Naryshkins as royal in-laws, and a certain *boyarina* named Feodosia Morozova.[23] The latter had dared to snub the tsar by choosing not to attend the wedding.

Of all the rebels who had ever defied him, Morozova must surely have been one of the most troubling. The *boyarina* was a formidable opponent not only because of her high birth and enormous wealth, but also because of her reputation for philanthropy and her courage in defending the old faith. She had also been a close friend of the deceased tsaritsa, who had also admired Avvakum and been sympathetic to the Old Believers. Alexis was plainly confounded by Morozova and tried repeatedly to persuade her to accept the new rituals and liturgy. Later, in anger and frustration, he had her arrested along with her sister, Urusova, and subjected to hours of harsh interrogation. Her defiance became so legendary that the nineteenth century artist, Vasily Surikov, was moved to celebrate it in a famous painting. The *boyarina* is shown in an open sleigh being hauled off to prison, her face shrouded in angry defiance. As she passes the tsar's palace, she dramatically crosses herself in the Old Believer two-fingered style before a crowd of onlookers.

Over the next few years, Morozova and her sister were held in at least four different places of incarceration. Their regime varied. Sometimes they were tortured and kept in seclusion; sometimes they were treated humanely and allowed some communication with the outside world. However, when they were finally taken to the Pafnut'ev Monastery in Borovsk, their conditions worsened dramatically. Confined to a dungeon lacking proper air and light, they were bound by heavy chains and allowed to starve to death. The guards who had been ordered to punish these women, however, grew to admire their courage and endurance. As the sisters grew weaker and weaker, their tormentors had a change of heart and tried to save them by giving them bits of food. Too late; Urusova died in September of 1675, and Morozova in November of the same year.

The Old Believer movement, however, flourished despite continued persecution. Convinced that Orthodoxy was doomed and anticipating the end of the world, they began to associate the tsar and his government with the Antichrist. In time, they became divided into two groups: the *bespopovtsy*, or "priestless," who generally lived monastically in remote regions without liturgy or sacraments, and the more numerous *popovtsy*, or "priestists," who sought to convert establishment clergy to their point of view. The latter tended to be less extreme in their views and, in many cases, became valued for their entrepreneurial and business acumen beginning with the reign of Peter the Great. (He allowed them to worship as they pleased in return for paying a double poll tax.) The *bespopovtsy*, however, usually refused any compromise with the increasingly secular Muscovite state. Some became *stranniki* or wanderers who had no home, no possessions, and no official status in the country.

As a fierce defender of the old faith, Feodosia Morozova insisted on making the sign of the cross in the traditional manner — with two fingers rather than three. The tsar eventually sent her to prison where she starved to death. V.I. Surikov (1848–1916). Tretiakovsky Gallery, Moscow.

It is entirely possible that the Old Believer movement would have died out entirely if Alexis had been able to reconcile with Nikon. As it turned out, the *raskol'niki* misunderstood the reason for the patriarch's removal and incarceration and took heart. They intensified their efforts to win others to their beliefs, which included opposition to westernization, serfdom, and the development of a centralized, autocratic state. Thus, not only did the tsar acquire a new source of antagonism to his policies, but the established Church was mortally wounded by losing many of its most spiritual, energetic, and devout members. This made the complete subjugation of the Church to the state during the reign of Peter the Great relatively easy to accomplish, although even he could not arrest the continued growth of the Old Belief. By the middle of the 19th century, *raskol'niki* would account for one-sixth of the tsar's subjects.

Selected Bibliogrpahy

An extremely useful source about Tsar Michael's reign and the early years of the Romanov dynasty can be found in J.L.H. Keep's "The Regime of Filaret, 1618–1633," *Slavonic and East European Review*, XXXVIII, no. 86 (1957), pp. 100–122. David Warnes' *Chronicle of the Russian Tsars* does an excellent job describing Michael's reign. Also recommended are two biographies of Tsar Alexis: Joseph T. Fuhrmann's *Tsar Alexis, His Reign and His Russia* and Philip Longworth's *Alexis, Tsar of All the Russias*. The best description and analysis of the Salt Mutiny of 1648 can be found in Valerie Kivelson's article "The Devil Stole his Mind: The Tsar and the 1648 Uprising." The following entries in the *Modern Encyclopedia of Russian and Soviet History* are also useful: "Avvakum Petrovich" (Joseph T. Fuhrmann), "Old Believers" (G. Douglas Nichol), "Nikon" (G. Edward Orchard) "Morozova, Feodosia Prokop'evna" (G. Edward Orchard) and the "Solovetsky Upsrising of 1668–1676" (G. Edward Orchard) are also informative and useful. Of scholarly interest is Georg Michel's *At War with the Church*. The author breaks new ground in clarifying certain widely-held misconceptions about the Church schism and the Old Belief.

Dmytryshin, Basil. *Medieval Russia. A Source Book, 750–1800*. New York: Harcourt Brace Jovanovich, 1991.

Fuhrmann, Joseph T. "Aleksei Mikhailovich." *Modern Encyclopedia of Russian and Soviet History*, ed. Joseph L. Wieczynski, 54 vols. With suppl. Gulf Breeze, Florida: Academic International Press, 1976–1990.

_____. "Avvakum Petrovich" *Modern Encyclopedia of Russian and Soviet History*, ed. Joseph L. Wieczynski, 54 vols. With suppl. Gulf Breeze, Florida: Academic International Press, 1976–1990.

_____. *Tsar Alexis, His Reign and His Russia*. Gulf Breeze, Florida: Academic International Press, 1981.

Hughes, Lindsey A.J. "Morozov, Boris Ivanovich." *Modern Encyclopedia of Russian and Soviet History*, ed. Joseph L. Wieczynski, 54 vols. With suppl. Gulf Breeze, Florida: Academic International Press, 1976–1990.

Kivelson, Valerie A. "The Devil Stole His Mind: The Tsar and the 1648 Uprising." *American Historical Review*, June 1993, pp. 733–756.

Lincoln, Bruce. *The Romanovs, Autocrats of All the Russias*. New York: Doubleday, 1981.

Longworth, Philip. *Alexis, Tsar of All the Russias*. New York: Franklin Watts, 1984.

Nicholl, G. Douglas. "Old Believers" *Modern Encyclopedia of Russian and Soviet History*, ed. Joseph L. Wieczynski, 54 vols. With suppl. Gulf Breeze, Florida: Academic International Press, 1976–1990.

Orchard, G. Edward. "Feodosia Prokop'evna." *Modern Encyclopedia of Russian and Soviet History*, ed. Joseph L. Wieczynski, 54 vols. With suppl. Gulf Breeze, Florida: Academic International Press, 1976–1990.

_____. "Nikon." *Modern Encyclopedia of Russian and Soviet History*, ed. Joseph L. Wieczynsky, 54 vols. With suppl. Gulf Breeze, Florida: Academic International Press, 1976–1990.

_____. "Solovetskii Uprising of 1668–1676." *Modern Encyclopedia of Russian and Soviet History*, ed. Joseph L. Wieczynski, 54 vols. With suppl. Gulf Breeze, Florida: Academic International Press, 1976–1990.

Vernadsky, George. *A History of Russia, Vol. 5*. New Haven: Yale University Press, 1963.

Zenkovsky, Serge A. ed. *Medieval Russia's Epics, Chronicles and Tales*. New York: E.P. Dutton, 1974.

5. Cossack Rebels
and Renegades

In the last decade of his reign (in addition to all his other difficulties), Tsar Alexis was confronted with a Cossack rebellion that proved a far more lethal challenge to his authority than anything he had experienced before. It was instigated by a prosperous Don Cossack of some status from the Don named Stepan (Stenka) Timofeevich Razin, who, in the spring of 1670, led a desperate band of rebels up the Volga proclaiming an end to serfdom and death to landlords and Muscovite officials. At his height, Razin commanded an enormous army of Cossacks, peasants, and tribesmen who massacred the upper classes and pillaged their estates. The rebellion ultimately engulfed the entire Volga basin and, for a time, threatened the very fabric of the Muscovite social order. The tsar eventually prevailed, but only after he had applied all the military power at his disposal.

The issues that had provoked the crisis had been a long time developing. It will be recalled that with the disintegration of the Golden Horde in the 15th century, groups of Tatar renegades began to form warrior communities in the no man's land between the forest and the steppe. The members of these Cossack brotherhoods were highly mobile and lived by fishing, hunting, and plunder. They were fiercely independent and recognized no outside authority, despite the fact that they often spent the winter months in Muscovite border towns to sell their fish, furs, hides, honey, and wax, and to buy such necessary items as powder, lead, and clothing. In time, this free and rootless way of life attracted others including tribesmen and an increasing number of Russians. The latter were usually desperate to escape military service, high taxation, and oppressive landlords in Muscovy.

For their part, the Cossacks were inclined to accept able-bodied new-comers, although the flood from the north proved more than they expected. By the middle of the 16th century, the Slavic element had become dominant as large hosts developed in the south and west. These included such groups as the Volga, Don, Terek, Kuban, Ukrainian, and Zaporozhian Cossacks.

The relationship between the Muscovite state and the Cossack hosts was often stormy, mainly because the latter often made their living by brigandage and theft, but there were other antagonisms as well that derived from their contrasting lifestyles. The Muscovites had emerged from the forests, lived in permanent settlements, and were dependent on agriculture. They were developing a form of land tenure that featured military service from the gentry and forced labor from peasants. Too, the Muscovites were ruled autocratically by a grand prince and, later, a tsar who inherited his office from his father and appointed his own *boyar duma* to help him govern. By the late 15th century, this tsar enjoyed a near God-like status. With his golden crown, orb, scepter, and ornate vestments, he was expected to deport himself in a regal manner. His subjects bowed before him as slaves.

In contrast, the Cossacks lived on the open steppe and eschewed farming, which they associated with bondage.[1] Originally, they had lived communistically, sharing their possessions among themselves, although later class distinctions based on wealth began to appear. They also practiced a rough form of democracy that featured an assembly or *krug* (circle) to which every man could belong. Decisions were arrived at by open discussion, although the process sometimes degenerated into wild shouting and even fighting. The *ataman* was elected by acclamation but did not automatically enjoy deference and high status. During the process of being chosen, the potential leader was expected to refuse the office at least twice before being dragged into the circle by Cossack elders and splattered with mud. This was to teach him humility before investing him with his lone symbol of authority: a horsetail banner. Of course, a strong Cossack *ataman* might wield considerable authority especially during times of war, but even the most formidable took care not to offend the will of the majority. Those who did were promptly deposed, and in some cases, beaten to death.

Despite these fundamental differences, Muscovy and Cossackdom were potential allies. Both adhered at least nominally to Eastern Orthodoxy, and both suffered from raids by the Muslim Tatars and Turks. In 1571, after Moscow was destroyed by the Crimean Tatars, Tsar Ivan the Terrible resorted to a practice employed by his grandfather a century earlier. He paid groups of Don and Volga Cossacks to settle down and garrison the new forts and watch posts that he built to protect the southern frontier. These were known as "town" or service Cossacks (*gorodovye kazaki*). At the same time, he also encouraged the enlistment of "free" Cossacks in the regular army as scouts and cavalry. Still, the relationship was tense; the Cossacks were notoriously mercenary and willing to fight for anyone who paid them. Too, the flow of peasants from Muscovy was depriving the service nobility of an important source of labor. Thus, Ivan the Terrible and Boris Godunov made serious attempts to stop anyone trying to flee to the *steppe*, as they pushed the border of the state farther and farther south. They also forbade Cossacks from retiring to Muscovite towns in winter. These were temporary expedients, however; at some point the Cossacks would have to be tamed and absorbed into the state.

This proved to be no easy task, especially with the onset of famine in 1601 and the subsequent Time of Troubles. Desperate to find food, peasants and slaves fled south in ever greater numbers. This so augmented the Don Cossacks that they were able to play a decisive role in helping the first False Dmitri attain the throne in 1605. One year later, when the unpopular boyar, Vasily Shuisky, assassinated Dmitri and himself became tsar, Cossacks dominated the forces of Ivan Bolotnikov and Istoma Pashkov that laid siege to Moscow. They became still more prominent in 1607 when the bogus Tsarevich Piotr brought several thousand of them from the Terek, Volga, and the Don to besiege government forces at Tula. Finally, it was mainly Cossacks who provided support for the second and third False Dmitris, drove the occupying Poles from the Kremlin, and whose backing made possible the election of the first Romanov tsar, Michael, in 1613.

In the aftermath of so much destruction and hardship, the new tsar and his government labored mightily to restore the tsardom. A primary concern was to secure the country's borders, particularly in the south. To this end, he offered powder, shot, and grain to buy the support of the Don, Yaik, and Zaporozhian Cossacks. The Don Cossacks in particular were more than ready to cooperate. Economically weakened and thoroughly exhausted after so many years of conflict, their numbers were now depleted to below 2000. Moreover, they felt increasingly threatened by the growing power of the Tatars and Turks, but the spirit of harmony and cooperation that was engendered by mutual self interest did not last long. By 1620, the Don Cossacks were strong enough to resume raids on shipping in the Black Sea. This antagonized the powerful Turks, who not only demanded that Moscow bring them to heel, but later sent the Nogay and Crimean Tatars to the Don to extract revenge. Tsar Michael, desperate to avoid war with the Sultan, sternly reprimanded the Cossacks for their piracy. This, however, did not prevent them from expanding their raids to the Crimea and even to the Turkish fortifications around Azov. Subsequently, the tsar resorted to other ploys to curb their aggression: first, he severed diplomatic relations, and later had his father, the Patriarch Filaret, threaten them with excommunication. Finally, in 1630, he sent a personal emissary with a detachment of soldiers to the Don to demand obedience, but this was in vain. The Cossacks murdered the emissary.

The tsar decided, however, to tolerate such defiance in order to accomplish an important military objective: he hoped to enlist the Cossacks to retake the strategic fortress city of Smolensk on the Dnieper from Poland, which had been lost during the Time of Troubles. In 1632, he offered pay and other rewards to both the Don and the Yaik Cossacks for their sworn loyalty and military support, but the war against Poland was a near disaster. Not only did it end in defeat, it also allowed the Tatars over a two-year period to penetrate the undefended southern border and take more than 10,000 Russians captive. This prompted the Cossacks to retaliate in 1634 against the Nogay Tatars by plundering their territory, kidnapping their women, and stealing livestock. The tsar was obliged to applaud this effort, although he continued to warn against forays into the Crimea or against Turkish settlements, but by now the Cossacks had their eye on the Ottoman fortress at Azov. With its eleven bastions, high walls, and three citadels, one within the other, it was perceived as a mortal threat to the inhabitants on the Don. Thus, in 1637, when Turkey became involved in war with Persia (and later Venice), and the Crimean Tatars were off fighting in Moldavia, the Cossacks resolved to take it. To this end, a 9,000 man combined force of Don and Zaporozhian Cossacks in April of that year began a nine-week siege of the great fortress. In the early going, little was accomplished except the unfortunate death of the Turkish ambassador on his way to Moscow. Still, the attackers finally prevailed by exploding a strategically placed charge in the fortress wall on June 18, which allowed them to pour through the breach and subdue the defenders.

The capture of Azov also seemed to be a victory for the Russians, since the Cossacks almost immediately turned to Moscow for aid. The tsar was inclined to be generous and sent money and large quantities of flour, biscuit, groats, liquor, and munitions. At the same time, he was able truthfully to tell the Turks that the fortress had been taken without his permission. Still, a crisis was soon to develop. As thousands of Cossacks, merchants, and laborers poured into the city from all over, it was clear that the residents needed more than Moscow could give. Food ran short and people began to leave. In addition, the Turks, having made peace with their enemies, made it clear that they were determined to recover the fortress. In the summer of 1641, they laid siege to Azov, and with their huge numerical superiority, began to wear down the defenders. The latter, aided by their women, fought like demons and appeared to have won when the Turks unexpectedly abandoned the siege in October. But most knew the victory was only temporary has since the Cossacks had suffered too much and could not afford to rebuild what was left of the fortress. Mindful that the Turks and their Tatar allies would eventually return, they decided to offer their prize to Moscow. Tsar Michael was sorely tempted and convened a *Zemsky Sobor* to decide what to do, but, in the end, it was the certainty of a war with Turkey and the cost of repairing the walls and defending the city that decided its fate. Thus, the Cossacks were ordered to destroy and abandon the fortress.

The capture of Azov represents a high point of sorts for the Cossacks both militarily and psychologically, but now they were both exhausted by their achievement and thoroughly demoralized that it had all come to nothing. In the years that followed, Cossacks everywhere were forced to be on the defensive. This was especially true in Ukraine where they were being led by Bogdan Khmel'nitsky in a struggle against the Poles, and on the Don, where they were attacked relentlessly by the Nogays, Tatars, and Turks. In April 1642, when the town of Manych was burned down and a number of others besieged, the Don Cossacks again turned to Moscow for help. The tsar responded to their calls by sending money, supplies, and some 3,000 recruits. In 1647, when the town of Cherkassk was under siege by the Turks for the second time, the new tsar, Alexis, sent another 1000 men under the command of Andrei Lazarev, but this man was no friend of the Cossacks. Not only did he treat them like subordinates, he also insisted on searching for runaways despite the long-held tradition that there was no extradition from the Don. The Cossacks retaliated by stealing money and supplies intended for the Russians, but this was of little consequence. The tsar answered by cutting their pay as he continued to encourage Muscovite landowners to move farther and farther south into Cossack territory. He also sent search parties to the Don to track down runaways.

Despite this, the number of illegal immigrants to the Don Cossacks grew to a flood throughout the 1650s and 1660s. In large part, this was caused by the legalization of serfdom in 1649 and by the war with Poland (and later Sweden) that began in 1654. Men, desperate to escape the increased taxes and military conscription, were prepared to risk death to get to the Don, but by now the free, egalitarian warrior brotherhood of yore with its emphasis on democracy, sharing, and mutual support, hardly existed. In its place was a virtual oligarchy, dominated by a group known as the "homeowners" or *domovitye kazaki*, who lived downriver near

Cherkassk and controlled the decisions of the *krug*. Subordinate to them were the more recently arrived "naked ones" or *golytba*, who owned nothing and were nearly destitute. To become an official member of the community, a newcomer might wait as long as seven years before being admitted by the *krug*. In the meantime, however, they had little to do, prohibited as they were by tradition from the one occupation most of them knew — farming. Thus, many of them ended up working as laborers for the "homeowners" who treated them like slaves. The "naked ones" were also obliged to help to guard the southern border from the Tatars and Turks, although they received no share of the money sent by the government for performing this service.

In time, more and more of these increasingly angry, poorer Cossacks turned to steppe piracy in order to survive. For more than a hundred years, Cossack raiding parties had ranged along rivers of the southeast and the Black and Caspian Seas to plunder and loot. By the middle of the 17th century, however, such ventures were becoming increasingly difficult and dangerous for two reasons: Muscovite troops were being deployed farther and farther south, and the Turks had constructed forts at the mouth of the Don and had slung chains across the river. By 1666, so desperate had many of the poorer Cossacks become that 500 of them set out for Moscow, with an obscure freebooter named Vaska Us (pronounced OOS), to offer their services to Tsar Alexis in return for pay, but he and his followers never made it to the capital. By the time they reached Tula, so many other destitute men had joined their ranks that he could not control them. They soon gave themselves to plunder and looting. This prompted the local gentry to organize into a militia and notify the tsar, who sent troops under Prince Yuri Bariatynsky. The rebels were easily driven off, which ended the immediate crisis but did not solve the larger problem. Thus, the very next year a new *ataman* emerged named Stenka Razin, whose restless energy and charismatic leadership was far more potent than had ever been seen on the Don. Soon he would lead an army of Cossacks, peasants, and lower class townsmen in one of the greatest social rebellions in Russian history.

Interestingly, Stenka Razin himself had little reason to rebel. He was a respected member of the prosperous "house owning" Don Cossacks and had served them as both a soldier and a diplomat. He was well-traveled and well-connected: not only had he been to Moscow on three occasions (twice on official business), but his godfather, Kornilo Yakovlev, was the elected *ataman* of the downstreamers. Still, at some point, and for reasons unknown, Razin began to identify with the "naked ones." In the spring of 1667, he led a gang of them to the Volga, and then to the Caspian, for a

A member of the prosperous Don Cossack family, Razin's exploits as a rebel made him a hero to the poor and oppressed. L.P. Bushchik, *Illustrirovanaya Istoriya SSSR, XV-XVII vv.* Moskva, Prosveshcheniye, 1970.

campaign of piracy and plunder. His exploits soon became known far and wide as he repeatedly confounded his enemies by employing bold tactics and outright trickery. The first such incident occurred at the formidably defended city of Yaitsk, located some 250 miles up the Ural River. Razin had some of his men dress up as pilgrims and appear at the city's gates requesting permission to pray at the cathedral. Once inside, the Cossacks took over the town and executed anyone who resisted.

Razin's early successes attracted a number of new recruits but also some serious notoriety. The Cossacks were forced to spend a difficult winter at Yaitsk, battling the elements and fending off raids from government troops. The following spring, however, they set sail for the Caspian with about 1,500 men in thirty small maneuverable vessels called *strugi*, each of which was fitted with a light cannon. For the next fifteen months, they proceeded to plunder coastal towns and merchant shipping, despite the relentless pursuit of the Persian navy. At one point, after a number of close calls, Razin seemed almost ready to give up. Having led his exhausted men to the Persian town of Isfahan, he promised the shah loyalty and service in return for a modest grant of land, but before any final agreement could be reached, the Cossacks absconded. Later, they turned up in the town of Farahbad along the southern shore of the Caspian disguised as ordinary merchants. After mixing with the local population for several days, they suddenly rose up, overwhelmed the unsuspecting inhabitants, and stole their goods.

During the winter of 1668–1669, the Cossacks took refuge in the forests of northern Persia where they were harassed not only by the shah's soldiers, but also by disease and starvation. Still, with the arrival of spring, they were sufficiently recovered to resume their raids along the eastern shore of the Caspian, although they found the going unexpectedly difficult. Their numbers eventually became so depleted that when a huge Persian fleet caught up with them in June of 1669, defeat and annihilation seemed imminent. Amazingly, however, Razin was able to rally his beleaguered force and rout the enemy. Only three Persian ships escaped destruction as the Cossacks took cannons, ammunition, and prisoners, including the enemy commander's son.

The triumph was exhilarating but costly. The Cossacks had lost at least 500 men, with hundreds more wounded. In addition, nearly everyone else was sick from the saltwater they had been compelled to drink when they ran out of fresh. Razin deemed the situation so critical that he resolved to return to the Don as soon as possible. However, when his fleet reached the mouth of the Volga, he succumbed to the temptation of attacking two richly laden Persian merchant ships bound for Astrakhan. This provoked the city's *voevoda*, Ivan Prozorovsky, who sent a powerful force to destroy the pirates and retrieve what had been stolen. Razin, seeing that he could not escape, decided to negotiate. In return for a complete pardon, he agreed to partially disarm, free his captives, and return the booty taken from the two Persian ships.

What seemed to be an important government victory, however, turned out to be something much less. Razin found that he had become a hero to ordinary people who were thrilled by his adventures and exploits. His entry into the city prompted wild celebration, and he became the honored house guest of Prince Semen Lvov, the very officer who had been sent to bring him to heel. Even the *strel'tsy*, whose main duty it was to protect the city, treated him with deference. Basking in all this adulation, Razin quickly took charge. He released his captives but refused to honor most of the terms of the agreement he had signed. Prozorovsky tried to insist, but the Cossacks were soon on the move again toward the Don. Along the way, however, they indulged in one last act of mischief. Upon entering the town of Tsaritsyn, they broke into the municipal jail and freed all the prisoners. They also captured the local *voevoda* and amused themselves him by dragging him through the streets by his beard. The captive was eventually released but only after he had paid a large ransom.

By the time Stenka Razin returned to the Don in the summer of 1669, he was a changed man. Intoxicated perhaps by his new found fame, he now saw himself not as a mere adventurer, but as a social revolutionary and a defender of the poor and weak. He dreamed of vast conquests and a new social order based on the Cossack concept of justice. To this end, he established a new base of operations on an island in the middle of the river near a village called Kagalnik, which he fortified with earthen ramparts and cannon. As new recruits streamed to his banner, he bade his wife, children and brother, Frolka, to join him from their old home in Cherkassk. All this activity, however, began to worry not only the "home owners" who felt their possessions and power threatened, but the government in Moscow, who wondered what he might do next. The tsar sent his personal representative, Gerasim Evdokimov, to Cherkassk to rally the downstream Cossacks against this outlaw.

Evdokimov was received by Razin's godfather, Kornilo Yakovlev, who had summoned a council or *krug* of Cossack elders to allow the emissary to make his case. Stenka, however, found out about the meeting and burst in unexpectedly. After denouncing Evdokimov as a tool of the *boyar* aristocracy, he had his men beat him up and drown him in the Don. He also killed several Cossack elders who had dared to support him. When news of this outrage reached Tsar Alexis, he immediately stopped all payments to the Don Cossacks and ordered all trading routes to the region cut. Stenka Razin was now declared the tsar's mortal enemy. Amazingly, however, the feeling was not mutual; the *ataman* himself claimed to be fighting *in the name of the tsar* and against the evil boyars and *voevodas* who were oppressing the people. Thus the new campaign that began in April of 1670 actually had the feel of a crusade as the rebels returned to the town of Tsaritsyn. Inspired by the belief that they were fighting for something noble, the Cossacks overran the town's defenses and subsequently destroyed a powerful detachment of *strel'tsy* sent from Moscow to defend the town. (The latter had arrived late and were unaware that Tsaritsyn had already been taken.)

Razin quickly followed with another victory upstream at Kamyshin where he disguised his men as Muscovite soldiers, which allowed them to enter the town unopposed and subdue it with little bloodshed.

At this point, Razin flirted with the idea of marching on Moscow, since the tsar's military at that moment seemed particularly disorganized and vulnerable. Ultimately, however, he decided to return to Astrakhan with its strategic position at the mouth of the Volga. The city's enormous wealth in fish, caviar, salt, and the silk trade had deeply impressed him during his previous visit, and the *ataman* was determined to possess it before turning north. The task was not expected to be easy, since the *voevoda,* Prozorovsky, was determined to fight and commanded a position that seemed impregnable. Astrakhan was situated on an island in the river and protected by a huge citadel. Moreover, the city's powerful walls were defended by as many as 500 brass cannon, a number of experienced foreign officers, 6000 *strel'tsy,* and a ship in the harbor named the *Orel.*[2] Still, the Cossacks won two easy victories because the government troops sent out to stop them sympathized with the rebels and refused to fight. Seeing this, the remaining defenders lost heart. They were outmaneuvered when Stenka faked an assault on one gate and sent his main force to attack another.

In the bloodbath that followed, the Cossacks plundered the city from top to bottom, destroying indiscriminately and terrorizing everyone, especially the wealthy and prominent. The *voevoda* Prozorovsky was savagely tortured before being flung to his death from a high tower. His two sons, aged sixteen and eight, received similar treatment; after being hung by their heels all night, the older boy was executed while the younger was returned to his mother barely alive. Other people of wealth and rank were hung by their ribs on fleshhooks until dead, and their corpses were dumped in a mass grave near a local monastery. In an attempt to curb these excesses and restore law and order, Razin tried in vain to establish a formal Cossack-style government for Astrakhan; but once he had left the city, it descended again into an orgy of rape and murder.

By mid–summer of 1670, as the Cossacks moved up the Volga, the rebellion gathered support not only from oppressed peasants and townsmen, but also from much of the lower class clergy and a number of non-Russian minorities. Stenka, however, was leaving nothing to chance. To enhance the high moral purpose of his campaign, he now claimed to be protecting the tsarevich Alexei, who had actually fallen ill and died earlier that year. To convince the credulous, he paraded a Circassian[3] prisoner on a special barge outfitted in red velvet for all to see. It was alleged that the boy had survived an assassination attempt by evil noblemen and had taken refuge among the Cossacks. Razin soon compounded this fable by another no less preposterous: that the deposed Patriarch Nikon also supported the Cossacks and was now among them.[4] Thus, as the rebel flotilla sailed north, it included a second special barge; this one was bedecked in black velvet and carried yet another impostor.

The long-expected showdown between the insurgents and government forces took place at Simbirsk[5] on the Volga River about three hundred miles southeast of Moscow. Early in September, as the rebels approached the city, they outnumbered the defenders four to one. However, the local *voevoda*, Prince Ivan Miloslavsky, was prepared to fight to the end and enjoyed some important advantages. He commanded four regiments of experienced *strel'tsy* and a cavalry detachment of Tatar *murzy*.[6] He also was protected by a hilltop citadel surrounded by a sturdy wooden wall (recently reinforced by sacks of earth, flour, and salt) and a moat. Finally, and most importantly, Miloslavsky was sustained by the belief that, if he held out long enough, he could expect to be reinforced by a powerful force from Moscow led by Prince Yuri Dolgoruky, one of the tsar's most distinguished officers.

The battle for Simbirsk raged for a full month and was far more intense than anything the rebels had previously experienced. It coincided with an enormous peasant uprising that was raging elsewhere in the region, featuring angry mobs plundering manors and murdering landlords. To an anxious Tsar Alexis in the Kremlin, the fate of the entire country seemed to hang in the balance. Razin's rebels first tried to smoke the defenders into submission by hurling incendiary bombs and flaming arrows into the citadel. They subsequently tried to punch holes in the wooden walls by firing their cannon at point blank range. Nothing worked. The turning point came in early October, when Muscovite reinforcements arrived not from Moscow as expected, but from Kazan, just as the rebels were beginning their fourth major assault on the citadel. Razin boldly led his force out to meet them and ordered a charge on some well-armed and disciplined *strel'tsy*. In the slaughter that followed, the rebels were thoroughly routed as their leader was severely cut by a sabre before being hit in the foot by a musket ball. As he lay helpless on the battlefield, he was rescued only when some retreating Cossacks returned to charge at the enemy and picked him up in the process.

The tsar's victory at Simbirsk was utterly decisive. Not only did it shatter the Cossacks militarily, but it ended the myth of invincibility that had surrounded their leader. Still, as the wounded *ataman* returned to his Kagalnik fortress on the Don with his dwindling gang of followers, he was determined to rekindle the rebellion. In February of 1671, he made a desperate attempt to overthrow the established Cossack leadership in Cherkassk but found he could no longer attract new followers or hold old ones. The attempt not only failed miserably, but increased the enmity of the "home owners" who, prodded by Moscow, resolved to put an end to Razin once and for all.

In April, Kornilo Yakovlev led a force to Kagalnik for a night raid on the island fortress in the Dnieper, which they surrounded and set on fire. Surprisingly, there was little resistance. Razin and his brother Frolka were taken captive, bound in chains, and sent to Moscow. Contemporaries have praised the *ataman* for enduring this reversal with courage and dignity, but in fact he seems to have been quite deluded about the fate that awaited him. He apparently believed that if he could speak with the tsar and explain his motives, he would be pardoned. It was not to be. Tsar Alexis did interrogate the renegade, but only to savor his triumph before ordering the prisoner to endure a prolonged and hideous execution. The Cossack was savagely beaten with a knout (a whip used for flogging), his limbs were yanked from their joints, and his torso was lacerated with a hot iron. The end finally came on June 6 (16), 1671, when Razin was quartered in Red Square. His head and other body parts were mounted on stakes for display. What remained was thrown to the dogs.

Thus Tsar Alexis had survived yet another ordeal without learning anything in the process. In the few remaining years of his life, he intensified his efforts to ensure that the Cossacks would never rise again by demanding that they recite loyalty oaths, increasing their military obligations, and forbidding them to accept new fugitives into their ranks. Such measures, however, accomplished little as resistance to Muscovite autocracy and expansion continued to grow. Indeed, as early as 1673, one of Razin's subordinates, planning to mount yet another rebellion against the state, announced that he was the tsarevich, Semen Alexeevich.[7] The movement was quickly suppressed but others followed, incited in many cases by Cossacks who had embraced the Old Belief. Thus, as the tumultuous 17th century drew to a close, Cossacks and peasants in Muscovy would continue to seethe with discontent that no despot, however fierce and determined, would be able to eradicate.

However, this lesson, more obvious perhaps in retrospect, was resisted by Tsar Alexis's youngest son, Peter the Great, who was crowned at ten in 1682 and ruled until 1725. In his obsession to modernize the Muscovite state and to expand at the expense of Sweden and Turkey, he had raised taxes, hired foreign advisors, and imposed a number of offensive western-style reforms. Resistance was especially strong in Astrakhan, where the lower class residents had rebelled in the spring of 1705, killing the military

This page and opposite: Razin comported himself with great bravery as he mounted the scaffold to endure torture and execution. The tsar was determined to make the Cossack's end as hideous as possible in order to deter others from rebelling against the state. *This page:* G.N. Gorelov (1880–1966). Katalog: *Vystavka Rabot,* and *opposite:* L.P. Bushchik, *illustrirovanaya Istoriya SSSR, XV–XVII vv.* Moskva, Prosveshchenye, 1970.

governor and hundreds of others.[8] The following year, the tsar had sent Field Marshall Boris Sheremetiev to suppress the insurgents. Sheremetiev employed some Don Cossacks to assist in the endeavor. The latter had previously been paid to act as defenders of the southern frontier and relished the opportunity to profit from their military prowess. However, the extreme brutality used against the rebels in Astrakhan made them wonder about their own future. They had long watched with concern as the Muscovite state encroached steadily on their territory, building forts and blockhouses, and stationing troops.

These Cossacks were also concerned by the continuing flow of Muscovite fugitives to the Don seeking to escape conscription and high taxation. The prosperous downstream elders in Cherkassk, led by *ataman*

Lukian Maksimov, no longer welcomed these newcomers and felt threatened by their increasing numbers. However, they were also alarmed by the prospect of Muscovite military intervention to stem the problem. Thus, when the tsar sent Colonel Yuri Dolgoruky in July of 1707 with a detachment of 300 men deep into their territory to return these fugitives by force, they debated whether they should resist or assist the government troops.

Reluctantly, they chose the latter option, knowing that to do otherwise would provoke retaliation and end the payments they received for defending the southern border.

Accordingly, Maksimov thought it prudent to assign a number of Cossacks to help Dolgoruky with his mission. Others, however, saw this as treason and a threat to Cossack independence. Among these was Kondrati Afanasievich Bulavin, a thirty-eight-year-old former downstream elder, who had long been an advocate of force to defend the rights of his people from Muscovite domination. Three years earlier he had destroyed a saltworks operation on the Northern Donets after the government had appropriated it by force. His opposition to Dolgoruky's present incursion was no less determined. On the night of October 8 (19), he and his followers annihilated most of the Muscovite force near a village on the Aidar River and disposed of their bodies by throwing them into wolf pits. Later, in a letter to the tsar, he justified his actions, complaining that the government troops had used torture and the knout, raped their women, hung innocent children by the legs from trees, and slit the nostrils of many Cossacks.

Bulavin's justifications notwithstanding, his assault on Muscovite troops provoked Maksimov and the elders to turn against him. What ensued nearly became a Cossack civil war. On October 18 (27), the downstreamers attacked and killed most of the rebels, although Bulavin escaped and led the other survivors through the forests to the village of Kodak on the Dnieper River, where they spent the winter. Maksimov claimed to have ended the rebellion, but in fact it was just beginning. Bulavin, whose daring and charisma much resembled Razin's, was soon attracting new followers among the Zaporozhian Cossacks. With the arrival of spring, he moved to the Don and sent out propaganda leaflets to rouse the population, many of whom were Old Believers. He promised to die rather than "remain silent and submissive before the wicked deeds of evil men — princes and boyars, profiteers and Germans— who are leading us into the Hellenic faith and away from the true Christian faith."[9]

Bulavin set up his new headquarters at Pristansky Gorodok and sent out more propaganda leaflets condemning Muscovite expansion and promoting the cause of Cossack independence. More volunteers came pouring in, and, by the end of April, 1708, rebel strength was at nearly 7000. At a general assembly of his followers, he announced his intention first to take Cherkassk and then Azov. He also directed one of his lieutenants, Lakashka Khokhlach, to destroy the tsar's shipbuilding works at Voronezh, which once again provoked Maksimov and other downstream elders, still determined to prevent a clash with Moscow, to attack Bulavin near the town of Panin on April 8. The result was a complete triumph for the rebels, who gathered cannon, powder, lead, and money. Later, Bulavin captured Cherkassk, had Maksimov and his followers beheaded, and was himself elected *ataman*. These were feats that even Razin had not been able to accomplish.

By the summer of 1708, the rebels' strength had swelled to about 30,000, although they probably more resembled a mob than an army. Bulavin seemed to have doubted that they could prevail against trained soldiers. He was also alarmed by the two regiments the tsar had dispatched to the Don under the command of Prince Vladimir Dolgoruky, brother of the slain Yuri. Thus, he made several attempts to find allies in the region but inexplicably failed to approach either the Bashkirs[10] or the Swedes, both of whom were determined enemies of the Muscovites. The former had been in rebellion since 1705, and the latter had been at war with Muscovy for eight years, and were now planning to invade Muscovy.[11] Perhaps, too, Bulavin was remiss not to exploit rumors about Peter's death by sponsoring a pretender as Razin had done thirty-eight years earlier.

In the meantime, dissatisfaction was growing among the remaining Cossack elders about the planned attack on Azov. They doubted that the rebel army could prevail against such a well-defended objective, and as usual, feared retaliation from the tsar. To protect their interests, a certain Ilya Zershchikov formed a conspiracy to overthrow Bulavin, and he informed the governor of Astrakhan of the impending assault. This deprived the rebels of any element of surprise when they appeared before the gates of Azov on July 6 (17), 1708. After some initial success, they were driven back and slaughtered. This defeat caused most of Bulavin's supporters in Cherkassk to turn against him. That night a mob of Cossacks surrounded the *ataman's* house and set it on fire. Eventually, they smashed down the door and killed him with a bullet to the head. The corpse was decapitated, preserved in alcohol, and later the head was displayed on a pike. What remained of the body was sent to Azov to hang by its heels as part of the victory celebration for the town's defenders.

The tsar was in Mogilev, a town 300 miles southwest of Moscow, when he learned of Bulavin's demise. The news was more than welcome, especially since his own army, now in its eighth year in a war against Sweden, was recovering from a loss inflicted just days earlier. He ordered cannon fired to celebrate the victory, although the rebellion was not yet over. On July 17 (28), part of Bulavin's old army captured Tsaritsyn, and two of his former lieutenants were preparing to return to Cherkassk to organize a new offensive. However, the Muscovite army under Prince Dolgoruky pursued the insurgents relentlessly, and finally won a decisive victory at Donetsky

Gorodok in late October. In the meantime, the tsar was preparing for an invasion by the Swedes, who were expected to march on Moscow. However, King Charles XII, mindful that his army was not at full strength and in need of supplies, decided to postpone his assault on the capital. Instead, he turned south to Ukraine for the winter to find rest and nourishment for his weary troops. He also hoped to join forces with the forces with a certain Ukrainian Cossack named Ivan Stepanovich Mazeppa, one of the tsar's most trusted allies.

Mazeppa, now in his late sixties, in many ways personifies the popular image of "the fur capped Cossack horseman, saber flashing, galloping across the empty steppe."[12] Born in the Polish-held area of Ukraine and raised as an Orthodox believer, he had been educated in Jesuit schools and had once served as a page at the court of the King of Poland. He was a physically imposing, uncommonly able soldier, and fluent in Polish, Latin, German, and Russian. His natural aptitude for leadership, however, was occasionally compromised by his excessive pride, temper, and lust for women. At one point, he had to abandon court life because of an affair with a nobleman's wife. The offended husband is alleged to have had him stripped naked, tarred and feathered, strapped to a horse, and sent wildly charging through thorned bushes and thickets. Mazeppa somehow survived this ordeal and fled to the Ukrainian Cossacks where he eventually became a diplomat. Later he was captured by the Zaporozhian Cossacks and turned over to an advisor of Tsar Alexis, Artemon Matveev. The latter was much impressed by Mazeppa's personality, intelligence, and apparent willingness to cooperate with the Muscovite government and allowed him to return to Ukraine as an ally.

During the regency of Sophia, Mazeppa also won the confidence of her chief advisor, Vasily Golitsyn, who supported his election as *hetman* of the Ukrainian Cossacks. However, the dynastic crisis of 1689[13] nearly proved to be his downfall, since he had initially backed Sophia over Peter. He switched his allegiance just in time and eventually became a confidante of the young tsar, who was charmed by the older man's wit, experience, and military skills. In the years that followed, the Cossack participated in campaigns against the Turks and the Tatars and advised Peter in diplomatic matters. For this, he was frequently rewarded by the tsar and, over the years, accumulated a fortune in money and land, but the patronage he received at court exposed Mazeppa to criticism by his fellow Cossacks that he was too subservient to Moscow. But the charge was unfair; Mazeppa was indeed a brazen opportunist, but he only pretended to be loyal to Peter. His real goal was someday to establish a Ukrainian state independent of Muscovite control, although, with the tsar opposed to such a plan, he saw no practical way of accomplishing his end. This changed, however, when Charles XII invaded Muscovy in the fall of 1708. Mazeppa and some two thousand Cossacks (far fewer than expected) suddenly defected to the Swedish king in return for his support of Ukrainian statehood.

The tsar was stunned by Mazeppa's defection, despite the fact that he had been repeatedly warned about the Cossack's potential for treachery. He got his revenge, however, when Muscovite troops under the command of Prince Alexander Menshikov[14] destroyed the Cossack capital of Burlatin in November killing all 7000 inhabitants. This came in the wake of an earlier Muscovite victory at Lesnaya over a Swedish force that was en route to bring needed supplies to Charles' army in Ukraine. Thus, the Swedes were forced to spend a fiercely cold winter in enemy territory on the edge of starvation. The following spring, the king, in an effort to regain the initiative, attacked the lightly defended fortress at Poltava with Mazeppa's help. Peter, however, anticipated the move, and came to the rescue with a much larger force. On July 8 (27), 1709, he overwhelmed the Swedes and achieved what is generally considered to be the greatest victory of his reign. Mazeppa did prove to be of some service to Charles by directing their escape to Turkey across the Bug River. Still, the future looked doubtful. After barely evading capture, they made it to the Sultan who was by no means eager to become involved in a war against Russia. In any case, the *hetman* soon fell ill and died some ten weeks later.

The tsar's victory over the Swedes stunned all of Europe and won acclaim and recognition for Russia as a great power.[15] However, it did nothing to pacify the large numbers of non-Russian steppe people struggling to preserve their traditional freedoms. By now, the most aggrieved of these groups were the Yaik Cossacks, many of whom had previously lived along the Don and the Volga but had moved eastward in the early 1600s to escape Muscovite tyranny. In the previous century, Tsar Michael had granted them full control of the Yaik River, its tributaries, and the surrounding territory in return for guarding the frontier against the Tatars, Kalmucks, and Kirghiz. They made their living by fishing, cattle herding, and salt production. During the time of Peter, however, all this was threatened by the development of a huge industrial and mining complex in the Ural Mountains. This brought an influx of Russian colonists into the region and encouraged the tsar in 1721 to place both the Don and the Yaik Cossacks under the authority of the War College. This so enraged the latter group that they burned their own capital city, Yaitsk, and fled to the Kuban. Peter countered by sending the army to return them by force. He also appointed one of his own Cossack supporters as *ataman* and built forts along the Yaik. In 1735, ten years after the tsar's death, the city of Orenburg was founded with a governor appointed from St. Petersburg.

The next few decades bought no respite for the Cossacks, whose way of life and traditional freedoms continued to suffer from Russian encroachments. Indeed, the process was accelerated in 1762 when the German-born princess and future Catherine the Great ascended the throne. The Yaik Cossacks lost their right to fish on the river when she made this activity a government monopoly. Other issues emerged as well: once when a corrupt *ataman,* accused of embezzling money from a general fund, was found guilty by a government commission, he was inexplicably allowed to go unpunished. The incident, which apparently seemed trivial to the authorities, infuriated the Cossacks. Worse still were the young empress' military policies. Service was now obligatory for all Cossack males, who were no longer allowed to elect their own officers. They were also to be assigned to regular army units, wear western style uniforms, submit to discipline by foreign officers, and shave their beards. During the war with Turkey, which began in 1768, the Cossacks made many attempts to petition Catherine about these issues but were repeatedly turned away. In time, she allowed them to return to their old units, but only because the war was going badly and she feared a mutiny. Only much later did she agree to establish a commission to investigate their grievances.

The officer sent to conduct the investigation, however, was probably the worst choice that could have been made. Not only did Major General von Traubenberg's German ancestry irritate the xenophobic Cossacks, but the man himself was not at all disposed to take their concerns seriously. One of his first acts after arriving in Yaitsk in December 1771 was to arrest seven "troublemakers," have them whipped in the town's square, and have them sent to Orenburg as army recruits. The Cossacks were outraged. They attacked the convoy transporting the prisoners, set them free, and later killed von Traubenberg and most of the other members of the commission. They also destroyed the homes of some of their own elders whose loyalty they doubted. Catherine countered by sending a force of loyal service Cossacks from Moscow, under the command of Major General Feodor Freiman, to Yaitsk to teach the rebels a lesson. Anyone remotely involved in the affair was punished by knouting, mutilation or exile. Those thought to be most guilty were taken to St. Petersburg for trial. Of these, sixty-two were executed.

As anger and frustration rose throughout the steppe region and Volga basin, threat of a rebellion simmered dangerously. Much of this discontent focused on Catherine and the fact that she came to power by ousting her German-born husband Peter III, who had died mysteriously just days

Yemelian Pugachev bore no resemblance to Peter III, but his claim to be the true tsar attracted huge numbers of Cossacks, peasants and tribesmen to his banner. The *jacquerie* he inspired, known as the *Pugachevshchina*, was one of the most destructive social upheavals in Russian history. L.P. Bushchik, *Illustrirovanaya Istoriya SSSR, XV–XVII vv.* Moskva, Prosveshcheniye, 1970.

after being deposed. Despite the fact that Peter himself was in many ways a loathsome individual who hated everything Russian, he gained a reputation as a good tsar because of two edicts he issued in February and March of 1762. The first reversed an unpopular policy of Peter the Great by freeing the nobility from compulsory service. The second converted monastic serfs into state serfs and thereby significantly improved their status and working conditions. Together these initiatives gave rise to a general expectation, at least among the low-born, that the tsar was planning to abolish serfdom altogether. However, when this possibility was dashed by Peter's overthrow and death, many peasants concluded that he had been murdered by the nobles who wanted to keep them in bondage. Inevitably, new rumors began to circulate, the most potent of which was that the tsar, like the child Dmitri in 1591, had escaped death and was somewhere in hiding.

It was in this charged atmosphere that the thirty-year-old Don Cossack, Yemelian Ivanovich Pugachev, entered the town of Yaitsk in November, 1772. Though he pretended to be an Old Believer engaged in fish trading, he was actually an army deserter, who, like so many others, longed to find a place where he could live in peace away from the tyranny of the state. In many ways, his entire life had been a series of injustices at the hands of the Russians. At seventeen, he was forced him into military service despite the fact that he had only just been married. Once, during the Seven Years War,[16] he was furiously whipped by a colonel when he failed to restrain the latter's horse which had bolted free during an enemy attack. At war's end, he went home to farm, start a business, and raise a family, only to be recalled in 1768 for the war against Turkey. Pugachev served with distinction and won a promotion for bravery. However, during the winter of 1770, he fell desperately ill and lay for a time so covered with sores that his chest and legs began to putrefy. With his life in danger, he was allowed to go to Cherkassk to apply for retirement, only to be denied.

Pugachev decided not to rejoin his unit but went to Taganrog on the Sea of Azov to visit his sister and brother-in-law. When the latter, a man named Pavlov, complained about their hard life under Russian rule, Pugachev suggested the Terek River in the Kuban as a possible refuge, a place well beyond the Russian border. Because it was a difficult journey, he agreed to take them part of the way. However, the migrants got lost after they were left on their own and were soon picked up by the authorities. Pavlov promptly blamed his army deserter brother-in-law for taking them into a forbidden zone, a crime that could be punished by hanging. For a while, Pugachev went into hiding, but he reappeared in Cherkassk when he learned that his mother had been arrested and was being held there. Despite his best efforts, he was unable to convince the authorities that they should release her and nearly got arrested himself in the process. He then fled 300 miles to the Terek River, presumably to start a new life.

Pugachev was not only welcomed by the Terek Cossacks, but was soon elected their *ataman*. So forcefully was he able to articulate their concerns that, in February 1772, he was sent to St. Petersburg to complain about the low pay they received for guarding the southern border. It was a dangerous place for a fugitive to want to go, but he never made it to his destination. Along the way he decided to visit his wife, got arrested twice, escaped twice, and eventually took refuge in a monastery at Starodub near the Ukrainian border. There he conceived of a plan to end his predicament. Having learned that Old Believer refugees in Poland would be allowed to return to the homeland if they agreed to settle in certain distant provinces, he decided to pose as an Old Believer. He crossed the border with a forged military pass and applied to enter Russia through another frontier post, where he was issued a passport allowing him to settle on the Irgiz River near the Caspian Sea. This, however, was on the condition was that he would spend six weeks in quarantine at a location near the border.

During this period, Pugachev lodged with an Old Believer merchant named Kozhevnikov, for whom he did odd jobs in return for room, board, and a few rubles. He also met another deserter named Andrei Semenov, who happened to remark one day how much Pugachev resembled the late Tsar Peter III. It must have been a joke: the Cossack was five-feet four-inches tall and of dark complexion, while the late tsar was taller, thin, and rather blond. Too, the Cossack's face and chest were pockmarked from scrofula,[17] and he was missing several teeth from having been punched in the face. Pugachev at first didn't seem to take it seriously, although the very suggestion may have aroused the trickster in him. Years earlier, while still in the army, he had been known to claim that his sword had been a gift of his "godfather Peter the Great." In any case, Kozhevnikov encouraged the comparison. He knew the fugitive would be going to an area populated by Yaik Cossacks, many of whom were Old Believers. The people had been persecuted mercilessly by the government and were eager to find someone to lead them. The merchant offered to give him food, money, and some letters of introduction for Old Believers he might meet along the way. In fact, these letters came in handy when he stopped at a monastery on the Volga and was helped by the abbot, Filaret. The churchman didn't believe Pugachev looked at all like Peter III but declared that it didn't matter; the Yaik Cossacks would want to believe that he was their good tsar, as long as he told them what they wanted to hear. To this end, he suggested Pugachev embellish his story to make it more enticing.

At Yaitsk, Pugachev soon became acquainted with an Old Believer named Denis Pianov, who told him about a recent Cossack rebellion against forced migrations to Azov and Taganrog. Not only was it brutally suppressed by government troops, but the local *ataman*, Stepan Yefremov, was deposed and sent into exile. Pianov went on to say that people were fed up and that many wanted to migrate to a new area free from Russian domination. It was at this point that Pugachev told his story, revealing that he was Peter III who had escaped death and had traveled as far as Constantinople and Egypt to amass a great fortune as a merchant. Now he offered to lead a migration of the Yaik Cossacks to the Kuban and, since he claimed to be a rich man, promised to pay twelve rubles to anyone who would follow him. Before anything could come of this, however, he was forced once again to flee. The authorities were on the lookout for a suspicious merchant in town resembling Pugachev whom they wanted to question.

Pugachev eventually was arrested in the town of Malykovka in December 1772, tortured and sent first to Simbirsk for questioning and then to a prison in Kazan, where he would spend the next five months. However , in late May 1773, once again, local Old Believers came to his rescue by helping him to escape and return to the Yaik. Apparently, the road back was not easy, and he was not seen again until August when he showed up at the cabin of a farmer named Tolkachev. By now, he had formed an entirely new resolve about his enterprise and talked not of migration, but of revolution and of saving the country. He declared his intent to go to St. Petersburg to claim the throne, reunite with his son, and put his wife in a convent. The response was amazing: people came from far and wide to kiss his hand and pledge their support. However, the local authorities soon got wind of what was happening and sent soldiers to make an arrest. Pugachev fled in the nick of time to another hideout sixty miles away.

By now, the pretender had acquired as a secretary a Cossack named Pochitalin, who helped him prepare his first manifesto for distribution. In this document, which was dated September 17 (28), 1773, he promised that "If you will stand up for your fatherland, then your Cossack glory will never leave you and your children from now and forever." He also declared forgiveness to those who had sinned against him and granted his followers "the river from the heights to the mouth, and the land, and grasses, and money and lead and powder, and bread provisions."[18] Pugachev did not sign the manifesto because he could neither read nor write. Still, the message fell on fertile ground. By the next day, he had an army of 200 men that would soon grow to many more. Later that day, when a detachment under Colonel Simonov from Yaitsk rode out to the Tolkachev farm to arrest Pugachev, they were met by a single Cossack waving a copy of the manifesto. When it was read to the soldiers, half of them defected to the rebels; the other half turned back.

But outnumbered by nearly two to one, and with no cannon, Pugachev was unable to take Yaitsk, whose commander could not be tricked into surrendering. Still, the pretender made his point by hanging a number of loyalists before turning north toward Orenburg, gathering volunteers among the Bashkirs and Ural industrial peasants[19] along the way. (The latter group felt particularly maltreated since they were tied for life to industrialists who exploited their labor and treated them like convicts.) In the next two weeks, the rebels captured a number of towns and military outposts, including Iletsk, which surrendered without a fight, and Fort Tatishchev, where they faced serious opposition. The latter fell after the rebels set fire to the stockade, encouraging the 600 Cossacks inside to mutiny. On October 5 (16) they attacked Orenburg, but were held off by the town's seventy cannon and 3000 defenders. Here Pugachev became resigned to a long siege and established military headquarters at the town of Berda, less than two miles away. Over the next few months, thousands more, many of them conscripts, streamed into the makeshift camp to join the rebels, living in tents and earthen huts. There was some reason for optimism. Early in November, Pugachev had soundly defeated two relief forces sent to raise the siege, although a third led by General Korf succeeded in resupplying the loyalists with 2,400 men and twenty-two cannon.

Over the winter months, Pugachev set up a court in imitation of what he believed the one in St. Petersburg to be. He took over the town's best house, paraded around in a black, lambskin hat lined with crimson, and wore a robe of red velvet. Surrounded by an elite guard of twenty-five Cossacks, the members of his court amused themselves by drinking, singing, and wild carousing, but life in the rebel camp could also be dangerous. Executions for even minor offenses were swift and frequent, and the diseases caused by the dead bodies lying about along with the absence of hygiene took their toll. Amazingly, in this raw atmosphere, prayers were offered daily for "Peter III," who sometimes grew somber talking about his plans for the future. As tsar, he would insist on Russian clothing and Cossack hairstyles for all. He would protect the Old Belief and not allow any man to shave his beard. He also promised to abolish serfdom and eliminate the boyars as a class (although the latter had been accomplished decades earlier by Peter the Great). Finally, he would make Berda the new Moscow, Kargala the new St. Petersburg, and Sakmarsk the new Kiev.

To administer his growing army, Pugachev set up a College of War, whose members were to devise strategy and tactics, coordinate troop movements, order munitions, and handle logistics. Pugachev was ably assisted by a number of skilled subordinates, including Kinzia Arslanov, the leader of the Bashkirs, and Andrei Ovchinnikov, who was his best military commander. The leader of the Ural industrial peasants was a certain Afanasi Sokolov,, whose nickname was Khlopusha or "the Cracker." As a convicted convict sentenced to work in a factory, he had been subject to the harshest discipline. He wore a net over his face to conceal his branded forehead, scarred face, and slit nostrils. Still, the man was a leader whose energy and charisma had inspired a rebellion of Ural workers against the authorities and placed them at Pugachev's disposal. He also did more than his share in keeping the rebel army supplied with money, weapons, and food from his old district.

The pretender rather enjoyed his exalted position — being addressed as "your excellency" or *batiushka* (little father) and having his hand kissed. However, it is difficult to know just what his followers thought of him. His closest cohorts, to be sure, knew he was an impostor and played along because they were eager for personal gain, but there were many others who solemnly believed that he really was the rightful tsar and that his survival was an act of divine intervention. Pugachev may not have fully appreciated the importance of all this. At times, he played his role to perfection, talking idealistically and using high sounding phrases, but he could just as easily lapse into the crudest vulgarity or start singing bawdy drinking songs. Ironically, the real Peter III behaved in much the same way, but the rebels who followed the pretender did not know this. They expected him to be their mythical savior and deport himself accordingly. Thus, in February when he decided to marry a young Cossack girl after whom he lusted, many were amazed. How could a tsar choose a low-born Cossack for a wife? And wasn't he already married to Catherine? Pugachev brushed these concerns aside and allowed the Church to sanctify the union. He seemed to have given no thought to his real wife and children.

Despite all his personal shortcomings, the pretender was quite a competent military commander and absolutely fearless in battle. He seemed to have had an intuitive grasp of tactics and was especially adept in the use of artillery. However, as the empress' war with Turkey ground to an end, he would soon need all these qualities just to survive. In late 1773, the government sent one of their best military commanders, Alexander Bibikov, to suppress the rebellion. The general was a veteran of the Seven Years War and had been decorated for bravery. He arrived in Kazan in December and worked to restore morale by organizing the local gentry into a militia. By

January, he went on the offensive and, aided by a number of able lieutenants, began to retake one town after another. However, Pugachev was determined to regain the initiative and, on the night of March 22 (April 2), attacked a force led by Major General Golitsyn that was attempting to break the rebel siege at Orenburg. Despite a significant numerical advantage, the pretender was forced to retreat to Tatishchev. There the rebels made walls of snow, over which they poured water, which quickly solidified into ice. Golitsyn's artillery, however, easily smashed down these defenses and his men overran the fort, killing 2000. Pugachev fled first to Berda, then Kargala, then Sakmarsk, where he found himself surrounded. Most of his army was captured, but somehow he and a few trusted comrades escaped and headed northeast into Bashkiria.

In the spring of 1774, with the rebels everywhere on the defensive, it seemed the game was nearly over. Bibikov tried to keep up the pressure, but the general's sudden illness and death at his headquarters on April 9 (20) profoundly demoralized his men. He was succeeded by the experienced but inflexible General Feodor Shcherbatov, whose tendency to quarrel with subordinates impeded the war effort. Still, the rebels remained mostly on the defensive, and on April 17 (28), they were forced to abandon the siege of Yaitsk. Now, it seemed that all that was needed to end the rebellion was to find Pugachev, but he was off rebuilding his army. His new force, however, had few Cossacks and, despite impressive numbers, little offensive punch. In May, the rebels were repelled when they tried to take the fort at Troitski. Many of them were captured, although not Pugachev. He escaped and soon turned up among the Bashkirs to attract more followers. In June, his new army appeared at Osa on the Kama River where he employed the services of a talented bombardier named Ivan Beloborodov. Under the latter's direction, the rebels set fire to the fort by rolling carts filled with burning straw into the wooden walls. The defenders, overcome by the fire and smoke, surrendered and joined Pugachev, who was much emboldened by the victory. With an army that now numbered about 7000, he decided to attack Kazan on the Volga.

This came as a complete surprise to the government, which had thought the rebellion all but over. But on July 12 (23), Pugachev ordered a frontal attack on the fortress setting fire to the wooden walls as he had at Osa. The 700 regular soldiers guarding the city retreated into the citadel as the attackers desecrated churches, dug up graves, plundered stores, destroyed houses, and killed anyone dressed in western clothes. Meanwhile, with the fires raging out of control, the rebels began emptying the jails. It was here that Pugachev saw his wife, Sophia, and their three children for the first time in more than two years. She had been forced to sell their home to feed the children and, because of her husband's notoriety, was eventually brought to Kazan for interrogation. The pretender was reluctant to embrace his family lest he give away his true identity. He set them up in a tent near his own, claiming they were the family of an old friend. In any case, their reunion was interrupted the very next day by the arrival of Lieutenant Colonel Ivan Michelson's force of 800 men, who had marched all the way from the Ural Mountains. Exhausted and ridiculously outnumbered, they quickly regrouped, attacked, and drove the rebels from the city. Three times Pugachev returned, and three times he was repulsed. By the time the fighting had ended, three-fourths of Kazan had been destroyed, including twenty-five churches and three monasteries.

Alexander Pushkin, who immortalized the pretender in his story, *The Captain's Daughter,* wrote a history of the revolt in which he likened Pugachev's flight to an invasion. It was true. As the rebels crossed the Volga, there was general fear that they would march on Moscow. Instead, they turned south where they continued to attract new followers, mostly peasants and tribesmen. The violence and destruction that attended their march now rose to fantastic proportions. Much of this furor was abetted by one of Pugachev's last manifestoes, disseminated in July of 1774, in which he grandly promised the peasants "the land, the woods, the hay meadows, the fishing grounds, the salt lakes." He also urged them to take vengeance on the gentry — to "seize them, punish them, hang them, treat them in the same way as they, having no Christian feeling, oppressed you, the peasants."[20] What followed has been called a *Pugachevshchina*[21] without Pugachev. Estates throughout the region were plundered and burned, and whole families were massacred. Town after town fell to the rebels with little resistance until Tsaritsyn, where they were forced to retreat after a five-hour battle. The rebels lost again four days later on August 25 (September 5) at Chernyi Yar when Mikhelson's army overtook them, killing thousands and taking all their cannon. The pretender had tried in vain to stave off defeat by suddenly turning on his pursuer and attacking, but this time the rout was complete. He was forced to flee southward some forty-two miles before he could find a place to cross the Volga. With only four boats to ferry hundreds of men, many tried to swim and were drowned.

The pretender was now down to about 200 men, and most of these were beginning to desert. Nevertheless, he still talked of carrying on by going to Astrakhan, Turkey, or westward to the Zaporozhian Cossacks, but, for the few remaining Cossacks who comprised Pugachev's inner circle, all this was pure fantasy. Worn out and bitter, they now began to openly question his identity, wondering why he was unable to write his name and why some called him Yemelian Ivanovich instead of Peter Feodorovich.

Possibly, they may have also begun to think about the 28,000 rubles offered for his capture and the hope of obtaining a pardon. In any case, they somehow agreed that they would return to Yaitsk to see their families and then go to the steppe area south of Orenburg to join the Kirghiz-Kaisaks still in revolt. Along the way, however, they got into an argument when Pugachev for some reason suggested they go to Guryev on the Caspian Sea instead. A scuffle ensued, and the pretender was subdued and bound. The next day he was handed over to Colonel Simonov at Yaitsk to begin the long trip to Moscow.

But first Pugachev was taken to Simbirsk, where he was interrogated by General Pavel Panin, under whom he had served during the Turkish war. He was also confined in a specially built iron cage that forced him to remain in a crouched position the entire journey. Much of the time he froze, since he had only a few rags to protect himself against the cold. When he reached Moscow on November 4 (15), the questioning was intense and virtually nonstop for many days. Some of his cohorts, as well as other people who had known him, were brought in to testify. For his own part, Pugachev insisted to the end that he had not been aided by foreign powers, noblemen, or Old Believers. He also claimed that most of the violence was perpetrated by the Yaik Cossacks who had used him as a front. Such disclaimers mattered little now, however, and when his trial began on December 30 in the Kremlin's Palace of Facets, the pretender wasn't even allowed to be present. He did appear on the second day, but only to receive a sentence that was designed to horrify anyone who saw or heard about it — being drawn and quartered *before* being beheaded.

Pugachev's execution took place on January 10 (21), 1775, not in Red Square, but in Bolotnii Square on the large, crescent-shaped island in the Moscow River just south of the Kremlin. As one of five to suffer capital punishment that day, he appeared in a tumbrel at the end of a procession accompanied by several priests. Shivering in a sheepskin coat and with a candle in each hand, he bowed to the onlookers as he was wheeled along. Pugachev made the sign of the cross as the sentence was read out, heard himself be excommunicated by a priest, gave up his coat, and was led to the block. As an act of mercy, Catherine had secretly countermanded the original sentence, ordering that he be decapitated before the body was drawn and quartered. This being done, his head was put on a pike and held high to the cheers of the crowd. The corpse was then cut up into pieces, each of which was attached to a wheel and displayed in different parts of the city.

This rebellion, the greatest social upheaval in Russian history, was not soon forgotten. As Pugachev's followers were hunted down, executions took place in other towns and cities as well. General Panin, operating along the Volga, was authorized to take harsh reprisals on anyone suspected of having contributed to the disorders, and he did. Whole villages were wiped out as the guilty were hanged by the neck or with hooks in their ribs. Others were broken by the wheel or flogged to death. Many were mutilated by having their nostrils slit, ears torn off, or foreheads branded. Those thought to be less guilty were beaten and forced to pay a fine; others had their hair or beards shorn. Pugachev's two wives, three children, and sister were incarcerated in Keksgolm prison for life. One of his daughters remained in captivity for sixty years until her death in 1834. The Cossacks who had betrayed and delivered the pretender received pardons.

Catherine's reaction to the rebellion was a mixture of shock, anger, embarrassment, and denial. In part, this confusion was because she believed herself an enlightened ruler whose only motivation was a sincere desire to improve the lot of her subjects. Thus, in the aftermath of the great calamity, she struggled not merely to understand what had happened, but also to address its causes. Accordingly, she lowered the price of salt, eliminated wartime taxes, and offered amnesty to debtors, army deserters, and fugitive state peasants. She also banned the use of force to convert Muslim tribesmen to Orthodoxy and improved the treatment of Ural factory workers. At the same time, she felt compelled to do something to support the landowner class, of which she was a prominent member. To this end, she issued her Statute of Provinces of 1775, which placed control of local affairs firmly in the hands of the nobility. Finally, Catherine resorted to some expedients that the Soviets would perfect in the 20th century. Places with unpleasant associations were renamed: the Yaik River became the Ural, the town of Yaitsk became Uralsk, and Zimoveiskaya Stanitsa (the birthplace of both Razin and Pugachev) became Potemkinskaya. In addition, whole populations were deported: the Zaporozhian Cossacks to the Kuban and the Volga Cossacks to the Caucasus. Finally, the truth about what happened and why was not to be admitted or even discussed, but doomed to "eternal oblivion and profound silence."[22]

Selected Bibliography

It would be difficult to imagine studying this topic without consulting Paul Avrich's *Russian Rebels* and Philip Longworth's older but still useful *The Cossacks*. Longworth's biography *Alexis, Tsar of All the Russias* also has much useful information about Stepan Razin. Robert Massie's *Peter the Great-His Life and World*, develops interesting portraits of Bulavin and

Mazeppa, and John T. Alexander's *Emperor of the Cossacks* offers a particularly arresting account of Pugachev and the *Pugashchevshchina*. Too, the *Modern Encyclopedia of Russian and Soviet History* has a number of important articles including "Mazepa, Ivan Stepanovich" (James Cracraft), "Pugachev, Emelian Ivanovich" (John T. Alexander), "Bulavin, Kondratii Afanas'evich" and "Razin, Stepan Timofeevich" (James G. Hart).

Alexander, John T. "Pugachev, Emelian Ivanovich." *Modern Encyclopedia of Russian and Soviet History*, ed. Joseph L. Wieczynsky, 54 vols. with suppl. Gulf Breeze, Florida: Academic International Press, 1976–1990.

Avrich, Paul. *Russian Rebels*. New York: W.W. Norton, 1972.

Cracraft, James. "Mazepa, "Ivan Stepanovich." *Modern Encyclopedia of Russian and Soviet History*, ed. Joseph L. Wieczynsky, 54 vols. with suppl. Gulf Breeze, Florida: Academic International Press, 1976–1990.

Hart, James G. "Razin, Stepan Timofeevich." *Modern Encyclopedia of Russian and Soviet History*, ed. Joseph L. Wieczynsky, 54 vols. with suppl. Gulf Breeze, Florida: Academic International Press, 1976–1990.

Lincoln, Bruce. *The Romanovs, Autocrats of All the Russias*. New York: Doubleday, 1981.

Longworth, Philip. *Alexis, Tsar of All the Russias*. New York: Franklin Watts, 1984.

Massie, Robert. *Peter the Great. His Life and World*. New York: Ballantine Books, 1981.

Schlafly, Daniel L. "Bulavin, Kondratii Afanas'evich." *Modern Encyclopedia of Russian and Soviet History*, ed. Joseph L. Wieczynsky, 54 vols. with suppl. Gulf Breeze, Florida: Academic International Press, 1976–1990.

Ure, John. *The Cossacks: An Illustrated History*. Woodstock and New York: The Overlook Press, 1999.

6. REBEL RELATIVES AND THE REVOLTS OF THE STREL'TSY

Not all the Romanovs ruled tyrannically. Some were able to engender a fair measure of cooperation between the rival factions at court. Such was the case with Tsar Feodor III, who ascended the throne in January 1676 following Tsar Alexei's death. Just sixteen years old at the time, he was intelligent, even-tempered, and better educated than any of his predecessors. Unfortunately, he was also afflicted by a scurvy-like disease that had so swollen his legs that he had to be carried during his own coronation. Bed-ridden for much of his reign, he was unable to participate fully in affairs of state. Still, he is remembered for one very important initiative, the abolition of *mestnichestvo*. This was a practice that allowed noblemen to obtain important positions in the military and government by virtue of their ancestry rather than their competence. The move antagonized many but was welcomed by those who hoped to minimize bureaucratic corruption and inefficiency. However, Feodor's death on April 27 (May 7), 1682. ended any hope of further reform for the immediate future and plunged the country into the first dynastic crisis of the Romanov era.

The deceased Tsar Feodor had been married twice but left no male heirs. He should have been automatically succeeded by his fifteen-year-old brother Ivan, but this was resisted by the *boyar duma* and the Patriarch Ioachim (Joachim), who were concerned that Ivan's frail health and various infirmities would make it impossible for him to rule. Many favored his half-brother, Peter, who was the son of Tsar Alexis' second wife, Natalya Naryshkina. The boy was only ten, but he was mentally competent and physically robust. To decide the issue, the patriarch called for a vote by acclamation before a crowd assembled near the Red Staircase in the Kremlin's Cathedral Square. Peter won, but the choice was far from unanimous. Indeed, there was vehement opposition from the Miloslavsky relatives of the tsar's first wife, Maria, and their supporters, who saw their privileges and positions at court threatened. They did not intend to give up without a struggle.

Surprisingly, one of the boldest of those who protested the young Peter's election to the throne was the deceased tsar's older sister, the tsarevna or princess Sophia. At a time when most women in her class were confined to the terem, one would have expected her to have been excluded from public affairs, but Sophia was no ordinary maiden. Born in 1657, and the sixth of Tsar Alexei's children by his first wife, she had previously violated convention by attending lessons with her younger brother, Feodor. Although this originally may have been for the purpose of looking after him, Sophia turned it into an opportunity to improve her status at court. Over the years, she became his indispensable helper and remained by his side even after he became tsar. Now that Feodor was dead, Sophia was outraged at the Naryshkin's suddenly ascension to power, and dared to confront the patriarch himself on behalf of her other brother, Ivan.

Opposition to the Naryshkins grew from other quarters as well, including an important part of the military establishment known as the *strel'tsy*. This once elite unit of fusiliers, created during the time of Ivan the Terrible as Muscovy's first professional soldiers, was a conspicuous presence in Moscow as they paraded around with their flowing beards and bright uniforms. Over the years, they had acquired a number of additional duties, and now served as sentries, bodyguards, escorts, internal security troops, frontier guards, builders, and firefighters, but the twenty-two thousand or so that lived in and around the capital had a fierce sense of entitlement and often a lot of free time on their hands. They were fond of strong drink and inclined to rowdiness and outright defiance. To keep them appeased and out of trouble, they were allowed to live in their own settlements, practice trades, and manage shops. They also paid no taxes. But in the spring of 1682, the *strel'tsy* were restless and unhappy. Some were Old Believers who mourned the loss of the true faith and hated the changes and innovations that were being urged on them by foreign advisors. Others had complaints against their own officers, who often forced them to work on their private estates and sometimes withheld their pay. Indeed, so acute did this latter issue become that, two days after the death of Tsar Feodor, twelve regiments marched on the Kremlin and demanded Tsaritsa Natalya punish the offenders by having them beaten with a cudgel. Hoping to avoid a crisis, the new regent acquiesced, but more trouble was soon to come.

Sophia was the half-sister of Peter the Great, who, as a woman, defied convention by governing Muscovy as regent for seven years. Eventually, Peter
ousted her from power and had her confined for life in the Novodevichy
Monastery. I.E. Repin (1844–1930). Tretiakovsky Gallery, Moscow.

The *strel'tsy* were also agitated by the selection of Peter over his older brother, Ivan, to the throne. They suspected foul play on the part of the Naryshkins, many of whom had been seen celebrating as they left Tsar Feodor's funeral service. They were also incensed by the elevation of the new tsar's uncle, Ivan Naryshkin, to the rank of boyar on May 7 (17) at the tender age of twenty-three. Not only was he thought to be too young for such an honor, but his arrogance and bad manners had made him an object of universal dislike. Among other things, he is alleged to have lounged on the imperial throne, paraded about in the tsar's crown and robes, and insulted Tsarevich Ivan. He was subsequently implicated in two more rumors that were even more serious: that Tsar Feodor had been poisoned (previously it was believed he had died a natural death), and that the tsarevich, Ivan, had been assassinated.

News of the tsarevich's alleged murder was conveyed to the *Strel'tsy* Quarter on the morning of May 15 by Alexander Miloslavsky and Piotr Tolstoy, who appeared on horseback urging the soldiers to take vengeance. Soon a small army in full battle array was marching on the Kremlin. Before anyone in the government could react, hundreds of angry men had penetrated the old fortress and gathered in front of the imperial palace. Brandishing their muskets, pikes, and halberds, they demanded to see Tsarevich Ivan. After some delay, Natalya, with Peter and Ivan hand-in-hand, stepped out onto the Red Staircase adjoining the Palace of Facets. The *strel'tsy* were dumbfounded. Not only did Ivan appear perfectly fine, but the boy declared that he was not being mistreated and had "no complaints against anybody."

With this, Natalya and the boys withdrew to the palace, and Artemon Matveev, former chief advisor to Tsar Alexis, stepped forward. Six years earlier, he had been convicted of practicing sorcery and sent into exile. Despite the fact that he had been allowed to return, he was generally considered to be a rather suspicious character and enjoyed no great popularity among the men. Still, his words struck a positive cord as he reminded the soldiers of their importance to the crown, and he gently urged them to withdraw. Unfortunately, the effect of this speech was immediately undone by that of Prince Mikhail Dolgoruky, whose father was the director of the *Strel'tsy* Department. The prince, himself a *strel'tsy* commander, denounced the men for their insubordination and threatened harsh reprisals. Hearing this, the men exploded in anger and began an orgy of violence that was to last three days and claim some forty lives.

The first victims were Dolgoruky and Matveev, both of whom were immediately hacked to pieces. A mob of soldiers then dashed up the Red Staircase and into the palace, searching for the enemies they hated. The

This page and opposite: The *strel'tsy* were members of an elite military unit founded by Ivan the Terrible trained in the use of firearms. In May of 1682, they went on a rampage in the Kremlin and murdered many of young Peter I's relatives and supporters. Among the victims was a family friend and adviser named Artemon Matveev, who is shown at right being thrown from the Red Staircase onto a pike. L.P. Bushchik, *Illustrirovanaya Istoriya SSSR, XV–XVII vv.* Moskva, Prosveshcheniye, 1970; Novosti, London.

most prominent of these were members of the Naryshkin clan, and especially the tsar's uncle, Ivan, who was now accused of plotting to seize the throne. For nearly three days, he was hunted like an animal, managing to avoid capture only by scurrying from one hiding place to another in the imperial palace. His sister, who could see no other way of ending the bloodbath, finally persuaded him to surrender. Others singled out for slaughter included a number of unpopular *strel'tsy* commanders and a corrupt state secretary named Averky Kirillov. Among the foreigners to be put to death was a Polish doctor named Daniel von Gaden, who was accused of poisoning Tsar Feodor. The doctor had been apprehended on the evening of May 15 (25) trying to sneak into the German Suburb dressed as a beggar. It was alleged that dried snakes had been found in his home — clear proof that he was indeed a sorcerer.

In the aftermath of this horrible bloodbath, Natalya and what remained of her family wandered about in a state of shock. The *strel'tsy* were quick to sense a vacuum and forcefully put forward a number of demands the regency was too weak to resist. These included complete amnesty, restoration of back pay, and the construction of a triumphal column in Red Square in their honor. By the end of May, they had even forced Natalya to renounce her position as regent in favor of Sophia, while insisting that Peter and Ivan henceforth rule jointly as co-tsars. This led to a most unusual ceremony in Moscow the following month. For the first time in history, two sovereigns were crowned at once. For the occasion, a special double throne was created, the back of which contained a small opening to allow one of the noblemen serving at court to whisper instructions to the boy-tsars.

Sophia's role in this complicated affair has long intrigued historians, many of whom have blamed her for instigating the revolt. Although hard evidence is lacking, it is probable that she was glad to see many of Peter's relatives eliminated. According to one account, it was she who convinced the Naryshkins to urge Ivan Naryshkin to give himself up in order to prevent a massacre. She also played a prominent role in the negotiations with the *strel'tsy*, who allowed her to act as a mediator and hoped she would become their patron in the new government. Indeed, one of Sophia's first acts was to appoint an Old Believer, Prince Ivan Khovansky, director of the *Strel'tsy* Department. The choice was a popular one. Khovansky had a record of service to the crown that spanned more than thirty years. He had been the military governor of a number of cities and towns and had served as head of the *Yamskoy Prikaz,* or Department of Transportation, during the reign of Tsar Feodor. However, he also had a reputation for debauchery, was notoriously ambitious, and was something of a loudmouth.

While serving as military governor of Novgorod, his incessant boasting won him the nickname *Tararui*, or "windbag."

Khovansky apparently believed the regency could not long endure and that his own star was on the rise. Just days after the rebellion had subsided, he prodded some Old Believers in the Titov regiment to present a petition to the government requesting a debate on religious matters. Sophia was not eager to confront these fanatics, but, under pressure, agreed to a meeting on July 5 (15). However, as large numbers of Old Believers began to stream into the capital (apparently anticipating a return to the Old Belief), she grew uneasy. To avoid an ugly scene, she insisted that the debate take place in the Palace of Facets, which was too small to accommodate everyone who wanted to attend. She also flouted tradition by attending the session herself, but she was not prepared for what transpired. At one point, an Old Believer named Nikita and the Archbishop Afanasy became so impassioned that they nearly came to blows. Sophia herself remained calm until she heard someone declare that her father, the late Tsar Alexei, had been 'perverted' by Nikon and other defilers of the true faith. She then jumped to her feet and loudly rebuked the dissenters. She also denounced the attending *strel'tsy* as 'rebellious blockheads,' and threatened to leave the country.

But Sophia did not leave the country. Instead she took steps to strengthen her position by currying favor with the military and take a hard line with religious dissenters. Thus, as she offered the *strel'tsy* material rewards to keep them loyal, she executed Nikita, whose strident attack on the government during the debate had particularly antagonized her. She would also like to have been rid of Khovansky, but his popularity among the soldiers made this a dubious move politically. However, that summer the prince undermined his own position by a number of blunders: He recklessly accused the *boyars* and other high officials of plotting against the *strel'tsy* and urged the government to turn them all over to him for punishment. He demanded more money for his men and suggested it come from the revenues of crown lands. He also tried to instigate a crisis in Novgorod by claiming that servitors in the region were planning to rise in mutiny. Finally, he attempted to have his son, Andrei, marry one of the royal princesses. This last act convinced many that he was planning to seize the throne.

Sophia pretended not to notice Khovansky's activities and spent much of July and August traveling around Muscovy visiting monasteries and royal estates. However, when Khovansky failed to appear as ordered on September 1 to attend a New Year's celebration, his fate was sealed. Two weeks later, she invited the prince and his son to attend a meeting with a visiting Ukrainian dignitary at Vozdvizhenskoe, just south of the Trinity Monastery. Everything went according to form until after a mass on September 17 (27) when she convened a special session of the *boyar duma*. Then, with neither Khovansky present, she denounced them both as traitors. The accused were arrested in a nearby village, brought to Vozdvizhenskoe, and condemned to death without a trial. The elder Khovansky tearfully begged to be allowed to answer the charges and offered to reveal the names of those who had incited the *strel'tsy* rebellion the previous May. All this fell on deaf ears, however, as father and son were unceremoniously beheaded in the square near the main road to Moscow. It was a fine present for Sophia, who was celebrating her name day.[1]

With the Khovanskys dead and the *strel'tsy* under control, Sophia was able to rule while the two tsars reigned. It was an odd arrangement. Tsar Ivan lived in the Kremlin under the watchful eye of his sister and did little more than perform at ceremonies. Because of his disabilities, he required constant assistance and showed little comprehension and no initiative. Tsar Peter took part in the same ceremonies with energy and zest but did not live in the Kremlin. To escape its hostile atmosphere and bad memories, he had been taken by his mother to the suburb of Preobrazhenskoe where he was introduced to the exotic German Suburb. This foreign enclave, with its attractive tree-lined boulevards, was off-limits to most Muscovites, but the boy-tsar became a frequent visitor. Soon he became intrigued by all things Western, especially as they related to the military. Over the next few years, he spent much time organizing elaborate war games with his friends under the tutelage of foreign officers.

Meanwhile, the new regent, ignoring Peter and his mother, pursued policies designed to promote stability and the status quo. She was assisted by a number of able advisors, including the sophisticated and cosmopolitan Prince Vasily Golitsyn, who may have become her lover. The prince became director of the Foreign Office in May of 1682 and the following year was awarded the title "Guardian of the Tsars' Great Seal and the State's Great Ambassadorial Affairs." Golitsyn was rather conservative on most questions and promulgated laws to improve tax collection, strengthen serfdom, and eliminate bribery and corruption. He also tried to humanize the law code by eliminating the death penalty for seditious language, and he ended the practice of burying women alive for murdering their husbands. However, like Sophia, the prince had no tolerance for the Old Believers, who were being burned at the stake for their continuing opposition to the state church.

The regency proved to be somewhat more adventurous in foreign affairs. In April of 1686, Muscovy entered into an alliance with Poland,

Austria and the Venetian Republic, who were then at war with the Ottoman Empire. The agreement included a treaty of "permanent peace" with Poland, by which the latter agreed to recognize the city of Kiev as a Muscovite possession. In return, however, the Russians had to attack the Crimean Tatars, who were vassals of the Turkish sultan. This treaty was hailed as a great diplomatic victory at the time, but the two campaigns that were subsequently carried out against the Tatars, in 1687 and 1689, were disappointments. Together they resulted in the death or capture of some 85 thousand men. However, when the troops straggled back to Moscow after the second campaign in July 1689, Sophia and Golitsyn arranged that they be hailed as conquerors. Many people were taken in by this charade, but not Tsar Peter. Not only did he refuse to receive the "victors," but he even resisted the distribution of the customary awards. Sophia, who had grown accustomed to her half-brother's non-interference in affairs of state, was dismayed by his new assertiveness, but Peter was now fully grown and officially of age. Six months earlier, he had taken a wife[2] and was now increasingly resentful of his half-sister's domination. Some of this bad feeling had surfaced earlier on July 8 at a religious festival in the Cathedral of the Assumption. Annoyed by Sophia's participation in the service, he demanded that she retire immediately. Her refusal to do so enraged him and helped set the scene for a nasty confrontation.

On August 7 (17), Sophia embarked on a pilgrimage to the nearby Donskoy Monastery[3] accompanied by an unusually large force of *strel'tsy*, allegedly because of a recent murder that had been committed in the area during a previous such excursion. But the real reason for the added security was that a mysterious letter had been delivered to the Kremlin warning of an imminent attack by Peter's forces. Sophia's anxiety was such that her director of the *strel'tsy*, Feodor Shaklovity, ordered the gates of the Kremlin closed as he summoned more soldiers to augment his already large force. However, this activity gave rise to a counter-rumor that the *strel'tsy* were planning to march on Preobrazhenskoe to assassinate Peter. Later that night, the young tsar was awakened by his uncle, Lev Naryshkin, and Prince Boris Golitsyn and warned of the danger. Terrified, he fled the palace in his nightgown and bare feet and hid in a grove of trees until his clothes could be brought to him. He then rode by horseback to the Trinity Monastery some forty-five miles to the northeast, arriving at dawn in a state of near collapse. As the tsar slept, and word spread of Sophia's alleged attempt to have him removed from power, his relatives and supporters hastened to the monastery. These included his wife and mother, his play regiments from Preobrazhenskoe, and one of the loyal *strel'tsy* units from Moscow.

In fact, Sophia had not ordered the *strel'tsy* to march, and Peter was not in any danger. It is probable that the rumor was planted by his own supporters who were hostile to the regency. Still, few doubted that Sophia longed to rule in her own right. Not only had she begun to refer to herself as autocrat, or *samoderzhitsa*, but in 1688, she commissioned a portrait of herself with the imperial crown and scepter. Such presumption caused resentment in many circles, and particularly among the Naryshkins, who had little difficulty persuading Peter to believe that his half-sister intended to do him harm.

For the next three weeks, Peter remained at Trinity, determined to force the issue. He began by writing Sophia a letter demanding to know why she had gathered such a large force of *strel'tsy* on August 17 (27). When she was not able to provide a satisfactory answer, he ordered the various *strel'tsy* commanders to report to the monastery with ten men from each regiment. Although Sophia tried to countermand this directive by threatening to behead anyone who complied, she knew she could not win an all-out struggle for power. Thus, to reassure Peter of her loyalty and affection, she sent messengers to Trinity to convey the same, only to have them rebuffed. She also implored the Patriarch Ioachim to intercede on her behalf. He, at first, agreed, but later defected to Peter. Finally, Sophia, accompanied by Golitsyn and some other supporters, decided to go to Trinity herself but got only as far the village of Vozdvizhenskoe before being informed that Peter would not receive them. When the regent tried to proceed, she was threatened with cannon fire.

On September 1 (10), New Year's Day,[4] Tsar Peter sent another letter to the Kremlin ordering that "blantant criminal" Feodor Shaklovity, and others who had recently conspired against him, to report to the Trinity Monastery. Sophia was enraged by the message and ordered the colonel who delivered it to be beheaded. (Fortunately for him, the command could not be carried out for lack of an executioner.) Later that day, the regent, trying to regain the initiative, gave a number of impassioned speeches before large crowds to justify her behavior and condemn those who had sown discord between herself and Peter. Still, her support continued to evaporate, and the formal arrest of Feodor Shaklovity on September 7 (17) ended any hope that her authority could be restored. Five days later, after hearings and interrogations, Shaklovity and two others were executed, and a number of *strel'tsy* were knouted and had their tongues cut out. Vasily Golitsyn was condemned to lifelong exile in the far north, and Sophia was to be confined to the Novodevichy Monastery.

With the abolition of the regency, one of Peter's first acts was to write his older brother, Ivan, for whom he had much affection. "And you know very well indeed how our sister the Tsarevna Sophia Alexeevna chose to rule our state by her own will and how in that rule there was much that was disagreeable to us and burdensome to the people...."[5] He then left for Alexandrovskaya Sloboda to pursue some of his favorite recreations such as hunting, riding, and drilling his troops. The running of the government was left to his advisors, who were delighted to be back in power, but the seventeen-year-old Peter would not be passive for long. At six-feet seven-inches tall and in robust health, he had a commanding presence. He was inquisitive, intelligent, furiously energetic, and increasingly critical of traditional Muscovite values. This last trait, which had been encouraged by his visits to the German Suburb, was disturbing to many and drew sharp criticism from the Patriarch Ioachim. When the aged prelate died in 1690, Peter was glad to be rid of him and hoped to name the enlightened and well-educated Marcellus of Pskov to take his place. However, his mother, supported by a number of conservative boyars, insisted on Adrian, the metropolitan of Kazan. Peter acquiesced, but the new patriarch's loathing of all things Western and his pedantic adherence to ritual and tradition soon alienated the young tsar.

Seeking to mock such attitudes, and to have some fun, Peter organized a gang of revelers called the Most Drunken Council. This group of assorted bureaucrats, noblemen, soldiers, ministers, and foreigners numbered between 80 and 200 and loved drinking, carousing, vulgar buffoonery, and gross masquerades. Those closest to the tsar had nicknames and mock titles by which they addressed one another. They also wore strange costumes in which they paraded around the city, occasionally dropping in on some unsuspecting nobleman to celebrate, sometimes for as long as three days. Such events featured huge feasts, binge drinking, speeches, games, pranks, raucous music, and blasts of artillery fire. The Council also enjoyed putting on silly skits that ridiculed that Roman Catholic Church, although it sometimes seemed that Russian Orthodoxy was also being parodied. Religious Muscovites were shocked by such rowdiness, but dared not criticize the tsar, who would tolerate no restraints on his behavior.[6]

Likewise, many of his subjects disapproved of Peter's interest in shipbuilding and sailing, but the tsar's love of the sea soon had important military applications. Troubled by Prince Golitsyn's two bungled military campaigns against the Ottoman Empire in 1687 and 1689, he decided to resume the attack in order to expand Muscovy's borders southward to the Black Sea. In 1695, he ordered an attack against the town of Azov and joined the army as an ordinary gunner. After a grueling march south, the Muscovites besieged the enemy fortress for many months but were not able to overcome the defenders, who were being supplied by sea. Peter finally called off the attack and withdrew to Voronezh on the Don, 325 miles to the north. There he constructed a fleet of galleys and mounted another offensive in the spring of 1696. This time the Muscovites captured the fortress, although they were not then able to establish a presence on the Black Sea.

Still, Peter was thrilled by his first military triumph, and he began to colonize Azov and the surrounding area. Thousands of peasants and strel'tsy were uprooted and forcibly sent south. He also planned the construction of a fleet of ten ocean-going warships for his new navy and soon found a way of building more. In 1696, he decreed that all large landowners and monasteries pay for the construction of one warship to be completed within eighteen months. He threatened to confiscate the property of anyone who failed to comply. Finally, in November of that year, and to the dismay of nearly everyone, Peter announced that he would be sending a number of men to western Europe to acquire the technological knowledge and skills necessary to run his fleet. What he did not announce was that he himself intended to go along disguised as an ordinary carpenter, Piotr Mikhailov. By so participating, the tsar had two goals: to avoid useless protocol while satisfying his curiosity about countries in the West and to seek an alliance in Europe against Turkey.

However, the journey that would eventually become known as the "Great Embassy" almost never got started. Just days before his departure, the tsar learned of a possible plot against his life involving a colonel in the strel'tsy named Ivan Tsykler and two boyars. The matter seems to have been blown out of proportion: the colonel had merely grumbled about being sent to a post far from Moscow, and the boyars had criticized the tsar's unregal behavior and his preference for foreigners. But Peter, suspecting that Sophia and the Miloslavskys were involved in something subversive, took the matter very seriously. To make his point, he sentenced the three to be beheaded in Red Square and ordered the remains of the long-deceased Ivan Miloslavsky (Sophia's uncle) to be dug up and hauled to the execution platform by a team of swine. The coffin was placed close to the block with the lid open so that when the chopping began, the blood of the condemned would splatter on Miloslavsky's corpse.

With the "conspiracy" quashed, the Great Embassy left Muscovy for Holland, where Peter resided for five months. He spent most of his time working in a shipyard but also took time to observe the dissection of cadavers, learn to pull teeth, and peer into a microscope. He then traveled to England to continue his apprenticeship as a shipbuilder, where he also enjoyed the generous hospitality of William III. The king admired the tsar's energy and curiosity and entertained him lavishly. He staged a mock naval battle in his honor, invited him to visit Parliament, and presented him with a magnificent yacht. Unfortunately, Peter was not one to show gratitude, especially when it was discovered that he had nearly destroyed his temporary Deptford residence.[7] Not only were the carefully manicured lawn and gardens dug up and completely ruined, but mud and grease were smeared all over the house. There were also torn drapes, broken windows, and expensive paintings riddled with bullet holes. The English were aghast, but Peter apparently shrugged it all off by paying for the damage with a huge, uncut diamond.

In May of 1698, the tsar journeyed to Vienna, which he found less interesting since there were fewer factories and no shipyards to inspect. Still, he had a pleasant interview with the Holy Roman Emperor, King Leopold, although he was disappointed by Austria's refusal to enter an alliance against Turkey. Later, he attended a Catholic mass, went to the opera, and participated in a masked ball dressed as a Frisian peasant. In sum, Peter found the Austrian capital pleasant enough but was eager to move on to Venice on the Adriatic Sea to learn the art of building war galleys. However, before he could continue his journey, his plans were interrupted by a letter from Feodor Romodanovsky[8] in Moscow. Four regiments of *strel'tsy* assigned to guard the Polish frontier had risen in revolt and were marching on Moscow.

With this news, the tsar immediately cancelled the rest of his trip and set out for home. As he approached the border of Muscovy in July, however, he was relieved to learn that the rebels had been stopped near the New Jerusalem Monastery some thirty miles northwest of Moscow. General Patrick Gordon[9] had tried to avoid bloodshed by promising the *strel'tsy* their back pay and pardons if they returned to their garrison duties, but the insurgents were determined to go to Moscow to be with their families and threatened to kill the old general and anyone else who dared to oppose them. Blasts of cannon fire soon brought them to heel, however, and within an hour most had surrendered. One hundred and thirty were executed on the spot, and the rest were marched to Moscow in chains to await the wrath of the tsar.

Peter arrived in the capital on September 5 (15), eager to learn the extent of the mutiny. Fourteen torture chambers had been constructed to accommodate the 1,714 surviving *strel'tsy*. For the next six weeks, Peter's officers inflicted unimaginable torments on the soldiers in an effort to get them to talk about how they had been induced to rebel. These included being beaten with the knout, broken on the rack, and roasted by fire. These tortures, horrific though they were, did not at first loosen any tongues. Finally, one of the rebels began to speak of two letters, allegedly written

The *strel'tsy* hated the influence accorded to foreigners during the reign of Peter the Great, and rebelled when the tsar was visiting western Europe. Peter had more than a thousand of these mutineers executed upon his return to Moscow. I.G. Korb, *Dnevnik puteshestviya v Moscoviyu* (1698–1699). St. Petersburg, Izdaniye A.S. Suborina.

by the Princess Sophia, urging the *strel'tsy* to restore her to power. The tsar went to the Novodevichy Monastery on September 27 (October 7) to personally interview his half-sister. The two had not seen each other in nine years, but neither took pleasure in this reunion. Sophia, unbowed by her long confinement, stoutly denied writing letters to the *strel'tsy* or participating in any conspiracies. Peter was skeptical but did not press the issue. Convinced, however, that she was still a threat, he sent her back to the monastery amidst tightened security. Three weeks later, Sophia was shorn as a nun.[10]

The execution of the rebels who had survived the torture chamber began on September 30 (October 10) and lasted several months. Most were hanged or beheaded at Preobrazhenskoe or in Red Square. Peter encouraged many of his closest associates to wield the executioner's ax, and it is alleged that he participated himself. There is no hard evidence to support this claim, but in his desire to punish the guilty and intimidate others, he did not shrink from harsh measures. He ordered 196 rebels hanged near the convent's walls in plain view of Novodevichy's residents. Of those, the three who were accused of having written Sophia were strung up outside her window in the Naprudnaya Tower. Their corpses dangled there for five months.

As the surviving *strel'tsy* were sent into exile, and the tension in Moscow eased somewhat, Peter turned his attention to other matters. His imagination and imperial ambitions having been whetted by his travels abroad, he now resolved to impose Westernization on his subjects in all things great and small. To this end, he forced Muscovites to adopt European dress and made men shave their sacred beards. (The latter was a particular affront to Old Believers.) He also dreamed of military conquest, and, in 1696, won significant territories in the south including the port city of Azov against Turkey. In August of 1700, however, he invaded Livonia to begin what is now known as the Great Northern War, only to have his army crushed at Narva by one of history's great military geniuses, Charles XII of Sweden.[11] The tsar fled the battlefield in terror but quickly recovered. He rebuilt his army and returned in 1704 to capture Narva. The victory was important because it accelerated the construction of nearby St. Petersburg, which would someday become the capital of his new empire. However, all this activity demanded the conscription of more soldiers, more workers, and a flood of new taxes.

Muscovites complained bitterly about most of Peter's initiatives, almost all of which violated sacred traditions, but he tsar was not deterred. In 1702, he created the Secret Office of the Preobrazhensky, whose agents used various kinds of harassment and torture to root out dissent. Not everyone was intimidated, however. Among his most determined opponents were the Old Believers, who watched in anger as the tsar melted down church bells for cannon, forced priests and monks to serve in the military, and imposed a Western-style calendar on the land.[12] Such blasphemy convinced many that Peter was the Antichrist and that the end of the world was near. Still, the flood of reforms continued. Using Sweden as a model, he reorganized the government bureaucracy and divided his tsardom into provinces. He established a nine-man Senate to administer the country in his absence and to minimize the Church's interference in affairs of state, eventually abolishing the office of patriarch. To replace it, he created the Holy Synod, a committee consisting of ten clerics supervised by a layman to be appointed by him. He also promoted education by sending students abroad to study and founding various kinds of schools, and he encouraged women to play a more active role in public life.

Many of the reforms cited above came late in his reign, and were less offensive in themselves than other aspects of Peter's rule. His blasphemous personal behavior, his preference for foreigners, his demand for conscripts, his suppression of tribal peoples, and his ravenous tax policies all provoked uprisings throughout his realm in the first decade of the 18th century. These occurred in the towns, and among tribesmen and Cossacks, and coincided with the invasion of Charles XII powerful Swedish army. So precarious was Peter's situation even after his great victory at Poltava of 1709 that he nearly lost everything to the Turks, who declared war against Russia the following year. Initially, the tsar had hoped to avoid another conflict but was confident that his army was invincible. Thus, not only did he accept the challenge, he declared his intention to liberate all Balkan Christians from Islamic rule. The result was near disaster. In July of 1711, the tsar found his army trapped by an enormous Ottoman force on the Pruth River, a tributary of the Danube. Outnumbered five to one, he made what seemed a futile offer to negotiate. To his amazement, the Turks not only accepted, but gave him terms that were far less harsh that he had expected. True, he was forced to give up vast territories in the south, including Azov and Taganrog, but he and his army were allowed to go free, and he was allowed to retain all the lands previously won in the Baltic. This included his beloved St. Petersburg, which officially became Russia's new capital in 1712.

Back home, however, the tsar's escape on the Pruth seemed like a miracle but was not cheered by all. Indeed, many Russians, fed up with war, high taxes, and increased demands for service, would have been happy to see him perish. Peter's unpopularity prompted some to look to Tsarevich Alexis, whose habits and interests were more traditionally Russian. In some ways, he seemed an attractive alternative to his father. At six feet tall, he was to some extent physically imposing and had a talent for foreign languages and a special interest in theology and the Church. Unfortunately, he was also a hopeless alcoholic, weak in character, and terrified of his father. He had no capacity for leadership, little understanding of affairs of state, and no desire to learn. Those who supported him did so in the belief that, with Peter out of the way, at least the wars and reforms would cease.

To be sure, many of the tsarevich's shortcomings derived from a tormented childhood. As a small boy, he had been forcibly separated from his mother, Eudoxia Lopukhina, whom the tsar hated and had forced into a convent. In 1698, Peter sent his son to live with an aunt, hired foreign tutors to educate him, and then mostly ignored him. At some point, he bade his barely literate friend, Alexander Menshikov, participate in Alexis' upbringing and to supervise his tutors. Menshikov was one of the tsar's most trusted soldiers, but he was in no way equipped to groom the meek and fragile tsarevich. Not only did he bully and humiliate the boy, but he often forced him to act as his personal servant. Peter seems to have been aware of all this but did not intervene. Not surprisingly, Alexis never developed any affection for his father or Menshikov, both of whom, thankfully, were usually off fighting the Swedes. The tsarevich was also ill at ease around his future stepmother, Catherine.[13] She was the daughter of a Lithuanian peasant, to whom the tsar had taken a fancy in 1702 and married in 1707.

In time, Peter began to think about preparing Alexis to rule and was particularly keen that he develop an interest in military affairs. When the tsarevich was thirteen, he was trained as a bombardier for an artillery regiment and subsequently spent much time traveling with the army. As he grew older, he was given specific assignments such as gathering provisions for the soldiers and rounding up new recruits. In 1706, he oversaw the strengthening of the defenses of Moscow against a possible Swedish attack, and in 1708 he was sent south to help suppress the rebellions near Astrakhan. Alexis tried hard to please his father and occasionally showed promise, but, at heart, he did not like the military and withered under Peter's relentless criticism. In time, the son came to fear and detest his father, avoiding him whenever possible. He retreated to his own circle of friends, many of whom hated the tsar and his reforms. These dissidents not only gave him sympathy, but encouraged him to drink and carouse to excess.

A major turning point in the tsarevich's life came with his father's victory at Poltava, which Alexis missed because of illness. In the aftermath, Peter decided that his son would study abroad and take a western wife. In 1710, Alexis was sent to Dresden, where he was to receive instruction in a variety of subjects including fortification, drawing, foreign languages, fencing, and dancing. It was during his stay that he was betrothed to Princess Charlotte of Wolfenbüttel, whom the tsar himself had selected because of her high birth and family connections. The two, who first met in the spa resort of Carlsbad, seemed to like each other and willingly agreed to the union which was formalized in October of 1712. However, the couple was not destined to know happiness. During the first year and a half of their marriage, Alexis was frequently away with the army, and it was not until late in the summer of 1713 that the newlyweds were able to live together in St. Petersburg. By this time, the dark side of the tsarevich's personality had begun to emerge. He now drank continually, often lashing out at his wife, who was pregnant with their first child. Charlotte tried in every way to please her husband, but she could not calm his tantrums or avoid his abuse. In the spring of 1714, Alexis was diagnosed with tuberculosis and forced to go to Carlsbad in Germany for the cure. He left without bothering to explain or say good-bye. During his absence, Charlotte gave birth to a baby girl and wrote to the father, hoping that he would be cheered by the good news. She never received an answer.

Alexis returned to St. Petersburg the following December, but only after being so ordered by his father. Still, for a while, he seemed a changed man. He showed consideration for his wife and affection for his daughter. Gradually, however, he slipped back into his old ways. At some point, he became infatuated with a Finnish serf girl, Afrosina, captured during the war against Sweden. The young woman was rather less smitten than the tsarevich, but soon became his mistress and moved into the imperial residence. Thereafter Alexis mostly ignored his wife, except to make love to her once a week, hoping to produce a male heir. Charlotte endured this humiliation long enough to give birth to a future tsar in October of 1715, Peter Alexeevich. It was a joyful occasion for everyone except the mother, who fell ill and died one week later.

The day after Charlotte's funeral, Peter's wife, Catherine, also gave birth to a son, named Piotr Petrovich. Now that the tsar had a second male heir in addition to Alexis, he took the occasion to send his son an angry letter denouncing him for neglecting his duties. He demanded that the tsarevich begin to behave more responsibly or be disinherited. To Peter's surprise, Alexis meekly agreed to step aside, asking only that he be furnished with a "bare maintenance during my life." At first the tsar seemed to accept this solution, but then began to worry. What if his son seized power after his death and undid his reforms? Six weeks later, Peter wrote again, this time insisting that the tsarevich either apply himself seriously or enter a monastery. He also demanded an immediate answer and threatened, "If you fail to do it, I will treat you as a criminal."[14]

The tsarevich was paralyzed with fear upon receipt of this second letter and turned to a certain Alexander Kikin,[15] one of Peter's former friends, for advice. Kikin, who was the head of the Admiralty, had grown to detest the tsar's despotic ways. He also appreciated Alexis' dilemma and thought he knew a way out. He advised him to become a monk and bide his time: "Remember, they do not nail the cowl to a man's head. One can always slip it off again and throw it away."[16] With this in mind, Alexis informed his father of his intention to leave the secular world, only to find that Peter's attitude seemed to have softened. The tsar, who was busy planning a second trip to western Europe, did not want such an important matter to be decided in haste. He urged his son to take some time to think it over and promised to wait six months for an answer.

However, Alexis soon forgot all about the issue that so concerned the tsar. In the two letters he wrote his father while the latter was abroad during the summer of 1716, he mostly complained about his health and made no mention of what he intended to do with regard to his father's ultimatum. But, in late August, the tsar wrote Alexis a letter that fully conveyed his exasperation: "I repeat it to you that I absolutely will have you resolve on something, for otherwise I must judge that you only seek to gain time to pass it in your usual idleness."[17] The receipt of this most recent letter in October was another shock for the tsarevich. Realizing that he would finally have to choose between becoming a monk or a serious heir-in-training under his father's tutelage, he pretended to do the latter. Soon he was borrowing money from a number of people, including Prince Menshikov, on the pretense that he was going to Copenhagen to join the tsar. In fact, he had decided to run away and seek refuge somewhere in the west. Once again turning to Kikin for advice, he chose Vienna, hoping to persuade his brother-in-law Charles VI to grant him asylum.

Thus, in October 1716, Alexis fled his homeland dressed as an officer and using the pseudonym Kokhansky. He was accompanied by his beloved Afrosina (disguised as a boy page) and three servants. His arrival at the Imperial Court on November 10 and plea for help presented something of a diplomatic dilemma, since the emperor was reluctant to become involved in what seemed a family dispute. Still, impressed by the intensity of his brother-in-law's panic, he agreed to provide sanctuary. Two days later, he sent the tsarevich to the castle of Ehrenberg in the Tyrol valley guarded by soldiers who did not know his true identity, but the following month, Peter, having become aware of his son's defection, suspected that he might have gone to Vienna and ordered him found. By March of 1717, his agents had spotted him in Ehrenberg, only to be thwarted by the emperor, who had him hastily transferred to Castle St. Elmo on the outskirts of Naples, Italy. Here Alexis felt safe, and, over the next few months, wrote several letters to the Senate[18] explaining his actions as he basked in the warm southern climate. Little did he suspect that he had been followed by a Captain of the Guards named Alexander Rumianstev, who soon informed the tsar of his son's whereabouts. Peter was furious at the emperor's duplicity and resolved to stop at nothing to secure his son's return. To this end, he sent his former ambassador to Turkey, Piotr Tolstoy,[19] to Vienna.

Tolstoy was in some ways an odd man to entrust with such a delicate family matter. He was related to the Miloslavskys and had once been a supporter of Sophia. Still, at seventy-two, no one was more qualified to deal with Charles VI or to appreciate the difficulty of his position. The emperor had promised Alexis protection but did not want to anger Peter, whose armies were stationed in Poland and northern Germany. Thus, the old diplomat skillfully applied the pressure until Charles agreed to set up a meeting at the viceroy's palace on September 26 (October 7), 1717. Charles allowed Alexis to be tricked into coming but made it clear that he was not to be repatriated by force.

Alexis reacted in terror when he saw his father's emissaries and feared they had come to assassinate him, but Tolstoy, speaking calmly, assured him that he came only to deliver a letter from the tsar promising forgiveness if the son would return. The tsarevich was too confused and shaken to decide then and there, but he promised to think it over. However, it is unlikely that he had forgotten Alexander Kikin's advice nearly a year earlier: "Remember, if your father sends somebody to persuade you to return, do not do it. He will have you publicly beheaded."[20] Two days later, at a second meeting, Alexis announced his intention to remain under the protection of the emperor. Hearing this, Tolstoy exploded in anger and warned that the tsar would make war in order to get him back. Moreover, he assured the tsarevich that no escape was possible, since he would be followed wherever he went.

While Alexis trembled and cried, Tolstoy also resorted to guile. He bribed an Austrian official to tell Alexis that he could probably not count on the emperor's protection much longer. He also lied that the tsar was already making plans to invade with his army and abduct his son by force. Then, sensing Afrosina's influence on the tsarevich, he promised her material rewards if she would persuade her lover to return. With this, Alexis' resistance all but collapsed. His only plea was that he and Afrosina be allowed to retire to a country house after their return and live unmolested. Tolstoy readily agreed to this arrangement, and, noticing the young woman was pregnant, offered to write the tsar and request permission for the couple to marry.

The first leg of the trip home passed without incident as the party traveled leisurely toward Austria, stopping occasionally to visit religious shrines along the way. Upon reaching Vienna, however, Afrosina was left behind to rest because of her condition. It was agreed that she would continue across the Alps in the spring. The tsarevich was loath to part from her, but Tolstoy was anxious to keep moving. He wanted to avoid having to pay a courtesy call on Charles VI, fearing that if Alexis spoke to his royal brother-in-law, he might reconsider his decision to return. Thus, after bidding farewell to Afrosina, the party slipped through Vienna in one night, stopping only when they reached the town of Brunn in Moravia. When the emperor learned of this maneuver, he suspected the worst and ordered the governor of the region to stop the party and to personally ensure that the tsarevich was returning voluntarily. Tolstoy tried desperately to prevent an interview, and, at one point, threatened to draw his sword. Forced finally to relent, he was enormously relieved when the tsarevich voiced no objection to returning home.

In January of 1718 the party crossed into Russian territory and on February 3 (14), Alexis was formally received in the Great Audience Hall of the Moscow Kremlin. The atmosphere was hostile and tense as he was stripped of his sword and compelled to beg on his knees. He renounced any claim to the throne and solemnly swore allegiance to his half-brother, Piotr Petrovich. But the tsar, contrary to his original promise, refused to grant a pardon until he had learned the names of those who had helped his son flee. Far from objecting to this new condition, Alexis promptly betrayed his servant, Ivan Afanasiev, and his friend, Alexander Kikin. Initially, Peter was satisfied with his son's account but later began to suspect that others had been involved. Thus, in a subsequent interview with the tsarevich, the tsar extracted the names of more potential traitors, although most of these had had little or no prior knowledge about Alexis' flight. They included an aunt, Maria Alexeevna, an uncle, Avraamy Lopukhin, two senators, a number of noblemen, his former tutor, Nikifor Viazemsky, and his confessor, Iakov Ignatiev.

It took a number of weeks to round up and interrogate everyone implicated, but the tsar, acting as judge and prosecutor, was determined to ferret out the whole truth. Many of those brought in for questioning were eventually condemned and beheaded on March 26 (May 6) in Red Square. Three were singled out for special tortures: Alexander Kikin,[21] who had encouraged the tsarevich to flee, Dositheus, the bishop of Rostov, who had publicly expressed sympathy for him, and an officer named Stepan Glebov, who had become the lover of Alexis' mother, Eudoxia Lopukhina, at her convent in Suzdal. Peter learned of the affair when he sent one of his agents to investigate the possibility that she had been in contact with her son.[22]

Typically, the tsarevich made no attempt to protect those who had supported him. His only thought was to avoid punishment himself and marry Afrosina. However, the young woman, who had apparently given birth to a child en route to St. Petersburg, had herself incarcerated upon her return in the Fortress of St. Peter and Paul.[23] Found among her possessions were some unsent letters from Alexis to the Senate and two archbishops. All were similar in content, explaining the reason for his flight and expressing his intention to someday return. Although the letters contained nothing that was overtly treasonous, the tsar was much troubled by their hostile tone. After some reflection, he decided to investigate further.

In May, Peter brought Alexis and Afrosina to the Peterhof,[24] to question them separately. Afrosina went first and freely admitted that the tsarevich had often expressed enmity toward his father and that he had conveyed these feelings in letters to the emperor, Charles VI. She added that the tsarevich had actually been cheered by bad news coming out of Russia, such as reports of mutinies and rebellions, and by an illness of the little tsarevich, Piotr Petrovich. Alexis, she said, hoped that he would someday become tsar so that he could abandon the navy, reduce the army, restore the power of the Church, and move the capital back to Moscow. When Peter confronted Alexis with these accusations, he flatly denied them, only to be contradicted when Afrosina later repeated her testimony in his presence. He also lied when the tsar asked about the letters written to the Senate and the archbishops, insisting that the Austrians had forced him to write them under threat of expulsion. The truth came out two weeks later when the Imperial Court in Vienna denied this claim.

The tsar, now convinced beyond all doubt that his son was a traitor, ordered him jailed in the Fortress of Peter and Paul. In June, he convoked two courts, one ecclesiastical and one secular, to judge the prisoner. This was probably unnecessary, since by now Alexis was so terrified that he was prepared to confess to treason or anything else his father might have suggested. However, the punishment was harder to decide, since the ecclesiastical court refused to render a clear verdict. The members merely acknowledged that, when a son disobeys his father, there was ample precedent for both the death penalty as well as for mercy. The secular court, however, wanted to hear more and decided to apply torture. On June 8 (19), they inflicted twenty-five blows of the knout, which left the tsarevich in near shock, his back bruised and bloody, but since he had revealed nothing new, fifteen more blows were applied on the morning of June 13 (24). Now, barely conscious and desperate to end the questioning, Alexis admitted that not only did he wish for his father's death, but that he would have been willing to pay Charles VI for troops to seize the Russian throne by force. Satisfied, the members of the secular court unanimously voted for the death penalty. All that was required now was the tsar's signature on the appropriate document. However, the tsarevich died the evening of June 15 (26) before this could be done.

In the days that followed, life seemed to go on in St. Petersburg almost as if nothing had happened. The ninth anniversary of the victory at Poltava was wildly celebrated, and a new ninety-four gun ship that the tsar had designed himself was launched amid much jubilation. Alexis was laid to rest on June 19 (30) in the Fortress of Peter and Paul's cathedral next to his wife with all the honors due a person of his rank. The father, who showed little emotion as his son was being laid to rest, was in fact gen-

The tsarevich Alexei was terrified of his father Peter the Great and wanted no part of his reforms. In 1617, he fled the country and sought refuge with the emperor of Austria. Eventually he was found and brought back to Russia by Peter's agents. Nikolai Ge's famous painting of an angry tsar interrogating his son at a palace near St. Petersburg offers some hint of Alexei's terrible fate. N. Ge (1831–1894). Tretiakovsky Gallery. Moscow.

uinely grievous. Still, he would always believe that he had acted according to duty. Thus, he discouraged any official display of mourning and invited no foreign ambassadors to the funeral.

However, pathetic and inconsequential Alexis may have seemed during his short life, his death had enormous significance for Russia, especially as Peter's own health began to decline. It forced the tsar to give much more thought about the future, especially with the passing of his only surviving son, Piotr Petrovich, in April of 1719. The new heir to the throne was now Alexis' son, Peter Alexeevich, and the tsar was nagged by the worry that he would attract support from those who hoped to undo his reforms. Thus, in February 1722, he undertook two initiatives to ensure that only the most able men rise to positions of power and importance. The most enduring of these was his celebrated Table of Ranks, which divided military, court, and civilian service into fourteen parallel grades, and based promotion on ability and length of service rather than birth. It was also at this time that he promulgated his Law of Succession, by which every tsar would henceforth designate his own successor. In this way, he hoped to ensure that power would pass only to those who were fit to rule.

Arguably, the Table of Ranks was at least somewhat successful in promoting men of merit into positions of responsibility. In any case, it remained in force until November of 1917. However, the new Law of Succession, which was undone at the end of the century by Tsar Paul, did the exact opposite, mainly because it undermined the traditional notion of legitimacy and thereby encouraged unscrupulous individuals at court to manipulate the selection process for selfish ends. Thus, as will be described in the next chapter, Peter's initiative actually allowed some of the most irresponsible and incompetent rulers in Russian history to ascend the throne. However, this same law also made it possible for an obscure German princess, the future Catherine the Great, to come to power and rule for more than three decades. Her reign was one of enormous territorial expansion and cultural development, although it, too, would engender an assortment of unintended consequences that would eventually bring the country to the brink of grave crisis.

Selected Bibliography

One of the best sources on the life of Peter I is M.S. Sumner's *Peter the Great*. Less thoroughly researched, but also useful, is Robert K. Massie's *Peter the Great: His Life and World*. The latter devotes much attention to the conflict between Peter and his son Alexei. Lindsey Hughes' *Russia in the Time of Peter the Great* makes use of primary sources previously unavailable to historians, and her *Sophia, Regent of Russia 1657–1704* is an excellent in-depth study of a bold and talented woman. James Cracraft has written three articles useful to the student of this period, all of which can be found in *Modern Encyclopedia of Russian and Soviet History*. They are: "Khovansky, Ivan Ivanovich," "Menshikov, Alexander Danilovich," and "Peter I the Great."

Avrich, Paul. *Russian Rebels*. New York: W.W. Norton, 1972.
Cracroft, James. "Khovansky, Ivan Ivanovich," *Modern Encyclopedia of Russian and Soviet History*, ed. Joseph L. Wieczynski, 54 vols. With suppl. Gulf Breeze, Florida: Academic International Press, 1976–1990.
_____. "Menshikov, Alexander Danilovich," *Modern Encyclopedia of Russian and Soviet History*, ed. Joseph L. Wieczynski, 54 vols. With suppl. Gulf Breeze, Florida: Academic International Press, 1976–1990.
_____. "Peter the Great," *Modern Encyclopedia of Russian and Soviet History*, ed.,

Joseph L. Wieczynski, 54 vols. With suppl. Gulf Breeze, Florida: Academic International Press, 1976–1990.

Crummey, Robert O. "Petrovich, Aleksei," *Modern Encyclopedia of Russian and Soviet History*, ed. Joseph L. Wieczynski, 54 vols. With suppl. Gulf Breeze, Florida: Academic International Press, 1976–1990.

De Jonge, Alex. *Fire and Water. A Life of Peter the Great.* New York: Coward, McCann and Geohegan, 1980.

Hughes, Lindsey, A.J. "Golitsin, Vasily Vasilievich," *Modern Encyclopedia of Russian and Soviet History*, ed. Joseph L. Wieczynski, 54 vols. With suppl. Gulf Breeze, Florida: Academic International Press, 1976–1990.

_____. *Russia in the Time of Peter the Great.* New Haven: Yale University Press, 1990.

_____. "Sophia Alekseevna," *Modern Encyclopedia of Russian and Soviet History*, ed. Joseph L. Wieczynski, 54 vols. With suppl. Gulf Breeze, Florida: Academic International Press, 1976–1990.

_____. *Sophia, Regent of Russia 1657–1704.* New Haven: Yale University Press, 1998.

Massie, Robert. *Peter the Great. His Life and World.* New York: Ballantine, 1981.

Sumner, M.S. *Peter the Great.* London: Thames and Hudson, 1978.

7. SCHEMING ARISTOCRATS—
PALACE COUPS

It is ironic that Peter — who, more than any other tsar, wanted to ensure that he would be succeeded by a competent heir — was too ill at the time of his death to invoke his own law of succession, despite the fact that he had long been mindful of his own mortality and had given much thought to finding a worthy successor. However, by the summer of 1724, his health had become a serious problem since he was now suffering from stranguary, an infection of the urinary tract. This malady became so acute that he was unable to urinate and had to have a catheter inserted into his bladder. This procedure, hideously painful though it was, for a time gave him some relief. Then as the symptoms returned, the tsar was further afflicted by chills and a fever that developed after he jumped into the Gulf of Finland on a cold November day to rescue some sailors whose boat had capsized. Again he recovered, only to fall ill one last time in January 1725 during the Blessing of the Waters to celebrate the Feast of the Epiphany.[1] Thereafter Peter's condition alternately improved and worsened, until it was clear on January 27 (February 7) that he would not recover. On that day, at about two in the afternoon, he asked for a writing pad, apparently to name a successor. However, he was able to scrawl only "Give all to..."[2] before losing consciousness. His death the following day set the stage for a series of palace coups that would unsettle the dynasty until the end of the century.

With no lawful heir, a serious crisis might have developed had not a few opportunists quickly stepped in to fill the void. The most aggressive of these was Alexander Menshikov, who, along with a few other self-serving favorites of Tsar Peter, brushed aside the candidacy of Peter Alexeevich (who would have been the legitimate heir had not Peter changed the law) and promoted Catherine to the throne. The new empress, who was in bad health, had neither the desire nor the aptitude to rule. She was quite happy to allow Menshikov and his cohorts to run the government for the next two years before her own death in March of 1727. Aside from the creation of the *Verkhovnii tainii Soviet*, or Supreme Privy Council,[3] Catherine accomplished little during her short reign. However, she did name a successor: the same twelve-year-old Peter Alexeevich whom her husband had hoped to deprive of the throne. The late tsar's worst fears were nearly realized when the boy, after being crowned in Moscow, refused to return to St. Petersburg. Indeed, the new capital might have been abandoned altogether had it not been for the young tsar's untimely death from smallpox on January 19 (30), 1730. In an odd twist of fate, Peter II expired on the very day he was to have been married to Catherine Dolgorukaya, the daughter of a prominent nobleman. And, like his illustrious grandfather, he died without appointing a successor.

The dynastic crisis that confronted Russia in January of 1730 must have seemed a great opportunity for the seven-member Supreme Privy Council, whose task it was to choose the next tsar. The situation was unique: for the first time in Russia's history, all the candidates for the throne were women. They included Peter the Great's first wife, Evdokia, his daughter Elizabeth, and the three daughters of Peter's half-brother and co-tsar, Ivan IV — Yekaterina, Anna, and Praskovia. The fact that all these women were politically weak and inexperienced encouraged the Council, largely under the influence of its two most prominent members Dmitri Golitsyn and Vasily Dolgoruky, to suppose that they might be able to dominate the next empress. For this reason, they were most attracted to Anna Ivanovna, a nearly destitute widow whom they thought to be docile and easy to manage. She had once been married to the Duke of Courland,[4] but his untimely death in 1711, just months after the wedding, had left her alone and miserable in a drafty thirteenth-century castle. Largely forgotten by Peter, she was forced to beg for money from anyone at the court in St. Petersburg who might show sympathy. Few did. As the years passed, Anna grew increasingly bitter about her dreary existence. Now thirty-seven, she was dull, unattractive, and seemingly without hope for the future. It was, however, precisely for these reasons that the members of the Council decided to offer her the crown. They expected that she would be grateful to those who had rescued her from poverty and anonymity.

Prince Golitsyn, however, was doubtful that gratitude alone would suffice to keep their prospective empress submissive. As a precaution, he urged his fellow Council members to insist that she sign a document formally limiting her power. The terms were severe: she could not levy taxes, spend state monies, decide questions of war and peace, punish nobles or promote men to high rank in the army or government without the advice and consent of the Council, nor could she marry or appoint an heir without permission. Had this arrangement been allowed to stand, Russia might have moved away from authoritarianism and toward some form of constitutional government. However, most nobles, many of whom were already in Moscow to attend Peter II's wedding, were suspicious that the agreement would be exploited by the Council for the benefit of a few. Some sent petitions to Anna urging her to reject the proposed conditions and arranged a meeting in Moscow on February 25 (March 8), just prior to her coronation. Thus, with Dmitri Golitsyn and Vasily Dolgoruky in attendance, Anna tore up the agreement and later dissolved the Supreme Privy Council.

Having now abolished all restraints, Anna ruled Russia autocratically for ten years, despite the fact that she was more interested in court gossip than in affairs of state. She is generally considered to have been among the worst of the Romanov rulers, in large part because she is wrongly believed to have allowed certain German favorites to dominate her government and ruin the country. The most hated of these was her lover, Ernst-Johann Biron, whose sole official responsibility was to arrange court affairs and celebrations. Although he was undeniably arrogant and corrupt, he had little influence in matters of public policy. Two other Germans, B.C. Münnich and Andrei Ostermann, did occupy high positions in the government but served rather well as head of the army and director of foreign policy respectively. In fact, Anna, for all her frivolousness, sponsored a number of worthy endeavors during her reign: she encouraged private enterprise, patronized the arts and education, founded a school for cadets, and hired foreign architects to embellish and beautify St. Petersburg. She also fought two successful, albeit horrendously expensive wars against France and Turkey. The first of these allowed Russia to determine who would be selected to become king of Poland, and the second won back the port city of Azov, which had been lost by Peter the Great in 1711.

Still, for most historians, the negative aspects of Anna's reign, particularly in the social and financial realms, have been impossible to ignore. She exacerbated the growing gap between the gentry and peasants by relieving the former of most of their service obligations while increasing the tax burden for the latter. She also helped plunge the country deeply into debt by spending over half the country's annual income to create a glittering court life. Finally, the cruelty and vulgarity of her personal amusements disgusted many of her contemporaries, Russian and foreign alike. Among these was the special delight she took in degrading high-ranking noblemen by forcing them to squat and cackle like hens or charge about mounted on each others' shoulders in mock jousting tournaments. She was also inclined to humiliate those who offended her religious prejudices. When General Alexei Apraksin married a Catholic, he was summoned to court and ordered to crawl on his knees and bray like a donkey. Later, when Prince Mikhail Golitsyn's Catholic wife died, the husband was forcibly remarried to an ugly Kalmuck[5] woman in an elaborate mock wedding. Guests were invited from all over Russia to participate in a grand procession in which they followed the bridal pair in carriages drawn by pigs, dogs, and goats. The newlyweds were then compelled to spend their first night together stark naked in a miniature palace constructed entirely of ice.[6]

In the final years of her reign, Anna suffered much from kidney stones and gout. When she was finally diagnosed with a kidney ulcer, the doctors deceived her by telling her that she was suffering from the onset of menopause. Still, as Anna sensed death approaching in October of 1740, she tried to provide for a smooth transition by naming as heir a two-month-old infant, Ivan Antonovich, the son of her elder sister's daughter. Unfortunately, she also named Biron as regent, a move that provoked serious opposition. Three weeks later, the parents of the new emperor, Anna Leopoldovna and Prince Anton Ulrich of Brunswick-Luneburg, conspired with Field Marshall Münnich to arrest Biron in the middle of the night. The ex-regent fought back desperately with his fists and had to be beaten down with the rifle butts of the soldiers assigned to depose him. He was finally gagged, bound hand and foot, and wrapped in a large cloak before being brought to the old Winter Palace to face his successor, Anna Leopoldovna, who promptly exiled him to the Arctic.

The new regent, however, just twenty-two years old, had few diehard supporters and a fair number of enemies. Among the latter were the friends and followers of Grand Duchess Elizabeth, Peter the Great's beautiful and pleasure-loving daughter. Elizabeth had never been especially keen to ascend the throne but was provoked to act by the rumor that Anna Leopoldovna would soon declare herself empress. Thus, at two in the morning on November 25 (December 6), 1741, yet another palace coup was set in motion when Elizabeth appeared at the barracks of the Preobrazhensky Guard, who had long held her in high esteem. "My children you all know whose daughter I am. It is my resolve this night to deliver you and all of Russia from our German tormentors. Will you follow me?"[7] The soldiers cheered their assent and were soon marching toward the

Winter Palace. As dawn was breaking, Elizabeth crept into the imperial bedroom and awoke Anna Leopoldovna to inform her that she had been deposed. The daughter of Peter the Great would remain in power for the next twenty years.

The new empress had good intentions but was ill-prepared for the task that confronted her. She promised to rule in the spirit of her father despite the fact that she had no work ethic and little desire to occupy herself with serious matters. Still, she often acted on good advice and accomplished much that was positive. Among other things, she restored the Senate to its former status, embellished St. Petersburg and its environs with impressive new structures, and commissioned the building of a new Winter Palace.[8] She founded Moscow State University and promoted industry and commerce. Unfortunately, she also extended and intensified the misery of the serfs by bestowing them freely on her favorites and increasing the legal and judicial powers of the landowners. In time, serfdom would come to be recognized as a monstrous evil and a threat to the very future of the country, but Elizabeth saw nothing of this.

Ironically, the one responsibility she did take seriously, that of choosing an heir, proved to be her most serious mistake. Almost immediately after ascending the throne, Elizabeth named as successor her orphaned nephew, the thirteen-year-old Charles Peter Ulrich, Duke of Holstein, and invited him to come to Russia. The young Duke, who would one day be known as Peter III, genealogically had much to recommend him. He was a grandson of Peter the Great and a great grandnephew of Charles XII of Sweden. However, not long after his arrival in January of 1742, Peter's behavior gave rise to doubts about his competence and even his sanity. Pale and thin, he had a lolling tongue and was prone to weird grimaces. He strutted about like a guardsman, spoke in a shrill voice, and behaved abominably. Elizabeth tried desperately to civilize and educate her nephew, but the boy refused to learn. He hated everything Russian and was especially contemptuous of the Orthodox Church. He spent most of his time drawing fortifications, dreaming about the military, and playing with dolls and toy soldiers. He also enjoyed fiddling, drinking, smoking, carousing, and training a pack of dogs that he kept in his personal living quarters.

Much of Peter's bizarre and antisocial behavior can probably by explained by the beatings and the systematic abuse inflicted upon him by Holstein tutors, who raised and educated him. In any case, Elizabeth soon gave up trying to influence him directly and decided to find him a wife. Acting on the advice of Frederick the Great, she chose the fourteen-year-old Sophia Augusta Frederika of Anhalt-Zerbst, the daughter of a Prussian soldier. The girl, who arrived in Russia in February of 1744 accompanied by her mother, soon proved to be the opposite of her future husband whom she managed to befriend. Elizabeth was delighted by the young woman's enthusiasm for learning Russian and embracing Orthodoxy and soon had her re-baptized with the name Catherine. Eighteen months later, Catherine and Peter were married in a grand ceremony, despite the fact that he had only recently recovered from a bout of smallpox that had left him pockmarked and hideous to look at.

For the rest of Elizabeth's reign, while Peter frittered away his time in fantasy and make-believe, Catherine did everything possible to improve her mind and status at court. She read the works of the great philosophers and ingratiated herself with people of importance. Still, in many ways her life was difficult. Not long after the wedding, her mother had been forced to leave the country because her political machinations had angered the empress. In addition, Catherine herself had been placed under constant surveillance to ensure that she would remain faithful to her husband. Finally, she was also forced to participate in Elizabeth's frivolous and decadent court life, which, among other things, featured masquerades that required men and women to dress as the opposite sex. Not only did she dislike the music and dancing, but she was thoroughly exhausted by the court's frequent excursions and irregular hours. Still, there were some pleasures: along with riding and duck shooting, Catherine enjoyed gambling. Unfortunately, she usually lost more than she won and was at times deeply in debt

After a few years of married life, Catherine grew estranged from her husband and sought affection in the arms of other men. In September of 1754, she gave birth to a child named Paul, whose paternity has always been in doubt. In her memoirs, Catherine claimed the father was a nobleman named Sergei Saltykov, although some historians doubt her veracity, since Paul grew to bear an uncanny resemblance to Peter both in appearance and behavior. Whatever the truth, Elizabeth seems not to have cared. She personally took over Paul's upbringing and began to groom him in a manner befitting that of a future tsar. It is not certain to what extent Catherine wanted to be involved with raising the boy, but, in any case, she did not resist the empress' initiative. In time, a fierce antagonism would develop between mother and son that would be of major significance for the dynasty.

Soon after the birth of Paul, Catherine's position at court was threatened when Peter fell in love with Yelizaveta Vorontsova, the niece of the vice-chancellor, whose ugliness and stupidity were the topic of much amusement around the capital. They seemed to have had no sex life, but Vorontsova won Peter's heart because she encouraged his fantasies and enjoyed participating in his games. Indeed, the heir was so infatuated with his new love that he wanted to divorce his wife and marry his mistress. This, however, was out of the question without his aunt's approval. In any case, Catherine had fallen out of favor at court for other reasons. The empress, who was now in bad health, suspected that the German princess was conspiring to position herself for the throne after Elizabeth had passed from the scene.

The final years of Elizabeth's rule were dominated by the Seven Years War, which began in 1756 when Frederick the Great of Prussia invaded Saxony. Elizabeth had grown to hate the Prussian king not only for his aggressive foreign policy, but also because of the lewd stories he told about her sex life. Working with uncharacteristic energy and commitment, she helped form a coalition against him that included Saxony, France, Austria, and Sweden. Over the next five years, Frederick struggled mightily to keep his enemies at bay, hoping eventually to split the alliance. Elizabeth, however, was determined to prevail, and, by early January of 1762, the Russians seemed on the verge of complete victory with the capture of an important fortress in Pomerania.[9] However, just as the army was planning to continue its advance, the empress died, elevating her nephew Peter to the throne. The new tsar, who had long idolized Frederick as "one of the greatest heroes of the world," promptly called for an armistice and ordered the army to withdraw to the Vistula River. Soon a Prussian envoy, Baron von Goltz, was in St. Petersburg to negotiate a peace that returned to Prussia all lands won by Russia for no compensation except for Frederick's promise to defend Peter's beloved Holstein against an attack by Denmark.

Ironically, Elizabeth, who had promised to deliver the country from "our German tormentors," now seemed to have done the exact opposite. So stunning was Peter's sabotage of Russia's victory, that, in the eyes of many Russians, it was as if the country were being ruled by a Prussian tsar. Although Peter caused outrage by his handling of foreign affairs, some of his domestic initiatives were actually quite popular. He abolished the secret police, outlawed the knout, and released the nobility from compulsory state service. He also tried to help the peasantry by reducing the salt tax and by making it easier for free serfs to buy their way into merchant status. Unfortunately, these positive measures were more than offset by his hatred of the Church and insulting admiration of all things German. Thus, after demoting the Senate, he created a new council composed mostly of German advisors, ordered the army to don Prussian uniforms, and abolished the Imperial Guard. He also antagonized the Orthodox faithful by confiscating Church lands and constructing a Lutheran chapel in the new Winter Palace. In short, Peter seemed to taunt the very people upon whom his power depended.

Another source of serious dissatisfaction was Peter's decision to wage war against Denmark in order to force the return of the province of Schleswig to Holstein.[10] Patriotic Russians were aghast at the thought of committing the army to such an unnecessary conflict and soon began to consider ways of ridding themselves of this "German tsar." Among those who had begun to plot and scheme, two deserve special mention: Nikita Ivanovich Panin, a former diplomat and tutor for Tsarevich Paul, and the Princess Yekaterina Dashkova, the sister of Peter's mistress. Both detested Peter and favored the elevation of seven-year-old Paul to the throne and the establishment of a regency. Yet neither anticipated Catherine's resourcefulness and determination to attain supreme power herself. Thus, while Peter recklessly alienated nearly everyone by his policies and public buffoonery, Catherine deported herself with dignity, spoke with moderation, and attracted supporters. The most ardent of these was a Guards' officer named Grigori Orlov who had become her lover. Moreover, he had four brothers, all of them officers, who did their best to promote the former German princess and to denigrate Peter.

However, in the spring of 1762, Catherine's position was precarious. She was many months pregnant with Orlov's child, a fact that she concealed by wearing large flowing dresses. At the same time, she was demoralized by her husband's frequent threats to send her to a convent. In April, not long after she had secretly given birth to a son,[11] Peter verbally abused her at a formal banquet and later ordered her arrest. Although her incarceration was prevented by the intervention of her uncle, Georg-Ludwig of Holstein, it was clear to all that both Catherine and Paul were in danger, and the time to act could not be long postponed. The conspirators had decided to arrest Peter as he was leaving for Denmark. However, in early July, their hand was forced when one of them, Captain Piotr Passek, was arrested while the tsar was residing at the imperial palace at Oranienbaum[12] as the final preparations for the campaign were being made. It was feared that under torture he might talk.

Catherine had also gone to Oranienbaum ostensibly to be with Peter and to attend a special performance at which he would play the violin. However, learning of the arrest and fearing that the plot might soon be discovered, the conspirators decided that she must return to St. Petersburg so that she could be proclaimed empress even before Peter could be arrested. Thus, on the morning of June 28 (July 9), Catherine was awakened at the Mon Plasir Pavilion at the Peterhof not far from Oranienbaum by Alexei Orlov, informed of the situation, and returned to the capital where she was cheered in turn by the Izmailovsky, Semenovsky, and Preobrazhensky Guards. She then went to the Kazan Cathedral on the Nevsky

Prospect to attend a short service and to hear herself proclaimed by the Church. Finally, she appeared on the balcony of the Winter Palace with her seven-year-old son, Paul, before a cheering crowd.

Meanwhile, Peter was still at Oranienbaum totally unaware that he had been deposed. He suspected something was amiss, however, on June 29 (July 10) when he traveled to the Peterhof. Expecting to enjoy a lavish celebration in honor of his name day, he was amazed to find the palace deserted. Moreover, the three officials he sent to St. Petersburg to find out what had happened had not returned. (All had defected to Catherine.) Only now did he guess that his throne was in danger. He tried to counter-attack by sailing to Kronstadt to find supporters only to be turned away by soldiers who had declared for Catherine. With this, Peter's resolve crumbled, and he meekly returned to Oranienbaum to await the end. In the meantime, Catherine, dressed in a borrowed military uniform, rode at the head of a large military detachment to arrest her husband. The two were not to meet, however. Along the way she received two letters from Peter: the first offered to negotiate, and the second pleaded to be allowed to return to Holstein in return for his abdication. Both were rejected. She did accept a third letter in which he announced his unconditional abdication. The ex-tsar was then taken to Peterhof, formally arrested, stripped of his uniform, and forced to don a dressing gown and slippers. He was also separated from Yelizaveta Vorontsova and sent to a nearby country estate named Ropsha where he had once resided as grand duke. There he was assigned to live in a large room where he was attended by his Negro servant and German doctor. He was also allowed to play his violin and keep his dog.

The conspirators had planned eventually to send the ex-tsar to the fortress-prison at Schlüsselberg[13] to be permanently incarcerated. However, it was soon apparent that as long as Peter remained alive he would be a potential rallying point for enemies of the new regime. Catherine undoubtedly worried about this possibility, but the Orlov brothers spared her the necessity of acting. On July 16, she received a note from Alexei informing her that her husband had been killed in a drunken scuffle with Feodor Bariatynsky, one of his jailers. The details of the incident were left suspiciously vague: "I don't know what we did but all of us are guilty and worthy of punishment. Have mercy upon me if only for my brother's sake. I confess it all to you, and there is nothing to investigate."[14]

Catherine's complicity in the murder is not certain, although she did help cover it up by listing the official cause of death as colic followed by an acute hemorrhoidal attack, despite the fact that the bruised and battered corpse left no doubt that the ex-tsar had been strangled and beaten.

The official cause of Peter III's death (in Catherine II's own words) was "an acute attack of colic after one of his frequent bouts of hemorrhoids." In fact, he was murdered by a group of her own supporters, who confessed to the deed and were never punished. H. Roger Violette Picture Library.

She also made no move to punish the murderers. In fact, Alexei Orlov was promoted to Major General "for outstanding service to the motherland," given 50,000 rubles and an estate with eight hundred serfs. Feodor Bariatynsky received 20,000 rubles. Finally, in an attempt to downplay the significance of Peter III and his short reign, Catherine had him interred not in the Cathedral of St. Peter and Paul with his grandfather, but rather in an obscure corner of the Alexander Nevsky Monastery.[15] Her excuse for this deliberate act of disrespect was that her husband had never bothered to have himself crowned.

The new empress was not about to make the same mistake. On Sunday, September 22 (October 3), her coronation took place in the Moscow Kremlin. The ceremony, which began at ten in the morning in the Palace of Facets, featured a grand procession across the square to the Cathedral of the Assumption. The mood was festive: cannon were fired, church bells rang, and thousands of silver coins were flung to the onlookers from large oak barrels. Once inside the cathedral, Catherine donned her imperial robes and placed on her head a magnificent crown studded with diamonds and other precious stones. Then, standing under the main dome, she solemnly swore to defend Holy Russia and rule according to divine guidance. This was followed by the sacred liturgy, after which the new empress returned to the square to visit two other nearby cathedrals, Archangel and Annunciation. There she paid homage to Russia's past rulers and kissed holy relics. Her last stop was a return to the Palace of Facets where she distributed gifts to her favorites.

Although Catherine's deportment throughout the ceremony and during the early months of her reign was regal and impressive, she was troubled by nasty whispers about her lack of legitimacy. She knew her potential enemies would want to exploit the fact that she had no Romanov blood in her veins. Coupled with this concern was the presence in Schlüsselberg of the former infant tsar, Ivan Antonovich, who, two decades earlier, had been overthrown by Elizabeth. Since then the young man, now twenty-two, had been languishing in cruel captivity. He was severely underdeveloped physically, mentally, and emotionally. His situation was especially tragic because Elizabeth had originally intended to send him to Germany with his parents but feared he might return later to claim the throne. Thus, she initially sent the family to the prison at Donnemunde for two years and then to Kholmogory on the White Sea, where the ex-tsar was separated from his parents and condemned to live in complete isolation.

In 1756, he was moved to the more secure fortress at Schlüsselberg where his true identity was kept secret even from his jailers. Here the ex-tsar's situation took a dramatic turn for the worse. Although he had never been treated well, the abuse he underwent now became deliberate and systematic. Confined to a dark, filthy, poorly ventilated cell, he was allowed no education, exercise, or amusement. Moreover, his guards, who were allowed to beat and scourge him, were instructed to kill him should anyone attempt a rescue. By the time of Peter III's ascension to power, the "nameless convict" (as Catherine always referred to him) was scarcely human. Half-starved, ill, and disoriented, Ivan Antonovich barely knew who he was and probably understood little about the reason for his incarceration. However, his condition interested both Peter and Catherine, who, in 1762, on separate occasions, brought the prisoner to St. Petersburg for interviews. Peter, who may have intended to disinherit Paul, was considering him as a possible heir. Catherine actually considered marrying him in order to legitimize her hold on power. Unfortunately, the ex-tsar's sorry state would not permit either possibility. Indeed, Catherine was so disturbed by his plight that she tried to persuade him to enter a monastery. This would have improved his living situation while making him ineligible to ever ascend the throne. However, Ivan Antonovich probably did not understand what was being suggested.

In any case, the prisoner's misery was not to last much longer. During the late night hours of July 5 (16), 1764, a Ukrainian army officer, Vasily Mirovich, whose garrison was stationed at Schlüsselberg, made a foolhardy and desperate attempt to rescue the ex-tsar in the hope of gaining a reward. The plan, poorly conceived to begin with, was complicated by the drowning death of his lone accomplice just before the attempt took place. Moreover, the thirty-eight soldiers he enlisted to provide the firepower for the attack on the fortress had not been at all prepared for their task and hardly knew what they were trying to achieve. Despite this, the insurgents, after some confused fighting with the sixteen defenders of the inner garrison, succeeded in reaching the jail only to find that the guards, in obedience to their long-standing orders, had stabbed and hacked the prisoner to death with their swords. Catherine, who was in the city of Riga at the time, was alarmed by news of the uprising, and feared that it was part of an extensive plot. A thorough investigation followed, in which some fifty officers and men were interrogated. Mirovich, who was found guilty and beheaded, was the only one to suffer the death penalty. However, several common soldiers who had obeyed his orders were forced to run a gauntlet of one thousand men, some as many as twelve times, before being sentenced to hard labor. Interestingly, the guards who killed Ivan Antonovich were promoted and given seven thousand rubles each.

For Catherine, the elimination of the ex-tsar was a mixed blessing. Though she was undoubtedly glad to be rid of a man whose name could be exploited by her enemies, the bad publicity engendered by his murder just two years after her husband's did not soon subside. Even more ominous was the effect these events had on her ten-year-old son, Paul, whom she had designated as heir. In time, he came to resent his mother's role in the coup against his father and the ruthless manner in which she had seized power pushing him aside. Catherine sensed her son's enmity but mostly ignored him, keeping him far from the center of power. As he grew older, she allowed him to set up his own court at nearby Gatchina,[16] which he organized and ran like a Prussian estate. She also appropriated his sons to raise as her own, just as Elizabeth had done with Paul. In time, the grand duke began to fear, rightly as it turns out, that his mother intended to disinherit him in favor of his eldest son, Alexander.

Traditionally, Catherine's reign of thirty-four years has been considered a glorious epoch in Russian history. However, some of her achievements and policies fell far short of their original promise. The celebrated Legislative Commission that she convened in 1767 to codify Russian laws and address certain social problems did neither. However, the effort was widely commended largely on the strength of the special instruction, or *Nakaz*, she issued to the delegates to guide them in their deliberations. Composed by the empress herself over eighteen months, the *Nakaz* was based on the highest ideals of the Enlightenment and was radical enough to be banned in France. In the end, however, nothing came of this project, largely because Catherine herself never ceased to believe that autocracy was the only feasible form of government for a country as vast as Russia. The empress also disappointed many in her dealings with the Church, which she had sworn to support. Just prior to her coronation, she cancelled Peter III's order to confiscate Church lands but quickly reversed herself once she had been crowned. This provoked such furious protest from the Metropolitan Arseni of Rostov, that Catherine had him tried in an ecclesiastical court in April 1763. The prelate was found guilty and exiled to a distant monastery where he was forced to perform hard labor.

However, Catherine has also been justly admired for her determination to promote the public good and the prestige of the state. The latter was especially enhanced by her foreign policy, which featured vast territorial acquisitions after military victories over Turkey and Sweden and the partition of Poland. The empress was a tireless promoter of education, establishing the Medical Collegium in 1763 and the Smolny Institute for aristocratic young women in 1764. She founded one of the world's great museums, the Hermitage, and supported it lavishly by buying works of Rembrandt, Van Dyke, Raphael, and Titian. She built hospitals and allowed herself to be inoculated against smallpox to encourage others to do the same. She encouraged French culture, literature, and drama at court and wrote a number of satirical reviews and plays. Her most visible legacy, however, belongs to the city of St. Petersburg and its environs, which she did so much to beautify with palaces and parks. Among her grandest achievements were the improvements she sponsored at the imperial estate at Tsarskoe Selo. Catherine also commissioned one of the capital's most visible landmarks, The Bronze Horseman, as a memorial to Peter the Great. She had it mounted on a huge plinth that had been hauled from the border of Finland and placed in the Senate Square where it inspired one of Alexander Pushkin's greatest poems.

Despite her many accomplishments, Catherine left a decidedly troubled legacy. The most serious of these was the continued expansion of serfdom, an evil that made a mockery of the very ideals she claimed to cherish. To be sure, the tradition of the gentry living off free peasant labor was so entwined in the economic and social fabric of the country that there could be no thought of abolishing it outright.[17] But the fury of the Pugachev revolt in the 1770s (described in Chapter V) should have alerted her at least to the need to regulate the relationship between landowner and serfs in order to mitigate its worst excesses. Had the empress also been less extravagant in awarding large land grants with serfs to her favorites, she would have set a helpful example and possibly reversed a dangerous trend. Unfortunately, much of what she did as empress served to aggravate the problem. Thus, in 1785, when she issued her famous Charter to the Nobility, in which she declared landlords free from taxes and state service, she also gave them such punitive powers over their serfs as to reduce the latter to near slavery.

In her final years on the throne, Catherine's health declined precipitously. She had lost most of her teeth, was dangerously overweight, and suffered from a kidney ailment that left her legs disfigured and swollen. Nevertheless, she continued to satisfy her sexual and emotional needs by cavorting with younger men. Most of these were handsome non-entities eager to exploit her generosity, although one, whom she had met years earlier, proved her intellectual equal and one of the most remarkable characters in Russian history. Gregory Potemkin[18] is remembered mostly for the facades of fake villages he constructed in the south of Russia to create the illusion for Catherine and other visitors of prosperity in newly conquered lands. However, he was also a man of solid accomplishment in politics, diplomacy, and war. His influence with the empress endured long after the couple's physical relationship had ended, and his sudden death in 1791, while the country was at war with Turkey, left her in deep despair.

By this time, however, she was involved with a Guard's officer named Platon Zubov, who was thirty-eight years her junior. Despite the fact that he was vain, arrogant, and of dubious intelligence, Catherine tried her best to groom and educate him by involving him in affairs of state. Zubov never did live up to Catherine's expectations, but, just a few years after her death, he would play an important role in changing the course of Russian history.

Almost completely ignored during these final years was the heir to the throne, Grand Duke Paul. This in large part was because Potemkin had long sensed his hostility to him and other like-minded advisers around the empress and had skillfully maneuvered to keep him without power or influence. Thus, not only was Paul rarely invited to court, but his relationship with his mother eventually became so strained that the two all but ceased to communicate. Indeed, the grand duke found satisfaction only when he was at Gatchina away from the capital, drilling his troops and managing his estate. Unfortunately, even this did not prevent him from being wounded by his insulting lack of status at court. By the time he reached middle age, the heir had become a curious mixture of admirable traits and frightening eccentricities. On the one hand, he was a man devoted to principle who tried to protect the people living on his estate from injustice and misfortune; on the other, he was a fierce martinet whose savage temper and unreasonable demands terrified everyone. Significantly, Paul was known to disapprove of virtually every aspect of Catherine's rule including her decadent court life, foreign policy, and territorial acquisitions, but all he could do was brood about his vulnerability and worry that he would soon be removed as heir.

Indeed, this almost certainly would have happened had Catherine lived only a bit longer, but a massive stroke suffered on the morning of November 4 (15), 1796, brought about her death two days later and thus elevated to the throne the son she so detested. For Paul it was a moment of triumph, though he was careful to behave solemnly and without celebration as the occasion demanded. Still, as he was planning his mother's funeral, he could not resist the temptation to take revenge on those who had murdered his father thirty-four years earlier. Thus, he ordered Peter III's remains exhumed from a neglected corner of the Alexander Nevsky Monastery and transferred to the Peter and Paul Fortress. Forced to participate in the lengthy funeral procession were the surviving conspirators including Alexei Orlov and Feodor Baryatynsky. The former was ordered to carry the deceased tsar's crown behind the casket while the latter marched out in front. Once in the cathedral, the remains of Peter III and Catherine II were lowered into the same crypt. In this way, Paul sought to maximize attention for his father at the expense of his mother. For many this was an ominous beginning, although the worst was yet to come.

The extent to which Paul hoped to obliterate his mother's memory was obvious in the way he reversed many of her policies. He began by freeing a number of important political prisoners, including Alexander Radishchev,[19] whose criticism of serfdom had initially earned him a death sentence that was later commuted to Siberian exile. He formally apologized for the dismemberment of Poland (which he felt could not now be reversed) and released 12,000 Polish prisoners who had been condemned to a life of hard labor in Russia. He recalled Russian troops from a war recently begun against Persia[20] and those recently sent by Catherine to assist Austria against France.

Many of these early initiatives were rather well received, especially since they allowed the new tsar to cancel an order to draft more soldiers. However, the edicts that were intended to reorganize society and eliminate all vice were another matter. To these ends, Paul established guard posts around the city to check internal passports, enforce a curfew, and impose a new dress code. The clothing regulations were particularly obnoxious since they required city residents to abstain from many of the most popular French fashions. Among other things, they banned frock-coats, high boots, laces on shoes and breeches, and the wearing of round hats for people not in traditional Russian attire. Paul also sought to make street life more decorous by outlawing the dashing *troika* and commanded that all persons, upon encountering the sovereign on the street or any other member of imperial family, alight from their carriages and fall to their knees or curtsy in obeisance.

The new regime was hated by everyone and seemed to testify to the tsar's obsession to control every aspect of Russian life. Still, his record during those first few months in power was by no means all negative: he improved the functioning of the Senate, granted common soldiers the right to submit complaints against their officers, and was the first tsar in history to attempt to alleviate the plight of the serfs. By this initiative, announced at the conclusion of his coronation in Moscow, he urged landowners not to demand more than three days of labor or *barshchina* per week from their peasants. Moreover, on this same occasion, Paul abolished Peter the Great's unworkable Law of Succession by which the sovereign could choose his own heir to the throne. This decree restored the principle that the eldest born male would inherit the throne and excluded females from ever ruling. Thus did Paul intend to end the political intrigue and uncertainty that had attended every reign in the 18th century. Unfortunately, he would be unable to protect himself from the same dangers that had destroyed his father.

Paul was not destined to reign for long, mainly because of his demeaning manner, violent temper, and utter disrespect for the nobility. Not only did he routinely violate his mother's charter of 1785 by subjecting nobles to taxation, corporal punishment, and exile to Siberia, but his inclination to bully, harass, and humiliate anyone who aroused his displeasure created fierce resentment. This was especially true during the army's daily parade-in-review, or *Wachtparade*. Having forced the army to adopt uncomfortably tight Prussian-style uniforms complete with high conical hats, he also required soldiers to arrange their hair in an elaborate coiffure that could only be held in place by a foul-smelling compound of grease, wax, and powder. During the two or three hours of drill that followed, Paul himself would tap out the cadence with a long spontoon, flying into a rage at the slightest infraction. Offenders, whatever the rank, could be flogged on the spot, strapped into a *kibitka*,[21] and exiled to Siberia.

There was also general concern about the tsar's conduct of foreign policy and his apparent lack of resolve in containing France. Paul had always been a fierce foe of the Revolution and perceived Napoleon and the new republics he had established to be a grave threat to the European order. Still, during most of his first year on the throne, he felt unable to honor his mother's pledge to aid Austria and Britain against Napoleon because of his preoccupation with domestic policy and reform in the army. However, by the fall of 1798, he was sufficiently alarmed by France's capture of the Ionian Islands and Malta to enter into a naval alliance with the Turks. Paul had a particular interest in the latter, having long been fascinated by the Knights of Malta,[22] a Roman Catholic crusading order that was founded in a monastery in Jerusalem in the 11th century. Having originally been set up to care for pilgrims and the sick, they soon became militarily involved in the effort to expel the Muslims from the Holy Lands. But now they had fallen on hard times, and, in gratitude for Paul's solicitude, the Knights named him their grand master. Many at court were amazed that a Russian Orthodox tsar would assume such a role, but Paul saw no contradiction. In fact, so fervently did he admire their virtues and ideals that he believed they could help him unite French royalists and Russian nobles to restore the *ancien regime* throughout Europe. However, the refusal of Austria and Great Britain to recognize his new title infuriated him and affected his judgment in foreign policy.

By this time, Russia had joined Great Britain and Austria in the Second Coalition as the main action against Napoleon switched to land. As the French continued to win victories, Paul was compelled to recall to active duty his best commander, Alexander Vasilievich Suvorov. The general had withdrawn to his estate because he had scorned the tsar's Prussian military reforms. But Suvorov, although now sixty-eight years old, was far too valuable to be allowed to retire. He had been in the army more than fifty years and had never lost a battle. In 1799, he would again prove his genius by defeating the French in three major engagements, capturing 25 fortresses and taking 80,000 prisoners. His most amazing feat came in September when his exhausted and starving army was surrounded in the Swiss Alps by a French force five times larger. Somehow he was able to inspire his men to fight their way to safety. Yet all this came to nothing because, in the spring of 1800, Paul abruptly withdrew from the coalition and for a time seemed ready to join Napoleon. He had been greatly angered by the failure of his allies to support Russian troops in Switzerland and the Low Countries and even more infuriated when Lord Nelson captured Malta and refused to hand it over to him as grand master. To retaliate, he sent the Don Cossacks to invade British India. For many, this was the ultimate act of insanity, but by now it didn't matter. The tsar had accumulated too many enemies at home, and another palace coup was in the making.

Interestingly, the first active conspirator against the tsar was not someone whom he had particularly abused. To be sure, Nikita Petrovich Panin had never been an imperial favorite, but until recently he had enjoyed a fair amount of influence and status as the tsar's special emissary to Berlin. However, his failure to bring Prussia into the coalition against Napoleon after long negotiations led to his recall and subsequent demotion. Still, Panin's primary concern was the tsar's increasingly erratic behavior and dubious mental health. Convinced that Paul had to be removed to save Russia, he enlisted the support of Admiral Josef Ribas and the governor of St. Petersburg, Count Peter von der Pahlen. He then took the dangerous step of meeting with the Grand Duke Alexander to reveal both his concerns and a possible solution. Alexander was aghast at what was suggested but was so fearful of becoming a victim to his father's raging paranoia that he raised no objection.

Ultimately, however, neither Panin nor Ribas participated in the coup that would topple Paul. The former was dismissed from government service in November 1800 for criticizing the tsar's foreign policy, and the latter died suddenly of natural causes the same month. Leadership of the conspiracy thus fell to Pahlen whose motivation for removing the tsar was at least in part personal. Not long after Paul's accession, the count had been exiled to his estate because of the favor he had enjoyed at the court of the late empress and his friendship with Platon Zubov. Pahlen concealed his anger and worked hard to be restored to his previous status. To this end, he developed a friendship with the tsar's barber, Ivan Kutaisov, who lobbied successfully on his behalf. Thus, in November of 1797, Pahlen was given command of the Horse Guards, the same regiment in which he had begun his service nearly four decades earlier. One month later, he was promoted to inspector of the cavalry in St. Petersburg and Finland.

To be sure, the count's return to imperial favor did not protect him from the tsar's increasingly unpredictable and savage temper, but these outbursts, terrifying to others, seemed not to faze Pahlen. Nor did he complain when his own son faced harsh punishment for a rules violation. Indeed, so effectively did the count impress his master with his ability to cheerfully absorb abuse that the tsar promoted him to the post of governor-general of St. Petersburg. It was a fatal miscalculation. Now his most dangerous enemy was in an ideal position to plot against him and recruit others to the cause. This blunder was compounded in February of 1801, when Paul transferred his residence from the Winter Palace into the recently constructed Mikhailovsky Palace.[23] Everyone had warned him that the move was premature since the masonry and the plaster in the new structure were still wet. But the tsar would not be dissuaded; he was convinced that the Mikhailovsky Palace's deep moat and four drawbridges would make him invulnerable. He was also confident that Pahlen, who knew all the passwords and secret passageways, would serve and protect him.

By the spring of 1801, Pahlen had assembled at least sixty-eight individuals who had pledged their support in overthrowing the tsar. The coup had originally been planned for March 15 (27), but was moved up a few days because of Paul's growing suspicion that something sinister was in the air. One morning, he surprised the count by asking him if he had been a part of the coup against his father, Tsar Peter III, in 1762. Pahlen assured him that he had been too young to have been a participant, but, as they had discussed this matter before, why bring it up now? At this point, Paul bluntly asserted that he knew a conspiracy was in the making and wondered why his governor-general was doing nothing about it. Pahlen's response was inspired: Not only was he aware of the conspiracy, but he had succeeded in infiltrating it as a member! The count further assured his master that he would act decisively when the time was right.

Ironically, March 11 (23) found Paul in relatively high spirits even as he contemplated the possibility of treason within his own family. At dinner that evening, he had alarmed his wife and sons with some cryptic remarks about the need for heads to roll and blood to be shed even among those he loved. At about the same time, seven of the more prominent members of the conspiracy had gathered at the apartment of Colonel Talyzin in the Winter Palace for supper and to make their final plans.

Among those present was a Guards officer from Hanover named Leo Bennigsen. He had been dismissed from the service two years earlier because of his association with the Zubovs but had recently been returned to favor. Known for his courage and coolness under pressure, he had been chosen by Pahlen to play a leading role in what was about to take place. Now, as the conspirators imbibed heavily, they discussed last minute details and speculated on what Paul's removal could mean for Russia. Some spoke hopefully about a new political order and even a constitution. Interestingly, of the main conspirators, only Pahlen was absent, although he did show up late in the evening to propose a toast to the soon-to-be new tsar.

Not long after midnight, the conspirators set out in two groups toward the Mikhailovsky Palace. The going was difficult since the night was windy and bitterly cold, and most of the officers were drunk. The first group, led by Platon Zubov and Bennigsen, was able to cross the moat and enter the residence. The second group, led by Pahlen, was to secure the front of the building while the Preobrazhensky and Semenovsky Guards were to hold the circumference. However, things did not quite go as planned: Pahlen's group fell behind and arrived fifteen minutes too late to make any difference,[24] and Zubov and Bennigsen upon entering the tsar's bedchamber did not find him asleep as they had hoped. Apparently, he had been awakened by a servant's shouts and had tried to flee, but with the door to his wife's room locked and no time to open the special trap door under his worktable, he had scurried behind a Spanish screen in front of the fireplace and held his breath. The conspirators saw the empty cot, but as the bedding was still warm, realized he could not have gone far. Searching the room with only one candle between them, they could see little until light from the moon appearing from behind a cloud flooded through a large window. Only then did they spot Paul's bare feet and legs at the bottom of the Spanish screen. It was Bennigsen who declared him under arrest by the authority of the Emperor Alexander.

There is some confusion about exactly what happened next. According to one account, as Bennigsen was promising to spare Paul's life provided he did not struggle, more conspirators entered the room. The tsar, confused and frightened, tried to make sense of what was happening. At one point, he demanded to know what he had done to deserve such treatment. "You have tortured us for four years" replied one voice. Others gave their own answers. Then, as another group of seven or eight conspirators entered the room, Paul apparently tried to fight back. The newcomers threw themselves upon the tsar, knocking down the Spanish screen and extinguishing the candle. At this point, Bennigsen left the room to get another light, warning Paul not to resist, but as the scuffling continued, the tsar's head was smashed against the bronze capital of his worktable, crushing his cheek and injuring his eye. One of the Zubovs also hit with a gold snuff box before someone began to strangle him with a guardsman's sash. Just before the end, Paul pleaded for a chance to pray but to no avail. When Bennigsen returned, the tsar was dead.[25]

The news of the coup brought enormous relief and great rejoicing for all who had suffered under Paul's tyranny. The official cause of death was announced as apoplexy, but anyone who saw the battered corpse knew the violent nature of the tsar's end. Indeed, Grand Duke Alexander, who claimed to have been asleep during the coup, was so overcome with guilt and remorse about the savagery employed against his father that he refused at first to accept the oaths of loyalty from his troops. Pahlen finally forced the issue when he seized the young man firmly by the arm and said, "You have played the child long enough; go reign. Come show yourself to the Guards."[26] This being done, Tsar Alexander left for the Winter Palace at 2 A.M., first to sleep and recover and then to issue a series of edicts to undo the worst of his father's abuses. In the days and weeks that followed, political prisoners were released from jail and fugitives invited back from exile. All kinds of bans and prohibitions were lifted, including those on the import of books and musical scores. The civilian dress code was dropped, and soldiers were no longer required to wear Prussian-style pigtails. Censorship was ended, the secret police abolished, and the Charter to the Nobility reaffirmed. Finally, to the relief of everyone, war with Britain was averted, and the Cossacks en route to India were recalled.

The conspirators, however, did not fare well under the new tsar, some of whom had hoped that he would agree to a constitution and limits on his own power. In fact, Alexander felt more fear than gratitude to those who had saved the country from his father and soon began to resent their encroachments on his prerogatives. This was particularly true of Pahlen, who felt entitled to offer advice and direction when it was not solicited. However, once Alexander sensed the army was firmly behind him, he resolved to rid himself of the man who was most responsible for bringing him to the throne. On June 29, he summoned the count to the Winter Palace ostensibly to explain why he had ordered the ex-empress to remove an icon from her chapel that bore the inscription, "God will avenge the assassins of Paul." Apparently, the explanation was not satisfactory. That same day, Pahlen was exiled to his estate in Courland where he would spend the rest of his life. It would be left to another group of officers nearly a quarter century later to again raise the issue of a constitution for Russia. Again, the outcome would not be encouraging.

Selected Bibliography

Bruce Lincoln's *The Romanovs, Autocrats of All the Russias* is an excellent source for those desiring more information about the various dynastic crises during the 18th century. Two older books that are also useful are Ronald Hingley's *The Tsars* and Virginia Cowles' *The Romanovs*. Also of interest is Philip Longworth's *The Three Empresses: Catherine I, Anne and Elizabeth of Russia*. To this must be added Suzanne Massie's *Land of the Firebird: The Beauty of Old Russia* which lovingly describes 1000 years of cultural development in Russia. There have been many fine studies of Catherine the Great, although none surpasses Isabel de Maderiaga's *Russia in the Age of Catherine the Great*. The best handling of Tsar Paul's short but important reign is Roderick E. McGrew's *Paul I of Russia*.

Alexander, John, T. "Orlov, Grigori Grigor'evich." *Modern Encyclopedia of Russian and Soviet History*, ed. Joseph L. Wieczynski, 54 vols. With suppl. Gulf Breeze, Florida: Academic International Press, 1976–1990.

_____. "Zubov, Platon Alexandrovich." *Modern Encyclopedia of Russian and Soviet History*, ed. Joseph L. Wieczynski, 54 vols. With suppl. Gulf Breeze, Florida: Academic International Press, 1976–1990.

Cowles, Virginia. *The Romanovs*. New York: Harper and Row, 1971.

Cracraft, James. "Ivan V (Ivan Alekseevich)" *Modern Encyclopedia of Russian and Soviet History*, ed. Joseph L. Wieczynski, 54 vols. With suppl. Gulf Breeze, Florida: Academic International Press, 1976–1990.

_____. "Peter I — the Great." *Modern Encyclopedia of Russian and Soviet History*, ed. Joseph L. Wieczynski, 54 vols. With suppl. Gulf Breeze, Florida: Academic International Press, 1976–1990.

Griffiths, David M. "Anna I (Anna Ivanovna)." *Modern Encyclopedia of Russian and Soviet History*, ed. Joseph L. Wieczynski, 54 vols. With suppl. Gulf Breeze, Florida: Academic International Press, 1976–1990.

_____. "Biron, Ernst Johann" *Modern Encyclopedia of Russian and Soviet History*, ed. Joseph L. Wieczynski, 54 vols. With suppl. Gulf Breeze, Florida: Academic International Press, 1976–1990.

_____. "Catherine II — the Great." *Modern Encyclopedia of Russian and Soviet History*, ed., Joseph L. Wieczynski, 54 vols. With suppl. Gulf Breeze, Florida: Academic International Press, 1976–1990.

Hingley, Ronald. *The Tsars*. New York: The Macmillan Company, 1968.

Hughes, Lindsey A.J. "Peter II (Petr Alekseevich)" *Modern Encyclopedia of Russian and Soviet History*, ed. Joseph L. Wieczynski, 54 vols. With suppl. Gulf Breeze, Florida: Academic International Press, 1976–1990.

_____. "Peter III (Petr Fedorovich)" *Modern Encyclopedia of Russian and Soviet History*, ed. Joseph L. Wieczynski, 54 vols. With suppl. Gulf Breeze, Florida: Academic International Press, 1976–1990.

Lincoln, W. Bruce. *The Romanovs. Autocrats of All the Russias*. New York: Doubleday, 1981.

Longworth, Philip. *The Three Empresses: Catherine I, Anne and Elizabeth of Russia.* Austin, Texas: Holt, Rinehart and Winston, 1972.

Madariaga, Isabel de. *Russia in the Age of Catherine the Great.* New Haven: Yale University Press, 1981.

McConnell, Allen. *Tsar Alexander I: Paternalistic Reformer.* New York: T.Y. Crowell, 1970.

_____. "Radishchev, Alexander Nikolaevich." *Modern Encyclopedia of Russian and Soviet History,* ed. Joseph L. Wieczynski, 54 vols. With suppl. Gulf Breeze, Florida: Academic International Press, 1976–1990.

McGrew, Roderick E. *Paul I of Russia.* Oxford: Clarendon Press, 1992.

Munro, George E. "Catherine I — the Great." *Modern Encyclopedia of Russian and Soviet History,* ed., Joseph L. Wieczynski, 54 vols. with suppl. Gulf Breeze, Flo., 1976-90.

Munro, George E. "Elizabeth I (Elizaveta Petrovna)." *Modern Encyclopedia of Russian and Soviet History,* ed. Joseph L. Wieczynski, 54 vols. With suppl. Gulf Breeze, Florida: Academic International Press, 1976–1990.

_____. "Munnich, Burchard Christopher." *Modern Encyclopedia of Russian and Soviet History,* ed. Joseph L. Wieczynski, 54 vols. With suppl. Gulf Breeze, Florida: Academic International Press, 1976–1990.

_____. "Orlov, Aleksei Grigor'evich." *Modern Encyclopedia of Russian and Soviet History,* ed. Joseph L. Wieczynski, 54 vols. With suppl. Gulf Breeze, Florida: Academic International Press, 1976–1990.

_____. "Pahlen fon der, Petr Alekseevich." *Modern Encyclopedia of Russian and Soviet History,* ed. Joseph L. Wieczynski, 54 vols. With suppl. Gulf Breeze, Florida: Academic International Press, 1976–1990.

_____. "Potemkin, Grigorii Alexandrovich." *Modern Encyclopedia of Russian and Soviet History,* ed. Joseph L. Wieczynski, 54 vols. With suppl. Gulf Breeze, Florida: Academic International Press, 1976–1990.

_____. "Supreme Privy Council." *Modern Encyclopedia of Russian and Soviet History,* ed. Joseph L. Wieczynski, 54 vols. With suppl. Gulf Breeze, Florida: Academic International Press, 1976–1990.

Ragsdale, Hugh. "Paul I (Pavel Petrovich)." *Modern Encyclopedia of Russian and Soviet History,* ed. Joseph L. Wieczynski, 54 vols. With suppl. Gulf Breeze, Florida: Academic International Press, 1976–1990.

Schweitzer, Karl W. "Ivan VI (Ivan Antonovich)" *Modern Encyclopedia of Russian and Soviet History,* ed. Joseph L. Wieczynski, 54 vols. With suppl. Gulf Breeze, Florida: Academic International Press, 1976–1990.

Warner, Richard. "Bennigsen, Leontii Leont'evich." *Modern Encyclopedia of Russian and Soviet History,* ed. Joseph L. Wieczynski, 54 vols. With suppl. Gulf Breeze, Florida: Academic International Press, 1976–1990.

Rheinlander, L. Hamilton. "Succession Crisis of 1730." *Modern Encyclopedia of Russian and Soviet History,* ed. Joseph L. Wieczynski, 54 vols. With suppl. Gulf Breeze, Florida: Academic International Press, 1976–1990.

8. Aristocratic Rebels: The Decembrists and Petrashevtsy

For the rest of his life, Alexander was tormented by guilt for the role he had played in his father's murder. The malaise was particularly acute during the first year of his reign, when he was nearly overcome by his sense of unworthiness. In time, his wife, Yelizaveta Alexeevna, was able to persuade him that he could expiate his sin by service to the Russian people. To this end, he created a kind of "chosen council" consisting of three friends: a soldier/diplomat named Nikolai Novosil'tsev, a Polish nationalist named Adam Czartoryski, and a Russian liberal named Pavel Stroganov. The members of this triumvirate were senior to the tsar by sixteen, seven, and three years respectively, but they shared many of his ideals and were eager to work for them. Among the most important of their goals was a constitution based on the separation of powers and the right of elected representatives to fix taxes. Alexander also planned to enact a new law code, increase the powers and responsibilities of the Senate, and compose a "Charter for the Russian People." Finally, the new tsar had expressed a desire to liberate the country from its barbaric past by abolishing serfdom. However, to the deep disillusionment of his most devoted supporters, Alexander never achieved any of these worthy goals and thereby provoked the first attempt ever to end autocracy in Russia by force.

Some historians have sought to explain the tsar's failure to follow through on his solemn promises and idealistic commitments by certain contradictory elements in his upbringing. He had been raised in large part by his grandmother, Catherine II, who had wanted to inculcate him with cosmopolitan values and with the ideals of the *philosophs*. She had him tutored by a Swiss republican, Frederic Cesar de La Harpe, who frequently lectured the grand duke about the importance of enlightened government and the development of a civil society in Russia. La Harpe was in many ways a strange choice for such a task, since he knew little about the country whose future monarch he was charged to educate. Nor did he oblige Alexander to take tests, do homework, or demonstrate any practical application of what he had learned. Still, the empress deemed the enterprise a success, since the boy seemed to enthusiastically absorb everything he was taught. Unfortunately, she did not appreciate the extent to which these wholesome influences were being undermined by his father's fiercely military regime at Gatchina, where her grandson also spent much time. In fact, the young grand duke became so fascinated with the art of drilling soldiers on the parade ground that he could at times be nearly as pedantic and demanding as his father. But Alexander had no desire to stimulate the antagonism between Catherine and Paul and thus strove to adjust his behavior to please each as the situation demanded. In time, however, he seems to have become confused as to what his own values really were.

For instance, although Alexander professed to hate the dissipation and immorality of his grandmother, his own behavior was hardly exemplary. Aside from the fact that he is believed to have dallied with almost every attractive woman he met, he took the wife of one of his own officials to serve openly as his mistress for some fifteen years.[1] He even encouraged his own wife, with whom he remained on good terms, to engage in love affairs of her own. No less inconsistent was his behavior on official occasions: in contrast to his father, he was unfailingly polite and courteous to others and strove to affect an air of humility and modesty. To this end, he wore no jewelry, discouraged displays of pomp in his honor, and traveled without a retinue. However, like his father, he could be harsh to those who dared to disagree with him. Such was the case in January 1803, when Count Severin Potocki wanted to invoke the recently affirmed "right of remonstrance" and have the Senate review a decree that he believed contradicted an earlier one. The tsar astonished everyone by getting angry and chastising those who had spoken out. He issued the disputed law anyway and then revoked the right of senators to criticize legislation in the future.

Nevertheless, Alexander also accomplished much that was useful during the first half of his reign and at times seemed to embody the best intentions of his illustrious grandmother. This was particularly evident by the way he embellished the capital constructing some of its most famous architectural landmarks. Thus the Admiralty, Senate and Synod Buildings, St. Isaac's Cathedral, and the huge semi-circular General Staff building the encompasses Palace Square all were erected during his reign. He also abolished censorship, corresponded with Thomas Jefferson about the intricacies of the U.S. Constitution, and commissioned Nikolai Karamzin to write a history of Russia. The young tsar was evidently sincere in his desire to promote good government and enlightenment among his subjects. To these ends, he reorganized the bureaucracy, created a system of modern ministries, improved secondary schools, and established new universities at Dorpat, Vilna, Kazan, Kharkov, and St. Petersburg.

Many were so encouraged by these initiatives that they dared to hope that reforms of a more radical nature were in the offing. Such optimism seemed particularly justified in 1807, when Alexander appointed Mikhail Speransky[2] to become his personal assistant. The son of a village priest, Speransky was brilliant, well educated, and dutiful. He reorganized the country's finances, helped to establish a lyceum at Tsarskoe Selo, began the recodification of Russian laws, and made examinations mandatory for promotion to the upper levels of the bureaucracy. The high point of his collaboration with Alexander occurred in January 1810 with the creation of a new kind of State Council. Its members were to be appointed by the tsar to advise him on legislative matters. This initiative, however, was to be only part of a complete overhaul of Russia's political structure. Speransky envisioned the Senate as the head of the legal system, a new ministry to act as the executive, and an elected *State Duma* acting as the legislature in cooperation with the emperor. Unfortunately, by 1812, the tsar, who was preoccupied with foreign affairs, had grown wary of any reform that might limit his own power. He had also begun to listen to Speransky's many enemies, who scorned his low birth, francophilia, and reforming zeal. Accordingly, on March 17 (29), Alexander summoned his loyal servant to a meeting to dismiss him. Speransky, who had had no hint that the tsar was dissatisfied with his performance, was later arrested and sent into exile. Alexander wept at the loss of this gifted man but believed that he had acted in the national interest. As he later justified his action to the duke of Württemberg: "One cannot judge sovereigns by the standard for individuals. Politics dictates duties that repel the heart."[3]

In the summer of 1812, Napoleon lead an army of nearly 600,000 men into Russia. It was a calamity that Alexander had long dreaded and tried to avoid. The tsar and the French emperor had already clashed in 1805 when the former had sponsored the Third Coalition in an attempt to prevent further French expansion. However, the effort had failed miserably as Napoleon smashed his enemies at Austerlitz, Jena, and Friedland. Ultimately, Alexander decided to make peace and negotiated with Napoleon on a raft in the middle of the Nieman River near Tilsit in July of 1807. He managed to make the most of his weak position by feigning enthusiasm for a proposed "treaty of peace and friendship" and by gracefully accepting the offensive and defensive alliance that bound Russia to France. This allowed him to save his ally Prussia from complete dismemberment and to occupy territory in Finland and the Danubian principalities. Unfortunately, the treaty also obliged Russia to participate in the onerous Continental System, by which she could no longer trade with Great Britain. This, of course, not only hurt England's economy, but Russia's as well.

In the years following Tilsit, Alexander's popularity and prestige at home plummeted. The country was torn by financial chaos as the ruble fell to one-fifth of its previous value. The big landowners and merchants were especially hard hit, since they were forbidden to export their hemp, flax, and timber to Britain. In addition, people in the western part of Russia feared a resurgence of Polish nationalism, since the new Grand Duchy of Poland was backed by French armies. Still, Alexander withstood all criticism during this period, secure in the knowledge that the true purpose of his policy was to gain time and to subvert his "ally" whenever possible. Thus, when Napoleon failed to withdraw his troops from Prussia as promised, the tsar did nothing to discourage the widespread smuggling that undermined the Continental System. Nor did he fulfill a pledge made at Erfurt in 1808 to help the French in their war with Austria. Finally, when Napoleon annexed the German duchy of Oldenburg early in 1811 (then ruled by Alexander's brother-in-law), the tsar acknowledged the inevitable and began to prepare for war.

The dreaded invasion finally came during the early morning hours of June 12 (24), 1812, when Napoleon's Grand Army crossed the Nieman River into Russian territory. Four days later they occupied Vilna, and, in August, Smolensk, after bloody but ineffective resistance. Patriotic Russians were aghast that the enemy had been able to advance so far in such a short time and were soon imploring the tsar to find a new commander. Up until now, he had relied mostly on an officer of Scottish descent, Mikhail Barclay de Tolly, whose policy of strategic retreat inspired little confidence among the defenders. Alexander was soon being urged to appoint Mikhail Kutuzov[4] as commander-in-chief, a man he did not like and whose abilities he did not trust. At sixty-seven, the general was fat, notoriously lazy, and ignorant about the latest innovations in warfare. He had only one eye due to an old battle wound, could hardly mount a horse, and seemed to prefer sleep to any other activity. Still, his credentials were impressive: he had once been a trusted lieutenant of the great Suvorov, had been awarded the order of St. George for his valor during the second Turkish War of 1787–91, and had won several important victories in a subsequent war with the

Turks in 1806. Too, Kutuzov had a rapport with his men that most officers could only envy, although even he had no quick answer on how to now stop the invader. Thus, the Russian retreat continued, although, when Kutuzov finally did engage the enemy at Borodino on August 26 (September 7), Napoleon would remember it as his most terrible battle. The fighting, which raged for fifteen hours and claimed some 80,000 men, ended in what most would consider a draw. However, the next day Kutuzov, appalled by the carnage and determined to preserve his army, withdrew to the southeast. This allowed the French to enter Moscow one week later.

Having now occupied the ancient capital, Napoleon expected a quick surrender, but it was not to be. Not only did Alexander refuse to negotiate, but the city caught fire on September 2 (14) and soon in lay in ruins, mostly uninhabitable. In the weeks that followed, the Grand Army, surrounded by a hostile population and their lines of communication stretched to the limit, began to suffer from a lack of food and shelter. When the inevitable retreat began on October 7 (19), the French army was much weakened by hunger and disease and had to struggle in freezing temperatures to defend itself against the guerilla tactics of Cossacks and peasants. At first, the situation did not seem critical because the Russians were not expected to pursue, but Alexander, who had recently undergone some kind of spiritual catharsis, ruled otherwise. The former religious skeptic was now convinced that God intended him to carry on the struggle until Napoleon had not only withdrawn from Russia but was removed from power. This was resisted not only by Britain and Austria, who feared Napoleon's genius, but also by Kutuzov, who believed the ordinary soldier had suffered enough. However, when the old general's death in April of 1813 removed him as an obstacle, the tsar persuaded his reluctant allies to fight on. After a number of defeats, a decisive victory was finally won at Leipzig[5] in October. Five months later, Alexander, entering Paris at the head of a great army, was acclaimed a hero.

When the Congress of Vienna convened in September of 1814, Alexander expected to play a leading role, and he did. Still, the negotiations proved to be extremely difficult and he did not get his way on every point. His conquests of Finland and Bessarabia were recognized, but he was not allowed to absorb all of Poland as he had hoped and eventually agreed to settle for a state much reduced in size. The tsar, although infuriated by the recalcitrance of his former allies, was distracted now by a concern that was far more profound — that of his own salvation. Desperate to find inner peace, he had begun to study the Bible and consult with mystics. One of these, a certain Baroness Julie von Krudener, dramatically appeared at his residence one night and pleaded for an audience. At fifty years of age, she was no longer beautiful, but she captivated the tsar for many months by her prophesies and moralizing. Not only had she predicted Napoleon's return at the head of a new army in March of 1815, but, after his final defeat two months later at Waterloo, she urged the tsar to create the Holy Alliance. By this agreement, signed in September, most of the states of Europe promised to abide by "the precepts of Justice, Christian Charity and Peace." Unfortunately, it was not taken seriously by anyone except Alexander. In November, however, the tsar forged the Quadruple Alliance of Russia, Britain, Austria, and Prussia, which did have some practical application, since it called for regular conferences to maintain peace in Europe.

His work in western Europe now concluded, at least for the time being, Alexander returned to Russia in December in a strangely depressed and somber mood. Those closest to him were disturbed by the change in his personality: he was on edge, easily irritated, and inclined to take out his frustration in petty ways on those who might have expected better.[6] This was especially true for the army, which was now subject to a more stringent code of behavior that, among other things, obliged his officers to wear their uniforms even when off duty. On New Years Day, 1816, Alexander published a manifesto to the nation thanking his subjects for their valor in defeating Napoleon but insisted that the victory was all due to the will of God. He also denounced the French people in the harshest terms and referred to Napoleon as "a commoner, a foreign bandit and a malefactor."[7] He predicted that the former emperor would one day "present himself drenched in the blood of peoples before the terrible tribunal, in the face of God, when each receives retribution for his acts."[8] Such language startled those who thought they knew this man, and even his former tutor La Harpe wrote him to express his dismay. But Alexander was now distracted by yet other voices. One of these was the deeply pious Alexander Nikolaievich Golitsyn, whom he had recently appointed Procurator of the Holy Synod. Another was the Grand Master of the Imperial Court, Koshelev, who had helped found the Russian Bible Society (of which Alexander was a member) and was known to be fascinated by mysticism and the occult.

Indeed, the tsar's obsession with spiritual matters made him oblivious to the yearnings of many of his civic-minded subjects, especially those who had observed freedoms unknown in Russia as they campaigned with the army in the west. These men could only wonder why "the blessed one" (as he was now known by the Orthodox faithful), who had established constitutions in Finland and Poland, had neglected to do the same at home.

Nor could they understand Alexander's ambivalence about serfdom, an institution he had promised to abolish but had so far failed even to ameliorate. Previously, he had issued a decree that would have allowed serfs to receive their freedom with the consent of their masters, but he had added so many qualifications that only a tiny fraction of those in bondage were affected. In 1816, he had acted more boldly by granting a request by the Estonian nobility (made in 1811) to free their serfs without giving them land, but this actually left the latter economically worse off. Finally, he had refused a petition from Prince Vasil'chikov and sixty-four other wealthy landowners for a cooperative emancipation. In this instance, he seems to have been annoyed by their presumption to address a problem that God had intended him to solve.

In 1816, Alexander revived an earlier scheme, set aside during the war, to create a network of military colonies of soldier-farmers. His motives were both practical and humanitarian: not only would such colonies obviate the need for massive conscription[9] needed to allow Russia to maintain her "military preponderance" in Europe, but they would make it possible for soldiers to live with their families while they served in the army. The idea had originated six years earlier during an imperial visit to Gruzino, Count Alexei Arakcheev's[10] home near Novgorod. The tsar had so admired the high level of discipline, cleanliness, and efficiency on this estate that he resolved to see it expanded to the public domain.

Ominously, the bureaucrat he chose to administrate this project was Arakcheev himself, a man notorious for his crude manners, malevolence, and vile disposition. He has been described by one historian as a "drab minatory presence whose bristling hair *en brosse,* staring eyes and gaunt, hunched figure in threadbare coat could demoralize the most glittering assemblage."[11] A remorseless taskmaster, Arakcheev took pleasure in tormenting his own servants. He kept canes in vats of brine on his estate to flog those who aroused his displeasure and sometimes forced his victims to wear collars studded with sharp iron points. His obsession with perfection bordered on the insane: he insisted that his soldiers hold their breaths during parade-in-review so that they could appear more military, and he allegedly bit off the ear of one man for a trivial mistake. Arakcheev's personal life was no less dispiriting. Having separated from his legal spouse, he made the wife of a sailor his mistress. A fat, vulgar, woman drawn to pornography and sadism, she eventually had her throat cut by a serf at Gruzino whose pregnant sister she had abused.

Alexander's attachment to this man mystified most people, but, in fact, it made good sense. Arakcheev had served Tsar Paul as Quartermaster General with absolute loyalty and devotion for a number of years despite his having twice been sent into exile for minor offenses. After Paul's assassination, he had earned the son's gratitude and trust by consoling him and ameliorating his sense of guilt. Arakcheev, however, did more than serve the new tsar's emotional needs. A subordinate by nature, he could be counted on to do exactly as he was told, discreetly and without question. Alexander soon came to depend on him to take on the more unsavory tasks that others wished to avoid. This included tedious and difficult military assignments. During the war years, the count had been charged with training the army and improving Russian artillery. General Gneisenau of Prussia was so impressed by his accomplishment that he personally thanked him for having made victory possible, saying: "Liberated Europe owes you an eternal debt."[12] The tsar, too, was pleased with his servant and had no doubt that this was the man to administer the military colonies that would allow Russia to remain strong militarily and to address some pressing social problems.

Even Arakcheev had doubts about the feasibility of the task before him and was especially troubled by the cost, which absorbed fifty-four percent of state budget in the first year. The tsar, intending to be generous, had decreed that all soldier-farmers were to reside on carefully planned settlements that featured security, order, and the strictest sanitation. Moreover, the property of each colonist was to be guaranteed and inviolable: each would receive a horse, a plot of land, and a cottage. Repairs and upkeep were to be at the expense of the government. There would be schools for the children, medical care for the disabled, and enough food to ensure no one went hungry. Colonists would not pay state taxes nor would they be subject to road repair duty. Women who married into these settlements would receive twenty-five rubles.

That these promises were never kept must in part be attributed to Arakcheev, who on his own had decided that this enterprise should pay for itself. The first colonies were established during the summer of 1816, when various army regiments set up camp in the provinces of Novgorod, Mogilev, Kherson, Yekaterinoslav, and Slobodsko-Ukrainsky. Without warning, the inhabitants of the affected districts were declared to be military personnel. Families were ordered out of their peasant huts, or *izby*, and moved into barrack-like cottages. The men were put into uniform, had their beards shaved and their hair cropped, and were forced to submit to a routine of at least thirteen-and-a-half hours of work each day. When they weren't toiling in the fields or doing other chores, they were engaged in military training. Everything was done to the sound of a drum. Inspections were frequent and discipline savage. Most infractions were punished with the cane, which sometimes proved fatal. Personal freedom, leisure, and privacy ceased to exist. Marriages were arranged by military officials and women who failed to give birth at least once a year were fined. Even the children were subject to the strictest regimentation: boys began military training at six and were expected to be ready for full military service at eighteen. The girls also received rigorous preparation for the day when they would be required to fulfill their communal obligations. These would include rising at four each morning to wash, cook, clean, care for the cattle, sweep the streets, sand the pathways, and raise the children.

At their height, the military colonies stretched from the Baltic to the Black Seas and included about one-third of the peacetime army, but few observers liked what they saw.[13] Shortages, overcrowding, and harsh discipline made conditions generally abominable, and in some ways, comparable to Stalin's forced collectivization in the 1930s. To be sure, there were many attempts to resist this totalitarian nightmare: some tried to run away and hide in the forests, while others resorted to outright rebellion. The most violent of these occurred at Chuguev in Ukraine. Scores of men and women were sentenced to run a gauntlet of 1,000 soldiers, causing many fatalities. Nor could one hope for mercy by appealing to higher authority. On one such occasion, four young women who were being forced to marry begged Alexander for redress during an imperial visit; for this they were sternly admonished. Later, the tsar was heard to declare, "There will be military colonies whatever the cost, even if one has to line the road from St. Petersburg to Chudovo with corpses" (a distance of about sixty-six miles).[14]

However, 1816 was also the year that a number of liberal officers, many of whom had served abroad during the war years, formed a secret political society called the Society of the True and Faithful Sons of the Fatherland, or the Union of Salvation. Its purpose was to find a way to abolish autocracy and serfdom and thus save the country. There was, however, no precise agreement among its thirty or so members on how to accomplish this end. Most believed it would be necessary to first raise the social consciousness of the people, but others thought this would not be enough. When a few members proposed killing the tsar as a means of forcing radical change, many recoiled in horror, and the union was disbanded. Its successor, called the Union of Welfare, was formed in 1818. It consisted of about 200 men, mostly army officers, whose avowed purpose was to promote the public good by emphasizing enlightenment and morality. It urged its members to behave according to the highest principles and to encourage others to do the same. Thus, the gentry were to be reminded of the need to treat their serfs humanely and not to break up families when selling individual peasants.

A few of its members, however, were drawn to a more radical, secret agenda, which included the granting of a constitution, freedom for the serfs, shortening the length of military service, and abolishing the military colonies. The most determined of these was a young army officer named Pavel Pestel'[15], who had previously been a member of the Union of Salvation. Pestel', educated in Germany, fought in the war against Napoleon. He had been wounded at Borodino and Leipzig and was decorated a number of times. Having been imbued with liberal ideals in his youth, he was particularly disturbed by the military colonies, which he feared would become a counterrevolutionary force. In 1819, he wrote a treatise "On the Regulation of the State" in which he argued the need for freedom from arbitrary despotism, equality before the law, and an end to corporal punishment. Later, he expressed his preference for a republican form of government rather than a monarchy, since he believed the latter to be inherently despotic. Unfortunately, Pestel' was not much trusted or liked by his comrades and was not able to convince others to embrace his program. Subsequent events, however, were to work in his favor.

In the fall of 1820, a rebellion in the Semenovsky Regiment startled those who still believed Alexander was committed to liberal principles. It was provoked by the brutality of a Colonel F.E. Schwartz who had forced his men to march barefoot to economize on shoe leather and exhausted them with interminable drill. The officer was also inclined to inflict punishments that were calculated to humiliate, such as pulling their mustaches, spitting in their faces, and other more painful forms of physical abuse. On October 19 (31), the men retaliated by refusing to answer a roll call and were promptly imprisoned in the Peter and Paul Fortress. The next night, however, eleven other companies rebelled, demanding that their comrades be freed. They, too, went to prison, although, remarkably, the protest went no further. In fact, the original mutineers, who had marched off to jail in good order, declared their willingness to accept any punishment as long as they did not have to serve under Colonel Schwartz. Unfortunately, the incident was complicated by the subsequent discovery of two proclamations: one, found in the courtyard right after the mutiny, denounced Russia's tyrannical system of government. A second, found several weeks later, urged the soldiers to arrest their officers and elect new ones. It was apparent to most that the men had not been influenced by either document, but Alexander was convinced that the men had been swayed by political radicals. Accordingly, the punishments he authorized were severe: the entire regiment was disbanded and even those who were not directly involved at all were sent to far away places to reflect on the crime of the guilty. The latter were each given 6,000 blows with the cane and sentenced to hard labor in the mines.

Somehow, the mutiny of the Semenovsky Regiment encouraged the members of the Union of Welfare to believe that the army could be counted on should force be necessary to promote reform. However, the incident also provoked inquiries by the tsar's secret police and made everyone feel at risk. To escape such surveillance, the Union of Welfare disbanded in 1821 to rid itself of those whose allegiance was questionable. In its place, two other groups came into being: the Northern Society, which was centered in St. Petersburg, and the Southern Society, which was centered in Tulchin in Ukraine. The former was headed by an army officer named Nikita Muraviev, who had helped to found both the Union of Salvation and the Union of Welfare. Originally, he had been in favor of regicide but later moderated his views. As the leader of the weaker, less numerous Northern Society, he began to draw up a constitutional project called the *Green Book,* which called for a limited monarchy and guaranteed basic human rights including freedom of speech, the press, and religion. Suffrage was to be based on stringent property qualifications. Muraviev also proposed that serfdom be abolished and that the peasants be given land from the military colonies, which he intended to disband. He also envisioned the country operating as a federation of thirteen regions modeled on the American system.

In the south, Pavel Pestel' was developing his own program in a book called *Russian Justice (Russkaya Pravda),* which was considerably more radical. One of its most interesting features was its proposal for the abolition of serfdom and agrarian reform, which called for the confiscation of up to one-half of landlords' holdings with some compensation from the state. This land, along with other crown lands, would then be distributed to emancipated serfs. Ultimately, Pestel' envisioned the creation of a highly centralized republic. He believed, however, that this would require a transition period of ten years or so under a provisional government with dictatorial powers to protect the gains of the revolution. The empire would then be divided up into regions and provinces and governed by a national assembly elected once every five years with separate executive and legislative powers. A *State Duma* of five elected men would act as the supreme executive body. To this would be added a supreme council of 120 men elected for life to oversee the functioning of the government and to ensure that the principles of *Russian Justice* were followed. Privilege based on class was to be abolished, and all men twenty and over were to have the vote. The military settlements would be ended, and the term of service for conscripts would be reduced from twenty-five to fifteen years. Pestel' also hoped to create a new capital at Nizhny Novgorod on the Volga, which would be renamed Vladimir after the famous religious center to the east of Moscow.

However, Pestel' frightened people with his authoritarian manner and emphasis on dictatorship. His ideal was a highly centralized, monolithic, totalitarian state that would control both the minds and bodies of its citizens. He envisioned the banning of all private associations and the mobilization of the clergy and police to spy on the population to eliminate all vice, including idleness, card playing, and alcohol. He also favored an aggressive policy of Russification for minorities throughout the empire. Interestingly, he had no use for socialism, and although he wanted to ensure that emancipated serfs got land, he had no plans to address economic inequality. He frankly admired the free enterprise system and thought it good that the wealthy would always be with us, although he did not want them to be accorded any special legal privileges. Chillingly, Pestel's proposal to exterminate the entire Romanov family in order to prevent any possibility of restoring the monarchy anticipated the brutal logic of the Bolsheviks by nearly a century.

Pestel' worked hard to bring about unification of the Northern and Southern Societies, but he was opposed by Muraviev, who not only denounced his radical program but accused him of self-promotion. Still, many aspiring rebels in both groups, aware that revolutions had already occurred in Spain, Italy, and Greece, were eager for some kind of joint action. To exploit this sentiment and to resolve some of the more prickly ideological differences, Pestel' traveled to St. Petersburg to in March of 1824. Although he met with considerable resistance, he did find one kindred spirit in Kondraty Ryleev, an important poet and revolutionary thinker who shared his sense of urgency. Unlike most in the Northern Society, Ryleev agreed that the imperial family would probably have to be liquidated, although he rejected Pestel's proposal for a dictatorship and highly centralized state. Thus, at the end of six weeks of discussions very little had been agreed upon except to meet again in two years time.

But support for action was growing from other quarters as well. In 1825, a group called the United Slavs was absorbed into the Southern Society. The Slavs had organized in 1818 and gradually developed a program that called for the abolition of serfdom and autocracy and the creation of a democratic Slavic federation. They had been recruited and won over by the optimism and exaggerated claims of a certain Lieutenant Mikhail Bestuzhev-Riumin, who declared: "The high deed will be accomplished, and we will be proclaimed heroes of the age."[16] The lieutenant also bragged of military support and foreign connections that didn't exist and predicted that the tsar would be overthrown swiftly and with minimal bloodshed. The Slavs were both impressed and worried. The proposed plan was entirely an upper-class army affair that did not encourage nor, indeed, want the participation of the masses, but without a broad base of support, many wondered how the establishment of some new kind of tyranny could be prevented.

In fact, the planning for the projected coup never got specific enough to warrant concern about what would happen afterwards. The main conspirators from both societies had never been able to agree on more than a few basics: Alexander would be assassinated during a trip south in May of 1826 to inspect the Third Army Corps, and troops would subsequently occupy Kiev, Moscow, and St. Petersburg. The grand dukes would be sent into exile, and the Northern Society would form a provisional government and draft a constitutional charter. However, the plotters failed to think through important problems such as where they would get weapons and supplies and what they should tell the common soldiers on whom they would have to depend, nor did they consider how to deal with discord and treachery in their own ranks, which was far more serious than anyone thought. Thus, when Muraviev became discouraged about his waning influence in the Northern Society, he simply abandoned the enterprise and went back to his estates. Pestel' himself was betrayed by a fellow officer whom he had recently recruited for the Southern Society. His arrest on December 13 (25), prevented him from supporting the coup that was about to occur.

Interestingly, Alexander had long known of the dissent brewing against him in the army, but, by this time, he had become so detached from public affairs that he showed almost no interest. Even though the commander-chief of the Guards, General Vasil'chikov, had identified most of the troublemakers and revealed their plans, the tsar refused to act. As he explained to the general, he, too, had once shared their "illusions and errors," and concluded that it was not for him to repress them. In part, his seeming indifference may have been due to other events. In June 1824, he had been deeply shaken by the death of his illegitimate daughter, Sophia Naryshkina, of consumption; and in November, an enormous flood in St. Petersburg had damaged the Winter Palace, causing much loss of life. Such events convinced Alexander that he was being punished by God for his sins and prompted him to seek consolation and forgiveness from his long estranged wife, Yelizaveta Alexeevna. During this period, she became a regular visitor to his apartments in the Winter Palace to read the Bible and chat about matters of mutual interest. However, when her health began to decline the following year, Alexander became alarmed. The coughing and heart spasms suggested consumption, and the doctors recommended that she travel to Taganrog on the Sea of Azov to convalesce in a milder climate. The tsar decided to go with her.

Taganrog, with its marshy terrain, hot sun and high winds, was thought by many to be a rather odd destination for a person in poor health, but Alexander was preoccupied with the possibility of a war against Turkey and did not want to risk leaving the country at such a crucial time. Thus, he accepted the doctor's recommendation without question and left before his wife on September 1 (13) to prepare their lodgings. Despite its population of 10,000, the city had few comforts and, in many ways, was something of a backwater. Still, a suitable dwelling was eventually found, and the tsar himself lent a hand to make it presentable driving in nails to hang paintings and engravings. Yelizaveta Alexeevna arrived about three weeks later and quickly responded to the milder climate. It was, however, the tsar's health that now became a concern. Having left Taganrog to go on a brief inspection tour of the Crimea, he returned ill and was diagnosed with "bilous gastric fever." Laxatives and purgatives were prescribed, and, when these brought no improvement, the patient was bled with leeches. This appeared to worsen his condition, and the tsar died on November 19 (December 1), just short of his forty-eighth birthday. The autopsy report, which was signed by nine doctors, was unclear about the cause of death, although modern experts believe that he likely succumbed to either typhoid or malaria.

The news of Alexander's passing reached the capital on November 27 (December 9), and, because the tsar had no children, it was assumed that the eldest brother and governor of Poland, Grand Duke Konstantin, would now succeed him, but because Konstantin had married a commoner in 1820, who could not be recognized as empress, he informed his older brother that he renounced his right to the throne. Accordingly, the tsar had authorized the drafting of a manifesto to this effect in August of 1823 in which he proclaimed Nicholas heir. For some reason, however, he decided not to promulgate it. Perhaps the delay can be explained by Alexander's desire to wait until his own promised retirement to announce the change. In any case, he ordered the document kept secret until further notice, or his death. What transpired now might have been comical had not the future of the country been at stake. Konstantin and his subjects in Poland swore allegiance to Nicholas as soon as they learned of Alexander's death, but Nicholas, the Russian army, and others in St. Petersburg swore allegiance to Konstantin. Apparently, the younger brother was fearful of seeming to act in violation of Tsar Paul's Law of Succession[17] and wanted the older brother to come to the capital to formally renounce his right to the throne. Konstantin refused for reasons still not entirely clear and a confusing interregnum followed. Only on December 12 (December 24) did Nicholas finally proclaim himself tsar. He set Monday, December

14 (December 26) as the day the guard regiments in St. Petersburg would again swear their allegiance — this time to him.

Although caught by surprise by these events, the conspirators in St. Petersburg believed they had to seize the moment. After much discussion on December 13 (25), much of it dominated by Ryleev, they agreed to a new plan that was based on a lie: they would pretend to act in support of Konstantin's legal right to rule by urging the soldiers not to swear allegiance to Nicholas.[18] To this end, they spread a number of other falsehoods including the preposterous claim that Alexander, in his will, had freed the serfs and reduced the term of military service to ten years. Konstantin, they asserted, intended to honor this while Nicholas did not. In the meantime, the conspirators would muster all the military strength they could in the Senate Square the following day and, confident that Konstantin would never try to assume the throne, force that body to issue a manifesto announcing the overthrow of the monarchy. This would be followed by the creation of a provisional government, the convening of a constituent assembly, and the adoption of a constitution. Should anything go wrong, the rebels intended to appeal to the military colonies for support. If that failed, they would retreat into the interior.

Of course, everything depended upon getting public officials and soldiers to join the rebellion *before* they swore allegiance to Nicholas, since many would find it difficult to violate a sacred oath once made. Thus, it was a major setback when the Senate and State Council took their pledge to Nicholas at 7:30 A.M. on December 14 (26). Despite this, the conspirators went forward and the first rebel troops from the Life Guards Moscow Regiment arrived at the Square at about 11:00 A.M. Apparently, it was hoped that if enough regiments joined the mutineers the new tsar would surrender. Unfortunately, this plan had not been explained to the soldiers, who were unsure what they were expected to do. Too, the man who had been chosen to be their "dictator," Prince Sergei Trubetskoy, never showed up to take command. Having lost his courage, he spent the day wandering the city and eventually sought refuge in the home of his cousin, the Austrian ambassador. In the meantime, the troops stood around on the Square, freezing in the wind and cold, occasionally firing their weapons into the air and shouting "Hurrah for Konstantin." At 2 P.M. they were joined by the Life Guards Grenadiers and Naval Guards which brought their numbers up to about 3,000 (including thirty "Decembrist" officers). Still, the general confusion and disorder continued as some of the men had gotten drunk on the spirits offered them by the growing crowd of onlookers. Finally, in an attempt to end the leadership vacuum, Prince Obolensky, a staff officer with little experience, agreed to accept overall command.

However, his weak voice and noticeable lisp made him a poor choice for such a task.

The new tsar, however, who had been informed beforehand of the conspirators' plans, had not been passive. At 5 A.M. that morning, he had assembled all his senior Guards officers at the Winter Palace to explain the situation regarding Konstantin's refusal to accept the throne. He now ordered them to swear allegiance to him and issued the following warning: "After this you will answer to me with your heads for the tranquillity of the capital. As far as I am concerned, even if I shall be Emperor for only one hour, I shall show myself worthy of the honor."[19] In fact, he acquitted himself well under difficult circumstances. Later that morning when rebel soldiers were sent to the Winter Palace, he and his family escaped capture only by the timely arrival of the Sapper Battalion. These same rebel soldiers encountered the tsar a short time later near the General Staff Headquarters but failed to recognize him. When ordered to halt, one of them shouted, "We are for Konstantin," whereupon the tsar pointed to the Senate Square and replied, "Very well, your place is over there." Not long afterwards, Nicholas himself appeared on the Square to take charge. Tall and sternly handsome in his uniform of the Ismailovsky Guard, he was determined to prevail if possible without bloodshed on the first day of his reign, but this was complicated by the presence of a huge crowd of civilians milling about the Square, most of them sympathetic to the rebels. Surrounding them were about 10,000 loyal troops who had been summoned to prevent more regiments from joining the rebellion.

Over the next few hours, various individuals went forward to reason with the insurgents. Two of these, the governor-general Miloradovich of St. Petersburg and General Sturler, were shot dead by the Decembrist Piotr Kakhovsky, who began the day fully intending to die for the cause. This was followed by a cavalry charge on horses improperly shod for the icy Senate Square, which the rebels easily drove back. Somewhat later, Metropolitan Serafim, fully attired in his robes and vestments, went forward to plead with the troops but was turned away. The last to try persuasion was Grand Duke Mikhail, the tsar's younger brother, who only barely escaped death when a pistol aimed at him misfired. This prompted another cavalry charge, which was again repulsed and the stalemate continued. By mid-afternoon with darkness descending on the capital and the temperature falling, the tsar finally made a decision. Mindful that he could not allow the day to end without the crisis being resolved, he ordered rounds of canister fired into the rebel ranks. This emptied the Square, killing at least seventy and wounding many more. Those who tried to escape by running across the frozen Neva drowned when the tsar ordered cannon to

The high-born army officers who challenged Tsar Nicholas I's right to rule in the Senate Square in St. Petersburg on December 14, 1825 demanded a constitutional monarchy and the abolition of serfdom. "Literaturnoe Nasledstvo," tom 59, Izdatel'tsvo AH SSSR, Moskva, 1954.

blast holes in the ice. By five o'clock, the confrontation was over and the police began the task of rounding up the surviving mutineers.

It took ten days for news of the rebellion to reach the Southern Society, whose members, without Pestel's leadership, had made no plans to act during the crisis. However, the government soon learned who the potential troublemakers were and ordered a number of arrests. Among these were Lieutenant Colonel Sergei Muraviev-Apostol and Lieutenant Mikhail Bestuzhev-Riumin of the Chernigov Regiment. Also with them was Matvei Muraviev-Apostol, who was no longer in the army, but still active in the Southern Society. When the three learned that they were wanted by the authorities, they saw rebellion as their only possible course of action. In fact, the two Muraviev-Apostol brothers were soon taken into custody in the town of Trilesy but were able to escape with the help of some fellow officers. They immediately began to recruit soldiers to their cause.

Leadership of the rebellion fell to Sergei Muraviev-Apostol, who enjoyed an unusual rapport with his men. He soon collected a force of more than 1,000, and marched them to Vasilkov, which fell without resistance. Taking stock of the situation, Muraviev-Apostol realized it was necessary to broaden his base of support and sent messengers to the Polish secret societies and to the United Slavs. He also decided that it was important for his men to understand what they were fighting for and why. To this end, he spent the evening of December 30 (January 11) composing *An Orthodox Catechism,* which described the tsars as accursed of God and who had stolen freedom from the people. He further asserted that only the republican form of government was sanctioned by divine law and that Tsar Alexander's death was a sign from God to throw off the bonds of slavery. This was read to the troops the next day during a special mass held in the market square. Unfortunately, it had been written in ecclesiastical language so difficult that many of the men missed the intended message. After the mass, one of them is alleged to have expressed his bewilderment by saying something like, "I'm all for a republic, but who is going to be our tsar?"

In fact, the rebels could have used a tsar or at least a decisive leader. Discipline among the ranks was poor, and there was little agreement among the officers, particularly about the means they would use to achieve their ends or what they would do next. Muraviev-Apostol, as a devout Orthodox Christian, hated violence and hoped to prevail by persuasion. Thus, he favored marching to Zhitomir to join forces with the United Slavs. Most of his officers, believing that the rebellion could not succeed unless the most extreme measures were applied, favored an assault on Kiev. In the end, Muraviev-Apostol got his way, but there was little enthusiasm among the rebels as they trudged through one town after another without gaining any new support. The end came quickly during the afternoon of January 3 (15), when the rebels, marching along a snow-covered road, saw a detachment of cavalry some distance away. At first they thought these troops were potential allies, but a few rounds of cannon fire in their direction convinced them otherwise. With several soldiers dead and Muraviev-Apostol wounded, the mutiny was over.

One of the most surprising features of the subsequent investigation is the extent to which the tsar himself became involved in the process. Shocked and angry that so many men of noble birth had betrayed the monarchy, Nicholas personally decided who would be incarcerated where, what kind of food would they be given, and whether they would be forced to wear hand fetters, foot irons, or both. In addition, he interrogated the principal conspirators at the Winter Palace with surprising skill. Most were quickly broken and groveled pathetically as they begged forgiveness—some more abjectly than others.[20] Prince Trubetskoy fell to his knees to kiss the tsar's boots. Prince Odoevsky, who had dreamed of a glorious death, confessed hysterically and begged for a chance to reveal more. Only Piotr Kakhovsky, who spoke with "great daring and frankness" during the interrogation, won some respect from Nicholas, although he, too, asked for mercy in the end.

Of the 579 men who stood trial, almost half were acquitted. One hundred and twenty-one officers were sent off to hard labor in Siberia. Enlisted men who had lent active support were forced to run the gauntlet, with some of the survivors being sent to Siberia for hard labor or resettlement. Many of the soldiers in the Chernigov Regiment were sent to fight insurgents in the Caucasus. Only five of the Decembrists were condemned to die: Pavel Pestel', Mikhail-Bestuzhov Riumin, Kondraty Ryleev, Piotr Kakhovsky, and Sergei Muraviev-Apostol. The hanging was carried out on the embankment of the Peter and Paul Fortress in the early morning hours of July 13 (25), 1826. The tsar had decided not to attend but was kept informed of the proceedings at half-hour intervals by special couriers. With representatives from each regiment present to witness the execution, it was hoped that the spectacle would horrify anyone who saw it.

Interestingly, the condemned, contrary to what was reported to the tsar, showed no contrition and did not seem much frightened by their fate. Possibly, the incompetence of the executioners had something to do with this. It seems there had been a rain the night before and the ropes had shrunk. Prison officials had to borrow a bench from a local school for the prisoners to stand on so they could reach the nooses. Finally, after much delay, and with the condemned all standing on the bench, the order was given to kick it away. But something went wrong, and only two of the five were immediately hanged. The other three had somehow slipped their nooses and fallen into the pit below. It took quite some time to find some more rope, but in due course the prisoners were again strung up, this time with the desired result. Muraviev-Apostol, who had broken both his legs in the mishap, is said to have remarked: "Poor Russia! Here we don't even know how to hang a man properly!"[21]

The Decembrists, however, were not soon forgotten. Not only would they be revered by a future generation of revolutionaries, but Tsar Nicholas himself ordered the compilation of a digest of the conspirators' testimony for future reference. Unfortunately, he seems to have learned all the wrong lessons and focused almost entirely on the need to preserve the status quo by rigidly adhering to three principles: Orthodoxy, Autocracy, and Nationality.[22] And to ensure that his policies would be carried out to the letter, he created the Third Section of His Imperial Majesty's Own Chancery, with General Alexander Benckendorff as its head. This new police force, which Nicholas called the "moral physician of the Empire," became increasingly oppressive over the years and in many ways may be considered a prototype for the Soviet KGB. It had sweeping powers to investigate and report on anything and everything. By the late 1840s, its agents were examining sheet music and the rows of dots in arithmetic books in order to discover hidden messages. Foreign travelers were also suspect. Beginning in 1844, visitors from abroad had to submit to interrogation upon arrival in St. Petersburg and could expect their mail to be intercepted and examined during their stay. The Third Section was also responsible for censoring and harassing some of the greatest literary figures of the age. These included Alexander Pushkin[23] and Mikhail Lermontov,[24] both of whom spent years in exile: the former for writing politically offensive poems and the latter for attacking the authorities for their treatment of Pushkin. Another who suffered abuse was Piotr Chaadaev,[25] who was labeled a lunatic for having published an article critical of Russian culture.

Over the years, Nicholas never questioned or modified his reactionary views nor his conviction that he alone was answerable to God for the state of the empire. Thus, he spent much of his reign traveling the country, making spot inspections and punishing those who fell short of perfection. At times, his zeal must have seemed a bit ridiculous. He once fired a schoolmaster because one of his pupils was leaning on a windowsill during a lecture. On another occasion, a foreign tutor who sat down during an Orthodox church service was put in a straitjacket and sent to an insane asylum. He also dismissed a doctor during the cholera epidemic of 1831 because his hospital had reported more deaths than any other. Unfortunately the tsar could also assign punishments that were far more vindictive. Once when he was informed that two Jews had been caught illegally crossing a river in the southwest marches of his empire, he countermanded the governor general's recommendation to have them executed, commenting cynically, "Thank God we have never had capital punishment and I shall not be found introducing it."[26] Instead, Nicholas ordered the trespassers to run a gauntlet of 1,000 men, which, as he well knew, was every bit as lethal as the death penalty and far more hideous.[27]

Of course, even Nicholas understood that certain adjustments in the way the country was governed needed to be made. In addition to banning the knout as an instrument of punishment, he recalled Mikhail Speransky to government service and charged him with the codification of all Russian laws issued since 1649. Not only did this allow the law to be clearly stated for the first time since the 17th century, revealed how weak the legal basis for serfdom in Russia really was. Actually, the tsar himself saw this institution as a great evil and favored its abolition. Over the years, he set up no less than ten secret committees to consider how this might be done. But, fearing that the gentry, deprived of their serfs, might demand a constitution, or that the wrong kind of change would provoke the latter to rebel, Nicholas never did take decisive action. Still, in 1837, to make serfdom more humane for state-owned peasants, and to provide a positive example for the nobility to follow, he transformed the Fifth Section into the Ministry of State Domains, building schools and model farms and making additional lands available for poorer communities. A decade later, he forbade the sale of family members to different buyers and permitted serfs to buy their freedom if the landlord's estate was being sold for debt. These initiatives, although well intended, did not come close to alleviating the misery that millions of serfs had to accept as their lot.

Some believed that the military colonies might play a role in solving the problem of serfdom, but this notion was largely discredited in 1831 when colonists in the Novgorod region went on a rampage that took hundreds of lives. Although the immediate cause of the rebellion was the severity of the quarantine imposed after an outbreak of cholera, there were other more fundamental reasons as well. These included harsh discipline, endless military drill, and insufficient land allotments. Typically, Nicholas paid little attention to these valid grievances and ordered court-martials for all the rebels. The culprits were flogged so savagely that of the 1,599 so punished, 129 died. Nor did the aftermath of the rebellion bring any meaningful redress, for although the tsar concluded that the policy of combining soldiering and farming was not so practical after all, the settlements continued to grow. By 1850, their population had doubled, the only difference being that now a distinction was made between those soldier/colonists who fought in the field and those who supported them at home. Henceforth, the latter would receive more land but would also pay rent and be subject to regular military conscription.

In addition to preserving the established order in Russia, the tsar also felt obliged to do it abroad. Thus the overthrow of Charles X[28] by a Paris mob in July of 1830, and the Belgian revolt against Dutch rule in September, alarmed Nicholas to such an extent that he announced his willingness to intervene. In both cases, however, he found no supporters among other European governments. These same allies who had promised to protect the principle of legitimacy at Vienna fifteen years earlier were now reluctant to do much of anything. However, when the Poles rebelled in November hoping to force an end to Russian occupation, the tsar was determined to prevail. His task was made more difficult by his own brother's (i.e., Grand Duke Konstantin's) failure to act decisively. As the rebellion spread, Nicholas was forced to commit Russian troops on a grand scale, many of whom were suffering from cholera. The disease claimed many lives, including Konstantin's, in June of 1831. Only after a year of fighting were the Poles finally suppressed. As a result, they were fully absorbed into the Russian empire and deprived of their constitution. The tsar also ordered that a fortress armed with powerful cannon be built in Warsaw so that the city could be quickly bombarded should there be any more trouble in the future.

Unfortunately, there was more trouble, although not right away and not in Poland. In February 1848, Louis Philippe of France,[29] the so-called "citizen king," was overthrown, and, the following December, Louis Napoleon was elected president of the Second French Republic. Nicholas initially reacted cautiously to this event, but he soon felt compelled to prepare an army to protect the status quo. However, before he was able to give the order to march, the revolutionary fervor had spread to Prussia, Austria, and Turkey. To stem the tide, he granted Austria a six-million-ruble loan; that summer, he dispatched troops to Moldavia and Wallachia to suppress a rebellion against the Turks. The following year, another army was sent to Austria to quash Hungarian rebels in a brutal operation that engendered a fierce anti-Russian hatred among the victims. Ironically, even the recipients of Nicholas' aid felt keen resentment because of his "overbearing solicitude" and domineering manner.

The tsar was even less popular at home than abroad, especially among those who took the country's domestic stagnation seriously. These included a group of intellectuals who had been meeting at the St. Petersburg home of Mikhail Buteshevich-Petrashevsky[30] every Friday night since January 1845. The initiator and host of these sessions was a graduate of the Imperial Lyceum at Tsarskoe Selo in 1839, who subsequently entered the Ministry of Foreign Affairs where he became a low-ranking civil servant. In his free time, Petrashevsky attended the lectures of V.S. Poroshin at the University of St. Petersburg where he became fascinated by the theories of the utopian socialist, Charles Fourier,[31] whom he called his "one and only idol." Among other things, Petrashevsky came to cherish the notion that all human beings possess innate dignity, regardless of their personal convictions or material status, and that the ownership of private property was immoral.

Petrashevsky was eager to convert others to his beliefs and hoped to obtain a teaching position at the Lyceum to teach foreign languages, but the authorities, remembering the applicant's poor behavior as a student, turned him down. Thus, he began to spread his ideas informally by turning his home into a kind of *salon*. During a period of about four years, more than 250 people, including the writers Feodor Dostoyevsky[32] and Mikhail Saltykov-Shchedrin, attended these Friday sessions to discuss religion, philosophy and literature and important social problems. But the *Petrashevtsy*,[33] as they came to be called, with few exceptions, were not particularly radical nor were they much interested in the problems of Russia's few factory workers. Many were simply lonely young men, alone in the capital, who wanted companionship and enjoyed the food and drink provided by the host. To be sure, they hated autocracy and serfdom and longed for an end to censorship and certain judicial reforms such as trial by jury, but most had no plans to use force to achieve their ends.

One notable exception to this was Nikolai Speshnev[34] who was heir to a huge estate with 500 serfs. Like Petrashevsky, he was educated at Tsarskoe Selo and later spent much time traveling in western Europe. In 1845, he began to study early Christianity to understand its influence and economic success as a secret society. He concluded that Russia's political transformation could be effected by a similar organization. He also became enthralled with socialism and soon began to write articles about the current situation in Russia for the Paris-based *Revue Independante.* Speshnev returned to Russia in 1847 because of lack of money and took up residence in St. Petersburg. Drawn, no doubt to Petrashevsky's lending library of banned books, he soon began to attend the Friday sessions where he impressed everyone with his knowledge of socialism, philosophy, and the revolutionary scene in western Europe. Yet Speshnev seemed to have been at odds with Petrashevsky on many issues, including the reluctance of most members to use violence to bring about social change. In time, he grew disillusioned with the lack of revolutionary ardor of most members and withdrew to a splinter group known as the Kashkin Circle. Oddly, he had grown close to the nonviolent Dostoyevsky with whom he worked to set up an illegal printing press.

In the final analysis, the *Petrashevtsy* posed little danger to Nicholas and probably would have been ignored had not Petrashevsky himself distributed a brochure about serfdom to the Petersburg provincial assembly of the nobility in February 1848. This caught the attention of Nicholas, who forbade any further discussion about this matter, and the Minister of the Interior, L.A. Perovsky, who had Petrashevsky's Friday gatherings infiltrated by one of his spies. Eager to emphasize his own importance, Perovsky was able to persuade the tsar that the Petrashevtsy were not only subversive, but preparing an attempt on his (Nicholas') life. On the night of April 22–23 (4–5 May), 1849, the police raided Petrashevsky's home and made several arrests. This led to a general roundup of more than two hundred suspects, although formal charges were made against only seventy-two. Of these, twenty-one were condemned to be executed by a firing squad and the others sent into exile — all for the crime of having taken part in a political discussion circle. Nicholas later decided to commute their sentences to Siberian exile. However, to teach them a lesson, he planned a mock execution. The condemned were marched into the Semenovsky

Square in St. Petersburg to the customary rolling of drums. There they were forced to kiss the cross, submit to having swords broken over their heads, and ordered to don white-hooded shrouds. All the while, a priest in his funeral chasuble stood nearby solemnly intoning prayers. When the first three were brought out and tied to stakes, the firing squad readied and took aim. Only then, at the last possible moment, were the commuted sentences announced.

By the beginning of 1851, however, after twenty-five years on the throne, Nicholas was tired and ailing. He had nearly died a few years earlier of an abdominal inflammation and was much concerned by the chronic bad health of his wife, Alexandra Feodorovna, with whom he had always been close. Nor could he be entirely at ease about the domestic situation in the country, with the problem of serfdom still unsolved. Of some solace perhaps were his accomplishments in foreign policy and diplomacy. Victories over Persia and Turkey in the late 1820s had allowed him to expand his empire and to build a fleet on the Caspian Sea. He had also gained the right for Russian merchant ships to navigate the Bosporus and Dardanelles and had forced the Turks to recognize Russia's annexation of Georgia and the Caucasus. He had fulfilled his self-appointed obligation as "gendarme of Europe" by facing down revolutionaries in 1830 and 1848 and, in so doing, believed that he had earned the good will and trust of other powers, particularly Austria and Great Britain. However, it was precisely this fatal miscalculation that helped bring his reign to a tragic end.

In 1851, Louis Napoleon[35] had begun to lobby the Porte in Constantinople to grant Roman Catholics more rights over religious shrines in the Holy Land. This was mainly a political move for domestic consumption, since Napoleon needed to curry favor with the Catholics in France in order to abolish French constitution, dismiss the parliament, and have himself proclaimed emperor. But Nicholas saw the French initiative in Turkey as a threat to his position as protector of all Orthodox believers. Thus, a quarrel developed between the two heads of state from which neither could back away. By February of 1853, the mood in St. Petersburg had become belligerent, and the tsar sent Prince Alexander Menshikov to Turkey to insist on a settlement that favored the Orthodox and recognized Russia's right to intervene on their behalf. The Turks naturally resisted this affront to their sovereignty, and, by October 1853, the two powers were at war.

The Russians would undoubtedly have prevailed if the conflict had stayed limited, but in March of 1854, Britain and France entered the war in support of Turkey.[36] Moreover, the Austrians, far from showing gratitude to Nicholas for his help in 1848, lent support to the allies, although they did not actually declare war. Thus, the tsar found himself diplomatically

Feodor Dostoyevsky was one of many young intellectuals who met at the home of Mikhail Buteshevich-Petrashevsky to discuss serfdom and other taboo subjects. For this crime, he and others were subjected to a mock execution and exiled to Siberia. V.G. Perov (1822–1882) Tretiakovsky Gallery, Moscow.

isolated. The main fighting was centered in the Crimean peninsula where the allies landed in September laying siege to the Russian port of Sevastopol. The defenders, struggling desperately, held out for eleven months despite their poor weaponry, outmoded tactics and lack of logistical support. Although Nicholas did not live to witness the bitter end (he died of influenza in March of 1855), he was probably aware of the extent to which his system had failed. It was left to his son and successor, Alexander II, to make peace. By the terms of the Treaty of Paris signed in 1856, Russia lost the mouth of the Danube and part of Bessarabia to Turkey. She was forced to accept the neutralization of the Black Sea and relinquish her claim to a protectorate over Orthodox Catholics in the Ottoman Empire.

The reigns of Alexander and Nicholas taken together represent a missed opportunity. Both men understood that the country suffered from a backward economy, weak finances, and a corrupt and inefficient bureaucracy. And, unlike their illustrious grandmother, Catherine the Great, both understood that serfdom was an evil that had to be abolished, and both gave serious thought as to how this might be done. However, believing as they did that autocracy was necessary for Russia's survival, neither was willing to ally himself with the honest and energetic men who were willing to sacrifice themselves in order to make Russia's transformation to a modern European state possible. Alexander had raised expectations with high-sounding phrases about the need for major reforms but ultimately did little. Nicholas not only promised far less, but sought to create a police state to terrorize his subjects into obedience. Thus, it fell to the next tsar, Alexander II, to deal with serfdom and other problems, although he, too, shied from fundamentally changing the system that had so stunted the country's development. His timidity in this regard bitterly disappointed a new kind of revolutionary, who eventually became convinced that only by terror and destruction could they hope to save Russia.

Selected Bibliography

One of the more useful biographies on the "enigmatic tsar" is *Alexander I: Paternalistic Reformer* by Allen McConnell. Also of interest is Henri Troyat's *Alexander of Russia — Napoleon's Conqueror.* Bruce Lincoln's *Nicholas I* offers an excellent description of the Decembrist Revolt and the suppression of the Petrashevtsy, and analyzes the reactionary policies that so characterized the reign of Nicholas I. Other good sources for the Decembrists and Petrashevtsy are *The Shadow of the Winter Palace* by Edward Crankshaw and *Road to Revolution* by Avrahm Yarmolinsky. Information about Tsar Alexander's project to create military colonies can be found in Michael Jenkins' *Arakchaev-Grand Vizier of the Russian Empire.*

Christian, David. "Speransky, Mikhail Mikhailovich." *Modern Encyclopedia of Russian and Soviet History,* ed. Joseph L. Wieczynski, 54 vols. With suppl. Gulf Breeze, Florida: Academic International Press, 1976–1990.

Cowles, Virginia. *The Romanovs.* Middlesex, England: Penguin, 1971.

Crankshaft, Edward. *The Shadow of the Winter Palace.* Middlesex, England: Penguin, 1976.

Evans, John L. "Petrashevtsy." *Modern Encyclopedia of Russian and Soviet History,* ed. Joseph L. Wieczynski, 54 vols. With suppl. Gulf Breeze, Florida: Academic International Press, 1976–1990.

Hingley, Ronald. *The Tsars 1533–1917.* New York: MacMillan, 1968.

Lincoln, Bruce. *Nicholas I.* DeKalb, Illinois: Northern University Press, 1978.

_____. "Nicholas I (Nikolai Pavlovich)." *Modern Encyclopedia of Russian and Soviet History,* ed. Joseph L. Wieczynski, 54 vols. With suppl. Gulf Breeze, Florida: Academic International Press, 1976–1990.

McConnell, Allen. *Alexander I: Paternalistic Reformer.* Thomas Y. Crowell Company, New York, 1970.

McConnell, Allen. "Alexander I (Alexander Pavlovich)." *Modern Encyclopedia of Russian and Soviet History,* ed. Joseph L. Wieczynski, 54 vols. With suppl. Gulf Breeze, Florida: Academic International Press, 1976–1990.

Nekina, M.V. "Decembrists' Uprising of 1825." *Modern Encyclopedia of Russian and Soviet History,* ed. Joseph L. Wieczynski, 54 vols. With suppl. Gulf Breeze, Florida: Academic International Press, 1976–1990.

O'Meara, Patrick J. "Pestel' Pavel Ivanovich." *Modern Encyclopedia of Russian and Soviet History,* ed. Joseph L. Wieczynski, 54 vols. With suppl. Gulf Breeze, Florida: Academic International Press, 1976–1990.

_____. "Ryleev, Kondratii Fedorovich." *Modern Encyclopedia of Russian and Soviet History,* ed. Joseph L. Wieczynski, 54 vols. With suppl. Gulf Breeze, Florida: Academic International Press, 1976–1990.

Payne, Robert. *The Fortress.* New York: Simon and Shuster, 1957.

Schlafly, Daniel L. "Arakcheev, "Aleksei Andreevich." *Modern Encyclopedia of Russian and Soviet History,* ed. Joseph L. Wieczynski, 54 vols. With suppl. Gulf Breeze, Florida: Academic International Press, 1976–1990.

Schweizer, Karl W. "Kutuzov, Mikhail Illarionovich." *Modern Encyclopedia of Russian and Soviet History,* ed. Joseph L. Wieczynski, 54 vols. With suppl. Gulf Breeze, Florida: Academic International Press, 1976–1990.

Warnes, David. *Chronicle of the Russian Tsars.* London: Thames and Hudson, 1999.

Yarmolinsky, Avrahm. *Road to Revolution.* Princeton: Princeton University Press, 1957.

9. Nihilists, Nechaev, and the People's Will

The death of Nicholas I led to an outpouring of joy and a sense of relief not seen since the assassination of Tsar Paul, fifty-four years earlier. Among those who rejoiced was Alexander Herzen,[1] an influential *émigré* journalist, publicist, and political thinker who had left Russia in 1847 and settled in London. As a young man, he had been twice punished by the tsar's police for minor transgressions: in 1834, for having been a part of a university discussion group that the authorities had deemed too political (for which he served four years in jail), and again in 1840, for having criticized the local police in a letter to his father. In the latter instance, he was charged with "spreading false and harmful rumors" and exiled to Novgorod for one year to work as a clerk. During this period, Herzen's bitterness about the essential injustice of the Russian system drove him nearly to despair. Renouncing all religion, he embraced agrarian socialism as the hope of the future. He also became fascinated by the philosophy of Hegel[2] in which he saw "the algebra of revolution."

In London, Herzen established a publishing house, The Free Russian Press, and exhorted the gentry back home to liberate their serfs. Failure to do this, he warned, would lead either to their emancipation by the tsar (which would strengthen his autocracy) or to a massive peasant uprising, which would result in a horrible bloodbath. So many other dissidents were attracted by his eloquence and logic that Herzen's home soon became a meeting place for other *émigrés*, whom he was able to help by publishing their articles, offering advice and, in some cases, providing financial assistance. Despite his success as a publicist and a writer and his relatively comfortable existence, Herzen was never at ease in the West. He was offended by the shallow materialism of Europe's middle class and dismayed by the economic and social side effects of industrialization, and he saw nothing to admire in parliamentary democracy, which seemed to serve only the interests of the propertied classes. Instead, Herzen placed his trust in the Russian peasants, who, living cooperatively on their *mir*, or commune, could teach the West how to create a higher, freer civilization. Thus, he longed for the day when Russia would be liberated from autocracy and serfdom so that a federation of peasant communes could come into being. This was the only way that a true democracy based on social and economic justice could be achieved and the evils of industrialization avoided.

With the accession of Alexander II to the throne, Herzen dared to hope that a different kind of man now resided in the Winter Palace. This prompted the publication of a new periodical, the *Polar Star*, the purpose of which was to propagate free ideas in Russia. The first edition appeared on July 13 (25), 1855, on the anniversary of the execution of the five Decembrists and featured their profiles on the cover. Herzen also began to write a series of public letters to the new tsar in which he spoke hopefully about a "revolution from above." He implored Alexander to abolish serfdom, provide land for the peasants, and grant freedom of speech to the people. The following year, Herzen and his friend Nikolai Ogarev[3] decided to create yet another shorter, more frequently issued journal *The Bell*. Named after the Assembly Bell of medieval Novgorod that once summoned free men to meetings in the town square, it eventually became a bi-weekly publication. Despite the fact that it had to be smuggled into Russia, by 1860, it had a circulation of about 3000, although the number of people who read it must have been at least ten times higher. So credible was *The Bell* thought to be in reflecting the realities of Russian life that many government officials and possibly the tsar himself were among its regular readers.

Indeed, Herzen's optimism with regard to the new tsar was not entirely unjustified. Alexander II was far more humane and intelligent than his father and seemed eager to create an atmosphere of good will. He lifted restrictions on the number of university students, eased censorship, made it easier to travel abroad, and gave amnesty to many political prisoners including the remaining Decembrists and most of the *Petrashevsty*. And although he was a conservative at heart who believed, as did his predecessors, that autocracy was necessary for Russia's survival, he was also realistic: Russia needed to develop economically and to reform militarily, and these would be impeded as long as serfdom remained in place. Alexander was convinced that serfdom was an unmitigated moral evil and a relic of the country's barbaric past that had no place in modern Europe. It had to be abolished as soon as possible, but in a way that would cause minimal domestic unrest. This meant, among other things, that the serfs would have to receive land, but whose land? How much? And how to pay for it? These were questions that he referred to a secret government committee in 1856. He also urged provincial assemblies and the nobility to offer their own suggestions on the topic. In 1859, an Editorial Commission was formed to sort out the many proposals and to compose the Act of Emancipation. When it was finally signed by Alexander on February 19 (3 March), 1861, twenty-two million serfs who had been the property of some one-hundred thousand landowning nobles received their freedom.

The immediate reaction to this epochal proclamation was euphoria, and the tsar was acclaimed as the "Great Liberator." Unfortunately, this mood was not to last. Once people began to sift through the details of the statute, they realized that it was not what most had expected. The nobles, many of whom had never favored emancipation anyway, were dismayed by their reduced political and economic power and had great difficulty adjusting to the new conditions. Even more dissatisfied were the peasants, who were allotted less land than they had previously farmed and who now were expected to compensate the nobles at inflated prices. Also, the peasants could not be considered entirely free, since they were still tied to their peasant commune, which was assigned the task of making land allotments, limiting their movement, and collecting redemption payments and taxes. Believing they were being cheated by those nobles who were trying to thwart the tsar's wishes, many refused to sign agreements with their former landlords, render services, or pay dues. As violence erupted in various parts of the country, the government resorted to force. In the town of Bezdna near Kazan, a former serf named Anton Petrov read the complex Act of Emancipation, which few other peasants could understand, and announced that it was a fraud perpetrated by the landowners. He claimed to have been in contact with the tsar and promised that the real statute would soon be delivered. In the meantime, he urged his fellow peasants to refuse to pay quitrent and to take over all the land. Soldiers were sent to arrest him, but he was protected by some 5,000 supporters, who refused to hand him over. In the violence that ensued, sixty-one died and 112 were wounded. Petrov himself was captured and executed.

Within three months of the Emancipation Edict, Herzen published an article in *The Bell* entitled "An Analysis of the New Serfdom" in which he announced that the people had been deceived by the tsar. His indignation was echoed by other younger radicals, including Nikolai Chernyshevsky[4] and Nikolai Dobroliubov, both of whom were important contributors to the St. Petersburg-based literary journal *The Contemporary*. Chernyshevsky and Dobroliubov differed from Herzen, however, since they believed that violence was an acceptable means of achieving their ends. Moreover, unlike the high-born activists and dreamers of an earlier era, these *raznochintsy*[5] had no faith in the tsar's good intentions. At first, they had refrained from commenting on the statute, but in March 1861 they registered their disapproval by publishing a translation of Longfellow's *Poems on Slavery* accompanied by an article about the condition of slaves in America. In fact, many of these younger activists were glad that the new law had antagonized nearly everyone and hoped the current unrest could be exploited to promote revolution.

This is very nearly what happened. Throughout the spring and summer of 1861, the disturbances in the countryside not only continued but spread to the villages and the universities. The students in St. Petersburg and other cities became so agitated during the months following emancipation that the school authorities issued a new statute reducing the number of scholarships and forbidding students from holding meetings. This led to more protests the following fall and the closing of the University of St. Petersburg for an entire year. Tension further increased in 1862 when a series of fires of unknown origin broke out in the capital and in towns along the Volga, and a number of new radical publications appeared attacking the Emancipation Edict. The most radical of these was *Young Russia*, or *Molodaya Rossiya*. Its author, Piotr Zaichnevsky,[6] rejected all proposals for reform and called for violent revolution. Predictably, the government's response was to arrest anyone who seemed even remotely involved in the unrest. Among these was Chernyshevsky and a former tsarist official named Nikolai Serno-Solovievich, who had created a short-lived revolutionary organization called 'Land and Liberty,' by which he hoped to completely undo the old feudal order in Russia.

The tsar was also distracted by unrest in Poland in 1863 when rebels, hoping to gain independence and promote certain social reforms, mounted a series of attacks on Russian occupation troops. This was the beginning of a rebellion that eventually spread to Lithuania, parts of Belorussia, and the right bank of Ukraine. It took nearly fifteen months to suppress the rebels, who were aided by a fair number of Russian radicals, some of them high-ranking officers. The operation entailed such brutality that Russia suffered greatly in the court of European opinion. In Britain and France, strikes were organized in support of the Poles, and Karl Marx and Friedrich Engels championed their cause at the First International. None of this, however, prevented Alexander from depriving the Poles of their autonomy and imposing Russification on them with new vigor. The only positive result for the rebels was that the social and economic reforms they had enacted during the rebellion were subsequently recognized by the tsar.

It is to Alexander's credit that the difficulties encountered during the early 1860s did not weaken his resolve with regard to emancipation and other kinds of reform. When conflicts and problems emerged that seemed intractable, the tsar appointed peace mediators to work them out. He also authorized a number of additional initiatives and reforms over the next few years. These included more autonomy for the universities, new educational opportunities for women, and a lessening of censorship. In 1864, he agreed to a complete overhaul of the judicial system by which equality before the law was proclaimed for all Russians, the abolition of secret interrogation, and the introduction of trial by jury. That same year, institutions of local self-government, or *zemstvos*, were created, whose elected members were to deal with education, welfare, health, communications, road repair, and the collection of state and local taxes.

All of this should been welcomed by the more progressive thinkers among the citizenry, but public support was far from overwhelming. Indeed, many radical students embraced a new intellectual movement called nihilism, a term coined by Ivan Turgenev[7] in his novel *Fathers and Sons*, published in 1862. The author applied it to those who flaunted their contempt for everything polite society held dear. The nihilists, convinced of their own superior intelligence and morality, rejected the authority of the state, the Church, and the family. They paraded about in blue-tinted glasses, preached free love, denied the existence of anything spiritual, and proclaimed their faith in scientific materialism. They also demanded utilitarianism in the arts and circulated pamphlets calling for the tsar's assassination.

Although most people were repulsed by the nihilists' message of negation, one man was inspired to act. On April 4 (16), 1866, a deranged student named Dmitri Karakazov fired a shot at the tsar as he was leaving the Summer Garden in St. Petersburg. He missed, but his attempt marked a turning point both in the rule of Alexander II and in the revolutionary movement in Russia. The would-be assassin was descended from a family of poor landowners near Saratov on the Volga. He had no great intelligence or ability and had been expelled from the universities of Kazan and Moscow. Later, he worked as a clerk for a rich nobleman and apparently so hated the experience that he became involved with a gang of terrorists called "Hell."[8] Although the very purpose of this group was to kill state officials, Karakazov stunned everyone when he declared his intention to go to St. Petersburg and assassinate Alexander II. To explain his motives, he composed an address to the workers in which he denounced "the nobility in their idleness and the swarms of wealthy officials and other privileged people living in glittering houses."[9] Most of all, he blamed the tsar for supporting the system of exploitation that brought misery to the people.

Having fired his shot, Karakozov was quickly apprehended and incarcerated in the Peter and Paul Fortress. His attempt to conceal his identity was foiled when the proprietor of the hotel where he was staying went to the police to report one of his tenants missing. Far more significant, however, was what a search of his room revealed: the Moscow address of his cousin, Nikolai Ishutin,[10] who was a prominent member of "Hell." This led to the arrest of some fifty other suspects, although only the eleven deemed most guilty had to stand trial. All were sentenced to imprisonment and exile except Karakozov, who was to be hanged. Some liberal officials, hoping to save the young man, persuaded him to write to the tsar expressing contrition for his crime. Indeed, Karakozov did write a letter but did not directly ask for mercy. He merely swore that he would not have acted as he did had he not been in anguish about the impoverished state of the Russian people. In any case, Alexander was not impressed. Later when his Minister of Justice urged him to grant the prisoner clemency, the tsar replied, "As a Christian I have long forgiven him in my heart, but as a sovereign I do not believe I have a right to pardon him."[11] Thus, Karakozov was executed in accordance with his sentence.

The aftermath of this unhappy affair brought on a period of personal malaise that seemed to accentuate the tsar's worse qualities. Depressed and disillusioned by the absence of gratitude for his reforms, he became further distracted by personal problems. The situation began with the death of his beloved twenty-one-year-old son and heir, Nikolai Alexandrovich, who had succumbed to tubercular meningitis in 1865. Overwhelmed with grief, Alexander began to experience mood swings that alternated between the deepest depression and spasms of uncontrollable rage. The following year, he acquired a teenage mistress named Katya Dolgorukaya, who was the daughter of a nobleman and a student at the Smolny Institute. The girl was actually the tsar's ward, since her father, having died in 1860, had left the family deeply in debt. Alexander agreed to pay the creditors and to see to her education, but soon he fell madly in love. The scandal was not merely in the fact that she was thirty years younger than he, but also in the timing, which could not have been worse. The empress, Maria Alexandrovna, still mourning the death of her son, could not bear the humiliation and withdrew into her own private world of piety and good works.[12] Moreover, the heir to the throne, Alexander Alexandrovich, thoroughly appalled by his father's behavior, began to listen to those who opposed his policies. These included his former tutor, the arch-reactionary Konstantine Pobedonostsev.

The next few years brought a fair amount of reaction that disheartened many of the tsar's supporters. The new minister of education, Count Dmitri Tolstoy, imposed a clamp-down on the schools and sought to discourage political and social activism by increasing the emphasis on classical languages in the curriculum. Alexander appointed another aristocrat to head the Third Department, Piotr Shuvalov, who quickly acted to limit freedom of the press, curtail the taxation powers of the *zemstvos,* and undermine regular judicial procedure during important court cases. Still, the spirit of reform was not entirely snuffed out. In 1870, important changes were introduced in municipal government, and, four years later, there was an overhaul of the military that featured the introduction of universal military service with a system of education for all soldiers. Problems involving inequality and abuse were also addressed, and the number of years a conscript was to serve was reduced from fifteen to six.

Alexander was also active in matters of diplomacy and foreign policy. In 1871, he agreed to the formation of the new Prussia-dominated state of Germany, never suspecting how this would affect Russia's security in the next century. In any case, this allowed him to repudiate the Peace of Paris of 1856, which forbade a Russian military presence on the Black Sea. He also joined the Three Emperors' League in 1873, which obligated Russia, Germany, and Austria to come to the defense of one another in the event of an attack by another European power. (Formed in 1873 with Russia, Germany and Austria-Hungary, the league provided a solid front against Great Britain in 1883 when the latter threatened war in Afghanistan.) This was no idle concern, since Russian territorial expansion to the south and east beginning in the late 1850s engendered suspicion and concern in many countries, especially Great Britain. These gains included a region just north of the Caucasus and some new lands along the northern banks of the Amur River. The latter acquisition permitted the founding of the important cities of Kharbarovsk in 1858 and Vladivostok in 1860. Finally, in the years between 1865 and 1876, vast territories were absorbed in Central Asia, including the khanates of Kokland, Bokhara, and Kiva and the Transcaspian region. Ironically, the tsar did not personally favor the acquisition of new territories, since he was wary of antagonizing other powers. Still, he found it difficult to object when military commanders, acting on their own, presented him with potentially valuable trophies.

Alexander was also uncomfortable with the public's growing enthusiasm for the Pan-Slav movement, which called on Russia to protect other oppressed Slavic peoples in the Balkans. In 1876, thousands of Russians volunteered to fight in the Serbian army when the Turks savagely suppressed rebellions against their rule. The tsar personally felt little sympathy for the Slav cause but was unable to resist the public pressure for supporting them. As the conflict intensified and the Turks gained the upper hand, Alexander was pressured by Pan-Slav enthusiasts to authorize a declaration of war on the Porte in April, 1877. The fighting that followed was bitter and costly, but the Russians ultimately prevailed despite shocking incompetence in the conduct of the war. Moreover, the advantageous peace that had been won by the Treaty of San Stefano had to be renegotiated that summer in Berlin at the insistence of Austria and Great Britain. The end result did allow some modest Russian gains in the Caucasus, but the subsequent redistribution of territories in the Balkans was not at all what the tsar had intended.

In the meantime, as Russia's economic and social problems continued to fester, the number of radicals determined to address them grew. Among these were two medical students, Mark Natanson[13] and Vasily Alexandrov, who, in the spring of 1869, organized a discussion group in St. Petersburg to explore ways to improve the country morally and socially. The members of this circle believed that only the masses could effect meaningful change in the country. Thus, they stressed the value of self-education and dedicated themselves to discovering the "truth" about conditions in Russia. Having established a communal residence, in part to save money, they debated among themselves the merit of various theories and ideologies as they looked for ways to expand their activism. They also collected books, many of them forbidden, on economic conditions, philosophy, and other pertinent subjects. The following year, such "circles of self-education" appeared in other cities.

Eventually, the Natanson-Alexandrov commune merged with a women's group led by Sophia Perovskaya[14] and subsequently became officially known as the Tschaikovsky Circle.[15] Some of the members were intent on agitating among the workers. Natanson tried to discourage this kind of activity, but his arrest in October 1871 for disseminating illegal literature temporarily ended his influence. In any case, there were many in the student movement, who, from the outset, had favored more confrontational tactics. One of these was a twenty-year-old named Sergei Gennadievich Nechaev, the son of an innkeeper from the factory town of Ivanovo, east of Moscow, who in 1867 had been hired to teach religion at a grammar school in St. Petersburg. Small and slightly-built, he was not an attractive or imposing man, but he was soon to become one of fiercest revolutionary fanatics in Russian history. His comrades would not only be mesmerized by his utter devotion to the cause but would also come to fear him. Even the tsar would soon know his name and worry about his influence.

Unlike many others who became involved in the movement, Nechaev was not much of an academic. Having graduated from his local school in 1865, he had some difficulty obtaining a teaching certificate after studying both in Moscow and St. Petersburg. Nor did he acquit himself well on the job: he failed to motivate the students, was often absent from class, and was known to get drunk and carouse with "suspicious" people. The school janitor was so offended by his behavior that he lodged an official complaint with the school authorities in January of 1869. The matter was dropped, however, when the accuser showed up at the hearing inebriated.

By this time, Nechaev was now fully absorbed in radical politics. He had been auditing classes for some months at the University of St. Petersburg and had become acquainted with Piotr Tkachev,[16] an important revolutionary theorist and writer, whose ideas were notoriously extreme. He once wrote about the need to liquidate everyone over twenty-five in order to prepare society for the coming revolution. But as much as most were repelled by such lunacy, Nechaev was inspired. Early in 1869, the two collaborated on a tract entitled *Program of Revolutionary Activities,* which called for the creation of revolutionary circles in university cities throughout the country. The two envisioned that the movement would spread to urban centers and eventually to the peasants who would finally understand how the emancipation edict had cheated them. Their goal was to incite a general rebellion on the ninth anniversary of the emancipation statute, February 19, 1870. Subsequently, Nechaev and Tkachev wrote a proclamation about the recent student troubles entitled *To Society.* They declared the essential rightness of their cause and the unanimity of the movement and promised "to die in exile or in dungeons rather than to stifle morally in our decadent colleges and universities."[17] In fact, Nechaev seems to have anticipated his own end with stunning accuracy.

Although Nechaev's intensity and devotion to the cause won admirers, his growing ambition and determination to lead the movement also made enemies. People were particularly put off by his lying. For example, having claimed that he hadn't learned to read until the age of sixteen, he pretended to quote from Immanuel Kant's *Critique of Pure Reason,* never having read the book. At first people were amazed but eventually most saw through the deception. Thus at some point in early February, Nechaev, having sensed that he was losing his hold on those who had previously seemed to admire him, changed his tactics. He began to talk about going to America, sold his belongings and disappeared. No sooner was he missed than Vera Zasulich,[18] a woman who herself would one day be acclaimed as a hero of the revolutionary movement, received an anonymous letter. The sender, whoever he or she was, claimed to have been walking along the street in St. Petersburg when a prison cart passed. Someone inside had thrown out a wrapped paper instructing that it be delivered to the addressee. Inside was another note in Nechaev's handwriting, which read:

> They are taking me to the Fortress. Do not lose heart, beloved comrades. Continue to have faith in me, and let us hope we meet again.[19]

Zasulich and others made inquiries with the police, who denied having arrested anyone named Nechaev. In the confusion that followed, no one seemed to have guessed that it was all a trick. Nechaev apparently foresaw that this little prank would enhance his reputation as a revolutionary and that his comrades would conclude that the police had lied about not having arrested him.

In the meantime, Nechaev was on his way to Moscow to get a fake passport. From there, he went to Odessa and finally to Switzerland to contact the exile community. In Geneva, he was immediately accepted by the famous anarchist, Mikhail Bakunin,[20] and Nikolai Ogarev, who had been Herzen's collaborator in London. At fifty-five, Bakunin was in poor health and deeply discouraged about the future of the revolutionary movement. He quickly became rejuvenated, however, when Nechaev described his daring, albeit fictitious, escape from the Peter and Paul Fortress and then told stories of widespread peasant rebellions in Russia. He also spoke of a revolutionary committee that was poised for a great upheaval in the near future. All that was needed was a little money. Ogarev, now a hopeless alcoholic and suffering from epilepsy, was captivated by Nechaev's performance. He wrote to Herzen, inviting him to come to Geneva to behold this vigorous young man of action and asking him to turn over a sum of money, 20,000 francs, that had been left to Herzen and Ogarev some years earlier by a mysterious eccentric named Bakhmatiev.[21] Herzen made the trip, met Nechaev, and was thoroughly appalled by his "bloodthirsty inclinations." He tried to talk sense to Ogarev, but the latter was hopelessly convinced that his new friend was the hero they had all been waiting for. Herzen soon left Geneva in disgust and died six months later in Paris. However, before he died, he gave in to Ogarev's continuing pleas and sent half the amount requested. Most of it was promptly turned over to Nechaev.

Yet Nechaev was interested in much more than money. He wanted credentials to bolster his reputation at home. Ogarev obliged by writing a poem entitled *The Student* in three verses, the first of which reads as follows:

To my young friend Nechaev

He was born to a wretched fate,
And was taught in a hard school,
And suffered interminable torments
In years of unceasing labor.
But as the years swept by
His love for the people grew stronger,
And fiercer his thirst for the common good,
The thirst to improve man's fate.[22]

This is hardly great poetry in any language, but it is remarkable for the way it emphasizes Nechaev's high moral purpose. To be sure, the former religion teacher was an unusually resourceful and ruthless revolutionary, but it is not known to what extent he cared about "the people" or thirsted "to improve man's fate." Still, he was prepared to use any means necessary to destroy the state, although, like so many other radicals, he had no clearly thought-out vision of a more humane future. In any case, having exploited Ogarev for what he could give, he persuaded Bakunin to forge a certificate that identified him (i.e., Nechaev) as one of the "accredited representatives of the Russian Section of the World Revolutionary Alliance." The document was affixed with a seal bearing the words "European Revolutionary Alliance, Central Committee" and was signed by Bakunin. Neither organization had ever existed.

Nechaev also polished his writing skills that summer. Aided at times by Bakunin, he wrote a number of manifestoes and pamphlets, including two articles for a periodical, *The People's Vengeance (Narodnaya Rasprava),* a tract entitled *Principles of Revolution,* and *The Revolutionary Catechism.* The last of these is the most interesting because it clearly reflects the author's utter ruthlessness. It is divided into four sections and contains a total of twenty-six articles. Among other things, Nechaev asserts that the revolutionary "knows only one science, the science of destruction." For him, morality is everything that promotes revolution, and immorality is everything that impedes it. Furthermore, the true revolutionary not only excludes all romanticism and sensitivity but also "private vendettas and personal hatred." This last tenet is significant because it is one that Nechaev himself would not honor.[23]

On September 3, Nechaev returned to Moscow after six months abroad and moved in with a fellow revolutionary activist, Piotr Uspensky. He assumed one of many aliases and set about recruiting members (none of whom were supposed to know Nechaev's real identity) for a revolutionary cell, which he called The People's Vengeance (so named after his journal), that would be part of the fictitious World Revolutionary Alliance.

It was to be supervised by a secret committee, which also didn't exist since Nechaev was its only member. Soon there were other cells operating in the Moscow area, which held biweekly meetings to discuss the revolutionary pamphlets produced by Nechaev and Bakunin over the summer as well as tactics for the struggle to come. They also raised money among the well-to-do by persuasion, physical intimidation, and/or blackmail. The goal of The People's Vengeance was threefold: to create a vast network of cells throughout European Russia, to infiltrate the Tula Arms Factory, and to prepare for a massive uprising that was to occur in the spring.

Nechaev worked especially closely with four within his own cell: Nikolai Nikolaev, a devoted follower whom he had known since child-hood, Ivan Ivanov, a student in the Petrovsky Agricultural Academy, Ivan Pryzhov,[24] the son of a retired soldier, and Alexei Kuznetsov, the scion of a merchant family. Each was given a specific area of focus; Nikolaev was to work among the peasants, Ivanov among the students, Pryzhov among the underworld (i.e., criminals, drunkards and prostitutes), and Kuznetsov among the merchant class. For a while, things went fairly well; new members were recruited, some money was raised, and the members for the most part worked harmoniously under Nechaev's leadership. Preserving his incognito, he liked to occasionally talk about the man in Ogarev's poem, who was rumored to have died in Siberia, and hint that he might still be alive. Although some of his comrades must have seen through the decep-tion, none dared to confront him or question his veracity or judgment in any way. Then on November 4, Nechaev ordered Ivan Ivanov to post some revolutionary leaflets around the dining hall and library of the Agricul-tural Academy. To the astonishment of everyone, the latter refused, declar-ing bluntly that such an action would be stupid, since it would only lead to a police crackdown and the arrest of innocent students. Furious, Nechaev demanded that Ivanov follow orders, but the latter held firm. From this moment on, the former religion teacher was determined have his revenge.

The next day, Nechaev disappeared and was not seen again for two weeks. It is possible that he went to Tula, but this is not certain. In any case, when he returned, he announced to Pryzhov, Nikolaev, Kuznetsov and Piotr Uspensky that Ivanov had become an informer and had to be eliminated. He proposed that they lure him to the Petrovsky Park near the Agricultural Academy on the pretext that a printing press had been found in an artificial grotto located on the grounds, which they were all to help retrieve. He then ordered Nikolaev to procure a pistol and a knife for what he really had in mind. None of the others believed, as they were later to claim, that Ivanov had done anything to deserve the death penalty, but neither did they contradict Nechaev, who clearly had personal reasons for acting as he did.

The park, which was situated to the northwest of Moscow, had previously been the site of a large 18th century palace built by the Empress Elizabeth's lover, Prince Razumovsky. Nearby there were some small chalets owned by wealthy nobles and a number of large gardens. Many years later, the government bought the land, tore down the palace, and offered it to Moscow State University. In 1865, university officials decided to make use of the gardens by building the Agricultural Academy. It was to this beautiful, snow-covered setting on the evening of November 21 (December 4), 1869, that Ivan Ivanov came, accompanied by Nikolaev and Pryzhov, to meet his doom.

Nechaev, Kuznetsov, and Piotr Uspensky were waiting when the victim arrived. The group entered the grotto, which was pitch-dark. Only Kuznetzov remained outside, presumably to stand guard. Once inside, Nechaev attacked Nikolaev, mistaking him for Ivanov, and seized him by the throat. The latter cried out, "Not me! I'm Nikolaev!"[25] and pulled away. This was followed by a free-for-all with grunts, cursing, and scuffling about. Ivanov, realizing that he was in mortal danger, broke free. He made it out of the grotto only to be caught and forced to the ground. Nechaev then pounced on his victim and tried to strangle him. Ivanov fended him off by biting deeply into his assailant's thumb. The murder was finally accomplished with Nikolaev working the throat, Nechaev sitting on his chest, and Kuznetsov his legs. To ensure the victim was dead, Nechaev shot the corpse in the head and then searched his pockets. Oddly, he took everything except a watch and a library card that had been issued to Kuznetsov. The body was then weighed down with bricks and forced under the thin ice covering a nearby pond. The assassins retired to Kuznetsov's apartment to collect themselves, get rid of Ivanov's belongings, and to change their clothes.

The police found the body four days later. The library card quickly led to the roundup of everyone involved or suspected except Nechaev. Somehow he had managed to flee the country, traveling first to Geneva and then Locarno to renew his relationship with Ogarev and Bakunin. The latter was especially glad to see him, since he was in serious difficulty. It seems the old anarchist, desperate for money, had accepted an advance from a Russian publisher to translate Karl Marx's *Das Kapital*, but, having spent the money, he was unable to finish the job, and the publisher was now demanding to be repaid. Nechaev promptly wrote the man a letter ordering him to stop bothering Bakunin or face punishment by the now non-existent organization The People's Vengeance. The bluff worked.

Once again, Nechaev's dynamic presence proved a tonic for the two older revolutionaries. Ogarev wrote to Herzen's brother and managed to secure the other half of the Bakhmatiev fund. The three also began to produce more revolutionary literature, and an attempt was made to renew publication of *The Bell,* although the endeavor collapsed after six issues. Herzen's daughter, Natasha, known to most as Tata, soon joined the group and seemed attracted to Nechaev. He, too, was interested in this young woman who had recently inherited much of her father's estate. For a while, a romance seemed to be in the making, but Nechaev's crude and abusive manner disenchanted her. Then, as the money began to dry up, Bakunin himself became disillusioned with his younger comrade. Not only had the peasant revolt planned for February 19 (3 March), 1870, failed to materialize, but the sordid facts about Ivanov's murder were becoming known. In June he wrote Nechaev a letter chastising him not only for his lies and deceptions, but also for his rude treatment of Tata. He urged him to mend his ways, but it was too late. In Russia, the authorities had learned all about Nechaev's role in the murder and were demanding his extradition. Nechaev knew he would have to move on. That July, he saw Bakunin and Ogarev for the last time. They urged him to go to America, but he had other ideas. After stealing important personal documents from them, he went to London to join the First International. However, his collaboration with Bakunin offended Marx and resulted in his being rejected. With nothing to do in London, Nechaev soon left for Paris. By March 1871, he was back in Zurich with a Serbian passport and was working as a house painter.

In July, a trial was held for the murder of Ivanov and included eighty others known to be associated with Nechaev. The court was open to the public and reported on at length in the newspapers. People were generally appalled by the extent of the conspiracy and by the youth of the defendants. Oddly, the focus of the proceedings was less on the murder than on the one suspect who had escaped. As various documents were read aloud during the trial, including *The Revolutionary Catechism* and Ogarev's poem, Nechaev took on the aura of a demon. Even the tsar was filled with dread as he received daily reports about the testimony of the defendants. Who was this creature and what did he want? Had the fugitive been present to answer, he might have quoted from his own *Catechism:* "Our task is total, terrible, universal and merciless destruction."[26]

The trial lasted ten weeks and ended with the acquittal of all except those who had actually participated in the murder. The verdict, which brought imprisonment for most of the defendants, did not satisfy those who wanted to see the main culprit receive his due. But Nechaev was far more miserable in Switzerland than he would ever be in jail. He had no

place to live, no money, and, worst of all, no followers. He had been sub-
sisting for some time on the few francs he was able to earn by painting
signs. Later, he joined some anarchists in a small town in the Jura Mountains, La Chaux-de-Fonds, but was unable to impress people as he had
earlier. Meanwhile, agents for the Russian police were closing in. This was
obvious even to Bakunin, who, remarkably, bore no grudge and wrote his
former protégé urging him to leave the country for his own good, but
Nechaev sneered at his old friend's advice, dismissing it as that of a jeal-
ous man eager to be rid of a competitor.

By August of 1872, Nechaev, attempting to revive his own status as a
revolutionary, had moved to Zurich to make contact with some Polish radicals. One of them was a paid agent of the Russian police named Adolf
Stempkowsky, who had agreed to meet him at a restaurant to discuss a plan
to infiltrate and disrupt Bakunin's organization. When Stempkowsky made
a gesture as if to call for a waiter, two Swiss plainclothes detectives walked
up and grabbed Nechaev and took his revolver. The fugitive fiercely resisted
and managed to break free. He might have escaped altogether had some
Serbian and Russian students congregating in the vicinity decided to help
him, but Nechaev's star had fallen too far for them to care very much about
him now. Thus, within days, he was handed over to the Russian police on
the Bavarian border. By October, he was in St. Petersburg, incarcerated in
the Peter and Paul Fortress while the government decided what to do with
him.

Some officials thought it prudent to execute Nechaev in secret, but
the tsar was persuaded of the necessity of holding a trial if only to destroy
the prisoner's aura of mystery. The proceedings opened in Moscow, where
the murder had been committed, on January 8, and lasted two and one-
half weeks. The tightest possible security precautions were undertaken to
discourage any attempt at a rescue. Nechaev relished the attention and
made good use of his moment in the limelight. Time and time again, he
interrupted the proceedings with loud objections. At one point he shouted,
"I am an émigré! I do not recognize your emperor or your laws!"[27] When
he wasn't calling out, he was making faces, weaving his beard into braids
or pretending to play an invisible piano on the ledge in front of him. Twice
he was removed from the courtroom because of his behavior; on the second occasion, he was taken into a back room and beaten by police officers.

The verdict, of course, was never in doubt: Nechaev was found guilty
and sentenced to twenty years in Siberia. Predictably he reacted with
defiance, shouting, "Long live the *Zemsky Sobor!*" and "Down with despotism!"[28] as he was dragged from the courtroom. He later wrote a letter to
a tsarist official about the injustice of his situation, comparing himself to

Sergei Nechaev became a revolutionary legend in his own time because of his ruthlessness and dedication to the cause. After his arrest in Switzerland in 1872, he survived for nearly a decade in the cold and damp prison in the Peter and Paul Fortress. Courtesy Staatsarchiv, Zurich.

the Cossack rebels, Stenka Razin, and Yemelian Pugachev. He claimed his only crime was a desire to bring happiness and prosperity to the Russian people, and he refused to show any remorse for the murder of Ivanov, which he dismissed as a political crime. However, the government was still determined to humiliate him. Just before Nechaev was to leave for Siberia, he was subjected to the customary ceremony of public degradation that such prisoners usually undergo. And still he continued to flaunt his contempt for the tsar's justice. Standing alone and fettered under symbolic gallows, with the drums rolling and a priest reading a prayer, Nechaev shouted his defiance, "The guillotine will soon be standing where I am! It will lop off all your heads! Don't fear, in two or three years your turn will come!" As he was being dragged away to the train that was supposed to take him to Siberia, he continued, "Down with the tsar! Hurrah for freedom! Long live the Russian people!"[29]

Nechaev never went to Siberia mainly because it was feared that he would escape. Instead, the tsar had personally decided that he be secretly returned to St. Petersburg to spend the rest of his life in the Alexei Revelin of the Peter and Paul Fortress. The Revelin was quite possibly the most dreaded prison in the country and had driven many inmates insane. Completely surrounded by water, its filthy, dripping interior saw almost no sunlight. The air, heavy and damp, was deadly for anyone susceptible to asthma. The cells were miniscule, with only the barest furnishings: an iron bed and table, a toilet, a thin woolen blanket, and a kerosene lamp. Yet the prisoner needed to be kept alive if only to make him suffer; thus, Nechaev would be allowed some exercise and fed three times a day. However, he was to be denied all human contact and was never again to be addressed by name. Henceforth, he was to be known only as the prisoner in cell number five. Moreover, the black-uniformed guards were never to converse with him; they were to observe him carefully and write weekly reports for the tsar about his behavior and health. As it turned out, Nechaev was far more diligent in watching them than they him.

The situation was not wholly intolerable. Nechaev was allowed a wide range of reading and writing materials and managed to keep himself busy. However, this did not prevent him from being obstreperous when provoked. During his third year in the Fortress, the chief of the Corps of the Gendarmerie paid him a visit and offered him his freedom if he would tell all he knew about revolutionary activity in Russia and serve the Third Section as a spy. Nechaev, enraged, jumped to his feet and punched the general in the face hard enough to bloody his mouth and nose. Amazingly, he was not punished; in fact, the prison governor returned six months later to talk to him about what might be done about the increasing revolutionary activity in the country. This time the prisoner agreed to write a letter to the tsar, although the content was not what the authorities had hoped. Nechaev merely ranted about the unfairness of his treatment and demanded to be retried as a political prisoner, threatening that, if this were not done immediately, he would somehow get his revenge.

This time his defiance brought serious retaliation and a rapid deterioration in his conditions. Henceforth, he was to wear ankle *and* wrist fetters, which caused the skin in the affected areas to suppurate. Forced now to spend much of his time chained to the wall, Nechaev was to be denied all writing materials and only occasionally allowed to read. This new regime nearly brought him to his knees. He now suffered from fits of shivering and insomnia and could sometimes be heard singing melancholy songs at night in a pitiful voice. His suffering was acute, but he would not give up. On Palm Sunday of 1880, he tried to communicate with the tsar by carving a message into the wall of his cell with a broken teaspoon and highlighting it with his own blood. Complaining bitterly of being denied books and of treatment he thought was designed to drive him to madness, he ended his "letter" with these words: "I have the honor to inform Your Majesty that the Third Division of the Imperial Chancellery may deprive me of my mind only by depriving me of my life: not otherwise."[30]

This was no idle boast; Nechaev's guile and cunning had not deserted him. Over the years, he had managed to develop a certain rapport with the guards, some of whom had begun to sympathize with him. By the summer of 1880, they were smuggling in various kinds of printed matter, including a plan of the prison. In November, they helped him communicate with a newly arrived prisoner, Stepan Shiraev, who told him about a new terrorist group, The People's Will. When the newcomer told Nechaev how much he was admired by its members, the latter saw new hope. He soon conceived of a plan to take over the Fortress and sent a letter via one of the guards to a certain Grigori Isaev, who was a member of that organization's executive committee. The recipient was astonished to hear from the legendary rebel. It was as if Nechaev had come back from the dead.

For a while, a correspondence flourished between The People's Will and Nechaev in the fortress as the former actually considered an attempt to rescue him. Eventually, however, the group decided to go ahead with a previous plan to assassinate the tsar, which they accomplished on March 1 (13), 1881, in a manner subsequently to be described. A few weeks later, after the assassination, the governor of the prison, having learned that Nechaev had suborned the guards, clamped down hard on his living conditions. The prisoner's response was to write the new tsar a letter complaining about the injustice of his situation. This time, however, there was no official reaction, and Nechaev's health began to decline. Suffering now from dropsy and scurvy, and barely able to breathe in the foul-smelling dungeon, he became seriously ill. The prison doctor began feeding him lemons and milk to alleviate the scurvy, but the patient did not improve. His decline continued for more than a year until the afternoon of November 21 (December 4), 1882, when Nechaev was found lying dead in a corner of his cell. It was the twelfth anniversary of Ivanov's murder.

Nechaev's tenacity and defiance had amazed even those who hated him, although most involved in the fight against the autocracy wanted to avoid his ruthlessness and elitism. The majority of student activists inclined more toward the populism, or *narodnichestvo*, of Alexander Herzen and Piotr Lavrov.[31] Interest in and enthusiasm for the countryside and the people who worked the land had long been growing and reached its peak at the end of the 1860s. Possibly it was Bakunin who captured the spirit best in his essay, *A Few Words to My Younger Brothers,* when he implored them to "forsake this world that is doomed to destruction, these universities, academies and schools.... Get off to the people!"[32] This is exactly what happened in the early 1870s, and especially during the "mad summer" of 1874, when more than 2000 students went to the countryside. They sought to establish ties with the peasants to learn more about them, to help them understand the unfairness of their plight, and to rouse them to action. It began as a moral crusade with groups of young people dressed in peasant garb, marching into the countryside. Confident that they could make a difference, some went into rural areas singing the revolutionary chorus from the final scene of Modeste Mussorgsky's opera *Boris Godunov.* Others drew inspiration from Ilya Repin's painting "Haulers on the Volga" and went to live among the Volga boatmen.

Their reception, however, was far different from what they expected. The Russian peasants they encountered were generally "sly, suspicious, envious, venal, drunken," and wholly lacking in revolutionary potential. The locals cared nothing for the high-minded ideals the students sought to convey and themselves hoped one day to be able to exploit others as they had been exploited, nor did they appreciate anyone who criticized the tsar. Those who tried were jeered, stoned, beaten up, and/or reported to the police. Between the years 1873 and 1877, some 1,600 students were arrested, many of whom were forced to languish in jail for three or four years before going to trial. Amazingly, however, the very harshness of this ordeal inspired an ever-increasing spirit of self-sacrifice among the best and the brightest.

One of these was Yekaterina Breshko-Breshkovskaya,[33] who left her husband in 1873 to start a commune with her sister in Kiev. The commune flourished but was soon infiltrated by the police, who arrested many of its members. Later that year, Breshko-Breshkovskaya went to St. Petersburg to make contact with others in the movement and soon became a staunch proponent of revolution. Thus, as she prepared to "go to the people" in the summer of 1874, she dyed her hair gray and applied acid to her hands and face, apparently to make herself appear older and more authentic. Traveling south along the Dnieper, she delivered her message not only to peasants, but to factory workers and anyone else who had reason to be dissatisfied with the existing social order. Yet she made few converts and was eventually arrested in September, charged with carrying subversive literature. After spending nearly four years in the Peter and Paul Fortress waiting to be tried, Breshko-Breshkovskaya was convicted in 1878 and sentenced to a long term of hard labor. Amazingly, she survived the ordeal and continued her activism with such fervor that she eventually came to be known as "the grandmother of the revolution."

Another remarkable individual whose life changed as a result of the summer of 1874 was Dmitri Lizogub.[34] The scion of an extremely wealthy family in Chernigov Province, he enjoyed a life of luxury in his early youth. He studied for a time in France, and at a gymnasium at Yekaterinoslav before enrolling at the University of St. Petersburg at the age of twenty-one. Although his first love was mathematics, he was eventually drawn to the juridical faculty to study political economy. Lizogub read a number of utopian socialist thinkers, including Blanc, Owen, St. Simon, and Fourier, and was particularly affected by Bervi-Flerovsky's[35] study of the working class in Russia. Having now embraced the socialist cause, he made contact with members of the Tschaikovsky Circle as he prepared to "go to the people" in 1874. His experience that summer, however, was profoundly disturbing. Not only were the peasants hostile, but he and his fellow students were relentlessly harassed by the police and Russian officialdom. The ordeal so radicalized Lizogub that he resolved to endorse terror and devote his life and fortune to the cause. With his long beard, sad blue eyes, and personal asceticism, he soon became known as the "saint of the revolution." As a revolutionary, his main job was to finance subversive activities and avoid arrest. Nevertheless, over the course of the next few years, he was incarcerated no less than four times. The last of these occurred in Odessa in the fall of 1878, where he was accused of participating in a plot to kill the tsar. For this, he was convicted and sentenced to death, a fate which he accepted with complete composure.

However, the government's best efforts to stifle revolutionary activism only encouraged more of it. In January of 1875, two new revolutionary journals appeared. Published in Geneva by the followers of Bakunin, *The*

Vera Figner studied in Switzerland so she could become a doctor and serve the peasantry. Increasingly frustrated by the government's reactionary policies, she became a member of the terrorist organization, The People's Will. Yelena Segal, *Sophia Perovskaya*, Zhin' Zamechatel'nikh Lyudei, Molodaya Gvardiya, Moskva, 1962.

Worker (Rabotnik) was addressed to Russian proletarians and peasants to prepare them for violent revolution. The other was started by Piotr Lavrov in London and was called *Forward (Vpered)*; it was aimed at the promotion of socialist values by peaceful indoctrination. It encouraged only such activism that was in accordance with revolutionary morality and warned that violent revolution would invite a social cataclysm. A third journal appeared at the end of the year, *The Tocsin (Nabat)*. Its main contributor, Piotr Tkachev, living in Geneva, agreed with the Bakuninists about the need for decisive action. However, Tkachev, much like Lenin after him, had little faith in the masses. He favored a revolution brought about by an elite minority, not to destroy the state, but to take it over. Moreover, as a disciple of Auguste Blanqui,[36] he favored a regime that would impose a new order on the masses from above. Tkachev's ideas appalled Bakunin and Lavrov, but they had enormous influence on those who would later called themselves Bolsheviks.

For many radicals, the lack of unity among the various revolutionary factions was troubling. Among those determined to do something about it was a group of young women which included Vera Figner[37] and Sophia Bardina, who were studying medicine in Zurich. By the end of 1874, they were on their way back to Russia, having joined forces with some other like-minded students from Georgia.[38] They soon formed the Moscow Circle, the purpose of which was to unite all existing revolutionary groups in the country. To this end, they avoided commitment to any specific ideology or faction while insisting on total dedication and discipline. They urged their members to forsake all possessions and personal ties and to devote themselves entirely to spreading propaganda among the peasants and workers. In February 1875, they produced a constitution that sanctioned the use of force if scrupulously applied toward worthwhile ends. The group also assumed a new name, the All-Russian Social Revolutionary Organization, and soon succeeded in starting some cells among the urban proletariat. However, their carelessness about security led to a steady stream of arrests so that within months they were completely wiped out.

In the south, there were other groups which were far more radical but no more successful. One of these was the Southern Mutineers, or *Yuzhnye Buntari,* who were centered in Odessa. These rebels tried to incite peasants in Korsun near Kiev to seize the land from the landlords. To this end, they raised money for weapons, ammunition, and horses, and planned to forge a manifesto from the tsar calling for a peasant rebellion. However, at some point they were betrayed by one of their own and arrested. Another such group, working in the Chigrin district near Kiev, tried to exploit a feud between two groups of peasants, one prosperous and one poor. In the wake of the Emancipation Edict, the first had received more land than thought fair by the second, who now demanded an adjustment. Representatives from the poor peasants, called *dusheviks,* went to St. Petersburg to petition the tsar but were turned back by soldiers. However, convinced that the tsar really was on their side, the *dusheviks* refused to sign their official deeds as required by law or to make their allotment payments. Once again, the tsar's soldiers intervened, arresting about 100 and auctioning off the lands of those sent to jail, which left many families destitute. By May 1875, all resistance was ended.

This defeat led to a caper devised by a certain Yakov Stefanovich, who had "gone to the people" in the summer of 1874, and later had been one of the agitators in the Korsun affair. During the winter of 1875–76, he visited some of the imprisoned *dusheviks* in Kiev and promised to go to the tsar on their behalf. Later, he brought back two bogus imperial documents. Each was gilt-edged with a large, gold "Seal of the Council of Commissars" showing a pike and ax crossed and signed by Alexander II. The first was a manifesto ordering the peasants to form *druzhinas,* or bands, to rise up and take what was theirs from the gentry. The second was some statutes that required peasants to swear fidelity to the *druzhina,* threatening death for those who failed to comply. Further, each member was to arm himself with a pike and to pay monthly dues. The result was electric. *Druzhinas* of twenty-five men multiplied, each with an elected *ataman* supposedly responsible to a fictitious council of commissars appointed by the tsar. By the middle of the following year, there were about a thousand members waiting for preparations for the uprising to begin. But, as usual, the police were tipped off, and, by May of 1878, the *druzhinas* had almost all been broken up.

Amid all this defeat and failure, a ray of hope for revolutionaries broke through in late 1875, although none recognized it at the time. This was the return of the former Tschaikovsky Circle member Mark Natanson to St. Petersburg. In fact, he was in the capital illegally, having recently escaped from his place of exile in order to become an active revolutionary once again. Appalled by the disarray in the movement, he resolved to form a new party, which in 1878 would adopt the name of an older one, Land and Liberty. Natanson, who believed that the revolution was inevitable, always sought to avoid direct confrontation with the state. He thought mainly in terms of helping the people resist oppression and in preparing society for the coming upheaval, but others, concerned about the spread of capitalism and its corrupting influence, were intent on a more radical agenda. This was reflected in the party's first program of 1876, which called for mass revolution leading to the elimination of the capitalist system. It also promised the dissolution of the Russian Empire, followed by anarchy, collectivism, and wide autonomy for the regions and communes that were expected to emerge. The new organization also encouraged more activism to assist the forces that would create the revolution. To this end, it helped Piotr Kropotkin make a spectacular escape from prison, and also organized what Soviet historians have called the "first mass workers demonstration in Russian history."[39]

This event took place on December 6 (18), 1876 in St. Petersburg, after a memorial mass in the Cathedral of Kazan[40] for Russian volunteers who had fallen in the Balkans fighting the Turks. At the end of the service, some two hundred Land and Liberty followers gathered in front of the cathedral to listen to a speech by George Plekhanov,[41] who would one day be known as the "father of Russian Marxism." The speaker denounced the government for punishing the idealistic youth of the country and declared the day to be in memory of such martyrs as Chernyshevsky, Nechaev, and Dolgushkin.[42] He ended his address by shouting "Long live Land and Liberty! Long live the people! Death to the tsar!" As the demonstrators unfurled a red banner and hoisted a sixteen-year-old working youth on their shoulders, the police moved in and started making arrests— thirty-two in all. Typically, many of those sent to jail were innocent bystanders while the organizers of the demonstration all escaped.

For the next year and a half, Land and Liberty continued to agitate and seek new sources of revolutionary potential. For a while it tried to assist the urban proletariat, but little was accomplished, since the latter resented the students' presumption to interfere in their affairs. Thus, the main focus of Land and Liberty's activism remained with the peasants. Renewed efforts were made by members to go to the people in rural areas along the Volga. This time the participants made little attempt to resemble peasants at work; instead they dressed in their regular attire and employed themselves in a manner befitting their education. The idea was to gradually win the confidence of the locals by helping them in various practical ways. In time, they were to recruit potential rebels and form armed detachments for uprisings that would occur in the future. All this activity was to be directed by a center in each province. Once again, the effort got nowhere: too few people went to the countryside, and most of those that did soon left. Moreover, the peasants continued to be either hostile or indifferent, and the police continued to make arrests.

By the spring of 1877, the jails had become so full of radicals that officials in the Ministry of Justice had decided to stage two Senate trials. The first began in March and became known as the Trial of Fifty and involved the former members of the Moscow Circle. At the time, patriotic feeling in the country was high because of the imminence of war with Turkey. The tsar and his advisers were confident that the accused would not only be found guilty in court, but would also be condemned by public opinion. However, things did not quite go as planned. When two of the defendants, Sophia Bardina and Piotr Alexeev, spoke eloquently in their own defense, the judge felt compelled to have it stricken from the record. Nevertheless, copies were made by their supporters and distributed to a sympathetic public. The second trial began the following October and is usually referred to as the Great Trial. It involved 193 of those who had "gone to the people" a few years earlier and violated the law by spreading revolutionary propaganda to the people. The number would have been greater, but a large number of those arrested had either died in jail or gone insane. Many of the accused rejected the legitimacy of the court and refused to testify, although a certain Ippolit Myshkin created quite a stir when he denounced the court and compared it to a whorehouse. Yet this did not affect the outcome: on January 23 (February 4), 1878, those convicted were condemned to years of imprisonment, exile, and hard labor.

Then, on January 24 (February 5), an incident occurred that was to change the course of the revolutionary movement in Russia. Vera Zasulich, now a humble typesetter in the press of Land and Liberty, marched into the office of the Chief of St. Petersburg police, General F.F. Trepov, with

In January 1878, Vera Zasulich boldly attempted to murder St. Petersburg General Trepov, the chief of police who had ordered the brutal flogging of a political prisoner. Her unlikely acquittal in the trial that followed made her a hero in the revolutionary movement. Yelena Segal, *Sophia Perovskaya*, Zhizn' Zamechatel'nikh Lyudei, Molodaya Gvardiya, Moskva, 1962.

a revolver and shot him at point blank range. Her deed was actually a reaction to something that had happened six months earlier. It seems that in July of the previous year, the general had himself violated the law when he ordered a man flogged for failing to remove his hat in his presence. The outrage was immediate, shrill, and widespread. Many swore revenge, but when time passed and nobody acted, it fell to Zasulich to act as she did. Somehow the victim survived, but the would-be assassin was arrested and tried as a common rather than a political criminal. It was a big mistake; this meant a jury trial that would be open to the public.

Of course, there hardly seemed any need for a trial, since Zasulich did not deny her guilt and was fully prepared to submit to any punishment the court cared to impose. Still, her cause was aided by an inspired defense lawyer, a sympathetic presiding judge, and a victim who was generally loathed as a crook and a scoundrel. The not-guilty verdict that was rendered on March 31 (April 12), 1878, astounded everyone, including the defendant, who was carried out of the courtroom on the shoulders of her ecstatic supporters. But she was not yet a free woman. Unknown to her, when the tsar heard the decision, he ordered her immediate rearrest, which was nearly accomplished when she returned to the prison to pick up her belongings. Fortunately, the message was not delivered in time and Zasulich walked through the gates unmolested. Later, the police caught up with her on the street, but she was protected by a determined crowd. Within days, she was out of the country and on her way to Geneva.

Zasulich's bold deed and her acquittal delighted a large part of the public, including many officials in the government. It also prompted other revolutionaries to act in the same manner. In February, an attempt was made on the assistant prosecutor in Kiev, and in May, the city's chief of police was assassinated. However, the most dramatic stroke of all occurred in St. Petersburg when the head of the Third Section, General Nikolai Mezentsev, met his end while walking along a city street. His assassin, Sergei Kravchinsky, the editor of the periodical *Land and Liberty*, had wanted to protest the treatment of political prisoners. On August 4 (August 16), 1878, he approached his victim from behind and stabbed him with a dagger before Mezentsev's lone aide could react. Kravchinsky was quickly picked up by carriage drawn by a specially trained racehorse and eventually escaped abroad. It took the police two years merely to establish his identity.

This assassination had important consequences as the tsar gave special powers to the military governors of Moscow, St. Petersburg, and four other cities. They could now try civilians in military courts, arbitrarily arrest and exile anyone, and forbid the publication of subversive journals.

But such measures did nothing to deter a member of Land and Liberty named Alexander Soloviev,[43] who had gone to the people years earlier. In the spring of 1879, he told his friend and comrade, Alexander Mikhailov,[44] of his intention to kill Alexander II. Mikhailov, who had helped Kravchinsky plan his deed, was also prepared to help Soloviev, although Soloviev insisted that his proposal first be presented to the other members of Land and Liberty for their approval. This revived a fierce debate within the organization that had been smoldering for some time. Many believed that murder and assassination served no useful purpose and would ultimately destroy the ideals for which the organization stood. Others thought such acts to be indispensable in overthrowing the old order. In the end, Soloviev could not get an official endorsement for his plan but resolved to go ahead anyway. Mikhailov helped him plan the deed and provided a revolver. On April 2 (April 14), Soloviev fired four or five shots at the tsar, who was crossing Palace Square on his daily walk. The tsar managed to escape by running zigzag and then crawling on all fours to reach safety. Soloviev tried to end his own life by taking poison but was quickly apprehended and given an emetic. He was tried and executed the following month.

This latest assassination attempt led to a showdown of sorts in Land and Liberty as its members prepared for its upcoming congress in Voronezh. Once and for all, it was to be decided whether the organization would continue its mostly nonviolent strategy of "going to the people" to prepare the peasants for the coming revolution, or whether it would endorse a program of all-out terror against the government to force political concessions. Of the twenty-one members who planned to attend, some of those who favored the latter position agreed to meet beforehand in the town of Lipetsk to discuss how they might prevail at the congress without splitting the party. These included Mikhailov, Lev Tikhomirov,[45] and Mikhail Frolenko. To strengthen their position, they invited the highly respected Andrei Zheliabov,[46] who had always operated as a traditional populist but whose support they were determined to win. Zheliabov agreed to embrace terrorism as long as the goal was regicide. However, when the congress met on June 20 (July 2) in Voronezh there were a number of objectors, including Georgi Plekhanov, who walked out in disgust. He was later to form the Black Partition, or *Cherny Peredel'*, which never did attract many members, especially after Plekhanov left the country in January of 1880. The remaining members of Land and Liberty became known as The People's Will, or *Narodnaya Volya*. The impact of this new party on events in Russia was to be profound.

The new party wasted no time deciding on a purpose. The Executive Committee chose August 26 (September 7), 1879, the anniversary Tsar

Alexander's coronation, to formally sentence him to death. This time the conspirators meant to employ dynamite, in part because they had among their members a former engineering student, Nikolai Kibalchich, who was something of an expert on explosives. The conspirators decided to mine the tracks near Alexandrovsk (now Zaporozheye) on the Dnieper River to attack the tsar while he was returning from his vacation home in the Crimea. To carry out the necessary excavation, Andrei Zheliabov posed as a merchant intending to build a tannery nearby. He was accompanied by his "wife," Anna Yakimova, and two "workmen." Having moved into a flat, they starting digging into a seventy-five-foot high embankment along which the train was to pass. The task of planting two cylinders of dynamite involved danger and difficulty: not only had the autumn rains turned the entire area into a huge pit of mud, but the tracks were patrolled on a regular basis. Still, all was ready on the morning of November 18 (30), when the conspirators went to the site to accomplish the deed. Using an electric battery for power, they attached an induction coil to wires leading to the explosive device. However, when the tsar's train passed over the appointed spot and Zheliabov closed the circuit, nothing happened.

But the conspirators had foreseen the possibility of failure, and another team of nine, including Alexander Mikhailov, Lev Hartman, and Sophia Perovskaya, was waiting in a suburb of Moscow to try in case the first effort failed. Hartman and Perovskaya, posing as a married couple, had bought a house and told their neighbors that they would be building an ice cellar. Their real purpose was to dig a tunnel from their kitchen to a point under the nearby railroad tracks, where they would bury eighty pounds of dynamite. The work was wet, filthy, cold, exhausting, and fraught with practical problems. They had difficulty getting rid of the enormous quantities of soil dug from the tunnel and had to scatter it around the yard at night, hoping no one would notice. At one point the tunnel flooded, and later its ceiling, which had been shored up with wood, became visible where it crossed under a road. Still, the conspirators somehow managed to keep the project going, although they later had to mortgage the house to buy an expensive steel drill to continue digging in the frozen ground. The bank required an official inspection to be conducted in the presence of a police officer, which occurred without incident. Finally, on November 19 (December 1), this second team of conspirators was ready when the tsar's train arrived at 10:25 A.M. This time the firing device worked, producing an enormous explosion, but it was the wrong train.

Perhaps the most ambitious attempt of all was made by a solitary young man who was not a full-time member of The People's Will. Stepan Khalturin, from the town of Viatka, originally came to St. Petersburg to emigrate to America. However, having missed his ship, he had to find a job. This was not a difficult task because he was highly skilled and knew a number of trades. Once employed, however, he became involved in radical politics and helped to found an organization called the Northern Union of Russian Workers. By the time the group was broken up by the police in 1879, Khalturin had become a determined revolutionary and was convinced of the need to kill the tsar. To this end, he got himself hired to work on a construction project in the Winter Palace, which provided him with lodging in the basement of the imperial residence with three other workers. Soon he was in contact with Andrei Zheliabov, who agreed to supply him with dynamite, which he accumulated little by little for three months, waiting for the right time to strike.

Since the workers' dormitory was located directly under the Guards' quarters and two floors below the imperial dining room, Khalturin calculated that if he detonated a bomb large enough, he could kill the tsar during his evening meal. This, of course, meant endangering a lot of innocent people, which Zheliabov would not allow. Thus, he limited Khalturin's supply of dynamite to about 100 pounds. At the beginning of February, when it became known that the workers were soon to be moved out of the Winter Palace, Khalturin resolved to act at the first opportunity. On the evening of the fifth, when he knew he would be alone in the basement, he lit the fuse connected to the detonator and walked out of the building. He had gone only a short distance from the Palace when he was met by Zheliabov. Suddenly, the ground shook with a tremendous explosion. The damage was extensive, with flames shooting up and smoke pouring out of the building. Congratulations seemed in order, but this was premature. Later it was learned that although the Guards' quarters on the floor above the explosion had been completely destroyed, the dining hall above had hardly been touched. Further, for all the casualties caused (eleven killed and fifty-six injured), the tsar was unharmed. In fact, he had not even been in the dining hall at the time of the explosion. Later, The People's Will issued a proclamation regretting the loss of innocent life but declaring that the fight would go on until Alexander II abdicated in favor of a freely elected Constituent Assembly.

Although the tsar survived physically, psychologically he was shattered. The assassins seemed to be everywhere. In desperation, he turned to his minister of the interior, Count Mikhail Loris-Melikov, and made him head of the new Supreme Commission for the Maintenance of State Order and Public Peace. The son of an Armenian merchant, Loris-Melikov had served with great distinction in the recent war with Turkey and was known for his bravery and coolness under pressure. One week after his appointment, a Jewish student named Mlodecki fired a pistol at him but missed. The count coolly disarmed his assailant and got on with the business of creating what many came to call "a dictatorship of the heart." To this end, he abolished certain security measures deemed unnecessary and freed many of those sent into exile whose guilt had been questionable. He also eased censorship and dismissed the hated Dmitri Tolstoy as Minister of Education. His most significant step, however, was to abolish the Third Section and turn its functions over to the Ministry of the Interior, where he remained as head.

Loris-Meliklov, however, had much more in mind than stop-gap measures. Ultimately, he hoped to create a new institution that would undermine the very foundation of revolutionary discontent in the country. He envisioned a general commission empowered to offer advice in the legislative process, the composition of which was to include not only civil servants and appointed experts, but also elected representatives of the *zemstvo* boards and the municipal councils of the larger cities. It was, to be sure, a timid step, and one that was not intended to limit the sovereign's power in any way, although Loris-Melilov may have secretly hoped that the powers of the commission would expand over time. In any case, Alexander had grave doubts about this initiative and is alleged to have compared it to the Estates General convened by Louis XVI in 1789. Still, he allowed Loris-Melikov to further develop his idea.

Coincidentally, it was about this same time that the police solved a murder case that had puzzled them for nearly a year. Grigori Goldenberg, a member of The People's Will, had been arrested the previous November at the Yelizovetograd railway station while trying to transport dynamite in his suitcase. When his jailers had been unable to make him talk, they planted one of their own in his cell, who listened to him brag about having murdered Prince Kropotkin, the governor-general of Kharkov. More important, however, Goldenberg also spoke of his high connections in revolutionary circles and showed himself to be the kind of man who could be tricked into giving up secrets. Soon the jailers were talking to him in solitary confinement to better exploit his extraordinary naiveté and gullibility. In time, they were able to persuade him that they shared his desire for a more just society, that terrorism was a tragic mistake, and that only he could save Russia from a horrible bloodbath. Soon Goldenberg was confiding in his jailers some of what he knew. Later, he was transferred from Odessa to the Peter and Paul Fortress in St. Petersburg, where Loris-Melilov twice came to visit him in his cell. This added to his growing sense of self-importance and prompted more revelations. It was not until he tried to convert other prisoners to his point of view that he realized that he had been duped. On July 15 (27), Goldenberg committed suicide in his cell, but the damage had been done.

There were two more attempts to kill the tsar in 1880: one in Odessa in May (led by Perovskaya), the other in St. Petersburg in August led by Zheliabov. Both had gone awry, and more arrests were made. But in November, a new sense of urgency arose among the conspirators after the arrest of Alexander Mikhailov; he had been picked up at a commercial studio after having copies of photographs made of two recently executed comrades. With time and resources running out, one last try to kill the tsar had to be made, and Sophia Perovskaya took the initiative. Having observed that every Sunday the tsar drove down Malaya Sadovaya Street to the Manege to inspect the Guards, she suggested that this would be a good opportunity to make an attack. To this end, Yuri Bogdanovich, a member of the Executive Committee, rented a three-room front basement on Malaya Sadovaya Street early in December. Once again it was decided to tunnel under the street to plant a mine, although this time, several bomb throwers would be poised in reserve to join the attack should anything go wrong. In addition, Andrei Zheliabov would be standing by with a pistol and a dagger should still more force be needed for finish the job.

The work began in earnest in January when Bogdanovich and Anna Yakimova moved into the basement, as husband and wife preparing to open a cheese shop. There they began digging a tunnel, aided by as many as ten others, coming and going at all hours. At one point the work was held up by the rupture of a wooden sewer, which emitted a stench so vile that the conspirators were nearly overcome, but by late February the fifteen-foot tunnel was completed and ready to be mined. In the meantime, Zheliabov had found four men willing to throw the bombs that were being prepared, although the inexperience of those recruited must surely have given him pause. They were: Ignaty Grinevitsky, a former engineering student, twenty-six years old; Timofey Mikhailov, a boilermaker, twenty-one years old; Ivan Yermelianov, a cabinetmaker, twenty years old; and Nikolai Rysakov, a student, nineteen years old. Rysakov seems to have been an especially odd choice, since he had only recently become active in the movement and the extent of his commitment could not be known.

Even more worrisome were the activities of the police. They got a major break in February when they recruited an informer named Ivan Okladsky, who had worked with Zheliabov at Alexandrovsk. This was soon followed by the arrest of an important member of The People's Will named Nikolai Kletochnikov, who had been employed with the Third Section. Over a period of two years, he had kept his comrades informed about what the police knew and when they could be expected to act. But the worst was yet to come: on February 27 (March 11), Andrei Zheliabov was arrested at the apartment of a friend. This particularly upset Perovskaya, who for some time had been his lover. Her first impulse was to try to rescue him, but the police acted first. The very next day they visited the cheese shop posing as sanitation inspectors. Incredibly, they failed to find the tunnel and saw nothing sinister in the poorly disguised containers of excavated earth placed about the flat. Nor did they bother about the piles of dirt covered with straw under the sofa.

With time now clearly of the essence, the conspirators worked feverishly to finish their work. It was decided to accomplish the deed on the first date possible: Sunday, March 1. By the morning of the fateful day, the mines had been planted in the tunnel, and the four bombs assembled. The cheese shop was to be manned by Yakimova and Frolenko. Her job was to warn him of the approach of the imperial carriage and then to leave; his to detonate the mine. The other conspirators met early that morning at the apartment of Gesia Helfman on Telezhnaya Street. Perovskaya, who was now in charge, gave the final instructions, emphasizing that when the mine was exploded, the bomb throwers were to rush up and check the damage. Only then were they to decide whether or not to use their bombs. If, however, Alexander avoided the mined block by taking a different route to the Manege, as he sometimes did, the bomb throwers were to wait for his return trip. If he again avoided Malaya Sadovaya Street, Perovskaya was to take out her handkerchief and blow her nose. By this signal, the four men were to go to the Yekaterinsky Canal to carry out the attack there.

At 11 A.M. the conspirators left the apartment for their assigned positions. Two hours later, Alexander left the Winter Palace in his carriage, guarded by six mounted Cossacks and followed by three sleighs carrying the chief of police and two security officers. The tsar was in high spirits, confident that the most dangerous terrorists had already been caught. Still, he avoided the Malaya Sadovaya Street and traveled along the Yekaterininsky Canal and then up the Bolshaya Italianskaya into Manege Square. This automatically postponed the attack by about forty minutes until after the maneuvers, and tension was high as the conspirators waited. Finally, after the tsar emerged from the walls of the riding academy and climbed back into his carriage, Perovskaya saw the royal procession turn back down the Bolshaya Italianskaya. She then gave the signal setting the alternate plan into motion. All but one of the bomb throwers hurried over to the Yekaterininsky Canal. Timofey Mikhailov lost his nerve and went to the apartment on Telezhnaya Street to return his bomb and then go home.

In the meantime, the tsar, having paid a brief visit to his cousin along the way, was soon riding along the Yekaterininsky Canal Quay, where the assassins were waiting. Rysakov threw his bomb first, only to have it explode under the carriage, fatally wounding a Cossack guard and a young butcher's assistant standing nearby. The tsar, who suffered only a minor cut, got out of the carriage to inspect the damage and to have a look at his assailant. When someone asked if he was hurt, he replied "No, thank God, but —" looking around at those who had been injured. At that point, Rysakov was heard to say, "Still thanking God?"[47] It was an utterance he would later regret and try to deny. In any case, Alexander hardly reacted. Instead he turned and started walking toward one of the sleighs. Suddenly, Ignaty Grinevitsky emerged from the crowd and stood before him. Holding the bomb with both hands over his head, he threw it down hard at the tsar's feet. The explosion mortally wounded both men, although it was the imperial victim who aroused the most concern. With his legs badly shredded and bleeding all over, Alexander's last request was to be taken to the Winter Palace to die.

Although the assassination aroused jubilation and anticipation among all who hated the regime, nothing much happened in its immediate aftermath. The Executive Committee of the People's Will subsequently issued a number of documents, the first of which declared that "anyone who oppresses the nation is an enemy of the people."[48] Another urged the people to petition the new tsar, Alexander III, to give land to the peasants and lower taxes, and warned: "If he doesn't listen to the people and gets to be like his daddy, he too will have to be *replaced.*"[49] A third proclamation compared the tsar's oppression of his own people to that of the Tatar yoke. Finally, a last communication was composed by Tikhomirov to Alexander III urging him to make reforms before "a terrible explosion climax[es] the process and destroy[s] irretrievably the old order."[50]

But the 36-year-old Alexander III was too busy planning revenge to heed any threats. One by one, the conspirators were rounded up with the help of Rysakov, who, suddenly terrified by what he had done, offered himself as an informer. Thus, by March 17 (30), Gesia Helfman, Timofey Mikhailov, Sophia Perovskaya, and Nikolai Kibalchich were all in custody. One more defendant was added to the list when Andrei Zheliabov demanded that he be allowed to share the same fate as his comrades. The trial of the six conspirators started at 11 A.M. on March 26 (April 8) when they were led into the court room and ordered to state their names, ages, religion, and occupation. Far from being in the least intimidated, Zheliabov relished his predicament and refused his court-appointed attorney so that he would be able to speak in his own defense. This he did with considerable eloquence. When asked about his religion, he answered:

I was baptized into the Orthodox Church. However I reject Orthodoxy, although I admit the teachings of Jesus Christ — this teaching has an honored place among my moral convictions. I believe
in the truth and justice of that teaching, and I solemnly declare
that faith without works is dead. I believe that every true Christian should fight for the truth and the rights of the oppressed and
of those who are too weak to assert their rights; and I am prepared
to suffer for them. Such is my creed.[51]

Also impressive was the diminutive Sophia Perovskaya. She had less
to say, but her demeanor was regal. Previously she had written to her
mother, asking her to be calm and not to grieve. She expressed her complete tranquility about her fate and had no regrets. "I have lived according to my conscience and it would have been impossible to have done
otherwise."[52] Kibalchich was also composed and practically gave a lecture
to the court about the intricacies of explosives which many found fascinating. When the government experts tried to assert that the bombs used
against the tsar were made of substances imported from abroad, he referred
them to an article in the *Russian Artillery Journal* from August 1878.

The other defendants could only arouse pity. Gesia Helfman did not
deny the charges or plead for mercy. She merely explained that she had left
her Orthodox-Jewish home at sixteen to avoid being forced to marry a man
she didn't love. Later, she had been taken in by revolutionaries and sympathized with their cause. Timofey Mikhailov also made no attempt to
defend himself. Barely literate, he cited his lack of an education, saying at
one point, "I belong to a party that defends the workers and not one that
seeks an overthrow of the government, because not being developed or
educated enough I do not know about such things."[53] Rysakov's performance was pathetic in every respect. Far too terrified to make a coherent
defense, he claimed that he had never taken part in the terrorist movement,
that he was against violence, and that he had only participated in the assassination hoping to end the terror.

The accused were all found guilty as charged and sentenced to death
by hanging. Some had hoped the tsar would pardon the murderers as an
act of Christian charity. These included the famous novelist Lev Tolstoy[54]
and the philosopher Vladimir Soloviev. But Alexander III was determined
that all would die, although Gesia Helfman's pregnancy gave her a temporary reprieve. Thus at six in the morning of April 3 (15), 1881, the prisoners were awakened and given tea. They dressed and donned black
shrouds over their clothes. Sophia Perovskaya broke down briefly but was
consoled by Mikhailov. Minutes later they all had placards hung over their
shrouds with the word "Regicide" written bold in black ink. They climbed

The tsar was in the habit of reviewing the troops every Sunday at the Mikhailovsky Riding School. However on March 1, 1881 he changed his normal route at the behest of his wife, who feared a terrorist attack. But the members of The People's Will had prepared for this eventuality and were able to carry out the assassination despite the heavy security. *Krasnaya Znamya*, No. 1, Moscow, 1913.

This drawing of Sophia Perovskaya and Andrei Zheliabov was made during their trial in St. Peterburg. Their courageous behavior during their incarceration and execution was a source of inspiration to later revolutionaries. Yelena Segal, Sophia Perovskaya, Zhizn' Zamechatel'nikh Lyudei, Molodaya Grardiya, Moskva, 1962.

into tumbrels in the prison courtyard, and at 8 A.M. began their journey to the Semenovsky Square where gallows had been erected the day before. Seated with their backs to the horses, their hands cuffed from behind, and their feet fettered, they were accompanied by Cossacks on horseback and marching drummers, the latter having been ordered to make enough noise to prevent any political speeches.

Once in the Square, the sentences were formally read out before the condemned and a crowd of 80,000. This took nearly thirty minutes. Documents were signed by officials in frock coats and high hats, and five priests held out crosses for the condemned to kiss. After white cowls were placed over their heads, the former conspirators bade farewell to one another, albeit with some difficulty. Zheliabov, his wrists and ankles still bound, hobbled over to kiss Perovskaya for the last time. The others offered each other whatever solace they could. Only Rysakov was shunned and ignored.

The hangings were to go according to a plan: those deemed most guilty would be forced to watch and wait. Thus, since Kibalchich was considered least guilty, he went first and died quickly. The heavy-set Mikhailov was next, but his execution was bungled. Twice the rope broke, and twice the condemned fell flat on his face and chest, unable to break his fall. He finally died on the third attempt, but only after the rope had been reinforced with another. The tiny Perovskaya was third on the list and expired quickly. She was followed by Zheliabov, who struggled in the noose for some time. Finally, it was Rysakov's turn. Ironically, the one conspirator who had cooperated with the government was somehow considered the most guilty. He had hoped that a pardon would be announced at the last moment. Such things had happened before, but not this time. When the executioner motioned him forward, Rysakov became hysterical. He wedged his feet in the railings and had to be forcibly pulled away. However, once he was in the noose with the bench kicked away, his convulsions were brief. At 9:30, the five bodies were cut down from the crossbeam, placed in black coffins, loaded onto carts, and taken to the train station. From there they were transferred to the Preobrazhensky Cemetery and buried together in an unmarked grave.

Yet the elimination of the main conspirators brought no sense of relief for the new tsar, who had moved his entire family from the Winter Palace to the more secure imperial residence at Gatchina. There was still much to do to complete the transition of power, and this included a decision about Loris-Melikov's general commission, which had been tentatively approved by Alexander II in February. On March 8, it was discussed at a Council of Ministers meeting. A few of those present declared their support for the measure, but the tsar seemed to be swayed by the passionate opposition of Konstantin Pobedonostsev, who had recently been named head of the Holy Synod. The project was temporarily shelved, which led some to hope that the tsar had not made up his mind. However, on April 29, Alexander dispelled all doubt about how he intended to rule when he issued a proclamation that had been composed by Pobedonostsev:

> The voice of God commands us to stand resolutely by the task of governing, relying on Divine Providence with faith in the strength and truth of autocratic power, which we have been called to confirm and protect for the good of the people against all encroachments.[55]

This was followed by Loris-Melilov's resignation.

Had Alexander III been a reflective man, he might have wondered about these thousands of young men and women who had agitated and rebelled after the Emancipation Edict. Many were extraordinary individuals who were prepared to sacrifice everything, including their lives for what they believed was a noble cause. True, most were revolutionaries and atheists, but they were also intensely patriotic and even spiritual. Most truly believed in Russia's inherent cultural superiority and in the country's sacred mission to save the world. What they wanted was to be allowed to work for that end in a society dedicated to justice and harmony. Had they been accorded some measure of meaningful participation, they might have been an enormous asset both to the dynasty and the country. This, however, would have meant some dilution of autocracy, which was a heresy that the new tsar would not even consider. Thus, unqualified reaction was soon to become the bedrock of Alexander III's domestic policy. On August 14 (26), 1881, a law for the security of the realm was promulgated which empowered the authorities to impose military rule more easily than ever before. They could now imprison and/or fine anyone who aroused their displeasure, close down factories and shops, deport individuals from their home districts, fire civil servants, and dismiss elected officials. This decree, which stayed in effect until 1917, was constantly invoked during the reign of Russia's last two tsars. Not only did it quicken the country's march to revolution and disaster, but it helped pave the way for another tyranny that would engulf the country for most of the 20th century.

Selected Bibliography

One of the great scholarly studies of this period is Franco Venturi's *Roots of Revolution*. Other informative and more recent works include

Adam Ulam's *In the Name of the People* and Edward Crankshaw's *The Shadow of the Winter Palace.* Also of interest is *Road to Revolution* by Avrahm Yarmolinsky. *The Modern Encyclopedia of Russian and Soviet History* has many useful articles about most of the individuals mentioned in this chapter. The best of these is "Herzen, Alexander Ivanovich" by Michael von Herzen, and "The People's Will Party" by G. Douglas Nicholl. Finally, the chilling details about Sergei Nechaev's revolutionary activism are best described in Robert Payne's *The Fortress* and Philip Pomper's *Sergei Nechaev.*

Cowles, Virginia. *The Romanovs.* Middlesex, England: Penguin, 1971.

Crankshaft, Edward. *The Shadow of the Winter Palace.* Middlesex, England: Penguin Books, 1976.

Herzen, Michael von, "Herzen, Alexander Ivanovich," *Modern Encyclopedia of Russian and Soviet History,* ed. Joseph L. Wieczynski, 54 vols. With suppl. Gulf Breeze, Florida: Academic International Press, 1976–1990.

Hingley, Ronald. *The Tsars 1533–1917.* New York: The McMillan Company, 1968.

Nicholl, G. Douglas. "People's Will Party." *Modern Encyclopedia of Russian and Soviet History,* ed. Joseph L. Wieczynski, 54 vols. With suppl. Gulf Breeze, Florida: Academic International Press, 1976–1990.

Payne, Robert. *The Fortress.* New York: Simon and Shuster, 1957.

Pollard, Alan P. "Movement to the People," *Modern Encyclopedia of Russian and Soviet History,* ed. Joseph L. Wieczynski, 54 vols. With suppl. Gulf Breeze, Florida: Academic International Press, 1976–1990.

Stites, Richard. "Figner, Vera Nikolaevna," *Modern Encyclopedia of Russian and Soviet History,* ed. Joseph L. Wieczynski, 54 vols. With suppl. Gulf Breeze, Florida: Academic International Press, 1976–1990.

Ulam, Adam. *In the Name of the People.* New York: The Viking Press, 1977.

Warnes, David. *Chronicle of the Russian Tsars.* London: Thames and Hudson, 1999.

Yarmolinsky, Avrahm. *The Shadow of the Winter Palace.* Middlesex, England: Penguin, 1976.

10. REACTION, RASPUTIN AND REVOLUTION

The aftermath of Alexander II's assassination brought a steep decline in the fortune of The People's Will. The failure of the organization's great success to ignite a revolution was profoundly discouraging for its members as the police continued to make arrests. So dangerous did the situation become that the party moved its center of operations to Moscow. All this was compounded by another setback in February 1882, when twenty defendants were put on trial for participating in numerous attempts to assassinate Alexander II. All but one was found guilty, and, of these, all were sentenced to death. In the end, only one was hanged because the new tsar had been persuaded to be merciful. The others ended up doing hard labor in Siberia, most of them for life. This outcome so discouraged Tikhomirov that he left the country, leaving Vera Figner as the sole remaining member of the party's Executive Committee.

Yet even before the trial, Figner had been alarmed by the low morale and apathy among the remaining activists. To revive the party's sense of purpose, she had organized the assassination of an especially hated prosecuting officer in the military courts, General Mezentsev. However, nothing more was accomplished than the removal of one bad man and the swift conviction and execution of the two who had carried out the deed. With the party's ranks dangerously depleted, Figner was determined to recruit new members. To this end, she invited a former army officer and engineering student named Sergei Degaev[1] to serve in the inner circle. There was no doubting the man's willingness to work, since he had previously helped to dig the tunnel from the cheese shop under Malaya Sadovaya Street for the assassination of Alexander II, but Degaev, who was given the task of operating a printing press in the south of Russia, soon got arrested and ended up cooperating with the police. Later, he tried to repent for his crime by killing the undercover officer assigned to work with him before fleeing the country. Among those subsequently arrested was Vera Figner, who spent the next twenty years incarcerated in the bleak prison fortress of Schlusselberg.

In the meantime, Alexander III set about the task of rooting out all sources of opposition in the empire. To this end, he contradicted many of his father's policies by increasing censorship and approving a statute that effectively deprived the universities of their autonomy. This latter decree was particularly obnoxious because it required that students wear uniforms and submit to monitoring by specially appointed inspectors. Still, his most controversial counterreform came in 1889, when he defied his own Council of State by creating the office of land captain *(zemsky nachalnik)*. These were salaried officials appointed and dismissed by the minister of the interior from the ranks of the gentry. They were expected to supervise and control the peasants by exercising their considerable judicial powers as well as their right to confirm elected officials and approve decisions made at peasant meetings. The following year, the government also took steps to limit the activities of the *zemstvos* and to increase the number of representatives from the gentry. In 1892, the activities of the city *dumas* were likewise restricted.

In the spirit of his grandfather, Nicholas I, the new tsar reinstituted "Orthodoxy, Autocracy and Nationality" as the regime's ideology, which justified the new tsar's determination to impose russification on all his subjects. Although this policy antagonized minorities all over the empire (including Poles, Baltic Germans, Finns, Georgians and Ukrainians), no group suffered more than did the country's five million Jews, most of whom lived in ghettos within the Pale of Settlement. Konstantine Pobedonostsev expressed the prevailing official attitude best when he spoke of solving the "Jewish problem" by thirds — one third conversion to Orthodoxy, one-third emigration, and one-third liquidation. Thus, when a series of pogroms broke out in the early 1880s, the government offered the victims precious little protection and at times seemed to encourage the perpetrators. Such episodes left little doubt about what could be expected from this tsar, who in 1887 signed a law that limited the number of Jews allowed to enter the universities. Even more ominous was the forcible eviction of some 20,000 Jews from Moscow to enforce certain archaic residency restrictions. Such episodes largely explain the large Jewish exodus from Russia that soon followed. In the first years of the 20th century, about one million Jews left Russia for North America.

By the mid 1880s, although organized opposition to the state had been largely diffused, the universities continued to breed aspiring revolutionaries. Among those who were drawn to the fight against autocracy was a brilliant biology student named Alexander Ulianov,[2] whose brother, Vladimir Ilich Ulianov, two decades hence, as Lenin was to become the most famous Russian revolutionary of all time. Ulianov, who had recently won a gold medal for his thesis about the habits of sea spiders at the University of St. Petersburg, seemed an unlikely rebel. In the fall of 1886, however, he underwent a profound change when he helped to organize a memorial march to the grave of the socialist writer, Nikolai Dobroliubov. The event was planned for November 28 (December 10), the twenty-fifth anniversary of Dobroliubov's death, but the march was banned by the police. The students went ahead anyway. Arriving at the cemetery, however, they found the gates locked and themselves surrounded by mounted Cossacks. This was followed by a number of arrests, outraging the students who were already angry about a wide range of social and economic issues. No one took the situation more seriously than Ulianov, who now concluded that the only possible response to such tyranny was a campaign of systematic terror against the state. To this end, he decided to assassinate the tsar.

Working with a fellow student, Piotr Shevyrev, and a few others, Ulianov started doing research in the university library to learn how to build bombs. These devices, which he designed and put together himself, featured hollowed-out leaden pellets filled with strychnine around a solid core of dynamite in a cardboard housing. The time chosen for the murder was the end of February or possibly March 1 (13), which would have been the sixth anniversary of the assassination of Alexander II. The plan was to have three bomb throwers attack the tsar's carriage as he rode down the Nevsky Prospect in St. Petersburg on one of his inspection tours. The preparations went well until one of the conspirators, Pakhomy Andreiushkin, made a fatal mistake. In January, he wrote to a friend in Kharkov bragging about the efficacy of terrorism as a weapon against the state. The police intercepted the letter, and, although Andreiushkin had used a false name, his identity was eventually established. Now forewarned that something was up, the authorities were waiting and watching on February 27 and 28, when three men were seen prowling about Nevsky Prospect much of the day carrying suspicious packages. When they appeared again on March 1, they were arrested and made to confess their intent.

In all, twelve men and three women were rounded up and put on trial in April. One of the defendants was Piotr Shevyrev, who had gone to the

Crimea to convalesce from an illness before the assassination attempt was made. Previously, he had been one of the most militant in demanding that the tsar be killed; now he denied all responsibility and blamed everyone else. In contrast, Ulianov insisted that he alone was to blame and tried to minimize the involvement of the others by claiming they had only followed his orders. Nor would he beg for clemency. When his mother came to visit him in his cell in the Peter and Paul Fortress to urge him to do just that, he refused. He likened his situation to that of a duelist, who, having fired his pistol and missed, could not very well ask his opponent to refrain from firing his. Nor did his courage desert him during the trial. Before being convicted, he gave a moving speech in which he defended terrorism as "the sole defensive weapon which a minority can resort to when it is only strong spiritually," adding, "Among the Russian people you will always find ten persons so loyal to their ideas and so filled with the misery of their country that it is no sacrifice to die for a cause. Nothing can frighten such people." But the court was not to be swayed, and on May 8 (20), Ulianov, Shrevyrev, and the three bomb throwers went to the gallows.

Tsar Alexander read a transcript of Ulianov's speech but did not reflect on it. Satisfied with the outcome of the trial, he turned his attention to more pleasant matters such as the economy. Here the news was mostly encouraging: the ruble was stable, the country was enjoying a favorable balance of trade, and the rate of industrial growth was on the rise. All this was accompanied by a great boon in railway construction, which featured the building of the Trans-Siberian Railroad in 1891. This was a time of peace despite more Russian expansion and annexation to the southeast, including the Ill Valley in Turkestan (1883) and Merv (1884). In March of 1885, Russian and Afghan troops skirmished briefly over boundaries but reached a negotiated settlement in September. Moreover, Russian diplomacy fared well on other fronts. The tsar had renewed the Three Emperor's League in 1881 and 1884, but realizing the irreconcilable nature of Russia's differences with Austria-Hungary, particularly in the Balkans, he refused to renew again in 1887. Gradually, Alexander turned to France and, in 1894, signed a treaty aimed at halting future aggression from Germany, Austria-Hungary, and/or Italy. The terms, which were kept secret until 1918, obligated Russia and France to come to the defense of one another other if attacked and not to make a separate peace.

Still, the domestic situation was in many ways quite worrisome. The tariff of 1891, which was supposed to protect home industries and promote a favorable balance of trade, did that, but it also drove up prices for domestic goods, hurting the poor. In addition, too much grain had been exported during these years, and this, coupled with the country's poor transportation facilities, brought on devastating famine made worse by the outbreak of cholera in the countryside. Russian medicine might have dealt with the ensuing epidemic were it not for the government's inability to organize its resources in rural areas where the situation was worst. Moreover, this crisis accelerated the migration of desperate peasants to the cities to seek factory jobs. This contributed to the rapid rise of an urban proletariat, working long hours for poor pay and living in the most degrading squalor.

Despite such problems, it is tempting to think that had Alexander III ruled for another two decades, Russia's fate might have been quite different. This tsar, to be sure, was not known for any great intelligence or ability, but he did possess some assets that might have helped him face the difficulties ahead. One of these was an ability to make up his mind and stick to his decisions. He was also receptive to good advice, realistic when confronted with unpleasant truths, and able to command the loyalty of his subordinates. Finally, he was happily married to a supportive and charming wife, the Danish princess Dagmar, who bore him six children. However, by the thirteenth year of his reign, Tsar Alexander was ill with Bright's disease,[3] which afflicted his kidneys and tormented him with head and back pains. This affliction, which had been aggravated over the years by his excessive drinking, had become critical by the fall of 1894. His son and successor, the soon-to-be Tsar Nicholas II, was terrified at the prospect of ruling and possessed none of his father's assets to help him cope with his responsibilities. However, he had no choice. When Alexander died on October 20 (November 1) at age forty-nine, Nicholas became tsar and autocrat of all the Russias.

The deceased tsar had never held his eldest son in very high esteem and had often referred to him as "girlie" because of his gentle nature and unassertive personality. Physically, Nicholas was anything but an imposing presence. Standing only five-feet-seven and weighing about 140 pounds, he had always been in awe of his father, who had intended his son's upbringing to be suitably rigorous for a future autocrat. To this end, Nicholas spent most of his childhood at Gatchina, slept on an army cot with a hard pillow, and bathed in cold water. He never went to a proper school with other boys but was taught at home by tutors. Among these was the aged Pobedonostsev, whose dismal view of human nature, hatred of parliaments, and prejudice against Jews deeply impressed his lone student. But Nicholas' education was not entirely negative. The tsarevich developed a remarkable memory, acquired a decent knowledge of history and literature, and became fluent in three foreign languages, English, French, and German. All this might have served him well had he been able to bring some critical intelligence and mature judgment to bear on the problems and issues that were his to decide, but this seems to have been beyond his capacity. Nor was the new tsar naturally inquisitive; he found formal learning tedious and was happy to see his schooling end at the age of twenty-two.

Many historians have opined that Alexander III did little to prepare his son to succeed him, but this is not entirely fair. At nineteen, Nicholas was made a colonel in the Horse Guards, which he enjoyed and took seriously. Later, he was assigned to various government committees, which he found less fulfilling but performed dutifully. In the fall of 1890, he was sent on a nine-month cruise with his younger brother, Georgi, to broaden his understanding of the world. He traveled across the Mediterranean to Egypt, through the Suez Canal to India, to Malaysia, Indochina, and finally to Japan, where, for some reason, he was attacked and nearly killed by a sword-wielding samurai in the streets of Otsu. His last stop was Vladivostok, where he laid the cornerstone of the eastern end of the Trans-Siberian Railroad. Only then did he return to St. Petersburg, curiously unedified by his trip, except that he now had deep contempt for the Japanese, whom he would henceforth refer to as "monkeys."

Upon his return to the capital in the summer of 1891, Nicholas briefly resumed an affair with a beautiful ballerina, Matilda Kschessinska, who had hoped to become his wife. But the tsarevich was even more smitten by a granddaughter of Queen Victoria, Alix of Hesse-Darmstadt. The two had met in 1884, when he was sixteen and she twelve, on the occasion of the marriage of her older sister, Elizabeth, to Grand Duke Sergei, a brother of Alexander III. Despite the fact that Nicholas and Alix over the years had rarely seen each other, by the spring of 1894, they were desperately in love and wanting to be married. The tsarevich, however, needed first to overcome the opposition of his parents, who favored a daughter-in-law of a higher social rank. It took some time, but Nicholas, in a rare display of backbone, finally convinced them that he would consider no other woman. Thus, the wedding took place on November 27 (December 10), one week after Tsar Alexander III's funeral.

Princess Alix was duly baptized into the Russian Orthodox Church and assumed the name Alexandra Feodorovna. Despite her beauty and aristocratic upbringing, she found it very difficult to adjust to her new life or relate to others in her social circle. At first this was due mainly to the language barrier: she spoke no Russian and French only poorly, the latter being the language of the court. She and Nicholas, of course, always conversed in English, but even this set her apart from those she might have befriended. Moreover, she was extremely shy, intensely religious and, over the years, became increasingly neurotic. She had no sense of humor, did not enjoy entertaining or appearing in public, and soon made it clear that she sternly disapproved of the immorality and decadence of St. Petersburg society. This feeling was more than reciprocated.

Alexandra was also rankled by the lack of respect that her husband was accorded by his advisors and members of his own family. Among the latter were his three uncles: Vladimir, who was head of the Imperial Guards; Sergei, who was governor general of Moscow; and Alexei, an admiral who was in charge of naval affairs. There was also a great-uncle, Mikhail, who was chairman of the State Council. These men were loud, physically intimidating, and used to getting their own way. Nicholas hated having to meet with any of them alone. Yet the worst offender proved to be his own mother, the dowager empress, Marie Feodorovna, who continued to boss him as if he were a child. She even insisted that the newlyweds share her residence in the Anitchkov Palace instead of establishing a home of their own. It was only after many months and with great difficulty that Nicholas and Alexandra finally succeeded in breaking away and moving to the Alexander Palace at Tsarskoe Selo. It was here that they began to raise a family. Over the next ten years, the empress gave birth to four girls and one boy.[4]

Wherever he was, the tsar had an uncanny ability to attract misfortune, which only encouraged his natural fatalism. Mindful that he had been born on the feast of St. Job (May 6 [18]), he always felt a certain helplessness about what the future might bring. As he once confided to one of his ministers, "I have a secret conviction, that I am destined for a terrible trial, that I shall not receive my reward on this earth."[5] This became a self-fulfilling prophecy as his reign was punctuated by a series of appalling disasters over the next two decades. One of these occurred during his coronation in Moscow in May of 1896. As part of the week-long festivities, a great celebration had been planned for the common folk at Khodynka Field, a military training ground, at which free beer and souvenir mugs were to be distributed. However, when a rumor was circulated that there would not be enough of either to go around, a stampede ensued in which 1,429 were trampled to death. When Nicholas learned of the tragedy, his first impulse was to call off a formal ball planned for that evening, however his uncles convinced him that he would gravely offend the French ambassador who was hosting the affair. This proved to be very bad advice indeed, and the tsar would forever be remembered as being calloused and indifferent to the deaths caused by the poor planning of his own officials.

Actually, Nicholas' fatal flaw was not a lack of sensitivity or concern for his subjects, but rather a solemn and inflexible conviction that his rule was the embodiment of God's will on earth. Neither he nor anyone else had the right to alter the responsibility divinely entrusted to him, and he therefore bristled at any suggestion that he accept limits to his power. Thus, when the *Zemstvo* of Tver sent a congratulatory letter to the tsar upon ascending the throne, the signers also pleaded that he heed the voice of the people and see that the law be applied uniformly throughout the country. Nicholas, prompted by Pobedonostsev, sent a reply dismissing these hopes as "senseless dreams," categorically asserting that he intended to "maintain the principle of autocracy just as firmly and unflinchingly as it was preserved by my unforgettable dead father."[6] For Russia's scattered revolutionary elements, this pronouncement was a veritable call to arms.

Among the many activists who heeded this call was Alexander Ulianov's brother, Vladimir Ilich, soon to be better known as Lenin. Two years younger than the tsar, not only was he better educated and far more ambitious, he was actually planning to change the world. His first task was to destroy autocracy in Russia and to construct a new economic and social order. The origins of his radicalism can probably be traced to his brother's execution as well as his own subsequent expulsion from the University of Kazan for participating in a student demonstration. However, in 1891, after receiving a law degree from the University of St. Petersburg, he became attracted to Marxism and soon became a dedicated activist. In December of 1895, he was arrested for agitating on behalf of strikers in the textile and cigarette factories. After waiting fourteen months in jail to be tried, he was convicted and exiled to the Siberian town of Shushenskoe near the Mongolian border. It was here he married Nadezhda Krupskaya,[7] who shared his devotion to Marxism and acted as his loyal help-mate for the rest of his life. Lenin's term in exile also coincided with the formal founding of the Russian Social Democratic Labor Party in Minsk in 1897, an event he could not attend but which he heartily welcomed. By this time, he had begun to study contemporary economics and wrote a book entitled *The Development of Capitalism in Russia*, which appeared in 1899. It was also during this period that Lenin began to think about the need for an émigré newspaper to spell out a common ideology and forge a close knit network of the various revolutionary cells in the country and abroad.

In July 1900, after completing his term of exile, Lenin left Russia for western Europe where he had little influence on affairs at home. Still, he was far from idle and helped to establish the periodical *Iskra (The Spark)* in Munich. He also wrote *Chto delat? (What is to be Done?)* in which he called for the creation of a conspiratorial, revolutionary elite to lead the proletariat to the overthrow of the existing order and the establishment of a socialist order. This, however, prompted the opposition of those dedicated to the idea of a mass labor party and the need to seek economic gains for the workers by legal means. This all came out at the Second Congress of the Russian Socialist Democratic Labor Party in 1903, which was held at first in Brussels but was later forced to relocate to London. In the end, Lenin and his followers gained a two-vote majority and became known as the Bolsheviks, or "those of the majority." This gave them control of the party organs including the Central Committee. The Mensheviks, or "those of the minority," however, included such important notables such as Yuli Martov,[8] Pavel Axelrod,[9] Vera Zasulich, and Lev Trotsky.[10]

Neither the Bolsheviks nor the Mensheviks were perceived to be a serious threat to the state, mainly because neither supported terrorism. Far more fearsome were the Socialist Revolutionaries, who considered themselves the direct descendants of The People's Will. Like its predecessor, this party, which had formally organized only in 1901, believed in the revolutionary potential of the peasantry, although they also sought to enlist the factory workers to help destroy the autocracy. To this end, they had their own elite Battle Organization, the purpose of which was to continue the tradition of terror that had so confounded the state during the last years of Alexander II. Its leader was Grigori Gershuni,[11] who, hoping to make maximum use of this tactic to disable the government, prompted a student, Piotr Karpovich,[12] to assassinate an unpopular minister of education, Nikolai Bogolepov, in February 1901, and Stepan Balmashev[13] to assassinate the minister of the interior, Dmitri Sipiagin, in April of 1902.

But the Battle Organization's campaign of terror took an odd turn after the arrest of Gershuni in 1903. Its new leader was an engineer named Yevno Azev,[14] who was both a party member and an agent for the secret police. A few years earlier, he had been recruited by the chief of the Moscow *Okhrana*, Sergei Zubatov, who was trying to devise a plan to infiltrate the leadership of the various revolutionary groups. At the same time, Zubatov was organizing a net of workers' unions in the city in order to direct their activities toward nonviolent ends. To be sure, this put Azev in a unique position: he could now help or harm either side as he saw fit. He proceeded to do both in such a way as to obscure what he really hoped to achieve. For instance, he would often help his Socialist Revolutionary comrades plan an assassination only to warn the police so they could foil the attempt and arrest the conspirators before they could strike. At other times, he would allow the assassination to take place, possibly believing that the victim deserved to die. Such was case with the minister of the interior, Viacheslav Plehve, who was loathed as a particularly reactionary and sinister force in Nicholas' cabinet. Azev, who was Jewish, hated him because he believed that the minister had instigated the pogrom at Kishinov in April of 1903.

In fact, although Plehve was indeed anti-Semitic, he had not encouraged the pogrom at Kishinov. Still, he was ruthless and corrupt and perceived by most as a self-serving careerist with no solid convictions beyond devotion to the monarchy. He was also extremely ambitious, and this helped him rise from a minor position in the ministry of justice to that of prosecutor of the St. Petersburg Chamber of Justice in 1879. The following year, a major turning point came in Plehve's career when he wrote the report on the explosion in the Winter Palace. This was followed by more promotions culminating in his appointment to the post of minister of internal affairs after Sipiagin's assassination in 1902. Plehve was now at the height of his power, but his repressive policies soon earned him the enmity of nearly everyone including Boris Savinkov,[15] who was one of Azev's chief lieutenants in the Battle Organization of the Socialist Revolutionaries.

Having concluded that Plehve was a scoundrel who had to be eliminated, Savinkov recruited Yegor Sazonov,[16] a former medical student, who was willing to sacrifice himself to accomplish the deed. Accordingly, he agreed to stage the attack on him while the latter drove along Izmailovsky Prospect in St. Petersburg enroute to his weekly meeting with the tsar. It was a difficult assignment: Plehve's carriage was heavily guarded and generally moved at high speeds. But on July 15 (28), 1904, a determined Sazonov ran through a crowd of onlookers and positioned himself in front of the approaching carriage just in time. When it swerved to avoid him, he threw his bomb through the side window. The explosion killed Plehve and left Sazonov badly injured. Still, the latter survived and was sentenced to fifteen years hard labor. The tsar's diary entry in reaction to the loss of his minister was as follows: "In the good Plehve I have lost a friend and a priceless minister of internal affairs. God is punishing us in His wrath."[17]

Actually, Nicholas was probably better off without Plehve, who had been one of those who had expressed the belief that a "short, victorious war" was needed to unite the country. In February 1904, some five months before the minister's death, the Japanese had bombarded and disabled much of the Russian Pacific fleet at Port Arthur. The attack had been prompted by Russia's expansion into Manchuria and Korea. The Japanese had themselves coveted these areas, but the tsar had refused to negotiate. What followed was a series of military disasters that horrified the public and undermined the public's confidence in the government. It also emboldened an Orthodox priest named Father Georgi Gapon[18] to lead thousands of striking workers from the Putilov engineering works to the Winter Palace on January 9 (22), 1905, to petition the tsar to address their grievances and demands. These included an eight-hour work day, amnesty for political prisoners, freedom of speech and religion, and the convening of a constituent assembly.

Gapon, who had been recruited by Sergei Zubatov to participate in his "police socialism" scheme, seemed to have believed that he was helping both sides by taking charge of a dangerous situation. Sympathizing with the workers and their plight, Gapon believed that it was in the government's best interest to address their concerns, but Nicholas, who resided some fourteen miles outside the city at Tsarskoe Selo, was not disposed to travel to the Winter Palace to receive the petition. The workers, trusting that he would come, went ahead with the march carrying icons and religious banners. When they arrived at the Winter Palace, they were blocked by troops, who, after some hesitation, were ordered to fire. In the massacre that followed, about 150 were killed and many more wounded. Nicholas, to judge from the entry made in his diary that evening, seemed not to have fully appreciated the gravity of the situation: "Serious disorders took place in St. Petersburg today when workers tried to get to the Winter Palace. In several parts of the city troops were compelled to fire: there were many killed and wounded. Lord, how sad and painful this is."[19] In the days and weeks that followed, however, he made no attempt to address the fundamental causes of the unrest. His lone initiative was to invite a delegation of workers to an audience in the Winter Palace to lecture them about the dangers of listening to revolutionaries.

Yet Bloody Sunday, as the incident came to be known, enraged the country and shocked the world. It also galvanized the Socialist Revolutionary Battle Organization to take vengeance and brought to the fore a revolutionary spirit of rare purity. This was Ivan Kaliaev,[20] who had been born in Warsaw and had come to Moscow in 1896 to study history and philology at the university. Later, he had transferred to St. Petersburg to take up law, only to be expelled and arrested for participating in student disorders. His punishment was to spend two years in exile at Yekaterinoslav, which made it impossible for him to reenter any Russian university. Determined to finish his schooling, he enrolled in 1902 at the university at Lvov in western Ukraine but was arrested that summer for carrying subversive literature. Once again, he was sentenced to a period of exile, this time in Yarolslavl', where he came into contact with some members of the Socialist Revolutionary party. He was soon recruited by Savinkov to the Battle Organization, where his life took on a new purpose.

Kaliaev has been described as having come to terrorism "by way of a luminous faith and a desperate desire to sacrifice himself for the salvation of all mankind."[21] A man of steely determination, somehow he did not much seem like a revolutionary. He was shy and quiet, had fair features, was slight of build, dressed fastidiously, loved to read poetry and often composed verse himself. He was, however, the kind of man who lived by

The workers marched to the Winter Palace that Sunday in January 1905 to present a petition to Nicholas II, but the tsar avoided the demonstrators by remaining at his imperial residence at Tsarskoe Selo outside St. Petersburg. The massacre that followed led to a wave of strikes that lasted for nearly a year. I.A. Vladimirov (1889–1947).

fiercely-held convictions from which he refused to deviate. Previously, he had participated in the plot to assassinate Plehve by serving as a back-up bombthrower to Sazonov. In the aftermath of this success, he and the other accomplices left the country and met in Geneva to decide the Battle Organization's next move. It was agreed that the next target should be someone in the imperial family, such as the tsar's uncle, Grand Duke Sergei, who was also the governor-general of Moscow. Not only was the grand duke thoroughly hated for his ruthlessness and reactionary policies, but he was also Alexandra's brother-in-law.

In fact, Grand Duke Sergei had resigned his post of governor general right after the Bloody Sunday massacre, but this was not generally known. In any case, Kaliaev decided to attack him with a bomb on the evening of February 2 (15), 1905, as he rode in his carriage to attend a performance at the Bolshoi Theater. The assassin took up his position on the Voskresensky Square near the Alexandrovsky Gardens just outside the Kremlin and waited. When the grand duke appeared, Kaliaev prepared to throw the device, only to hold back at the last second. Riding with the grand duke was his wife, Elle, and their two children, and Kaliaev could not bring himself to kill the innocent. Still, he was determined to try again. On the afternoon of February 4 (17), Kaliaev walked through the Nikolsky

Gate into the Kremlin and threw a bomb at the grand duke's carriage as it passed by. The explosion blew the carriage and its royal passenger to pieces and left the driver mortally wounded. The assassin survived with only minor cuts and scratches, although the noise left him partially deaf. He was quickly arrested.

The evening after the murder, Grand Duchess Elle came to visit Kaliaev in his cell. Not having expected the visit, he tried to be civil, as did she, but the two did not understand each other. She had come to forgive him, and he would not be forgiven. After accepting a holy icon, he said simply, "My conscience is clear, I am sorry I caused you so great a sorrow. I acted with a deep sense of responsibility, and if I had a thousand lives, I would give them all, not only one. And now again I will say how sorry I am for you, but still I did my duty and I'll do it again to the very end, whatever happens. Goodbye. We shall never see each other again."[22] But a few days after the grand duchess's visit, Kaliaev began to hear rumors alleging that he had tearfully begged the woman to ask the tsar to pardon him. Immediately, he wrote her a letter full of bitterness, accusing her of spreading vile falsehoods, "I should not have sympathized with you and I should have refused to speak with you. I behaved with kindness, momentarily suppressing the natural hatred I felt for you. I have revealed the motives which moved me: you have proven unworthy of my generosity."[23]

Kaliaev went to St. Petersburg to be tried before a closed session of the Senate on April 5 (18), 1905. Various witnesses were called to confirm what was already known. The prisoner remained proud and defiant throughout and showed no remorse. When it was his turn to speak, he refused to admit that "the gentlemen of the court in their senatorial togas" had any right to judge him. "You cannot judge because you are a party in the dispute." He then listed the crimes of Grand Duke Sergei, which included tyrannizing poor Jews and innocent workers. The outcome was as expected: guilty on all counts; the punishment: death by hanging in the Schlüsselberg Fortress. Kaliaev was nearly euphoric: "I rejoice at your verdict. I hope you have the courage to carry it out openly and publicly as I executed the sentence of the Socialist Revolutionary party. Learn to look the advancing revolution straight in the eyes."[24]

Even before the grand duke's assassination, Nicholas had been preoccupied by the ever-increasing number of demonstrations, strikes, and terrorist acts that had come in the aftermath of Bloody Sunday. Added to all this was a stunning naval defeat at the hand of the Japanese at Tsushima on May 14 (27), which was followed by a mutiny aboard the battleship *Potemkin*[25] in the Black Sea. Assaulted by disaster on all sides, the tsar was forced to recall a man to his service whom he did not like. Sergei Witte was a mathematician of Dutch ancestry who had served Alexander III as minister of transportation and as minister of finance. He was brusque, opinionated, and extremely knowledgeable. Nicholas had long resented both his manner and his advice. Still, the magnitude of the crisis caused by the war compelled him to utilize the man's ability to negotiate the peace.

To this end, the former finance minister traveled to Portsmouth, New Hampshire, and secured terms that were far more lenient than anyone had dared to hope. Russia was forced to cede only Port Arthur, the southern line of the Chinese Eastern Railroad, and the southern half of Sakhalin Island to the Japanese. Thus, Witte returned to Russia in triumph to be awarded the rank of count, but he did not get a rest. In October, the country was nearly shut down in a massive general strike organized by the newly formed St. Petersburg Soviet of Workers, who were greatly inspired by the oratory of Lev Trotsky. The turmoil was intensified by the activities of a right-wing organization called the Union of the Russian People, whose special combat group attacked the Jews and other minorities. Once again the tsar turned to Witte for a solution, who outlined two possible courses of action: either grant constitutional reforms or impose a military dictatorship. It is to Nicholas' everlasting shame that he actually preferred the latter. However, when he offered the job of military dictator to his close relative, Grand Duke Nikolai Nikolaevich, the general threatened to shoot himself rather than wage war on the Russian people.

Thus, it was with a deep sense of shame and failure that Nicholas announced the Imperial Manifesto on October 17 (30) that promised "freedom of conscience, speech, assembly and association," and the establishment of an elected *Duma*[26] to approve all new laws. Witte was named chief of the council of ministers, or prime minister, and was expected to establish the new system and restore order to the country, but the general distrust of the government was such that the situation continued to get worse. There were peasant uprisings in the Baltic, mutinies in the military, and demands for independence in Poland and Finland. However, the worst unrest of all occurred in Moscow where the local soviet inspired some 2000 workers and students to set up barricades in the streets and hold out for ten days. Only when the Semenovsky Regiment arrived from St. Petersburg and used artillery to pound the insurgents into submission did the rebellion cease.

The opening of the so-called *Duma* of Popular Hope on April 27 (May 10), 1906, was a tense occasion for everyone involved, especially Nicholas. To prevent the new legislature from writing a constitution, he had previously instructed Witte to draw up the Fundamental Laws for the empire, the first article of which stated: "To the Emperor of the Russias belongs

In December of 1905, even after Tsar Nicholas had promised to establish an elected *Duma* and grant basic civil rights, defiant revolutionaries blockaded a section of Moscow. Russian artillery bombarded the insurgents for three days to force their submission. I.A. Vladimirov (1869–1947).

the supreme and unlimited power." Although the document did affirm basic civil rights, it also stipulated that cabinet officials would be responsible only to the tsar.

One week before the opening of the Duma, Nicholas dismissed Witte as prime minister and replaced him with a dull, uninspired bureaucrat, Ivan Goremykin. Then, with no legislative program having been offered for the *Duma* to consider, the members began to rant against the government and argue among themselves. The tsar soon tired of the commotion, dissolved the *Duma* in July, and called for new elections. At the same time, he replaced Goremykin with the younger more vigorous Piotr Stolypin, who would now serve both as minister of the interior and prime minister.

Although Stolypin was a confirmed monarchist, he was determined to cooperate with the *Duma* and submitted an ambitious legislative agenda for its consideration. However, before he could get down to work, he nearly became a victim when a bomb destroyed his summer residence, killing thirty-two people and wounding his daughter. He reacted by introducing a state of emergency and conducting a protracted campaign against terrorism. To this end, special military courts were empowered to apply the death penalty to those convicted of political acts of violence within twenty-four hours. At the same time, he promoted a scheme for land reform, which would allow peasants to leave their village communes and establish themselves as independent farmers. Legislation was passed the following year allowing individual peasants to claim their share of communal land in a consolidated plot rather than in communal strips. This initiative, introduced in November 1906, enjoyed some popularity but ultimately did little to raise productivity in the countryside.

The second *Duma*, which met in February 1907, included a large radical element and proved to be no more cooperative than the first. Stolypin soon concluded that it would not only be necessary to dissolve this body, but to change the election law itself to insure a composition more cooperative for the government. A pretext was found when some Social Democrats were accused of subverting the armed forces. When the *Duma* refused a request to waive the immunity of those accused, the tsar ordered its dissolution on June 3 (16). That very day, a new electoral law was introduced favoring the more conservative elements, despite the fact that such action was in clear violation of the Fundamental Laws. This initiative was not challenged, however, and the Third *Duma* which met the following November, lasted its full term of five years.

Although this was a more cooperative body than the first two, Stolypin suffered a number of defeats during this period, the most embarrassing of which came in 1911 when he introduced a bill to expand the *zemstvos* to six provinces in the Polish territories. The initiative was passed in the lower house of the *Duma* but was vetoed by the State Soviet, despite the prime minister's hard work to secure its passage. The measure eventually did become law in June when Nicholas agreed to suspend the *Duma* and invoke Article 87, which gave him and his ministers the right to legislate when the *Duma* was not in session. Although this was a victory of sorts, Stolypin did not regard it as such. Convinced that the tsar no longer had confidence in him, he submitted his resignation, which Nicholas, unfortunately as it turns out, did not accept.

In late August (early September) 1911, the tsar, Stolypin, and other government officials journeyed to Kiev to participate in a series of public ceremonies. These included the unveiling of a monument to Alexander II, the opening of a museum, and the laying of a foundation for a future agricultural and industrial exposition. On September 1 (14), Stolypin attended the opera at the Municipal Kiev Theater and took his seat in the first row of the pit, not far from the box of honor occupied by the tsar and his four young daughters. During the second intermission, a well-dressed young man walked past the security police right up to the chief minister and shot him twice at point blank range, once in the right hand and once under the right breast. Stolypin slumped into his seat, tried to open his jacket, and looking in the direction of the tsar's box made the sign of the cross. He was then taken to the Makovsky Hospital, where he was treated and seemed to be recovering. However, on September 4 (18), his condition took a drastic turn for the worse and he died the following day.

The assassin was a twenty-four-year-old lawyer named Dmitri Bogrov, who had been hired by the police to prevent the very crime he had just committed. Not much was known about him, except that his father was a wealthy attorney who had abandoned Judaism for Christianity, apparently to further his social ambitions. The young Bogrov had enjoyed all the privileges of wealth and class, including a good education and extended travel in western Europe. Still, he seemed somehow adrift and unable to find a purpose in life. Having begun a law program at Kiev University, he dropped out, went to Munich, developed a fondness for gambling, and returned to St. Petersburg deeply in debt. For a time, he fraternized with some Socialist Revolutionaries and later some anarchists, which drew the attention of the police. After a search of his apartment, he was subsequently questioned by the *Okhrana*, who, learning of his debts, invited him to work for them. He was to receive 100 rubles a month to provide the *Okhrana* with information about anarchists and Maximalists.[27]

For a while, this arrangement worked well for both sides: Bogrov got his money, which allowed him to return to law school, and the police got information that led to the arrest of revolutionaries both in Russia and abroad. However, at some point the informer seemed to have been bothered by his double game. In November 1910, he approached the Socialist Revolutionary leader, E.E. Lazarov, about a plan to assassinate Stolypin. Lazarov consulted with others in the party but ultimately rejected the offer because he had heard rumors about Bogrov's connections with the police. Disappointed, the aspiring assassin returned to Kiev to work in a law firm.

In August 1911, Bogrov was visited by a former friend named Stepa, who warned him that some of his anarchist comrades in Paris had learned of his treachery and planned to execute him. Stepa suggested that Bogov atone for his crimes by killing the *Okhrana* chief, Colonel N.N. Kuliabko, during the upcoming festivities in Kiev, but Bogrov was determined that the victim should be Stolypin and soon developed a daring scheme to accomplish the deed. On August 27 (September 9), he visited the *Okhrana* and told officials there that a man named Lazarov and two other Socialist Revolutionaries were planning to assassinate both the prime minister and the minister of education, L.A. Kasso. He called the two fictitious terrorists Nikolai Yakovlevich and Nina Alexandrovna and described the appearance of the former in some detail. Both, he claimed, would be staying in his apartment, but, as he insisted to Kuliabko, to catch them in the act and prevent Stolypin's murder, he needed tickets to the events the chief minister was likely to attend. Thus on September 1, Bogrov was in position at the opera house to murder the prime minister.

Stolypin's assassination sent shock waves through the city and the country. People wondered about the privileged young man who had sided with the revolutionaries. But Bogrov had little to say: "It may be there is no logic [in all this], but I had my own logic." The fact that he was Jewish, however, provoked a number of attacks on Jewish students and businessmen in the days that followed. Many left the city to escape the pogroms they feared might erupt, and troops were brought in as a precaution. However, the biggest issue of all in the aftermath of the assassination was the stunning incompetence of the police, and Colonel Kuliabko in particular, which had made the crime possible. Indeed, many believed that Stolypin was the victim of a police conspiracy, although there is no compelling evidence to support this allegation. For his own part, Bogrov insisted all along that he acted alone and that he regarded Stolypin "as the main architect of reaction and decided that his activities were harmful to the people."[28] The assassin was tried and convicted on September 23 (October 6) and hanged in the early morning of September 25 (October 8).

In the few years remaining before the Revolution, Nicholas would be hard-pressed to find competent ministers like Stolypin, who could act decisively during times of crisis. Such was especially the case after the Lena River Goldfield Massacre in April of 1912, when 5000 workers went on strike for better conditions and higher wages. The tragedy that ensued was caused by a drunken policeman who ordered his men to open fire, killing 200. This led to a wave of strikes elsewhere and enormous public indignation. The government authorized a commission to investigate, but its credibility was challenged by the *Duma,* which appointed its own committee headed by a young lawyer named Alexander Kerensky.[29] It was he who wrote the report condemning the government's management of the mines, which led to the resignation of the minister of the interior. Indeed, Kerensky's work gained him such popularity that he was elected to the fourth *Duma* that convened in November, but the pivotal role that he would play in Russian history was still in the future.

Not all was gloom and doom, however. In February 1913, the imperial family moved from Tsarskoe Selo into the Winter Palace to prepare for the 300th anniversary of the founding of the Romanov Dynasty. The celebrations were meant to surpass anything the country had ever seen. The opening event was a Te Deum in Our Lady of Kazan Cathedral on

Nevsky Prospect, although a steady downpour kept the crowds disappointingly thin. The occasion was further marred by an unpleasant incident in the cathedral when the president of the *Duma*, Mikhail Rodzianko, physically ejected a peasant who had dared to take a seat in front reserved for special guests. This was Rasputin, who had long been a favorite of the imperial family. He was thought to be a man of God by some and a debaucher and a charlatan by others. In any case, the incident was quickly forgotten, and, in the days that followed, a series of receptions took place in the Winter Palace where the tsar received dignitaries and ethnic delegations from all over the country. Nicholas and Alexandra also attended a gala performance of Glinka's great opera, *A Life for the Tsar*. Only the empress seemed not to enjoy herself, withdrawing from the royal box at the first opportunity.

At Easter that year, Nicholas presented Alexandra with a golden egg, made by the master Carl Peter Fabergé,[30] that was so exquisite as to defy description. Covered with miniature portraits of all the Romanov tsars and empresses, it opened up to reveal two tiny maps: one depicting Muscovy in 1613 and the other the Russian Empire in 1913. In May, there was a royal excursion up the Volga to the city of Kostroma to commemorate sixteen-year-old Michael Romanov's election to the Muscovite throne. Supporters of the monarchy took satisfaction in the difference brought about by three centuries of change and development: the land Michael would rule was a small territory recovering from many years of war, famine, and pestilence; the Russia of 1913 was a vast empire at peace and enjoying a period of relative prosperity. Workers, of course, still went on strike, and terrorists still lurked in the shadows, but both Nicholas and Alexandra were convinced by the success of the tercentenary celebrations that they were loved and admired by the overwhelming majority of their subjects.

While the tsar felt he had little to fear from revolutionaries and other enemies, he was extremely concerned by the health of his hemophiliac son, Tsarevich Alexei, who had been born in 1904. The disease, which had been transmitted to him from his great grandmother, Queen Victoria, through Alexandra, often left him in pain and, at times, too ill even to walk. The boy's illness was a closely guarded secret, for it was feared that if the public knew of the affliction, he would be deemed unfit for the throne. However, the fact that he had to be carried about on public occasions by a sailor from the imperial navy provoked much curiosity. It was also a source of anxiety and guilt for Alexandra, who felt responsible for her son's condition. Her single-minded determination to find a cure or at least relief for Alexis' condition in large part explains her stiff demeanor and seeming disinterest during public events. It also paved the way for a number of charlatans to exploit the credulity and generosity of the imperial family, including a bogus holy man from the remote Siberian town of Pokrovskoe, the aforementioned Grigori Efimovich Rasputin.

The name Rasputin, which means "dissolute" in Russian, was not his real surname. It was given to him by neighbors who observed his drunken behavior and lust for the village girls. More ominously, they also suspected that he was a horse thief. The young man, who was born into a relatively wealthy family, seemed to have had little to recommend him. He had no education, knew no trade, and seemed doomed to spend his life as a wagoner, transporting goods and passengers from town to town. However, a visit with some pilgrims to the monastery at Verkhoturoe brought him into contact with a renowned holy man named Makari, who made a deep impression on him. The monastery served both as a place of retreat for monks seeking peace and solitude and as a jail for heretical sectarians. Most of the latter were members of the Khlysty, a group that allegedly sought enhanced spirituality through orgies of flagellation and sexual intercourse. Later, Rasputin's enemies would charge that he was a member of this sect, although this was never proved. In any case, when he returned to Pokrovskoe, he married a peasant woman three years older than himself named Praskovie Feodorovna Dubrovina.[31] He tried to become a farmer, but, when a vision of the Holy Mother in the field one day inspired him to make a pilgrimage to the Holy Land, off he went.

Two years and many miles later, Rasputin returned home seemingly completely cleansed of his dissolute past. He now neither drank nor seduced women and, for a while at least, behaved like a holy man — quoting the Bible, blessing people, and tending the sick. However, when the local priest, doubting his sincerity, accused him of heresy, he set out on the road once again. Over the course of the next decade, he traveled far and wide. Although many of his old sinful habits returned during this period, he developed a reputation as a seer, a healer, and a preacher. In 1903, he arrived in St. Petersburg for the first time and made a series of acquaintances that was to change his life forever. These included the great preacher, Father Ioann of Kronstadt, and the rector of the St. Petersburg Theological Academy, Feofan, who was also Empress Alexandra's confessor. Finally, he made the acquaintance of a monk named Iliodor,[32] who was then a student at the academy. Iliodor had the makings of a true religious fanatic. Not only did he want to revitalize the Church, but he was determined to purify society of its weak nobility, brutal police, and corrupt imperial court. In Rasputin, he thought he saw a kindred spirit and was especially taken in by what he supposed was the peasant's deep spirituality.

To the modern observer, it must seem amazing that Rasputin could have attracted anyone, let alone society's most privileged and powerful. Filthy and foul-smelling, his table manners were gross and his language vulgar and crude. He was barely literate and spoke in jerky, disconnected sentences that often made little sense, but the steady gaze of his deep blue eyes exuded a magnetism that few could resist. And by preaching his personal doctrine of "salvation through sin," Rasputin was able to convince many that physical contact with him would enrich them spiritually and absolve them of guilt. As his fame grew, his alleged special powers became known to two Montenegrin princesses, Militsa and Anastasia, both of whom were married to uncles of the tsar. These women, bored as they were by polite society, not only saw something mystical and exotic in Rasputin, but recognized him as a true *starets*.[33] Thus, in November of 1905, they introduced him to Nicholas and Alexandra.

Despite the fact that Rasputin made a favorable impression during his first appearance at court, he did not automatically gain access to the inner circle. However, early in 1907, he made the acquaintance of Anna Vyrubova,[34] a plump, rather unattractive woman who had recently become a lady-in-waiting to the empress. By most accounts, Anna was a naïve and wholly innocent young woman who had little to offer in terms of intellect. Still, her utter devotion to the imperial family so endeared her to Alexandra that the empress resolved to find her a husband. To this end, the empress introduced her to a young naval officer, and a romance soon developed. The two became engaged, but Anna's apprehensions about the upcoming marriage led her to Rasputin, who paradoxically advised her to go ahead but predicted that there would be serious problems. This proved to be exactly the case. The husband, a veteran of the war against Japan, was afflicted by some mental illness and became so abusive toward his young wife that the marriage had to be dissolved. For consolation, Vyrubova turned to Rasputin, who, without taking advantage of her sexually, used his powers to ease her anguish. At the same time, Anna was virtually adopted by Alexandra, who felt guilty for having arranged the match. The two became close, and, when the tsarevich injured himself in 1908 and was near death, Vyrubova urged that Rasputin be called to minister to the boy. The latter was duly summoned to Tsarkoe Selo where he performed his first "miracle." Acting with calm and confidence, he prayed over Alexis until he fell asleep. When the patient awoke, he was well on the road to recovery.

This was indeed a major turning point in the relationship between Rasputin and the imperial family, but the favor shown to the *starets* also gave rise to powerful enemies. Much of this was due to the jealousy and dismay of those who, not knowing of the tsarevich's hemophilia, could not understand the attachment of Nicholas and Alexandra to a common peasant. Yet where some felt envy, others saw opportunity, and people seeking imperial favors now called on Rasputin offering money and gifts for his help. The temptation to exploit his situation sometimes proved to be too much for the *starets*, especially when the petitioner was an attractive woman. Things often got out of hand as he became involved in lurid sex scandals and wild orgies. These activities soon caught the attention of the police, who now began to watch the holy man and compile reports on his behavior.[35]

Historians have generally excoriated Nicholas for his failure to heed the many eye-witness accounts of Rasputin's drunken and licentious behavior, but the tsar was plainly caught in a dilemma he could not resolve. He had always been sustained by a deep conviction that the roots of his power lay with the peasants, who truly loved and revered him. In many ways, Rasputin seemed to embody that ideal, and his uncanny ability to cure his son and calm others around him (including the empress) seemed clear evidence of divine favor. Thus, the tsar was at first inclined to dismiss stories of Rasputin's sinful behavior as lies and exaggerations by those who resented the fact that a man of low birth had influence at court.

On the other hand, Nicholas had to know something was wrong when accounts of Rasputin's debauchery came from people who were entirely credible, but how could he banish a man whose presence was necessary for the well-being of his son, the future tsar? Possibly, he concluded that Rasputin's dual nature was simply one of those mysteries of God that no mortal being could ever fully comprehend. This put him in the uncomfortable position of trying to decide when the *starets'* advice was divinely inspired and when it was bogus. In any case, the tsar's wary approach was in stark contrast to the empress' blind faith in Rasputin and her unyielding hostility to anyone who criticized "Our Friend," as she and Nicholas referred to him.

That Rasputin was now a formidable political force can be seen in the help he was able to provide his friend Iliodor, who had finished his theological studies at the St. Petersburg Academy and had gone to the Pochaevsky Monastery in Volynia to become editor for the monastery's religious publications. In his zeal to re-establish a holy union between the tsar and his people, Iliodor began to inveigh against "liberalism, socialism, capitalism, Jews, students, the intelligentsia, factory workers, bureaucrats, aristocrats, courtiers, and hypocritical ecclesiastics who indulged themselves at the expense of the peasantry."[36] For this, he was reprimanded by the Holy Synod in February 1907 but to no effect. Iliodor merely responded by calling upon the tsar to confiscate the land of the nobility and redistribute it to the peasants. Later, he sent an open letter to the Synod denouncing the members for their lack of spirituality and denying their authority. For this, Iliodor would have been severely punished had not Rasputin prompted the tsar to intervene. Even so, Nicholas felt compelled to transfer the rebel monk to Tsaritsyn.

Thus began the second phase of Iliodor's rebellion. After gathering money from all kinds of well-wishers in Tsaritsyn, he build a monastery/fortress, where he established his base of operations, and then traveled up and down the Volga organizing regional chapters of the Union of the Russian People. He also called on the Black Hundreds[37] to rise up and terrorize the "enemies of God and Russia." It was almost as if a new Pugachev had emerged on the scene. The local authorities tried to arrest him, but he was protected by his supporters. Finally, in April 1909, Rasputin urged Iliodor to come to St. Petersburg to call on the empress. Alexandra made the monk promise to cease his agitation and to stop insulting the tsar's ministers. He agreed but did not keep his word. Upon returning to Tsaritsyn, he declared it his right to chastise even the tsar if he disobeyed the will of God. This prompted Nicholas to exile Iliodor to Minsk. Once again, however, Rasputin intervened and persuaded Nicholas to countermand his own order.

In November of 1910, Rasputin traveled to Tsaritsyn to visit Iliodor and received a rapturous greeting from the latter's supporters. He stayed about two weeks and then left with his friend for Pokrovskoe by steamer, a journey that would take nine days. According to the book Iliodor later wrote, it was at this time that he became fully aware of Rasputin's utter depravity. The latter spent most of the time boasting about his intimacy with the imperial family and his sexual exploits in society. He also showed Iliodor some personal letters from the empress and her daughters, which the younger monk found shocking. Hiding his emotions, Iliodor resolved to discredit the fraudulent *starets* when the time was right. To this end, he stole some letters, one of which was made public in 1912. It confirmed the worst suspicions of those who hated Rasputin and the empress. A portion of this letter reads as follows:

> My soul is only rested and at ease when you my teacher are near me. I kiss your hands and lay my head upon your blessed shoulders. I feel so joyful then. Then all I want to do is to sleep, sleep for ever on your shoulder, in your embrace.[38]

Eventually, Iliodor felt secure enough to force a showdown. In December of 1911, after learning that Rasputin had raped a nun, he conspired with the fiercely conservative Bishop of Saratov, Hermogen,[39] to lure the *starets* to the Yaroslavl' Monastery so he could be taught a lesson. After a list of misdeeds was read out, Hermogen punched him with his fist and beat him with a large wooden cross. Finally, the *starets* was forced to swear before a holy icon that he would stop seducing women and stay away from the imperial family. However, within days of the beating, Rasputin was back at Tsarkoe Selo to inform the tsar of the incident. Retribution was swift: Hermogen was deprived of his offices and sent into exile, and Iliodor was confined in the Florishchev Monastery. But the latter did not go quietly. He wrote the Holy Synod a letter demanding that the real culprit be punished:

> Either indict Rasputin on religious grounds, or defrock me. I cannot reconcile myself to the fact that the synod, the bearer of the blessing of the Holy Ghost, should shield the holy devil who desecrates the Church of Christ. Know that I am willing to rot in a dungeon, but that I shall not reconcile myself to the desecration of God's name.[40]

Rasputin, who was in Pokrovskoe at the time, did not hesitate to defend himself. He wrote the following to Nicholas and Alexandra:

> Iliodor has allied himself with demons. He is rebellious. They used to flog monks like him. Yes, tsars had them flogged. Now bring him to heel. Have no mercy.[41]

In December 1912, Iliodor was formally defrocked.

But the *starets* was by no means in the clear. Articles continued to appear in the newspapers about him, and his public image remained bad. He no longer went to the imperial palaces to see the tsar and empress but met them in the nearby cottage of Anna Vyrubova, who called him on the phone every day. He also spent time in Pokrovskoe and other places, partly in an effort to stay out of the public eye, but his indispensability to Nicholas and Alexandra soon became clear once and for all in the crisis that followed.

In the fall of 1912, after visiting the battlefield of Borodino to commemorate the 100th anniversary of the great battle with Napoleon, the imperial family went west into Poland to enjoy a holiday on their family estates at Belovezhe and Spala. At Belovezhe, the eight-year-old tsarevich bumped his knee against a ledge in the bathroom and was unable to walk. However, the injury did not seem life-threatening, and the family traveled on to their other estate at Spala to enjoy the beautiful forests and country roads. It was during a bumpy carriage ride one day with his mother that Alexis injured himself again, this time causing massive internal bleeding and the formation of a large tumor in his groin. The pain was so excruciating that the boy screamed himself hoarse. Doctors were summoned from St. Petersburg but were unable to stop the bleeding or relieve the pain. "When I'm dead, it won't hurt anymore, will it, Mama?"[42] he moaned. It was only on the eleventh night of the crisis that a desperate Alexandra urged Anna Vyrubova to send a telegram to Rasputin in Pokrovskoe asking him to pray for her son. His reply was swift and exactly what the empress needed to hear: "God has seen your tears and heard your prayers. Do not grieve. The Little One will not die. Do not allow the doctors to bother him too much."[43] One day later the bleeding stopped, and Alexis survived.

This incident, more than any other, solidified Rasputin's position at court and enhanced his prestige in St. Petersburg. People now came to his apartment in ever increasing numbers to achieve through the *starets* what they could not hope to otherwise. In many cases, this did not require an appeal to the tsar or the empress, but rather to other highly placed persons who wished to curry favor with the imperial couple. In any case, Rasputin helped some, exploited some, and ignored some. Those who fared worst were women who refused his advances. More than a few left his apartment screaming that he had tried to rape them. Those he decided to help generally received a scrap of paper with a cross drawn at the top with a few scribbled words such as, "My dear and valued friend. Do this for me. Grigori," or "My dear chap, Fix it up for her. She is all right. Grigori."[44] It was up to the petitioner to explain what they wanted to the person addressed. Sometimes Rasputin was approached by the rich and powerful and offered piles of banknotes or expensive gifts on the mere chance that his influence might be helpful. These he accepted to spend or give away as he saw fit. He was especially gracious to curious peasants who had come to visit him and marvel at his success.

Rasputin had lived at many different addresses in St. Petersburg, but the last two years of his life were spent on a third floor apartment at 64 Grokhavaya Street. It was a modest five-room dwelling and conveniently close to the train that took him to Tsarskoe Selo. It also had a back staircase, which allowed him come and go without being seen from the street. This was important because he was now at the height of both his fame and notoriety and sometimes needed to move in secret. His followers now attended to most of his needs, which included washing, cleaning, and preparing his meals. He often had guests for dinner and liked to subject them to little exercises in humility, which they dare not refuse. Thus, after passing out the knives and forks, the genial host might take a bite of something offering the rest to the person sitting beside him, or he might dip his fingers in jam so that others might lick them clean. Meals were also accompanied by his often incomprehensible preaching and sometimes interrupted by singing and dancing. And there was always lots of wine, Russian Madeira, which was specially fortified to affect even the strongest drinker.

Rasputin also had a more serious side, however, which was brought out by a crisis in the Balkans in the fall of 1912. In October, Montenegro had attacked Turkey and was soon joined by Serbia, Bulgaria, and Greece. The Turks lost heavily as the fighting continued on and off until May. By the peace of London, Turkey was deprived of most of its territory in Europe. However, discord among the victors soon led to another conflict that summer when Bulgaria attacked Greece and Serbia. This prompted Rumania, Turkey, and Montenegro to join forces to stop the aggressor. The second Balkan war ended with Bulgaria losing territory and Turkey regaining some of what it had previously lost. Ominously, Serbia emerged from the conflict greatly emboldened and eager to unite with other Serbs captive in the Austro-Hungarian empire.

During the crisis, the tsar had been under considerable pressure by Slavophiles urging him to intervene on behalf of their co-religionists in Serbia, but Rasputin was firmly opposed to any such military venture and pleaded with the tsar not to get involved. Ironically, the *starets*, who was so reckless and irresponsible in other matters, was far more perceptive than most about the horrors of war. He especially feared for the peasants, who would suffer the most in any future conflict, and once made his pacifist views known to a journalist who had asked for an interview:

> Let the Turks and the foreigners devour each other. They are blind and that is their misfortune. They will gain nothing simply advance the hour of their death. While we, leading a peaceful harmonious life, will rise above all others.[45]

Unfortunately, Rasputin's dissolute side soon reasserted itself. In the spring of 1914, he followed the imperial family to Yalta in the Crimea, where he took up residence in a fashionable hotel. He behaved with his usual abandon, carousing, getting drunk, and seducing women. He also loudly bragged about his intimacy with the imperial family to anyone who would listen. Apparently many did, and fantastic rumors spread quickly throughout the resort. At last, Nicholas decided it had gone too far and ordered Rasputin to return first to St. Petersburg to collect his relatives there on visit and then to Pokrovskoe, where he was to stay until further notice. The *starets* obeyed, unaware that he was was being stalked by an ex-prostitute named Kionia Gusyeva, who was an admirer of Iliodor. During the previous year, she had conspired with some other women to castrate Rasputin, but, for some reason, the attempt had not been carried out. Now she was in Yalta to kill him. However, when she learned that he had left town and was on his way to Pokrovskoe, she went directly there and waited. On June 15 (27), having disguised herself as a beggar, she approached him on the street asking for money. When he tried to oblige her, she stabbed him in the stomach, shouting "I have killed the Antichrist!" In fact, she had only wounded him, although Rasputin very nearly died in the days that followed. In any case, he was forced to convalesce in a hospital for many weeks.

Coincidentally, the following day, in the faraway Balkan city of Sarajevo, a completely unrelated event occurred. The heir to the Austrian throne, Archduke Franz Ferdinand, who was visiting Bosnia Hercegovina, was assassinated by Gavrilo Princip, a Serbian teenager and member of a terrorist organization called The Black Hand. The group had acted in protest of Austria's domination of Bosnia Hercegovina, the population of which was largely Serbian. In 1908, Austria had formally annexed the area in a move so sudden that both Serbia and Russia had been caught by surprise. Now, six years later, the Austrians were determined to use the assassination as a pretext to invade Serbia. To this end, they presented the Serbian government with an ultimatum so extreme that the Austrians were confident it would have to be rejected. In fact, the Serbs accepted all but two points and offered to negotiate, yet this was in vain; on July 17 (29) the Austrians, assured of German support, bombarded Belgrade.

The Serbs turned to Russia for help. Nicholas, remembering the crisis of 1908, was determined not to back down. However, he tried to play for time by ordering only a partial mobilization hoping to avoid war. This was followed by a flurry of telegrams between Nicholas and his cousin, the German Kaiser Wilhelm, to save the peace, but, in the end, it all came to nothing. At seven o'clock P.M. on August 1, the German ambassador in St. Petersburg delivered a declaration of war to the Russian foreign minister, Sergei Sazonov. On August 2, when Nicholas appeared on the balcony of the Winter Palace overlooking Palace Square, he was greeted by an enormous crowd of hysterically cheering people, welcoming the chance to go to war against Germany and Austria for the sake of Serbia. The patriotic fervor also prompted the renaming St. Petersburg to Petrograd.

However, the war could not stay localized. The Germans, long aware of Russia's alliance with France, were resigned to the necessity of fighting on two fronts. Their strategy was first to mount a massive attack on France and win a quick victory before turning on the Russians. It was assumed that the latter would take longer to mobilize, but the German plan also called for its army to pass through Belgium, which Great Britain had pledged to defend. Thus, by mid-September, the armies of Germany, France, and England were locked in combat in northern France, while the Russians, having mobilized more quickly than expected, were advancing into east Prussia. In panic, the Germans assigned Generals Paul von Hindenberg and Erich Ludendorff to confront the Russian second army under General Samsonov. The destruction of this Russian force set the tone for the entire conflict from which the Romanov dynasty and the country would not emerge.

Military defeats and mounting casualties continued in the west for nearly a year until Nicholas decided to relieve his top general, Grand Duke Nikolai Nicholaevich, and assume command of the army himself. Though the move was intended to be mainly symbolic, most of his ministers did not understand this and were aghast; the tsar was not qualified to lead troops on any scale, let alone a vast army. Still, Nicholas was convinced that his presence at the front would raise morale among the soldiers and reassure Russia's allies of the country's commitment to victory. Some members of the *Duma* used the opportunity to encourage the tsar to cooperate with the Progressive Bloc, a coalition of mostly liberal parties, to create a government that enjoyed the confidence of the people. But the tsar would have none of it. Instead he prorogued the *Duma* and called upon his "dear wifey" to come to the aid of her husband, giving her virtual control of the government.

To be sure, Alexandra generally knew little and cared less about anything having to do with affairs of state. Moreover, she was already fully involved with her two eldest daughters in running a field hospital for wounded soldiers at Tsarskoe Selo. Still, she accepted her new duties with a fervor that was to have dire consequences for the country. Her new activism was made even more damaging by Rasputin's return to St. Petersburg in January 1915. Having barely recovered from his near assassination, the *starets* had been banned by Nicholas from Tsarskoe Selo because of his opposition to the war, but he was returned to favor when he appeared to bring Anna Vyrubova back to life after she had her legs crushed and was nearly killed in a train accident.[46]

Alexandra's first major initiative was to urge her husband to dismiss those ministers who had tried to resign in order to protest Nicholas' decision to take command of the army. This began a series of bewildering ministerial changes that greatly undermined both the government and the Russian war effort. The first to go was the minister of interior, Prince Nicholas Shcherbatov, followed by the Procurator of the Holy Synod,

Samarin. Both were fired in October without reason. The minister of agriculture, Krivoshein, left in November and the state controller, Kharitonov, in January. Then in February 1916, Nicholas had to replace the one man in his cabinet whose loyalty both he and Alexandra very much valued, the prime minister Goremykin. The problem was the old man was so disdained by his colleagues in the *Duma* that he was unable to function. Every time he stood up to speak, he was drowned out by whistles and the sound of hissing. Still, the man chosen to replace him, a friend of Rasputin, was far worse.

Boris Sturmer, at sixty-seven, was held in contempt by virtually everyone who knew him. Of German ancestry, he had served previously as master of ceremonies at court and as governor of the Yaroslavl' province. Words used to describe him by those in a position to know included "utter nonentity," "false and double-faced" "third rate intellect" and "low character." Yet Sturmer got the job because, as Alexandra put it, "he very much values Grigori which is a great thing."[47] Nicholas, anticipating the resistance his appointment might engender, shrewdly appeared in person before the *Duma* for the first and only time. Its members were apparently so pleased that the tsar deigned to honor them with his presence that they temporarily forgot about Sturmer's appointment.

However, the good feeling was not to last. Soon the empress decided that it was time to purge the minister of war, Alexei Polivanov, a man whose ability in training and equipping the army had been described as "miraculous," but his competence in running his ministry was overshadowed by other considerations. As Alexandra put in a letter to Nicholas: "Is he not Our Friend's enemy?" Thus, Polivanov was replaced in March by General Shuvaiev, whose most desirable trait was his unswerving loyalty to the throne. In July, Sazonov was dismissed at the Foreign Ministry and replaced by, of all people, Sturmer, who had no diplomatic experience whatever. Worse still was the fact that the latter was to continue as prime minister.[48] In October, the tsar appointed a friend of Rasputin's, Alexander Protopopov, to be minister of the interior, despite the fact that he was suffering from either paralysis of the spine or chronic syphilis and was often unable to carry out his duties. As if that wasn't enough, the empress, without the tsar's approval, assigned Protopopov the additional task of organizing the nation's food supplies, this at the behest of Rasputin, who reasoned that, as minister of the interior, Protopopov would have the police to enforce his decisions.

To be sure, none of these appointments worked out very well, and by November, even Nicholas had to concede that Sturmer had to be dismissed from both his positions. Alexandra, prompted by Rasputin, pleaded that he be allowed to keep one of his jobs, but for once the tsar stood firm. Still, the matter was complicated by the fact that the new prime minister, Alexander Trepov, had agreed to serve only on condition that Protopopov also be dismissed. It seems the latter's behavior had actually become rather frightening. He had a strange habit of rolling his eyes while conversing with his colleagues, wore a police uniform to sessions of the *Duma*, and spoke to the icon on his desk as if it were a real person. Still, Alexandra's reaction to Protopopov's proposed dismissal was horror, and she used a previously planned visit to Headquarters late in the fall to force Nicholas to change his mind. After two days of nagging, not only did he relent, but he thanked his wife for setting him straight and apologized for his behavior. "You were so strong and steadfast — I admire you more than I can say. Forgive me if I was moody or unrestrained — sometimes one's temper must come out."[49]

By the beginning of 1916, Alexandra was hated by nearly everyone, although she little suspected that this was the case. This was because Protopopov had ordered police officials from all over the country to have ordinary citizens write letters to her expressing their support and affection. In fact, nearly everyone, at least in Petrograd, was convinced not only that she and Rasputin were lovers, but that they were passing military secrets to the Germans. Although both were intensely patriotic, the latter concern was not entirely unfounded. Nicholas, it seems, was in the habit of confiding to his wife the most sensitive military information. She would generally pass on what she knew to Rasputin, who was prepared to talk to anyone who would listen. This was especially true when he was in his cups. Thus, every Wednesday evening, Rasputin was invited to dine at the home of a Petrograd banker and German sympathizer named Manus. The latter always provided beautiful women as company and lots of wine.

The members of the *Duma* knew these things and suspected much more. In November, the leader of the Constitutional Democrats, Pavel Miliukov,[50] gave an impassioned speech in the Tauride Palace in which he read off a list of charges against the government, asking rhetorically after each, "Is this stupidity or treason?"[51] In December, a right-wing monarchist named Vladimir Purishkevich[52] gave another speech in which he described the "dark forces" that were destroying the monarchy and undermining the war effort. He ended by imploring all those who were patriotic to go to the tsar and tell him that "the multitude is threatening its wrath. Revolution threatens and an obscure *muzhik* shall govern Russia no longer."[53] Among those who were deeply moved by the appeal was the heir to the greatest fortune in Russia, Prince Felix Yusupov.

The prince was a rather unlikely person to bother himself much about civic matters. He had been raised in almost unimaginable luxury and was fond of all kinds of decadent amusements. These included dressing up like a woman to sing French songs in a nightclub or flirting in drag with young officers, many of whom were fooled and found him attractive. He was also known to use opium from time to time and was fascinated by spiritualism and the occult. He had first met Rasputin in 1909 and, although intrigued by the peasant's mystical powers, had thought him cunning and mean. Still, in February 1914, after Yusupov was married to the beautiful Grand Duchess Irina (a close relative of the tsar), he paid a visit to Rasputin hoping to find a "cure" for his homosexuality. To the prince's dismay, the *starets* nearly seduced him.

During the war, Yusupov, who had not volunteered for military service, became increasingly alarmed at the perceived damage Rasputin was doing to the monarchy and the country. By November 1916, he was convinced that the *starets* had to be assassinated. The first to be recruited to help was Purishkevich, who shared Yusupov's sense of urgency about what needed to be done. The conspiracy was also joined by the prince's longtime friend, Dmitri Pavlovich, an officer named Ivan Sukhotin, and a physician, Dr. Stanislav Lazovert. The plan was to invite Rasputin to Yusupov's Moika Palace[54] on December 29 to meet the Grand Duchess Irina, who was actually in the Crimea. The victim would be taken to a specially prepared basement room to await the beautiful lady who would supposedly be entertaining guests upstairs. In the meantime, Yusupov would sing to his guest on the guitar while plying him cakes and wine laced with potassium cyanide.

Rasputin spent the last day of his life going to church and visiting the bathhouse before receiving visitors around 11 A.M. One of these was a mysterious old woman who came and asked him a number of difficult questions: Did he appreciate the damage he was doing? Did he know anything about Russian history? Did he love the tsar? Rasputin was uneasy with his visitor and claimed somewhat defensively that he was just a plain, ignorant peasant who knew nothing of history but who truly loved the tsar. He knew that he had done much against the tsar and his family, but "I swear to you little mother that I did not mean to...Little mother I feel my end is near. They'll kill me, and then the throne won't last three months. I thank you for coming, I know you listened to your heart. I feel good with you, and also afraid."[55] Somewhat later, he received an anonymous telephone call warning him of his assassination.

That afternoon, Rasputin drank a lot of wine and fell into a deep depression. For some time, he had been troubled by a fear that he would not be alive much longer. In the previous days, he had written a chilling letter of prophecy entitled "The Spirit of Grigori Efimovich Rasputin-Novykh of the village of Pokrovskoe," in which he warned the tsar of dire consequences should he be assassinated by people of high birth:

> But if I am murdered by boyars, nobles, and if they shed my blood their hands will remain soiled with my blood, for twenty-five years they will not wash their hands from my blood. They will leave Russia. Brothers will kill brothers, and they will kill and hate each other, and for twenty-five years there will be no nobles in the country.[56]

He also promised that if the tsar's relatives were involved in his death, "none of your children or relations will remain alive for more than two years."[57]

Later that evening, Anna Vyrubova came to give him an icon signed by the empress and the children. Rasputin mentioned that he was going to visit the Yusupovs around midnight because Irina was in need of some kind of "treatment." At this, Vyrubova sensed something sinister. Why so late? Were they ashamed to meet with him during the day? She pleaded with him not to go, and Rasputin seemed to acquiesce. Still later, he was visited by Vladimir Protopopov, who also warned him of a plot against his life. Once again, Rasputin agreed not to go out that night.

However, he did go out. He was picked up at his residence by Yusupov with Lazovert acting as driver. Rasputin was unusually well-dressed for the occasion with his hair and beard combed, and his normal goat-like smell was covered by that of cheap soap. He also had an elegant fur coat and a beaver-skin hat to protect him from the cold. Arriving at the Moika Palace, they went downstairs. Upstairs, a gramophone played "Yankee Doodle" to simulate Grand Duchess Irina entertaining her guests. Yusupov was nervous and had some difficulty getting Rasputin to try the poisoned food and drink. At last, the *starets* did eat one of the cakes and swallow some wine, but nothing happened. In fact, he continued to cheerfully nibble and sip at the refreshments for the next two hours while Yusupov played his guitar and sang. At about 2:30 A.M., the prince went upstairs, pretending to look for his wife. Frantic, he consulted with his co-conspirators who agreed Rasputin would have to be shot. Yusupov understood that he would have to do it. He went to his study to retrieve his Browning revolver and descended the cellar stairs with the weapon hidden behind his back.

By now, Rasputin was feeling some effect from the poison and the wine, although he still did not suspect that he was in danger. The prince tried to divert his attention by admiring a crystal and bronze Italian crucifix standing on an inlaid wooden chest. When Rasputin staggered over for a closer look, Yusupov pulled out his gun and shot him in the side. The victim fell onto a bearskin rug and was soon pronounced dead by Dr. Lazovert, but the judgment was premature. When the conspirators went upstairs to discuss their next move, Yusupov wandered back down into the cellar. After feeling Rasputin's seemingly lifeless pulse, he began to shake the corpse in anger. Suddenly, the *starets'* eyes opened. He got to his feet and tried to strangle the horrified prince, who pulled away and ran back upstairs. Rasputin followed him but then headed for a door leading outside to the courtyard. As he ran to make his escape, he shouted, "Felix, Felix, I will tell the empress!"[58] Purishkevich hurried out into the courtyard after him and fired his pistol four times, hitting Rasputin twice. With the *starets* on the ground and motionless, he kicked him savagely in the head. Minutes later, when the body was brought back inside, Yusupov began pounding it with a rubber blackjack.

Originally, the conspirators had thought that one of them would dress up in Rasputin's hat and coat and return to his flat to make it seem that the *starets* was coming home after one of his long nights, but this plan was abandoned as they struggled to clean up the mess and get rid of the victim. They wrapped the body in a large curtain, placed it in a car, drove three miles to the Petrovsky Bridge, and heaved the body over the parapet into the Neva River. They then went to the home of Dmitri Pavlovich to clean the blood from the seat covers and dispose of one of Rasputin's overshoes left in the car, but it was all in vain. The shots had been heard, the police were called to investigate, and the murderers were identified. Moreover, according to the autopsy, the victim had not succumbed to the poison, the bullets, or the beating; he had drowned.[59]

Ordinary Russians rejoiced when they learned of Rasputin's assassination, but his demise did nothing to forestall the national calamity that was fast approaching. The members of the immediate imperial family were now in a state of shock and strangely resigned to whatever fate might bring. Rasputin's body was interred on the grounds of Tsarskoe Selo December 21 (January 4). After the funeral, Nicholas wrote in his diary, "At nine o'clock we went to...the field where we were present at a sad spectacle; the coffin with the body of the unforgettable Grigori, killed on the night of the 17th (29th) by monsters in the Yusupov house already stood in the grave."[60] The tsar returned to the front early in late February (early March) with a heavy heart and tried to carry on, but it was too late. Just two days after his arrival at military headquarters, serious disorders broke out in Petrograd.

The revolution that so profoundly affected the course of the 20th century did not start at the instigation of professional agitators or ruthless conspirators. It was the action of desperate women standing in breadlines who had decided that they had finally had enough. On February 23 (March 8), they began to break into stores to take what they needed. They were not firmly resisted by the Cossacks, who were supposed to keep order. Two days later, most of Petrograd was on strike. The tsar was informed, but did not believe the situation serious. His ministers pleaded with him to form a government responsible to the *Duma,* but he refused. He ordered his troops to restore order, but they joined the rebels. He tried to dissolve the *Duma,* but the members refused to obey. Finally, Nicholas agreed to board his train for Petrograd only to find that mutinous troops blocked the route further down the line. He got only as far as Pskov, where he was met by a delegation from the *Duma* demanding his abdication.

The tsar ultimately agreed to this, but only after his generals unanimously urged him to do so for the good of the country. At first, he was prepared to be succeeded by his son, but a conversation with his court physician, Professor Fedorov, convinced him that this was not feasible. For one thing, the boy's hemophilia was incurable, and, as tsar, Alexis would be often unable to carry out his official duties, but there was another consideration: the likelihood that the father and mother would be obliged to live in exile, separated from their son. This made abdication in favor of the tsarevich out of the question, and Nicholas named his brother, Grand Duke Mikhail, to succeed him. Late in the evening of March 2 (15), 1917, the tsar signed in pencil the document announcing his abdication. In effect, this action also ended 370 years of tsarist rule, because Mikhail would later refuse to ascend the throne.

Although it is probably an exaggeration to assert, as did Alexander Kerensky, that without Rasputin there would have been no Lenin, there can be no doubt that the *starets* did great harm both to the dynasty and the country. Not only did his debauchery tarnish the throne, but his desire to have his own supporters in positions of power ultimately immobilized the government. That Nicholas could have accorded him so much influence testifies to the solemn religious nature of his coronation oath. As tsar, he could allow himself to be guided and influenced by a man of God but never by ordinary mortals. Thus, it is highly unlikely that the tsar could ever have accepted the role of a constitutional monarch, which might have eased the country's transition into modernity. True, he had previously authorized the creation of the State *Duma,* but only after he was unable to find a military man willing to apply force to suppress those demanding change. In any case, he never intended to cooperate with the new assembly and hoped one day to reduce its powers to mere consultation. In this, he was true to his predecessors, who had fiercely resisted anyone who questioned their authority or sought to share in governing the country.

Selected Bibliography

Much has been written about the end of the Romanov Dynasty, especially in the form of biographies about Nicholas II. The popular favorite is Robert K. Massie's *Nicholas and Alexandra*. Although the author's approach is highly sentimental, he explains the significance of the tsarevich's hemophilia and how the scandal regarding Rasputin played an important role in the collapse of the government. More detailed information about Rasputin is provided by Edvard Radzinsky in *The Rasputin File*. Domenic Lieven's *Nicholas II: Twilight of the Empire* and Helene Carriere d' Encausse's *Nicholas II: The Interupted Transition* reflect more recent research and offer more detached analyses of the reign of the last tsar. One of the most comprehensive and penetrating studies of the period leading up to the Bolshevik victory and the civil war is by Orlando Figes, entitled *A People's Tragedy: A History of the Russian Revolution*. Finally, Robert Service's *Lenin* is a thoroughly researched and well-written study of the most successful revolutionary who ever lived.

De Jonge, Alex. *The Life and Times of Gregori Rasputin*. New York: Coward McCann, 1982.

Elwood, R.C. "Lenin, Vladimir Illich." Modern Encyclopedia of Russian and Soviet History, ed. Joseph L. Wieczynski, 54 vols. With suppl. Gulf Breeze, Florida: Academic International Press, 1976–1990.

Figes, Orlando. *A People's Tragedy: A History of the Russian Revolution*. New York: Penguin Books,1999.

Lieven, Dominic. *Nicholas II: Twilight of the Empire*. New York: St. Martin's Press, 1993.

Massie, Robert K. *Nicholas and Alexandra*. New York: Ballentine, 1967.

Payne, Robert. *The Fortress*. New York: Simon and Shuster, 1967.

Purishkevich, V.M. *The Murder of Rasputin*. Ed. Michael E. Shaw, trans. Bella Costello. Ann Arbor, Michigan: Ardis, 1985.

Rollins, Patrick J. "Iliodor." Modern Encyclopedia of Russian and Soviet History, ed. Joseph L. Wieczynski, 54 vols. With suppl. Gulf Breeze, Florida: Academic International Press, 1976–1990.

Rollins, Patrick J. "Rasputin, Grigorii Efimovich." Modern Encyclopedia of Russian and Soviet History, ed. Joseph L. Wieczynski, 54 vols. With suppl. Gulf Breeze, Florida: Academic International Press, 1976–1990.

Tobias, Henry J. "Azev, Evno Fishelevich." Modern Encyclopedia of Russian and Soviet History, ed. Joseph L. Wieczynski, 54 vols. With suppl. Gulf Breeze, Florida: Academic International Press, 1976–1990.

Warnes, David. *Chronicle of the Russian Tsars*. London: Thames and Hudson, 1999.

Warth, Rober D. "Nicholas II (Nikolai Aleksandrovich)" Modern Encyclopedia of Russian and Soviet History, ed. Joseph L. Wieczynski, 54 vols. With suppl. Gulf Breeze, Florida: Academic International Press, 1976–1990.

_____. "Stolypin, Peter Arkadevich." Modern Encyclopedia of Russian and Soviet History, ed. Joseph L. Wieczynski, 54 vols. With suppl. Gulf Breeze, Florida: Academic International Press, 1976–1990.

EPILOGUE

The Romanov dynasty was not the only ruling house to be destroyed in the turmoil of World War I. The Austrian Habsburgs, the German Hollenzollerns, and the Turkish Ottomans were all toppled for reasons having to do with weak monarchs unable to cope with war and modernity. By 1918, however, amid the defeat and devastation, a consensus emerged in each of these countries for a fundamental reordering of the political, social and economic order. This was followed by profound change and destructive upheavals the scale of which was nowhere exceeded than in Russia. The reasons for this can best be understood by reviewing some of the causes and conditions that impelled the many agitators, dissidents, and usurpers over 370 years to challenge Russia's autocrats. In almost every instance, the tsars were goaded into actions that were irrelevant, insufficient, or inimical to their best interests.

Among the earliest of the nobles to oppose the tsar's abuse of power was Prince Andrei Kurbsky. So infuriated was he by Ivan the Terrible's refusal to respect the rights of his *boyars* that he defected to the king of Poland and served in his army, but his actions served no useful end. Ivan responded by creating the dreaded *oprichnina*, which for a time ravaged the country and threatened to eliminate the high aristocracy altogether. Self-interest and privilege were also prime motivations during the Time of Troubles when a group of *boyars* led by Vasily Shuisky engaged in conspiracy and murder to arrange his elevation to power in 1606. In the ensuing civil war, he was abandoned by his own nobles who agreed to accept a Polish prince as tsar and invited a foreign army to occupy the Kremlin. Another such example of unintended consequences occurred in 1722 when Peter the Great, prompted by the treachery of his own son, changed the

Law of Succession to allow the sovereign to choose his or her successor. His goal was to promote stability, competence, and strong leadership, but the new law did mostly the opposite as ambitious nobles schemed to support candidates who would serve their interests. Over the next eight decades, eight autocrats occupied the throne, although only one, Catherine the Great, ruled in a manner that Peter might have approved. And she came to power in a military coup, which resulted in the murder of her husband.

In time, the motivation of some of these high-born and privileged dissidents changed to reflect principles beyond self-interest. However, it was not until the end of the 18th century that one of them, Alexander Radishchev, began to agitate against serfdom as a moral wrong. For his efforts, he gravely offended Catherine the Great and barely escaped the noose. A generation later, the Decembrists, who mustered troops in the Senate Square to protest the ascension of Nicholas I, and who urged the abolition of serfdom, were not so lucky. Five went to the gallows and the rest to Siberia. Alarmed by such activism, the new tsar set up the Third Section to ferret out subversives, hopefully, before they could act. Unfortunately, by this new system, the innocent were as likely to be punished as the guilty. Even the civic-minded *Petrashevtsy*, whose only crime was to meet on a regular basis to discuss issues such as serfdom, were treated like criminals.

Of course, serfdom was an especially controversial subject that offered no easy solution. Its very origin derived from the tsar's need to support a vast military establishment while guaranteeing his servitors a reliable source of free labor on their estates, but this arrangement provoked determined opposition from the serfs, who shirked, rebelled, or ran away. Ultimately, many took refuge with the various Cossacks hosts, who occupied valuable territory on the steppe. The state's efforts to recover these fugitives were usually thwarted by these independent warrior brotherhoods, which sometimes served the Turks and the Poles, and thus the tsars took steps to bring them under control. As the boundaries of Muscovy and Russia pushed inexorably southward, intrepid *atamans* such as Stepan Razin and Yemelian Pugachev led massive rebellions in defense of their land and way of life. However, they could not arrest the growth of the state or the expansion of serfdom.

By the beginning of the 19th century, however, even the autocracy recognized that serfdom was a moral blight and an obstacle to progress, but no one knew how to free the serfs with land without ruining the gentry, which had always been a bulwark of support for the throne. Alexander I talked much about this problem during his reign but ultimately did little. He finally offered military colonies as a solution, which proved to be a totalitarian nightmare. Nor did his successor, Nicholas I, for all his many secret committees to study the problem, dare to take action. It was not until Russia's disastrous defeat in the Crimean War that a new tsar, Alexander II, became convinced of the need to force the issue and deal with the consequences. Even so, the Emancipation Edict of 1861 was judged to be a failure by the country's growing intelligentsia, many of whom began to agitate for the establishment of an agrarian socialist society, which they believed was consistent with Russia's communal peasant traditions.

True to form, the autocracy resisted any popular participation with regard to questions about good government and the social order. Still, in the 1870s, thousands of mostly young students went to the countryside to bond with and assist the long-abused Russian peasant. When they were rejected by the very people they sought to help, many joined an ever growing campaign of activism that culminated in the formation of The People's Will in 1879. The members of this terrorist group were similar in mindset to the Old Believers of an earlier age, who chose to immolate themselves in their churches rather than accept changes in their faith that

Vladimir Lenin was living in Switzerland when the revolution broke out and played no direct role in the overthrow of the tsar. However, in the spring of 1917, he accepted a German offer to transport him by train to Russia through Finland. Within six months of his return in April of 1917, he helped to bring about the overthrow of the Provisional Government and the establishment of the world's first socialist state. A.A. Rylov (1870–1939). Tretiakovsky Gallery, Moscow.

would endanger their souls. In a like manner, the assassins of Tsar Alexander II were prepared to die in order to destroy autocracy, which violated their most cherished ideals and convictions. Unfortunately, their great triumph only brought more repression. Within weeks of ascending to the throne, Alexander III abandoned his father's tentative plan to establish an elected consultative assembly and promulgated a new law for the security of the realm, which made it easier for the authorities to impose martial law and summary justice.

In the roughly three and a half decades remaining before the first world war, the last two Romanov tsars tenaciously defended autocracy. Not only did Alexander III and Nicholas II see this as their religious duty, but also as a practical necessity given the country's vast size and diversity. However, the abolition of serfdom in 1861 had already prompted the creation of elective bodies of rural administration called *zemstvos*, and many concluded that such institutions could become a valuable resource to help the government cope with its ever-expanding duties. Such thinking seemed even more compelling because in the final years of the 19th century, as Russia began to industrialize, many poor peasants had migrated to the cities to take low-paying factory jobs amid squalid living conditions. Tormented and exploited beyond endurance, they had no one to turn to but the tsar, who they believed would help them if only he knew of their plight. Unfortunately, the massacre that took place on the morning of January 24, 1905, proved otherwise.

In the weeks and months that followed Bloody Sunday, a wave of strikes and violence swept the empire. By October, the country, which had just lost a war in the far east to Japan, was nearly shut down as the workers in some cities formed soviets to promote their demands. Nicholas, desperate to restore order and save his throne, called for the formation of a national legislature. This initiative might have led to a permanent solution had the tsar been willing to cooperate with the new *Duma*, but his obstinacy in defending his autocratic prerogatives coupled with the outbreak of war in 1914 created challenges that were above and beyond what the government could handle. Not the least of these was a string of military defeats during the first year of the conflict, which prompted the tsar to go to the front and leave the politically incompetent and unpopular empress in charge in the capital. The damage done by her was compounded by Rasputin's interference in affairs of state, which ultimately shattered the public's confidence in the government. At the end of 1916, five conspirators took it upon themselves to murder the *starets* to save Russia, but it was too late. When food riots broke out in St. Petersburg three months later, they were not suppressed by the normally pitiless Cossack troops who could not bring themselves to fire on unarmed people to save a corrupt regime.

It remains the dubious distinction of Nicholas II that he antagonized every faction in Russian society like no other tsar since Peter the Great. This included the nobles, the army, the gentry, the intelligentsia, the proletariat, and even much of the peasantry. Only the official Church remained nominally loyal to the crown, and by 1917 their influence and authority was much diminished. Yet the worst was yet to come; with the return to Russia of Lenin, Trotsky, and other Bolsheviks from self-imposed exile, the country became embroiled in radical politics that seriously undermined the new Provisional Government. In November, the Bolsheviks carried out another revolution to complete the destruction of the old order, but the new rulers, who based their authority on a secular "scientific" ideology, proved in many ways to be no wiser than their predecessors. Over the next seven decades, their most conspicuous folly was to try to rule Russia autocratically, tolerating no popular participation and no opposition, loyal or otherwise.

NOTES

1. Renegade Prince

1. Now, Tartu in Estonia.
2. Known in Russian as the Troitsa-Sergeeva Lavra, it was founded by St. Sergius of Radonezh in 1337, and has long been famous for its architecture and as an important religious center.
3. Muscovy became known as Imperial Russia during the reign of Peter the Great (1672–1725).
4. A title given by the grand prince, and later the tsar, to favored servitors. Usually these were large landowners of princely blood, who were then offered important offices and invited to participate in an advisory council that would later be called the boyar duma.
5. The title derives from the Latin "Caesar." Previous rulers of Muscovy had been crowned as grand prince, although Grand Prince Ivan III (r.1462–1505) and Grand Prince Vasily III (r.1505–1533) had also used the title from time to time. Ivan's decision to enhance his stature by crowning himself tsar provoked controversy both at home and abroad.
6. Turkic-speaking and Islamic descendents of the Mongols in Russia. With the disintegration of the Mongol Empire, they formed three major principalities, or khanates. These were at Kazan, Astrakhan, and in the Crimea.
7. This child was born in 1553 and died later the same year when a nurse accidentally dropped him into the Volga River while the tsar and his wife were traveling to the north on a pilgrimage. This Dmitri is not to be confused with Ivan's last child by his seventh wife who was also given the same name.
8. The chosen council was an informal group of advisers who assisted Ivan IV and whom he favored over the boyar duma. However, because the content of this body is not known, not all historians are willing to assert that Kurbsky was a member.
9. An area along the Baltic that is today part of Latvia and Estonia.
10. These included a large standing force of *strel'tsy*, or fusiliers, using Russian-made muskets and cannon foundries capable of producing sophisticated artillery. In fact, the world's most powerful mortar at that time was produced in Russia. It weighed more than 14,000 pounds, had a 36-inch bore, and could launch a one-ton stone projectile.
11. The name means "White Lake" in Russian and is located about 290 miles north of Moscow.
12. "Letter, Prince Kurbsky to Ivan the Terrible." J.L.I. Fennell, ed. and tr., *The Correspondence Between A.M. Kurbsky and Tsar Ivan IV of Russia 1664–1679*, p. 3.
13. "Letter, Ivan the Terrible to Prince Kurbsky." Fennell, p. 21.
14. "Letter, Ivan the Terrible to Prince Kurbsky." Fennell, p. 31.

15. In addition to numerous letters, Kurbsky is also alleged to have written *A History of the Grand Prince of Moscow*, and another work entitled *Novyi Margarit,*, which is actually a book of translations of the lives of the saints. Other writings credited to him include an introduction to a book about the Fathers of the Church and a short history of the Council of Florence.

16. Although Inge Auerbach in her biography of the prince asserts that he actually began to study Latin about three years after his arrival in Lithuania, it is not known whether he ever achieved written proficiency in this language. The few surviving Latin signatures of his name that exist reveal an awkward and unsteady hand. No signatures by Prince Kurbsky in Cyrillic have ever been found.

17. Scholars may approximately date the parchment of the letters using either paleographic or watermark evidence.

18. Thomas Owen has argued that the author of Kurbsky's first letter copied parts of it from another source. See "Quotations from a Common Source in the Kurbsky-Grozni Correspondence: A Research Note" by Thomas C. Owen, *The Russian Review*, vol. 49, 1990, 157–65.

19. See Edward L. Keenan, *The Kurbskii-Grozni Apocrypha.* Harvard University Press, 1971. Professor Keenan has altered his opinion somewhat over the years about how the correspondence came to be written, but his basic argument that Prince Kurbsky and Ivan the Terrible had nothing to do with it has not changed.

20. Keenan and many other scholars have found it suspicious that although originals are alleged to have been written between 1564 and 1579, the complete correspondence appears nowhere in a single manuscript. Moreover, the two dozen copies that exist were produced over a long period of time and just happen to be in chronological order.

21. The author interviewed Boris Morozov in Moscow on July 31, 2001.

22. Known in the 16th century as Alexandrovskaya Sloboda, it was Ivan's residence on and off for some fifteen years.

23. Many victims of the *oprichnina* terror were large landowners who had had their estates confiscated. Ivan would then redistribute these territories to personal favorites who had pledged to serve him.

24. Russian for Young Maiden's Monastery, it was founded in 1524 to commemorate the return of the city of Smolensk to Muscovy from Lithuania.

25. Maliuta Skuratov (?–1570) *Oprichnik* and favorite of Ivan the Terrible, was notorious for his ruthlessness and cruelty in carrying out the will of his master.

26. A city located on the Volkov River near Lake Il'men, 105 miles south of St. Petersburg. It was founded in the 9th century and became one of the most important trading centers in medieval Russia. However, by 1300, it had become involved in a power struggle with Moscow, which it eventually lost.

27. Henri Troyat, *Ivan the Terrible,* p. 151.

28. A town located on the Velikaya River just south of Lake Peipus near Estonia. From 1347 to 1510, it had commercial links to the Hanseatic League before being annexed by Moscow.

29. Hugh F. Graham, "Viskovati, Ivan Mikhailovich," *The Modern Encyclopedia of Russian and Soviet History,* p. 132.

30. According to Inge Auerbach, Kurbsky was also notorious for his harsh treatment of Jews who lived on his estates and sometimes had to defend himself in court against charges of abuse.

31. See Edward L. Keenan's article "Vita: Ivan Vasil'evich, Terrible Czar: 1530–1584." *Harvard Magazine,* Jan.-Feb. 1978, p. 49.

32. By the Treaty of Yam Zapolie, concluded with Poland in January of 1582, the Russians were forced to abandon all of Livonia, including Polotsk. The Poles agreed to evacuate the Russian towns that they had conquered. The treaty also included a ten-year armistice.

2. The Great Pretender

1. Many historians refer to this tsar by his first name and patronymic, although he is also known as Feodor I.

2. The members included Nikita Yuriev, Feodor Mstislavsky, Ivan Shuisky, Bogdan Bel'sky, and Boris Godunov.

3. In fact, Dmitri is known to have been an epileptic and had suffered a number of seizures just prior to his fatal accident.

4. This same icon was taken into battle in 1381 by Dmitri Donskoy in his great victory over the Mongols.

5. This wall was constructed between 1586 and 1591 by order of Boris Godunov. It was dismantled at the end of the eighteenth century and today forms a ring of boulevards and parks around the center of town.

6. An area formed by a loop in the Moscow River just south of the Kremlin known as "wooden town," through which enemies often attacked the great fortress.

7. Boris used the occasion of an unexpected state visit by the patriarch of Constantinople, in 1588, to lobby for the establishment of a patriarchate in Moscow. On January 26, 1589, the metropolitan of Moscow, Iov, was ordained in the Cathedral of the Assumption as Russia's first patriarch.

8. Boris had suspended the traditional right of peasants to leave their masters' estates to seek better working arrangement during a three-week period around The Feast of St. George, which fell on November 25. This enabled the gentry to retain and exploit their labor force without the need to offer improved conditions of service.

9. The tower stands 275 feet high and contains 52 bells, many of which are huge. An inscription at the top to reads: "By the Grace of the Holy Trinity and by Order of the Tsar and Grand Prince Boris Feodorovich, Autocrat of all Russia, this temple was finished and gilded in the second year of his reign."

10. The beard in Orthodox Russia was a fundamental symbol of religious belief and self-respect. Many priests would not bless a man with a shaven face.

11. See Jacques Margaret's *The Russian Empire and Grand Duchy of Muscovy*, p. 58. The events described by Margaret are generally considered to be the beginning of Russia's Time of Troubles, which began with the famine of 1601 and ended with the coronation of the first Romanov tsar in 1613. During this period, the Muscovite state nearly disintegrated as the populace suffered from starvation, civil war and foreign invasions.

12. A law or decree signed by the tsar.

13. The term is Turkic in origin and was first applied to migrant workers or freebooters who were not tied to the land. The earliest Cossacks were Tatar renegades who, after the breakup of the Golden Horde, formed warrior brotherhoods of up to 100 men. They lived on the *steppe* in small settlements called *stanitsas* and supported themselves mainly by fishing, hunting, and plunder. In the second half of the 16th century, their numbers were steadily augmented by Russians fleeing high taxes, punishment, debt, poverty, military service, and oppressive landlords in Muscovy.

14. This site is located just a few miles from what is today the city of Chernobyl.

15. Many historians believe that this version was concocted by Semyon Godunov and the Patriarch Iov to discredit rumors that the Tsarevich Dmitri was still alive. The true identity of the pretender remains a mystery.

16. Boris' sudden death after a meal has led many to suspect that he was poisoned. This has not been proved, but the possibility cannot be discounted.

17. A raised circular platform constructed in 1534 where executions were performed and proclamations read.

18. Known as both the Cathedral of St. Basil and the Blessed (Khram Vasiliya Blazhennogo) and the Church of the Intercession (Pokrovsky Sobor), this structure was built between 1555 and 1561 by order of Ivan the Terrible. It commemorates victories won over the Tatars at Kazan and Astrakhan.

19. Known as the *Blagoveshchensky Sobor* in Russian, this was the tsars' private chapel, used for weddings and christenings. It was built between 1484 and 1489 and is especially renowned for its beautiful *iconostasis*, or icon screen, separating the main body of the church from the sacristy.

20. The name literally means Chinatown but has nothing to do with the Chinese. It is actually an old trading section of Moscow, located east of the Kremlin and surrounded by a great wall, parts of which are still standing. The name was probably derived from

the bundles of poles (or *kit*) that were used to strengthen the early earthen walls.

21. Completed in 1508 to serve as the residence for the imperial family, the Terem Palace is a tiered structure with old-style window frames of white stone. It contains a number of small churches that in the late 1600s were united under a single cornice and room and adorned with eleven cupolas and faced with multi-colored tiles.

3. Boyars, Cossacks, and More Pretenders

1. It is worth noting that Shuisky was not properly elected tsar by a *Zemsky Sobor* but was proclaimed by a partisan crowd in Red Square. His main competitor had been Feodor Mstislavsky, whose indifferent personality had actually won few supporters.

2. The prince's description of Shuisky is one of several tsars and important personages in this time period. See Serge Zenkovsky's *Medieval Russia's Epics, Chronicles and Tales*, pp. 388–389.

3. This was the elderly metropolitan of Kazan, Hermogen (1530?–1612), who later proved to be one of the new tsar's staunchest supporters. He became a priest only at age 50 after living for a time among the Don Cossacks. He was well-educated, an excellent speaker, and known for his spiritual intensity and ruthlessness toward those of other faiths. He was also defiant in the face of authority and refused to sign Boris Godunov's coronation charter.

4. Known as Arkhangelsky Sobor in Russian, this cathedral contains forty-six tombs of Muscovy's grand princes and tsars from 1340 to 1700. Its present appearance is the result of a reconstruction project supervised by the Italian architect Alevisio Novy between 1505 and 1509.

5. Although Molchanov introduced himself as tsar to Bolotnikov, he did not intend to claim the throne himself, probably because his true identity was too well-known in Moscow.

6. A beautiful wooded area that was part of the tsars' country estate from the 15th to the 17th century. Today it is a popular park with a spectacular view overlooking the Moscow River.

7. The tsar left little doubt that he would support the interests of the landed aristocracy at the expense of the lower classes. In March of 1607, he signed legislation denying peasants their time-honored right to leave their landlords at will. Shuisky also accorded serf-owners considerable latitude in recovering fugitive peasants who had fled illegally in the previous fifteen years. See Robert Crummey's *The Formation of Muscovy 1304–1613*, p. 233.

8. Ivan Funikov was taken prisoner by vengeful peasants who sought to punish him for his lustful behavior with local girls. He seems to have been unbowed by the experience, however, and subsequently wrote a letter to a friend in humorous, rhymed verse in which he described his misfortunes. See Zenkovsky, pp. 487–489.

9. Paul Avrich, *Russian Rebels*, p. 44. Quoted in Rerun rossicarum scriptures exteri, I, 79; II, 156–157.

10. Built in the thirteenth century for Prince Daniel, who ruled from 1276 to 1303, it was also one of several monasteries intended to help defend the southern approach to Moscow from Tatar raids. Over the years, it was occasionally restored and expanded until the communist period, when some churches were destroyed and others turned into factories.

11. An excellent account of this moment can be found in Paul Avrich's *Russian Rebels*, pp. 43–44.

12. The identity of the second False Dmitri has long been the subject of much speculation. Members of the pretender's entourage believed him to be from Belorussia and reported that he could read and write Russian and Polish. Some thought he was Jewish and had been a scribe for the first pretender. See Ruslan Skrynnikov's *The Time of Troubles–Russia in Crisis*, pp. 62–63.

13. Today Tushino is located well within Moscow's city limits and is a stop on the metro.

14. Tsar Vasily and King Sigismund had signed a three-year armistice in July of 1608. The terms of this agreement featured the release of all Poles taken captive during the May, 1606, uprising in Moscow. Sigis-

mund, for his part, promised to withdraw all Polish troops from Russian soil.

15. Jerzy Mniszech was promised a sum of 300,000 rubles and the province of Severia from the new pretender for Marina's hand if and when he came to power.

16. One of the most prominent of these was the bishop of Rostov, Filaret Romanov, who was captured and brought to Tushino against his will. The pretender soon elevated him to the position of patriarch, although Filaret seemed to have served only under duress.

17. To avoid confusion with the first False Dmitri, many historians refer to the second as "the Thief."

18. Tsar Vasily was childless and had already lived to what was then considered a ripe old age.

19. Jealousy and a desire for revenge may have been a factor here, since Sigismund, who was Swedish by birth, had been heir to the Swedish crown before his uncle, Karl IX, had usurped the throne.

20. This agreement was quite similar to the one made seven months earlier at Tushino. Wladyslaw was expected to convert to Orthodoxy and to honor the property rights of the Church and aristocracy.

21. The term is thought to be of Turkish origin and denotes an elected Cossack military leader.

22. Like Bolotnikov, he had been taken captive by the Tatars while still a youth and had escaped to join the Cossacks. Zarutsky, however, had briefly served the first False Dmitri and, later, Bolotnikov himself.

23. He had also wanted to restore social order by creating what amounted to a constitution, which favored the landed aristocrats and ignored the Cossacks.

24. The patriarch at that time was still being held by the Poles and suffering from a lack of food and adequate clothing. However, he still wrote messages to the Russian people urging them to resist the invader, which were smuggled out of the Kremlin only with great difficulty.

25. Situated on the Volga River, Nizhni-Novgorod had a population of about 8000 people early in the 17th century. It was a prosperous trading center and was well-defended by a strong brick kremlin.

26. The term roughly translates as village elder or headman.

27. A Russian courtier considerably lower in rank than a boyar.

28. Derived from the German *Hauptmann* or captain, it denotes an elected Cossack military leader.

29. The beverage of choice in those days was a dark brew fermented from grain called *kvass*.

30. Known as the Uspensky Sobor in Russian, it was built between 1475 and 1479 under the supervision of an Italian architect, Aristotle Fioravanti. It was in this cathedral that many of Russia's most prominent metropolitans and patriarchs were buried and all the tsars crowned.

31. Mikhail Glinka's dramatic opera *A Life for the Tsar* or *Ivan Susanin*, which glorifies a common peasant's devotion to his sovereign, has long been a staple in Russian opera houses.

32. Known in Russian as the Granovitaya Palata, it is the oldest civil structure in Moscow. Constructed between 1487 and 1491 under the direction of Marco Ruffo and Pietro-Antonio Solari, its name derives from the prism-like blocks that adorn its facade. The palace was once part of the tsar's residence and is famous for its magnificent throne room.

33. This crown was allegedly worn by Vladimir Monomakh, a 12th century Kievan ruler, who successfully waged war against rival princes and aggressive nomadic tribes.

34. A monument to honor Minin and Pozharsky was erected in Red Square two centuries later with the inscription: "To Citizen Minin and Prince Pozharsky — Russia Is Grateful — 1818."

35. There was no patriarch at this time, since Hermogen had died in February, 1612, while being held captive by the Poles in the Kremlin.

4. Mobs, Mutinies, and the Church Schism

1. The central and most ancient part of the Kremlin formed by three major cathedrals, the Bell Tower of Ivan the Great, the Palace of Facets, and the Terem Palace. The tsar and his family resided in the latter.

2. The tsar kept in close contact with Morozov in exile and urged that his guards treat him with respect and see to his comforts. On October 26 (November 5), 1648, Alexis, sensing that the danger had passed, allowed his former tutor and adviser to return to Moscow.

3. The tsar violated an important tradition when he refused to receive the petition on June 1. See Valerie Kivelson's article "The Devil Stole His Mind," *American Historical Review*, June 1993, pp. 745–746.

4. The concept of the Church and State being in symphony and of the dyarchy formed by the patriarch and tsar was proclaimed at Filaret's ordination in 1619 by Patriarch Theophanes of Jerusalem.

5. Chapter X of the *Ulozhenie* stipulated that if an abbot or monk offended a man of high status, even if it occurred during the sermon in church, he had to pay a fine or be flogged daily until the offended individual agreed to a settlement.

6. Many Muscovites referred to this so called "German Quarter" as "Cockville" since it bordered on the Yauza and the Kukui rivers. The latter sounded like "khui," an obscene word for the male sex organ. See Bruce Lincoln's *The Romanovs*, pp. 81–82.

7. Elected *hetman* of the Zaporozhian Host, a group of Cossacks whose main settlement centered around Khoritsa Island in the Dnieper River, he had been educated by Jesuits at a Catholic college in the western Ukraine. Khmel'nitsky had previously lived among the Poles and fought with their army but became their sworn enemy when a neighbor stole land from him and killed his son. The *hetman's* attempt to get justice through the Polish courts landed him in jail.

8. Smolensk guarded the upper Dnieper River with a large fortress that was constructed by order of Boris Godunov but was lost to the Poles during the Time of Troubles.

9. A group of reformist clergy who sought to raise the spiritual and intellectual level of the Russian Church. They frowned on all popular forms of entertainment and were suspicious of anything foreign.

10. Plural for the word *staroobriadyets*. Another term used to identify a person who broke with the official Church is *raskol'nik*, or schismatic. However, as Georg Michel in his book *At War with the Church* has pointed

out, the *starooabriadtsy* and *raskol'niki* are not synonymous. The former is a more respectful term meant for those who really were devoted to the traditional rituals. The latter was applied to those who seemed determined to split the Church. In any case, Michel's recent research indicates that most people who were active during the early years of the movement were less concerned about the changes in ritual and liturgy than they were the Church's attempts to intrude on the autonomy of areas far from Moscow.

11. Icons painted in the western manner and deemed sacrilegious by the patriarch.

12. A gifted but ambitious Greek scholar who had originally come to Moscow in 1661 hoping to exploit the rift between Nikon and the tsar for his own personal advancement. Ligarides had originally been ordained a Roman Catholic priest, had converted to Islam, and then to Eastern Orthodoxy. He apparently had no deep religious convictions but was able to impress the tsar with his erudition and resourcefulness in the battle against Nikon.

13. Written in colloquial Russian while Avvakum was in exile, it describes his life and experiences and is considered one of the most important primary documents of that age.

14. Sergei Zenkovsky, *Medieval Russia's Epics Chronicles and Tales*, p. 404.

15. Zenkovsky, p. 415.

16. Historians are not exactly certain what happened at this encounter between the tsar and his former mentor. Alexis probably wanted the meeting to be secret because so many boyars opposed any reconciliation, and he was offended when Nikon arrived with a large retinue.

17. In 1681, Nikon was allowed to return to the New Jerusalem Monastery but died before he could reach his destination.

18. Avvakum was contemptuous of his two younger sons, who had agreed to accept the Church reforms to escape punishment. However, despite their willingness to cooperate, they were buried alive along with their mother who remained steadfast to the end.

19. Many sources record the year of Avvakum's execution as 1681.

20. The monastery had long been of military value and was also important for its salt works.

21. Another tsarevich, Semen Alexee-

vich, had died in June of 1669 at age four.

22. The daughter of Kyril Naryshkin, who was a landowner who lived far from Moscow. The father had persuaded Artemon Matveev to allow his daughter to live with his family in the capital to better her chances for social advancement.

23. The sister-in-law of the tsar's former tutor and adviser, Boris Morozov, she angered authorities by allowing her house to become a meeting place for Old Believers.

5. Cossack Rebels and Renegades

1. This eventually did change. By the 18th century, it was not unusual for Cossacks to engage in farming.

2. Muscovy's first ocean-going vessel ever, it was built on the Oka river and commanded by an Irishman named David Butler. It had a mostly European crew that had been recruited in Amsterdam.

3. An area in the northern Caucasus.

4. Razin had actually sent envoys to the ex-patriarch to suggest an alliance but had been firmly rebuffed.

5. Today the city of Ulianovsk, renamed in honor of Vladimir Ilich Ulianov (Lenin), who was born there in 1870.

6. Plural of *murza,* a Tatar of noble birth.

7. The tsarevich had died in June of 1669 at the age of four.

8. The uprising was prompted in large part by a fantastic rumor — that Astrakhan's single women would be forced to marry foreigners. This led to a frenzy of hasty weddings of Russian women to local men. Another rumor circulating at the time was that Peter, whose armies were at war with Sweden, had died in Stockholm and had been replaced by a German. This caused the rebellion in Astrakhan to spread to other towns.

9. Paul Avrich, *Russian Rebels,* p. 156. Quoted in *Krest'ianskie i national'nye nakanune obrazovania Rossiiskoi imperii: Bulavinskoe vostanie,* pp. 450–51; *Pis'ma i bumagi,* VIII, part 1, 600–1.

10. Semi-nomadic, Turkic-speaking Muslims, who lived mostly in the Ural region, hunting, trapping, herding, and beekeeping.

They gradually fell under Muscovite control after Ivan the Terrible's conquest of Kazan and Astrakhan in the 1550s. By the end of the century, Russian settlers were streaming into the area to build their farms and estates, accompanied by soldiers and missionaries. The latter made themselves particularly obnoxious by destroying mosques and baptizing devout Muslims at gunpoint. In addition, the Muscovite government soon took over the salt trade and imposed tribute and military service on the local population.

11. After Charles XII great victory at Narva, he spent a number of years campaigning in Poland.

12. Philip Longworth, *The Cossacks,* p. 1.

13. During this crisis, which will be described in the next chapter, the young Tsar Peter had forcibly ended the regency of his older half-sister, Sophia.

14. Alexander Danilovich Menshikov (1673–1729) was one of Peter's closest friends and advisers. As a child, he sold pies on the street but rose to become a nobleman, general, and one of the richest men in Russia. Though he was a notorious embezzler of state funds, Peter valued him for his loyalty, bravery and support for reform and westernization.

15. The victory at Poltava not only won vast territories for the Muscovite state, but also recognition as a great power by other European states. Henceforth, the author will use the term Russia, rather than Muscovy, to refer to the tsar's territories.

16. Fought between the years 1756–1763, the war began as a quarrel over Silesia between Frederick the Great of Prussia and the Archduchess Maria Theresa of Austria. The main belligerents were Prussia and England against Austria, Russia and France. Fighting also took place in America (where it was known as the French and Indian War) and in India. Prussia was slowly worn down by the struggle, but averted defeat when Russia's Empress Elizabeth died at the end of 1762. Her successor, Tsar Peter III, was a great admirer of Frederick the Great and chose to make peace on terms favorable to Prussia.

17. A form of tuberculosis attacking the lymph glands and sometimes the bones and joints. The latter often break down forming pus-filled boils, which leave scars. But far from trying to conceal these marks, Pugachev

actually showed them to others claiming they proved he really was Tsar Peter III.

18. John T. Alexander, *Emperor of the Cossacks*, pp. 59–60. Quoted from *Pugachevshchina*, comp. S.A. Goliubov, 3 vols. (Moscow and Leningrad, 1926– 1931), I, 25.

19. Beginning in 1721, Peter the Great, eager to exploit the country's rich deposits of iron and copper, began the process of virtually enslaving large numbers of peasants, convicts, and tribesmen by authorizing industrial entrepreneurs to arbitrarily transport whole towns to foundries and mines in the Ural Mountains. In 1736, the tsar issued an edict declaring these unfortunates and their families bondsmen, forever tied to their factories. The conditions under which they lived and labored were abominable, featuring low pay, back-breaking labor, fierce discipline, and savage punishments. See Avrich's *Russian Rebels*, pp. 199–202.

20. Paul Avrich, *Russian Rebels*, p. 227. Quoted in *Russkaia Starina*, 1875, p. 441; B. H. Sumner, *Survey of Russian History* (2nd ed., London, 1947, p. 146).

21. A brutally violent and widespread uprising or *jacquerie*.

22. Avrich, p. 245. Quoted in *Sbornik Imperatorskogo russkogo Istoricheskogo obshestva* XXVII, I; Polnoe Sobranie zakonov, XX, 85.

6. Rebel Relatives and the Revolts of the Strel'tsy

1. In old Russia, people were traditionally named after saints, each of whom was honored on a particular day during the year. A Russian was more likely to celebrate his or her name day, or *imyenitsa*, than birthday.

2. Peter's bride was Eudoxia Lopukhina (1669–1731), the daughter of a Muscovite nobleman. She had actually been chosen by Tsaritsa Natalya in the hope that she would settle him down, but the marriage was doomed from the beginning because Peter detested Eudoxia's narrow-mindedness and lack of intelligence. After a son, Alexei Petrovich, was born in 1690, the young tsar became estranged from his wife, refusing to have anything to do with her.

3. Founded by Tsar Feodor in 1591 to help guard the southern boundary of Moscow from Tatar raids, Donskoy was one of several monasteries constructed both for religious and military purposes.

4. Before the adoption of the Julian calendar in 1700, New Year's Day in Russia was celebrated on September 1. To Orthodox Believers, logic suggested that the new year could only have begun in the fall when apples were ripe to be picked. Otherwise, how could Eve have tempted Adam with the forbidden fruit?

5. Lindsey Hughes, *Sophia, Regent of Russia*, p. 239. Quoted in *Pis'ma i bumagi Imp. Petra Velilogo*, vol. 1, (St. Petersburg, 1887), pp. 13–14.

6. Actually, Peter had a serious side, which he cultivated with great determination. Painfully aware of his own lack of formal education and his inability to read and write fluently, he sought to compensate by acquiring a knowledge of anything that could be put to practical use. He loved to tinker with clocks and navigational instruments, work with wood on his own lathe, and lay stone at construction sites. In time, he claimed mastery in some fourteen different specialties, including surgery and dentistry. However, the tsar's eagerness to display his expertise in medical matters terrified members of his entourage, since he was inclined to practice on anyone suspected of having an ailment.

7. The house was an exceptionally beautiful structure that had been rented to him by the author, John Evelyn.

8. Feodor Romodanovsky (1640–1717) whose father had been murdered in the *strel'tsy* uprising in 1682, was one of the tsar's most loyal servitors. As head of the Secret Office, he had a reputation for ruthlessness and cruelty. However, he was also an enthusiastic member of the Most Drunken Council, and was given the mock title King of Pressburg and later, Prince Caesar. At times, Peter pretended to pay homage to him, mostly to consternate others who didn't understand the game that was being played.

9. Patrick Gordon (1635–1699) was a Scot who had come to Muscovy during the reign of Tsar Alexis. He became one of Peter's most important advisers on military matters.

10. Sophia spent the rest of her life at Novodevichy and died in 1704 at age 47.

11. Charles XII (1682–1718) ascended the throne at the age of fifteen and almost immediately attacked Denmark to break up a coalition of hostile powers that was forming against him. After the Danes were forced to sue for peace in 1700, he defeated the Russians at Narva and, from 1702 to 1707, waged war against Poland.

12. In 1700, Peter ordered the adoption of the Julian calendar, which according to the Russian practice of reckoning time from the beginning of the world, was the year 7,208. Ironically, the Julian calendar was already out of date and had been replaced in many countries by a more accurate one authorized by Pope Gregory in 1582. However, the Gregorian calendar was not recognized in Russia until after the Bol'shevik Revolution when the Soviets imposed it in February of 1918.

13. Catherine (1684–1727) was born Martha Skavronskaya, and captured as a young girl by the Russian army in 1702. She eventually ended up as a servant in the household of Prince Menshikov, where she caught Peter's eye and became his lover. Their marriage in 1707 was kept secret for a number of years even after she had given birth to a number of his children. A public wedding was performed in 1712 with Tsarevich Alexis acting as her godfather.

14. Robert K. Massie, p. 677. Quoted in *Manifesto of the Criminal Process of the Czarewitz Alexei Petrowitz*, The Hague, 1718, p. 103 (printed in Volume II of the *Present State of Russia by Friedrich Christian Weber*). Hereafter referred to as *Manifesto*.

15. Kikin had participated in Peter's play regiments as a youth and had gone to western Europe as part of the Grand Embassy. He later fell into disfavor when he was charged with embezzlement and corruption.

16. R. Massie, p. 677. Quoted in *Manifesto*, p. 116.

17. R. Massie, p. 679. Quoted in *Manifesto*, pp. 107–8.

18. An institution created in February of 1711 consisting of ten men. Its most important function was to govern the country in the tsar's absence.

19. This is the same Piotr Tolstoy who helped to incite the *strel'tsy* in May of 1682 by claiming that the Naryshkins had murdered Tsar Ivan. Later, however, he became a firm supporter of Peter's reforms and a diplomat. His most important service to the tsar was probably the twelve years he spent in Constantinople as Russia's ambassador to the Ottoman Empire.

20. R. Massie, p. 680. Quoted in *Manifesto*, p. 126.

21. Kikin's motives in opposing the tsar were somewhat similar to those of Prince Kurbsky, who defected to the King of Poland in 1564 during the reign of Ivan the Terrible.

22. A second round of executions took place in December of the same year.

23. An oblong hexagonal structure with six bastions, it was first built of earth and wood on Hare Island in the Neva River in 1703. Later, its walls were rebuilt of stone and its importance to St. Petersburg became similar to that of the Kremlin to Moscow. Within its walls was a prison for political offenders and the Cathedral of Peter and Paul, which serves as a mortuary for the later Romanov tsars, beginning with Peter the Great.

24. A palace located on the Gulf of Finland famous for its gardens, fountains and summer pavilions. Much of the Peterhof was the creation of Alexander Jean Baptiste LeBlond (1639–1719) who was inspired by Louis XIV's Versailles.

7. Scheming Aristocrats — Palace Coups

1. A holy festival observed on January 6 by the Gregorian Calendar. At one time it celebrated both the birth and baptism of Jesus, although, beginning in the fourth century, it honored the meeting of the Three Wise Men or Magi with the infant Jesus. In Russia, it called the blessing of the waters of the "Jordan," and was traditionally celebrated on the banks of the Moscow River and later on the banks of the Neva River.

2. Robert K. Massie, *Peter the Great*, p. 845. Quoted in Bernard Pares' *A History of Russia*, Alfred A. Knopf, 1960, p. 225.

3. The council members reduced the power of the Senate and made it subordinate to them.

4. An area in what is now western Latvia bordering on the Baltic Sea and the Gulf of Riga.

5. A member of a Buddhist Mongol people, who lived mainly northwest of the Caspian Sea.

6. Actually, the palace in question was rather imposing. It was twenty feet high and nearly three hundred feet long with glacial columns, statues, and a balcony. There were numerous ice sculptures including a life-size elephant with a man inside to simulate a trumpet sound. There were also ice dolphins that were somehow made to spew fire.

7. Virginia Cowles, *The Romanovs*, p. 68.

8. The original structure was built in 1711 on the banks of the Neva River and reconstructed in 1754 by Bartolomeo Rastrelli to serve as the imperial residence. Enormous by any standard (250 yards long and 160 yards wide), Catherine the Great set aside part of it to house her growing art collection, which she called the Hermitage.

9. An area along the Baltic Sea in what is now Germany and Poland.

10. Schleswig and Holstein form two continuous duchies on the southern border of Denmark. They form part of a peninsula between the North and Baltic Seas.

11. In order to give birth without Peter finding out, Catherine arranged for a servant to set fire to his own wooden house (which was located near the palace), confident that her husband would be lured to the site of the conflagration.

12. An estate built by Prince Menshikov in 1710, it is situated on the Gulf of Finland 18 miles west of St. Petersburg.

13. Originally called Noteborg, the fortress was built by the Swedes near the origin of the Neva River and Lake Ladoga. In 1702, it was captured by the Russians and renamed Schlüsselberg.

14. Letter, Alexei Orlov to Catherine. Quoted in Isabel de Madariaga, *Russia in the Age of Catherine the Great*, p. 32.

15. Founded by Peter the Great in 1710, it includes a burial ground for members of the tsar's family and certain other high born individuals.

16. A large estate located twenty-eight miles southwest of St. Petersburg that had been given by Catherine first to Gregory Orlov. After his death in 1783, the empress gave it to Paul.

17. In fact, Catherine squashed any hope that she would do anything about serfdom

while the Legislative Commission was still in session. In 1768, she issued a decree threatening any serf who petitioned the government against his landlord with the knout and exile to Siberia for life.

18. Gregory Alexandrovich Potemkin (1739–1791) was the son of a colonel from Smolensk who studied at the University of Moscow and later joined the Horse Guards in St. Petersburg. Academically brilliant, he was deeply pious and had a keen interest in theology. At the same time, he was known for his extravagant lifestyle. The Orlovs became so envious of his influence that they beat him up, blinding him in one eye. Thereafter, he was often referred to as "Cyclops."

19. Alexander Nikolaevich Radishchev (1749–1801) achieved both fame and notoriety for his tract *A Journey from St. Petersburg to Moscow*, in which he exposed serfdom as a grave injustice.

20. In 1795, when the Shah of Persia invaded the Caucasian principalities, Catherine sent Valerian Zubov with 30,000 men to drive him out.

21. A two-wheeled horse-drawn cart.

22. The knights had a small priory in Poland, which had passed to Russia during the partitions. Paul had offered them a generous settlement, which had led them to declare him their protector in December 1796.

23. Built between 1797 and 1800 by Vincenzo Brenna on the site of the old Summer Palace, which had burned down. Today it is known as the Engineers' Castle.

24. Some historians believe Pahlen intended to be late so that if the coup failed he could arrest the conspirators and pretend to have acted only to protect the tsar.

25. This account of Paul's assassination is based on Roderick E. McGrew's description of the same in *Paul I of Russia*, pp. 352–353.

26. Allen McConnell, *Tsar Alexander I: Paternalistic Reformer*, p.17.

8. Aristocratic Rebels: The Decembrists and Petrashevtsy

1. Maria Naryshkina bore him two illegitimate children.

2. Mikhail Mikhailovich Speransky

(1772–1839) is considered by many historians to be one of the most gifted bureaucrats in Russian history. Between 1810 and 1812 he trebled the governments revenues by increasing the soul tax and by introducing and income tax. These measures were appreciated by the tsar, but angered conservatives.

3. Allen McConnell, *Alexander I: Paternalistic Reformer*, p. 79.

4. Mikhail Ilaronovich Kutuzov (1745–1813) was blamed by Alexander for the disastrous defeat at Austerlitz in 1805, although it was the tsar himself who, acting in defiance of the general's advise, ordered a premature attack that enabled Napoleon to rout the Russian and Austrian armies.

5. Known as the "Battle of Nations," Alexander must be credited with persevering when his officers and foreign allies thought the battle was lost. At one point, he ordered his own bodyguard to attack the French cuirassiers, following closely behind at considerable risk to himself.

6. Once while reviewing his troops in St. Petersburg as they were returning from France, a peasant happened to wander across Alexander's path at the very moment his unsheathed sword was lowered in salute to his mother, the Dowager Empress. The tsar seemed to take this as a personal insult and slashed at him with his sword, whereupon some police officers beat the man with their clubs.

7. Henri Troyat, *Alexander of Russia*, p. 238.

8. Troyat, p. 239.

9. At that time, the government would routinely demand that landowners and village communes provide a quota of men for the army according to the military's needs at the moment. Once chosen, a recruit was expected to serve for twenty-five years under savage discipline and with minimal pay. There was no such thing as leave nor was there any compensation for soldiers who become ill or wounded. Those who survived their full terms were often completely used up, with no means of support and no place to go.

10. Alexei Andreevich Arakcheev (1769–1834) was the son of a minor nobleman from Tver province whose motto was *Bez lesti predan* (Devoted without flattery). In 1818, he was called upon by Alexander to devise a plan for emancipation that was intended to be so favorable to the landowners that they would welcome it. Typically, the plan was received well by Alexander but was never implemented. At least one historian believes that the tsar's failure to act represents an opportunity missed that might have saved the country from the strife and turmoil that was soon to come. See Allen McConnell's *Tsar Alexander I*, pp. 145–147.

11. Ronald Hingley, *The Tsars*, p. 229.

12. McConnell, p. 141.

13. Some, however, actually liked what they saw. The historian, Nikolai Karamzin, praised the enterprise, commenting that "where eight years ago stood impassable marches, you see orchards and towns."

14. McConnell, p. 142.

15. Pavel Ivanovich Pestel' (1799–1826) was the son of the governor general of Siberia, who was notoriously rapacious and corrupt. Pavel Ivanovich, however, was quite a different kind of man, having been decorated for bravery at Borodino by General Kutuzov himself. In the spring of 1821, he was sent to Moldavia during the Greek uprising to collect information about Alexander Ypsilanti. Tsar Alexander was much impressed by his "lucid and detailed account." In November of that year, he was promoted to colonel and given command of what was considered the worst regiment in the Second Army. In less than two years, this same regiment had so improved that the tsar rewarded Pestel' with a large grant of land.

16. Avrahm Yarmolinsky, *Road to Revolution*, p. 32.

17. According to Bruce Lincoln, it was Alexander who acted in violation of Tsar Paul's Law of Succession. Only Grand Duke Konstantin had the right to designate a successor, since he was the rightful heir to Alexander's throne. See Lincoln's *Nicholas I*, p. 24. However, Roderick E. McGrew believes Tsar Paul intended a strict law of primogeniture in which there was room for choice. Thus, when Konstantin abdicated, as he did, Nicholas automatically became his successor.

18. The conspirators were convinced that the common soldier would be willing to act decisively to support the legitimate tsar but that they would be hostile to any attempt to end the monarchy.

19. Lincoln, p. 40. Quoted in N.K. Shilder, *Imperator Nikolai Pervyi: Ego zhizn'*

i tsarstvovania, 2 vol., St. Petersburg, 1903, p. 281.

20. One man who behaved with exceptional composure was Mikhail Sergeevich Lunin (1787–1845), who was a veteran of the Napoleonic Wars and decorated many times for bravery. Lunin had lived for some months in Paris in 1816–1817, where he embraced Roman Catholicism. He returned to Russia upon the death of his father only to learn that the latter had accumulated many debts. To settle with his father's creditors, Lunin restored the family estates and cloth factory and, in the process, took a keen interest in the well-being of his serfs whose condition he was determined to improve. He helped to found the Union of Salvation in 1818 and took an active part in the discussions about government reform and emancipation. Later, his ardent Roman Catholicism drew him to Warsaw, where he became involved with some Polish patriotic societies. Though he played no part in the Decembrist Revolt, Tsar Nicholas insisted that he be returned to St. Petersburg to stand trial. Lunin was sentenced to twenty years in prison and exile. He died in Aktui near Nerchinsk in 1845.

21. Bruce Lincoln, p. 82. Quoted in I.D. Iakushkin, *Zapiski, stat'i, pisma dekabrista I.D, Iakushina* (Moscow, 1951), pp. 82–83.

22. Known as the ideology of "Official Nationality," it was defined by the tsar's minister of education, Count Sergei Semenovich Uvarov (1786–1855). He promised the tsar that Russia would be protected from revolutionary strife as long as the school system, from primary grades through the university, adhered rigidly to those three principles.

23. Alexander Sergeevich Pushkin (1799–1837) is Russia's greatest poet, famous also for his plays and short stories. Born into a noble family of modest means, his maternal grandfather was an Ethiopian who had risen to the rank of general under Peter the Great. Tsar Nicholas admired his wit and volunteered to personally review his work to free him from government censors. This proved to be a dubious arrangement that the poet probably regretted, especially when the tsar suggested that the young man rewrite his great play *Boris Godunov* in the form of a novel. In 1837, Pushkin was killed in a duel by a French-

man who he suspected had become his wife's lover.

24. Michail Yureevich Lermontov (1814–1841) was exiled to the Caucasus for a year for his poem *Death of a Poet*. Famous for his romantic poetry and short novel *A Hero of Our Time*, he was killed in a duel in 1841.

25. Piotr Yakovlevich Chaadaev (1793–1856) served in the Napoleonic wars and traveled in western Europe for three years. In his *Lettres Philosophiques* in 1836, he expressed his admiration for Western values and the Roman Catholic Church. He condemned Russia for having no past and claimed that she had contributed nothing to world culture.

26. Hingley, p. 255.

27. Nicholas could also show compassion when it was least expected. Once when he saw a hearse being drawn through the streets followed by no mourners, he decided to walk behind it to the cemetery. His example attracted a crowd of thousands. On another occasion, he discovered a porter asleep at his desk with an unfinished letter in front of him. In it he expressed his despair about his financial situation and wondered who would pay his debts. Without waking the man, Nicholas wrote on the letter: 'I, Nicholas I.'

28. Charles X (1757–1836) was a brother of the guillotined Louis XVI. He became King in 1824 at age sixty-six and immediately compensated the old aristocracy for the property they had lost during the Revolution. However, his reactionary ways antagonized so many people that he was forced to flee the country in 1830.

29. Louis Philippe (1773–1850) had initially been sympathetic to the goals of the French Revolution and had joined the National Guard to participate in the revolt. He later had to leave France for plotting against the republic. Having become king in 1830 after Charles X was forced to abdicate, he ruled for eighteen years but was generally unpopular. "France is bored" was a complaint frequently heard.

30. Mikhail Vasilievich Buteshevich-Petrashevsky (1821–1866) was the son of a doctor who had earned noble status by his long service in the Russian army. He was drawn to revolutionary ideas as a student and, in 1845, helped author a book with N.S. Kirilov called *A Pocket Dictionary of*

Foreign Words, which explained the meaning of many socialist and radical terms.

31. François Marie Charles Fourier (1772–1837), a French socialist who was harshly critical of all of institutions, proposed the reorganization of society into "phalansteries" of 1650 people each. People would be encouraged to live cooperatively while doing the work for which they were best suited.

32. Feodor Mikhailovich Dostoyevsky (1821–1881), one of Russia's greatest novelists, was condemned to death for his participation in the Petrashevsky discussion group. His sentence was communed to jail and exile in Siberia where he described his experiences in *Notes from the House of the Dead* in 1861.

33. Plural of the word *Petroshevets,* it refers to a participant in the discussion group organized by Mikhail Buteshevich-Petrashevsky.

34. Nikolai Alexandrovich Speshnev (1821–1882) so impressed Dostoyevsky that he made him the model for the character of Stavrogin in *The Possessed.* After Speshnev's arrest and trial, he was sentenced to ten years in the mines at Nerchinsk. He was then transferred to the Alexandrovsky Smelting Plant on the Shilka River, where he and fellow prisoner, Nikolai Mombelli, opened a school for children. He was amnestied in 1856 and moved to Irkutsk where he became editor of a weekly newspaper *The Irkutsk News.* He wrote articles on many topics including local history, geography, scientific discoveries, trade, commerce, and navigation on the Amur River. In 1860, he returned to his family estate near Pskov, just before the liberation of the serfs. In the years that followed, he became extremely unpopular among other nobles because of his sympathy for the plight of the peasants.

35. Louis Napoleon (1808–1873) was the son of Louis Bonaparte, King of Holland, who was the brother of Napoleon I. After the fall and exile of his uncle, the Bonapartes were sent into exile. Thus, Louis lived for a time in Italy, Germany, and Switzerland. He made two attempts to overthrow the government of Louis Philippe, in 1836 and 1840. He spent time in jail, escaped, went to England in 1846, and returned to France with the Revolution of 1848. He was elected first to the Assembly and, in December, was elected President of the Second French Republic. In 1852, he proclaimed himself emperor.

36. In 1855, Sardinia joined England and France in support of Turkey in order to gain a seat at the peace conference.

9. Nihilists, Nechaev, and the People's Will

1. Alexander Ivanovich Herzen (1812–1870) was the illegitimate son of a Russian nobleman and a German mother and became one of the most prominent socialist thinkers and writers of the 19th century. Among his most important works are *From the Other Shore,* published in 1850, and *My Past and Thoughts,* the first chapters of which appeared in 1854.

2. Georg Friedrich Hegel (1770–1831) was one of the most influential German philosophers of the 19th century who emphasized the need to study the past in order to understand any aspect of human culture. To this end, he developed a theory of history known as the *dialectic,* which features the steady march of progress in human events caused by the clash of conflicting forces.

3. Nikolai Platonovich Ogarev (1813–1877), the son of a wealthy landowner in Penza province, studied at Moscow State University where he met Alexander Herzen and helped him form a political discussion group. Later, he joined his friend in London where he supported his theory of Russian socialism, which called for the creation of a federal republic of self-governing communes. Ogarev was also respected for his talent as a poet.

4. Nikolai Gavrilovich Chernyshevsky (1828–1889), the son of a priest, became one of the most influential radical thinkers in 19th century Russia. His most important work was a novel entitled *What Is to Be Done?,* written during his first year in prison. It was to become a revolutionary classic and deeply influenced many socialist activists, including the future Bolshevik leader, Vladimir Ilyich Lenin.

5. A 19th century term that applies to educated men and women who did not belong to any previously recognized class. Such people often taught or wrote for a living and formed the bulk of the intelligentsia.

6. Piotr Grigorievich Zaichnevsky (1842–1896) was an influential radical activist in the early 1860s who had been attracted to the theories of Alexander Herzen as a university student in Moscow. His hatred of the monarchy was so intense that he called for the execution of all the Romanovs.

7. Ivan Sergeevich Turgenev (1818–1883), the son of an impoverished nobleman studied at the Universities of Moscow, St. Petersburg, and Berlin. After a brief career as a civil servant, he turned to writing where his interest in social issues soon became apparent. In 1847, he published *A Sportsman's Sketches,* which so graphically depicted the misery of the serfs that it profoundly influenced the future Tsar Alexander II to address the problem upon ascending the throne.

8. "Hell" was actually a subgroup of a larger group called "Organization," which was established in 1866. The purpose of Organization was to agitate and spread propaganda among the lower classes throughout the country.

9. Robert Payne, *The Fortress,* p. 153.

10. Nikolai Andreevich Ishutin (1840–1879) became attracted to socialism while a student at Moscow University and soon became the leader of a circle to discuss social problems and the need for a revolution. Deeply influenced by Chernyshevsky's *What Is to Be Done?,* he set up a number of cooperative economic enterprises and started a tuition-free school for poor working boys. He was also the founder of a Mutual Aid Society as well as "Organization."

11. Payne, p. 155.

12. In fact, the scandal got much worse. Although Alexander had always been considerate of his wife, in February of 1880 he did the unthinkable. While the empress lay mortally ill in the Winter Palace, the tsar moved Katya and their bastard children into the same residence for security reasons. When his wife died in May, Alexander waited only a little more than a month before marrying Katya, to whom he bestowed the title Princess Yurovskaya.

13. Mark Andreevich Natanson (1850–1919), the son of a prosperous Jewish merchant, generally favored nonviolence in promoting the cause of agrarian socialism in Russia. He was widely acclaimed as a tireless organizer whose sincerity of purpose and devotion to the cause was admired even by those who were far more radical.

14. Sophia Lvovna Perovskaya (1854–1881) was the daughter of the governor-general of St. Petersburg, Lev Nikolaevich Perovsky, and came to hate her despotic father, who frequently abused her mother. When Perovsky lost his position in 1866 because of Karakazov's assassination attempt against Alexander II, life at home became intolerable. The antagonism between father and daughter was further increased by Sophia's determination to get an education and by her interest in women's issues.

15. So named after Nikolai Vasilievich Tschaikovsky (1850–1926), whose good looks and dominating personality made him a natural leader. The *Tschaikovsty,* as they came to be known, were devoted to the idea of revolution although they were not particularly dogmatic about ideology. However, they generally endorsed neither terror nor the seizure of power by a revolutionary elite. Most hoped to establish a society based on socialism and producer cooperatives in the cities.

16. Piotr Nikitich Tkachev (1844–1885) was an important literary critic and Marxist thinker who has been called "the first Bolshevik" because of his conviction that only an elite minority in the radical intelligentsia could bring about the overthrow the state and set up a socialist dictatorship.

17. Adam Ulam, *In the Name of the People,* p. 178.

18. Vera Ivanovna Zasulich (1849–1919) was born in Mikhailovka near Smolensk and studied at a boarding school in Moscow, intending to become a governess. She later worked as a clerk, a weaver, and also taught literacy classes for workers. She became a revolutionary in 1868 after being influenced by Sergei Nechaev. Over the

years, she became active in a number of revolutionary organizations despite the fact that she was not an original thinker and had little talent for political organization, nor was she the least bit interested in feminism.

19. Robert Payne, *The Fortress*, p. 166 (i.e. the Fortress of St. Peter and Paul).

20. Mikhail Alexandrovich Bakunin (1814–1876), one of the most influential leaders of the international anarchist movement, was born the son of a nobleman and served briefly as an officer in the army. He was deeply influenced in his youth by the teachings of Fichte and Hegel and established a long friendship with Alexander Herzen. Bakunin's ultimate goal was to see a federation of self-governing communes in Russia organized on socialist principles. However, he left his homeland in 1857 after spending six years in jail, never to return. He frequently quarreled with others about ideology, especially Karl Marx, whose ideas he loathed. One of Bakunin's works, *God and the State,* published several years after his death, called for the abolition of all religion and the destruction of the state.

21. A wealthy Russian landowner who left Herzen and Ogarev a large sum of money before leaving for the Marquesas Islands in the Pacific to found a communist settlement. He was never heard from again.

22. Payne, p. 168.

23. The Revolutionary Catechism is printed in full in Robert Payne's *The Fortress,* pp. 173–176. Quoted in the *Pravitel'stvenniye Vestnik,* July 11, 1871 (from microfilm provided by the Library of Congress).

24. Ivan Gavrilovich Pryzhkov (1827–1885) was born into a peasant family, studied at Moscow University, and was later employed in the Moscow Office of Civil Justice. His revolutionary activities earned him a prison sentence of nine years after which he was resettled in Siberia. There he began to write history and is credited with some works on unusual topics, including the history of taverns in Russia and the poor.

25. Ulam, p. 192.
26. Payne, p. 176.
27. Payne, p. 211.
28. Payne, p. 213.
29. Payne, p. 215.

30. Payne, 229. Quoted in P.E. Shchegolev's *Alexeevsky Ravelin,* pp. 196–197 (Moscow, Izdatel'stvo APN, 1953).

31. Piotr Lavrov (1823–1900) was a colonel of artillery and professor of mathematics who abandoned his career in the 1860s to become a revolutionary socialist. As a founding member of the first Land and Liberty Party in 1862, he believed that the intelligentsia should help educate the peasants and work toward the creation of a socialist society. His philosophy is best described in a series of articles entitled "Historical Letters" in which he emphasized the importance of the individual in history. Later, he became editor of the journal *Forward (Vpered)* and in 1872 joined the First International. Although he eventually became a member of the radical People's Will, he was never comfortable with the use of terror, always insisting that such tactics be applied only as a last resort.

32. Alan P. Pollard, "Movement to the People," *Modern Encyclopedia of Russian and Soviet History,* p. 148.

33. Yekaterina Konstantinovna Breshko-Breshkovskaya (1844–1934) was born into a gentry family and deeply influenced by her father's liberalism and her mother's unorthodox religious beliefs. The latter had always emphasized the social message of the Gospels and the need to devote one's self to a higher cause. For Breshko-Breshkovskaya, this became the well-being of the peasantry.

34. Dmitri Lizogub (1849–1879), as a young man, had been much attracted to the ideals of the Gospels and the principles of equality and brotherhood and had intended to become a missionary. However, during his student years at the University of St. Petersburg, he renounced religion in his determination to devote his life to the alleviation of human suffering.

35. Vasily Vasilievich Bervi-Flerovsky (1829–1918) fiercely criticized the Emancipation Edict and attempted to subvert it, which led to his confinement in an insane asylum and banishment to Astrakhan. His two most famous works are *The ABCs of the Social Sciences* and *The Status of the Working Class in Russia.*

36. Auguste Blanqui (1805–1881) was a French socialist and intellectual who

became a professional revolutionary at the age of nineteen. He became a member of the Carbonari in 1824 and participated in riots to oppose the monarchy of Charles X and later that of Louis Philippe. As a revolutionary, he stressed the importance of reeducating the masses and the need for an organized elite to make the revolution. Always a vigorous man of action, he paid the price by spending thirty-three years of his life in various prisons.

37. Vera Nikolaevna Figner (1852–1942) was one of the most respected names among revolutionary activists, and she was the product of a happy childhood and a relatively privileged upbringing. She decided on a career in medicine because she thought it the best way to serve Russia's impoverished masses. Although she was slow to involve herself in revolutionary politics, she eventually performed heroically in the battle against the autocracy. Moreover, her service on behalf of the less fortunate lasted well into the Soviet period, although she always declined to become a party member. In 1941, she refused to be evacuated as the German army approached Moscow, saying to her rescuers, "Concern yourself with the living." She died in June of 1942 at ninety years of age.

38. Figner stayed to finish her degree, since she believed that only with a knowledge of medicine could she serve the peasantry in any meaningful way.

39. Ulam, p. 252.

40. Built between 1801 and 1811 by a former serf of the Stroganov family, Andrei Voronikhin, at the behest of Tsar Paul, who had admired St. Peter's in Rome. Four semi-circular rows of fluted columns extend out toward the Nevsky Prospect with a massive portico at each end. It was from this cathedral that General Mikhail Kutuzov rode off to war during the French invasion of 1812. It was in this cathedral that he was buried in 1813.

41. Georgi Valentinovich Plekhanov (1856–1918) was born into a gentry family and originally wanted to become an army officer. However, as a student in the Mining Institute, he became attracted to populism and soon became a member of Land and Liberty. In 1880, he went into exile to avoid arrest and did not return to Russia until 1917.

42. Alexei Vasilievich Dolgushin (1848–1885) was the son of a minor official and became an active revolutionary as a student at the St. Petersburg Technological Institute. In 1872, he became the leader of the Dolgushin Circle, the members of which were dedicated to an immediate peasant uprising. He was arrested in 1873 and sentenced to ten years hard labor, which was doubled when he slapped the face of a prison inspector at Krasnoiarsk. During this time he wrote *Buried Alive (Zashivo pogrebonnye)*, which was about the inhuman conditions in Russian prisons. He apparently had good reason to complain. In July of 1885, he died in the Schlüsselburg Fortress because of those same inhuman conditions.

43. Alexander Konstantinovich Soloviev (1846–1879) was originally a schoolteacher who abandoned the classroom because he couldn't stand the fact that his students enjoyed so many privileges. Later, he participated in the 'to the people campaign' and stayed in the countryside for nearly three years working as a laborer and a carpenter.

44. Alexander Dmitrievich Mikhailov (1855–1884) joined the revolutionary movement in 1875 after his expulsion from the St. Petersburg Technological Institute for participating in a student protest. The following year he helped to organize the new Land and Liberty Party as he gradually became convinced of the need to submit to a highly centralized organization based on unity, discipline, and conspiracy. Mikhailov became the party's most energetic organizer, who took it upon himself to warn others about the importance of security.

45. Lev Alexandrovich Tikhomirov (1852–1923) was a famous revolutionary theoretician and writer who became a member of the Moscow branch of the Tschaikovsky Circle as a medical student at the university. He was arrested in 1873 and spent four years in jail awaiting trial. He was eventually set free and joined the editorial board of Land and Liberty. Later, he became active in various assassination plots against the tsar, although he mourned the victim's death when it actually occurred. In 1882, he went to Switzerland where he later experienced a mental breakdown followed

by a complete change of heart. In 1888, he wrote a petition to Alexander III expressing remorse for his radical activities and received a full pardon. He returned to Moscow the following year to become the editor of the Moscow News (*Moskovskie Vedomosti*) and a staunch defender of the monarchy. Amazingly, the Bolsheviks took no action against him for his apostasy when they took power in 1917.

46. Andrei Zheliabov (1851–1883) was the son of household serfs and attended school at Kerch in Tauride Province and later became a student in the juridical school in Odessa. He became a revolutionary after being expelled from school for having participated in a student protest. Zheliabov's imposing presence, personal charisma, intelligence, and bravery made him a natural leader. Lenin considered him one of the most important revolutionaries of the 19th century.

47. Ulam, p. 356.

48. Ulam p. 360.

49. Ulam, p. 360.

50. Ulam, p. 361.

51. Payne, p. 291.

52. Payne, p. 290.

53. Ulam, pp. 363–4.

54. Lev Nikolaevich Tolstoy (1828–1910). In his later years, he became ashamed of his dissolute past and accomplishments and sought to reject both by living ascetically and doing manual labor on his estate. He also developed a keen interest in the plight of Russia's long suffering peasants. He concluded that both the state and the Orthodox Church were guilty of having exploited and abused an entire class of humanity, and urged his countrymen to defy both through passive resistance. Tolstoy was excommunicated from the Church in 1901, but his influence in society remained troublesome to the government even after his death.

55. Edward Crankshaw, *The Shadow of the Winter Palace*, p. 324.

10. Reaction, Rasputin, and Revolution

1. Sergei Petrovich Degaev (1849–1921)

emigrated to America where he changed his name to Alexander Pell. He always lived in fear that his true identity would be discovered. After the death of his first wife, he married one of his students at the University of South Dakota. Later, he worked at the Armour Institute of Technology in Chicago. He died in Bryn Mawr, Pennsylvania, where his young wife had taken a teaching position.

2. Alexander Ilich Ulianov (1866–1887) was the oldest of six children, and he was a quiet, sensitive youth whose academic brilliance shown most brightly in science. Indeed, he had civic concerns that reveal a high-mindedness unusual for such a young person. At sixteen, he wrote an essay entitled "What does a man need in order to make himself useful to society?"

3. Nephritis, an inflammation of the kidneys that reduces the amount of urine produced causing waste products to accumulate in the body.

4. These were Olga (1895), Tatiana (1897), Marie (1899), Anastasia (1901) and Alexis (1904).

5. Robert K. Massie, *Nicholas and Alexandra*, p. 114. Quoted in *An Ambassador's Memoirs* by Maurice Paleologue, p. 98 (3 vols. Translated by F.A. Holt, New York, Doran, 1925).

6. R. Massie, p 68. Quoted in *The Fall of the Russian Monarchy*, p. 57 (New York, Harper, 1958).

7. Nadezhda Konstantinovna Krupskaya (1869–1939) was born into a family of the minor nobility; her father had served as a military officer in Poland. She was drawn to revolutionary activities at an early age, was arrested in 1896, and exiled to Ufa. She corresponded with Lenin, who invited her to join him in Shushenskoe. She was allowed to do so only on condition that the two be married.

8. Yuli Osipovich Martov (1873–1923) was a member of the Social Democratic Party since 1892 who worked closely with Lenin until 1903, when the two split because of ideological differences. He became leader of the Mensheviks in 1917 but eventually settled in Berlin, where he edited the journal *The Socialist Courier*.

9. Pavel Borisovich Axelrod (1850?–1928) was born to a poor Jewish family in

Ukraine, and he was initially attracted to the ideas of Bakunin. He eventually joined the Black Partition, which emphasized the need to seek support for socialism among the peasants. He later became an important Menshevik ideologist and a determined critic of the Bolsheviks in exile after the Revolution.

10. Lev Davidovich Trotsky (1879–1940) was the son of a prosperous landowner named Bronstein, and he became an activist for the Social Democratic Party in 1896. He was arrested and sent to Siberia but escaped and returned to St. Petersburg to work for *Iskra*. He joined the Mensheviks in 1903 but would eventually become a Bolshevik and a close collaborator of Lenin.

11. Grigori Andreevich Gershuni (1870–1908) was the son of Lithuanian Jews and was trained as a pharmacist but was drawn to revolutionary activity while still a student. He had strong leadership qualities and eventually played an important role in the founding of the Socialist Revolutionary Party. He also wrote poetry and published a dramatic memoir of his life.

12. Piotr Vladimirovich Karpovich (1874–1917) studied at the universities of Moscow and Yuriev but was banned from all institutions of higher learning for having participated in student protests. In 1899, he went to the University of Berlin and briefly joined the Russian Social Democratic Labor Party. However, he soon returned to St. Petersburg to assassinate Bogolepov.

13. Stepan Valerianovich Balmashev (1881–1918) as a student at Kiev University had been arrested in January 1901 along with 182 others. He was condemned to serve nine months in the army. Upon his return to school, he joined the Battle Organization of the Socialist Revolutionary Party. In April 1902, he assassinated the minister of the interior, Sipiagin, and was tried and executed within the span of a month.

14. Yevno Fishelevich Azev (1869–1918) was the second of seventeen children raised in a poor Jewish family in Ukraine. He completed his studies at a local gymnasium and later became a reporter for a newspaper in Rostov. While he was employed in a business firm, he managed to steal a large

sum of money, went to Germany, and earned a degree electrical engineering.

15. Boris Viktorovich Savinkov (1879–1925), the son of an assistant procurator in Kharkov, was educated in Poland and was attracted to the revolutionary movement as a youth. He had originally joined the Social Democrats but later switched to the Socialist Revolutionaries. Having emigrated to France, he joined the French Army in 1914 and subsequently began to write novels. He returned to Russia in 1917, served as assistant minister of war under Kerensky, and later fought in the civil war against the Bolsheviks. After the defeat of the White Army, he fled to Poland. Savinkov returned to Russia in 1924, was arrested and condemned to ten years in jail. According to Soviet sources, he died on August 29, 1925 when he jumped from the fifth floor of the Lubianka Prison.

16. Yegor Sergeevich Sazonov (1882–1910), the son of a rich lumber merchant, had enrolled at Moscow University and initially heeded the advice of his father, who warned him to pay no attention to the "young hotheads" at the university. However, the brutality of the police in suppressing the strike drove him to desperate measures.

17. Quoted in Margaret H. Pertzoff, "Plehve, Viacheslav Konstantinovich," *Modern Encyclopedia of Russian and Soviet History* (ed., Joseph L. Wieczynski, 54 vols., with suppl., Gulf Breeze, FL., 1976–90).

18. Georgi Apollonovich Gapon (1870–1906), the founder of the Assembly of Russian Factory and Mill Workers in St. Petersburg in 1903, escaped punishment for his role in the Bloody Sunday debacle. However, even though he subsequently met with Lenin, he was never trusted by revolutionaries. In 1906, he was murdered in Finland under mysterious circumstances.

19. R. Massie, p. 104. Quoted in the tsar's diary *Journal Intime*, p. 207. Translated by A. Pierre (Paris, Payot, 1925).

20. Ivan Platonovich Kaliaev (1877–1905) was born in Poland of a Russian father and a Polish mother, and he studied history and philology at Moscow University. Later he took up the study of law at St. Petersburg University, where he joined a student movement, was arrested, and was

sent into exile, unable to return to the university. He joined the Social Democratic Party and was given the nickname "the Poet."

21. Robert Payne, *The Fortress*, p. 361.
22. Payne, p. 384.
23. Payne, p. 387.
24. Payne, p. 392.
25. A cruiser in the Black Sea fleet, its crew rose in mutiny after being served meat infested with maggots. The sailors killed their officers and took over the ship. They sailed to Odessa, where they bombarded the city to support a strike that was in progress. The ship continued on to Romania, where the crew surrendered to authorities.
26. The *Duma* actually consisted of two chambers. The upper house or State Soviet, which was partly appointed by the tsar, had veto power over any initiative passed by the lower house or State *Duma*.
27. Originally members of the Socialist Revolutionary Party, the Maximalists broke away in 1904 to form their own terrorist group. After the revolution of 1917, most joined the Bolshevik Party.
28. Abraham Ascher, *P.A. Stolypin: The Search for Stability in Late Imperial Russia*, p. 382.
29. Alexander Feodorovich Kerensky (1881–1970), the son of a teacher and school administrator in Simbirsk, became a moderate socialist and a foe of autocracy. He served in the Provisional Government as minister of justice, minister of war, and eventually prime minister, where he was ousted by Vladimir Lenin. Ironically, Kerensky's father had written a letter of recommendation for Lenin, to assure university authorities that he was not a revolutionary.
30. Carl Peter Fabergé (1846–1920), the descendent of Swiss jewelers who had come to Russia during the reign of Catherine the Great, was famous for his workmanship, ingenuity, and extravagance. He first began the tradition of producing special eggs at Easter during the reign of Alexander III.
31. Rasputin's wife was a strong, good-looking woman with fair hair and dark eyes. She was apparently unperturbed by her husband's extramarital liaisons, claiming that "he has enough for all." She gave birth three times: Dmitri (1897), Maria (1898), and Varvara (1900).
32. Iliodor (1880–1952), the religious name of Sergei Mikhailovich Trufanov, was a Don Cossack who had been ordained a priest at age twenty. He subsequently studied in St. Petersburg for five years to become a monk. His ruthless determination to restore purity to the Church got him in trouble with his superiors, and he was eventually forced into exile. He went to New York City in 1921, became a Baptist, and published a book about Rasputin entitled *The Mad Monk of Russia*, for which he earned a considerable sum of money. However, he lost it all in the stock market crash of 1929 and later worked for a time as a janitor in the New York Metropolitan Life building in Madison Square. In 1952, he died destitute and alone in Bellevue hospital.
33. A term that generally refers to a highly respected elder in the Orthodox Church whose deep spirituality enabled him to console troubled souls.
34. Anna Alexandrovna Vyrubova (1888–1964) was the daughter of Alexander Taneev, who was director of the private chancellery of Nicholas II. She was arrested several times during and after the revolution and eventually escaped to Finland, although little is known about her life as an émigré.
35. The worst scandal of all occurred in March of 1915. Rasputin went to the fashionable Yar Restaurant in Moscow with three prostitutes and two journalists and got roaring drunk. Soon he was bragging about his intimacy with the empress and even claimed that "the old girl" had made the shirt he was wearing. When someone demanded that he prove his identity, he unzipped his pants and began waving his penis about. Eventually, Nicholas received a full report of the incident and summoned Rasputin to Tsarskoe Selo for an explanation. The *starets* was contrite; he admitted to being a sinner like everyone else but claimed he was encouraged to drink too much by those who sought to discredit him. Nicholas apparently accepted the explanation and took no sterner measure than to banish him to Pokrovskoe for a time.
36. Patrick J. Rollins, *The Modern Ency-*

clopedia of Russian and Soviet History,
"Iliodor," p. 146.

37. Reactionary groups which formed in
1905 in support of the tsar. They were notorious for their hatred of Jews, university
students, and members of free professions.
They frequently employed violence against
their enemies.

38. Alex De Jonge, *The Life and Times of
Gregory Rasputin,* p. 192. Quoted in *Voprosi
istorii,* 1964, no. X, p. 131.

39. During the revolution of 1905, Hermogen had unsuccessfully petitioned the
tsar to restore the patriarchate. Ironically,
this goal was eventually accomplished by the
Soviet dictator Josef Stalin, who had been
expelled in 1899 from the Tiflis Theological
Seminary by Hermogen himself. At the
time, Hermogen was the school's rector.

40. De Jonge, pp. 223–224. Quoted in
Sergei Trufanov's *The Mad Monk of Russia,*
p. 207 (New York, 1918).

41. De Jonge, p. 224. Quoted in A.I.
Spirodovich's *Les dernières années de la cour,*
p. 190 (Paris, Payot, 1928).

42. R. Massie, p. 183. Quoted in
Baroness Sophie Buxhoeveden's *The Life
and Tragedy of Alexandra Feodorovna,
Empress of Russia,* p. 132 (New York and
London, Longmans, Green, 1928).

43. R. Massie, p. 185. Quoted in Anna
Viroubova's (Vyrubova) *Memories of the
Russian Court,* p. 93 (New York, Macmil-
lan, 1923).

44. R. Massie, pp. 335–336.

45. De Jonge, p. 221. Quoted in *Peter-
burgskaya gazetta,* 13x13.

46. On January 15, 1915, Vyrubova was
brought unconscious to the hospital at
Tsarskoe Selo. The doctors were pessimistic
about her recovery. Rasputin arrived at her
bedside only the following day when the
end seemed near and spoke to her in a commanding voice, "Annushka, wake up, look
at me!" Not only did she regain consciousness, but answered, "Grigori, is that you?
Thank God." Vyrubova recovered, but was
never able to walk again — exactly as
Rasputin had predicted.

47. R. Massie, p. 350. Quoted in *Letters
of the Tsaritsa to the Tsar 1914–1916,* p. 307.
(Introduction by Sir Bernard Pares, London, Duckworth, 1923).

48. It was also in the summer of 1916

that the Russian army began a successful
campaign against the Austrians in Galicia.
This so alarmed the Germans that they
diverted eighteen divisions from the siege
of Verdun and prevented the Austrians
from following up their victory over the
Italians at Caporetto. But Alexandra,
prompted by Rasputin, demanded that
Nicholas halt the advance to prevent more
Russian casualties. The tsar finally issued
the order in October.

49. R. Massie, p. 363. Quoted in *The
Letters of the Tsar to the Tsaritsa 1914–1917,*
p. 307 (London, Bodley, Head: New York,
Dodd, Mead, 1929).

50. Pavel Miliukov (1859–1943), the
founder of the Constitutional Democratic
Party, or Kadets, admired Great Britain's
form of government and desired the same
to be established by legal methods in Russia.

51. Quoted in DeJonge, p. 294.

52. Vladimir Mitrofanovich Purishkevich (1870–1920) was a right-wing member
of the *Duma* and had previously been a
founding member of the Union of the Russian People. The son of a wealthy landowner in Bessarabia, he was elected to the
second, third, and fourth *Dumas.* However,
as a firm believer in autocracy, his main
activity was to disrupt its proceedings by
calling out insults, making faces, and, on at
least one occasion, parading about with a
carnation in his zipper. Purishkevich actually hoped that the tsar would eventually
abolish the Duma. However, he was
extremely patriotic, and during the war he
spent much time and his own money
procuring supplies for the army.

53. R. Massie, p. 369. Quoted in Sir
Bernard Pares' *The Fall of the Russian
Monarchy,* pp. 396–397 (New York, Vintage
Books, 1961), and *Paleologue* III, p. 111.

54. One of the oldest residences in St.
Petersburg, it was partially rebuilt in the
1760s by Vallin de la Mothe. It contains a
suite of ceremonial rooms including a
rotunda, several drawing rooms, and a theater that seats 200 people. After the revolution, it became known as the Teacher's
Palace.

55. De Jonge, p. 312. Quoted in N.D.
Zhevakhov, *Vospominaniya,* p. 272 (2 vols.
Munich, 1923).

56. Robert K. Massie, *Nicholas and Alexandra*, p. 374.

57. R. Massie, p. 374. Quoted in Pares, p. 399.

58. R. Massie, p. 377. Quoted in Vladimir Pourichkevitch's (Purishkevich) *Comme j'ai tue Raspoutine*, pp. 106–107 (Paris, Povolozky, 1923).

59. Many historians suspect that the conspirators exaggerated or lied about some aspects of the murder. A good source for further reading on this topic is Edvard Radzinsky's *The Rasputin File*, pp. 475–489.

60. Quoted in Radzinsky, p. 486.

BIBLIOGRAPHY

Alexander, John T. "Bulavin, Kondratii Afanas'evich." *Modern Encyclopedia of Russian and Soviet History*, ed. Joseph L. Wieczynsky, 54 vols. With suppl. Gulf Breeze, Florida: Academic International Press, 1976–1990.

_____. *Emperor of the Cossacks*. Lawrence, Kansas: Coronado Press, 1973.

_____. "Pugachev, Emelian Ivanovich." *Modern Encyclopedia of Russian and Soviet History*, ed. Joseph L. Wieczynsky, 54 vols. With suppl. Gulf Breeze, Florida: Academic International Press, 1976–1990.

Ascher, Abraham. *P.S. Stolypin: The Search for Stability in Late Imperial Russia*. Stanford, California: Stanford University Press, 2001.

Avakumovic, Ivan. "Black Hundreds." *Modern Encyclopedia of Russian and Soviet History*, ed. Joseph L. Wieczynsky, 54 vols. With suppl. Gulf Breeze, Florida: Academic International Press, 1976–1990.

_____. "Kropotkin, Petr Alekseevich." *Modern Encyclopedia of Russian and Soviet History*, ed. Joseph L. Wieczynsky, 54 vols. With suppl. Gulf Breeze, Florida: Academic International Press, 1976–1990.

Avrich, Paul. *Russian Rebels*. New York: W.W. Norton, 1972.

Barbour, Philip. *Dmitri, Called the Pretender, Tsar and Great Prince of all Russia 1605–1606*. Boston: Houghton Mifflin, 1966.

Baron, Samuel L. "Plekhanov, Georgii Valentinovich." *Modern Encyclopedia of Russian and Soviet History*, ed. Joseph L. Wieczynsky, 54 vols. With suppl. Gulf Breeze, Florida: Academic International Press, 1976–1990.

Blakely, Allison. "Mikhailov, Timofei Mikhailovich." *Modern Encyclopedia of Russian and Soviet History*, ed. Joseph L. Wieczynsky, 54 vols. With suppl. Gulf Breeze, Florida: Academic International Press, 1976–1990.

_____. "Pisarev, Dimitrii Ivanovich." *Modern Encyclopedia of Russian and Soviet History*, ed. Joseph L. Wieczynsky, 54 vols. With suppl. Gulf Breeze, Florida: Academic International Press, 1976–1990.

Bobrecht, Benson. *Fearful Majesty: The Life and Reign of Ivan the Terrible*. New York: G.P. Putnam's Sons, 1987.

Bulganov, V.I. "Pretenders to the Throne in Russia." *Modern Encyclopedia of Russian and Soviet History*, ed. Joseph L. Wieczynsky, 54 vols. With suppl. Gulf Breeze, Florida: Academic International Press, 1976–1990.

Chmielewski, Edward. "Third Section of His Imperial Majesty's Own Chancellory." *Modern Encyclopedia of Russian and Soviet History*, ed. Joseph L. Wieczynsky, 54 vols. With suppl. Gulf Breeze, Florida: Academic International Press, 1976–1990.

Christian, David. "Speranskii, Mikhail Mikhailovich." *Modern Encyclopedia of Russian and Soviet History*, ed. Joseph L. Wieczynsky, 54 vols. With suppl. Gulf Breeze, Florida: Academic International Press, 1976–1990.

Cowles, Virginia. *The Romanovs*. New York: Harper and Row, 1971.

Cracraft, James. "Khovansky, Ivan Ivanovich." *Modern Encyclopedia of Russian and Soviet History*, ed. Joseph L. Wieczynsky, 54 vols. With suppl. Gulf Breeze, Florida: Academic International Press, 1976–1990.

_____. "Mazepa, Ivan Stepanovich." *Modern Encyclopedia of Russian and Soviet History*, ed. Joseph L. Wieczynsky, 54 vols. With suppl. Gulf Breeze, Florida: Academic International Press, 1976–1990.

_____. "Menshikov, Alexander Danilovich." *Modern Encyclopedia of Russian and Soviet History*, ed. Joseph L. Wieczynsky, 54 vols. With suppl. Gulf Breeze, Florida: Academic International Press, 1976–1990.

_____. "Peter I the Great." *Modern Encyclopedia of Russian and Soviet History*, ed. Joseph L. Wieczynsky, 54 vols. With suppl. Gulf Breeze, Florida: Academic International Press, 1976–1990.

Crankshaft, Edward. *The Shadow of the Winter Palace*. Middlesex, England: Penguin, 1976.

Crummey, Robert O. *The Formation of Muscovy, 1304–1613*. New York: Longman, 1987.

_____. "The Kurbskii-Groznyi Controversy." *Modern Encyclopedia of Russian and Soviet History*, ed. Joseph L. Wieczynsky, 54 vols. With suppl. Gulf Breeze, Florida: Academic International Press, 1976–1990.

_____. "Petrovich, Alexei." *Modern Encyclopedia of Russian and Soviet History*, ed. Joseph L. Wieczynsky, 54 vols. With suppl. Gulf Breeze, Florida: Academic International Press, 1976–1990.

De Jonge, Alex. *Fire and Water: A Life of Peter the Great*. New York: Coward McCann and Geohegan, 1980.

_____. *The Life and Times of Grigorii Rasputin*. New York: Coard McCann, 1982.

D'Encausse, Helene Carriere. *Nicholas II: The Interrupted Transition*, trans. George Holoch. New York: Holms and Meier Publishers, 2000.

Dmytryshin, Basil. *Medieval Russia: A Source Book, 750–1800*. New York: Harcourt Brace Jovanovich, 1991.

_____. "Shuisky, Vasilii Ivanovich." *Modern Encyclopedia of Russian and Soviet History*, ed. Joseph L. Wieczynsky, 54 vols. With suppl. Gulf Breeze, Florida: Academic International Press, 1976–1990.

Dunning, Chester S.L. *Russia's First Civil War*. University Park: Pennsylvania State University Press, 2001.

_____. "Shuiskii, Vasilii Ivanovich." Modern Encyclopedia of Russian and Soviet History, ed., Joseph L. Wieczynski, 54 vols. With suppl. Gulf Breeze, Florida: Academic International Press, 1976–90.

Engel, Barbara Alpern. "Perovskaya, Sof'ia L'vovna." *Modern Encyclopedia of Russian and Soviet History*, ed. Joseph L. Wieczynsky, 54 vols. With suppl. Gulf Breeze, Florida: Academic International Press, 1976–1990.

Evans, John L. "Saltykov-Shchedrin, Mikhail Evgrafovich." *Modern Encyclopedia of Russian and Soviet History*, ed. Joseph L. Wieczynsky, 54 vols. With suppl. Gulf Breeze, Florida: Academic International Press, 1976–1990.

Figes, Orlando. *A People's Tragedy: A History of the Russian Revolution.* New York: Penguin, 1999.

Freeze, Gregory, ed. *Russia: A History.* New York: Oxford University Press, 1997.

Fuhrmann, Joseph T. "Avvakum, Petrovich." *Modern Encyclopedia of Russian and Soviet History*, ed. Joseph L. Wieczynsky, 54 vols. With suppl. Gulf Breeze, Florida: Academic International Press, 1976–1990.

_____. *Tsar Alexis: His Reign and His Russia.* Gulf Breeze, Florida: Academic International Press, 1981.

Graham, Hugh F. "Copper Revolt." *Modern Encyclopedia of Russian and Soviet History*, ed. Joseph L. Wieczynsky, 54 vols. With suppl. Gulf Breeze, Florida: Academic International Press, 1976–1990.

_____. "Fedor Ivanovich." Modern Encyclopedia of Russian and Soviet History, ed. Joseph L. Wieczynski, 54 vols. With suppl. Gulf Breeze, Florida: Academic International Press, 1976–90.

_____. "Filipp." *Modern Encyclopedia of Russian and Soviet History*, ed. Joseph L. Wieczynsky, 54 vols. With suppl. Gulf Breeze, Florida: Academic International Press, 1976–1990.

_____. "Viskovatyi, Ivan Martynovich." *Modern Encyclopedia of Russian and Soviet History*, ed. Joseph L. Wieczynsky, 54 vols. With suppl. Gulf Breeze, Florida: Academic International Press, 1976–1990.

Graham, Stephen. Boris Godunov. Ann Arbor, Michigan: Archon Books, 1970.

Griffiths, David M. "Biron, Ernst Johann." *Modern Encyclopedia of Russian and Soviet History*, ed. Joseph L. Wieczynsky, 54 vols. With suppl. Gulf Breeze, Florida: Academic International Press, 1976–1990.

_____. "Catherine II (Catherine the Great: 1729–1796)." *Modern Encyclopedia of Russian and Soviet History*, ed. Joseph L. Wieczynsky, 54 vols. With suppl. Gulf Breeze, Florida: Academic International Press, 1976–1990.

_____. "Ivanovna, Anna." *Modern Encyclopedia of Russian and Soviet History*, ed. Joseph L. Wieczynsky, 54 vols. With suppl. Gulf Breeze, Florida: Academic International Press, 1976–1990.

Hart, James G. "Razin, Stepan Timofeevich." *Modern Encyclopedia of Russian and Soviet History*, ed. Joseph L. Wieczynsky, 54 vols. With suppl. Gulf Breeze, Florida: Academic International Press, 1976–1990.

Heilbronner, Hans. "Loris-Melikov, Mikhail Tarelovich." *Modern Encyclopedia of Russian and Soviet History*, ed. Joseph L. Wieczynsky, 54 vols. With suppl. Gulf Breeze, Florida: Academic International Press, 1976–1990.

Hellie, Richard. "Serfdom in Russia." *Modern Encyclopedia of Russian and Soviet History*, ed. Joseph L. Wieczynsky, 54 vols. With suppl. Gulf Breeze, Florida: Academic International Press, 1976–1990.

Herzen, Michael von. "Herzen, Alexander Ivanovich." *Modern Encyclopedia of Russian and Soviet History*, ed. Joseph L. Wieczynsky, 54 vols. With suppl. Gulf Breeze, Florida: Academic International Press, 1976–1990.

Hill, William H. "Alexander II." *Modern Encyclopedia of Russian and Soviet History*, ed. Joseph L. Wieczynsky, 54 vols. With suppl. Gulf Breeze, Florida: Academic International Press, 1976–1990.

Hingley, Ronald. *The Tsars.* New York: Macmillan, 1968.

Hughes, Lindsey A.J. "Alekseevich, Fedor," *Modern Encyclopedia of Russian and*

Soviet History, ed. Joseph L. Wieczynsky, 54 vols. With suppl. Gulf Breeze, Florida: Academic International Press, 1976–1990.

_____. "Golitsyn, Vasilii Vasil'evich." *Modern Encyclopedia of Russian and Soviet History*, ed. Joseph L. Wieczynsky, 54 vols. With suppl. Gulf Breeze, Florida: Academic International Press, 1976–1990.

_____. *Russia in the Age of Peter the Great*. New Haven: Yale University Press, 1998.

_____. *Sophia, Regent of Russia 1657–1704*. New Haven: Yale University Press, 1998.

Jenkins, Michael. *Arakcheev–Grand Vizer of the Russian Empire*. New York: Dial Press, 1969.

Johnson, Richard. "Grinevitskii, Ignatii Ioakimovich." *Modern Encyclopedia of Russian and Soviet History*, ed. Joseph L. Wieczynsky, 54 vols. With suppl. Gulf Breeze, Florida: Academic International Press, 1976–1990.

_____. "Natanson, Mark Andreevich." *Modern Encyclopedia of Russian and Soviet History*, ed. Joseph L. Wieczynsky, 54 vols. With suppl. Gulf Breeze, Florida: Academic International Press, 1976–1990.

Jones, David R. "Breshko-Breshkovskaia, Ekaterina Konstantinovna." *Modern Encyclopedia of Russian and Soviet History*, ed. Joseph L. Wieczynsky, 54 vols. With suppl. Gulf Breeze, Florida: Academic International Press, 1976– 1990.

Keenan, Edward. *The Kurbskii-Groznyi Apocrypha*. Cambridge Mass.: Harvard University Press, 1971.

Keep, J.L.H. "The Regime of Filaret, 1618–1633." *Slavonic and East European Review*, XXXVIII, no. 86 (1957), pp. 100–122.

Kimball, Alan. "Karakozov, Dmitrii Vladimirovich." *Modern Encyclopedia of Russian and Soviet History*, ed. Joseph L. Wieczynsky, 54 vols. With suppl. Gulf Breeze, Florida: Academic International Press, 1976–1990.

_____. "Lavrov, Petr Lavrovovich." *Modern Encyclopedia of Russian and Soviet History*, ed. Joseph L. Wieczynsky, 54 vols. With suppl. Gulf Breeze, Florida: Academic International Press, 1976–1990.

Kivelson, Valerie. "The Devil Stole His Mind: The Tsar and the 1948 Uprising." *American Historical Review*, June 1993, pp. 733–756.

Krasnodaev, B.I. *The Cossacks*. New York: Holt, Rinehardt and Winston, 1984.

_____. "Supreme Privy Council." *Modern Encyclopedia of Russian and Soviet History*, ed. Joseph L. Wieczynsky, 54 vols. With suppl. Gulf Breeze, Florida: Academic International Press, 1976–1990.

Levin, Sh. M. "Zheliabov, Andrei Ivanovichl." *Modern Encyclopedia of Russian and Soviet History*, ed. Joseph L. Wieczynsky, 54 vols. With suppl. Gulf Breeze, Florida: Academic International Press, 1976–1990.

Lieven, Dominic. *Nicholas II: Twilight of the Empire*. New York: St. Martin's Press, 1993.

Lincoln, Bruce. "Lunin, Mikhail Sergeevich." *Modern Encyclopedia of Russian and Soviet History*, ed. Joseph L. Wieczynsky, 54 vols. With suppl. Gulf Breeze, Florida: Academic International Press, 1976–1990.

_____. *Nicholas I*. DeKalb, Illinois: Northern University Press, 1978.

_____. *The Romanovs, Autocrats of All the Russias*. New York: Doubleday, 1981.

Longworth, Philip. *Alexis, Tsar of All the Russias*. New York: Franklin Watts, 1984.

_____. *The Cossacks*. Austin, Texas: Holt, Rinehardt and Winston, 1967.

_____. *The Three Empresses: Catherine I, Anne and Elizabeth of Russia*. Austin, Texas: Holt, Rinehart and Winston, 1972.

Lupinin, Nickolas. "Hermogen." *Modern Encyclopedia of Russian and Soviet His-*

tory, ed. Joseph L. Wieczynsky, 54 vols. With suppl. Gulf Breeze, Florida: Academic International Press, 1976–1990.

Maderiaga, Isabel de. *Russia in the Age of Catherine the Great*. New Haven: Yale University Press, 1981.

Margaret, Jacques. *The Russian Empire and Grand Duchy of Muscovy*. Trans. and ed. by Chester S. L. Dunning. Pittsburgh: University of Pittsburgh Press, 1983.

Massie, Robert K. *Nicholas and Alexandra*. New York: Atheneum, 1967.

_____. *Peter the Great. His Life and World*. New York: Ballentine, 1981.

Massie, Suzanne. *Land of the Firebird: The Beauty of Old Russia*. New York: Simon and Schuster, 1980.

Mazour, Anatole G. 1825. *The First Russian Revolution*. Stanford, California: Stanford University Press, 1937.

McConnell, Allen. "Alexander I." *Modern Encyclopedia of Russian and Soviet History*, ed. Joseph L. Wieczynsky, 54 vols. With suppl. Gulf Breeze, Florida: Academic International Press, 1976–1990.

_____. *Alexander I: Paternalistic Reformer*. New York: T.Y. Crowell, 1970.

_____. "Radishchev, Alexander Nikolaevich." *Modern Encyclopedia of Russian and Soviet History*, ed. Joseph L. Wieczynsky, 54 vols. With suppl. Gulf Breeze, Florida: Academic International Press, 1976–1990.

McGrew, Roderick E. "Cholera in Russia." *Modern Encyclopedia of Russian and Soviet History*, ed. Joseph L. Wieczynsky, 54 vols. With suppl. Gulf Breeze, Florida: Academic International Press, 1976–1990.

_____. *Paul I of Russia*. Oxford: Clarendon Press, 1992.

Micciche, Pasquale E. "Lizogub, Dmitrii Andreevich." *Modern Encyclopedia of Russian and Soviet History*, ed. Joseph L. Wieczynsky, 54 vols. With suppl. Gulf Breeze, Florida: Academic International Press, 1976–1990.

_____. "Zaichnevskii, Petr Grigor'evich." *Modern Encyclopedia of Russian and Soviet History*, ed. Joseph L. Wieczynsky, 54 vols. With suppl. Gulf Breeze, Florida: Academic International Press, 1976–1990.

Michels, Georg. *At War with the Church: Religious Dissent in Seventeenth-Century Russia*. Stanford, California: Stanford University Press, 1999.

Miller, Forrest A. "Nihilism." *Modern Encyclopedia of Russian and Soviet History*, ed. Joseph L. Wieczynsky, 54 vols. With suppl. Gulf Breeze, Florida: Academic International Press, 1976–1990.

Mohan, John M. "Dobroliubov, Nikolai Aleksandrovich." *Modern Encyclopedia of Russian and Soviet History*, ed. Joseph L. Wieczynsky, 54 vols. With suppl. Gulf Breeze, Florida: Academic International Press, 1976–1990.

Moynahan, Brian. *The Russian Century*. New York: Random House, 1994.

Munro, George E. "Elizabeth Petrovna." *Modern Encyclopedia of Russian and Soviet History*, ed. Joseph L. Wieczynsky, 54 vols. With suppl. Gulf Breeze, Florida: Academic International Press, 1976–1990.

_____. "Munnich, Burchard Christopher." *Modern Encyclopedia of Russian and Soviet History*, ed. Joseph L. Wieczynsky, 54 vols. With suppl. Gulf Breeze, Florida: Academic International Press, 1976–1990.

_____. "Pahlen (von der Palen), Petr Alekseevich." *Modern Encyclopedia of Russian and Soviet History*, ed. Joseph L. Wieczynsky, 54 vols. With suppl. Gulf Breeze, Florida: Academic International Press, 1976–1990.

Nekina, M.V. "Decembrists' Uprising of 1825." *Modern Encyclopedia of Russian and Soviet History*, ed. Joseph L. Wieczynsky, 54 vols. With suppl. Gulf Breeze, Florida: Academic International Press, 1976–1990.

Nicholl, G. Douglas. "Nikon." *Modern Encyclopedia of Russian and Soviet History*, ed. Joseph L. Wieczynsky, 54 vols. With suppl. Gulf Breeze, Florida: Academic International Press, 1976–1990.

_____. "Old Believers." *Modern Encyclopedia of Russian and Soviet History*, ed. Joseph L. Wieczynsky, 54 vols. With suppl. Gulf Breeze, Florida: Academic International Press, 1976–1990.

_____. "People's Will Party." *Modern Encyclopedia of Russian and Soviet History*, ed. Joseph L. Wieczynsky, 54 vols. With suppl. Gulf Breeze, Florida: Academic International Press, 1976–1990.

Noonan, Norma C. "Zasulich, Vera Ivanovna." *Modern Encyclopedia of Russian and Soviet History*, ed. Joseph L. Wieczynsky, 54 vols. With suppl. Gulf Breeze, Florida: Academic International Press, 1976–1990.

Nutsch, James G. "Northern Society of the Decembrist Movement." *Modern Encyclopedia of Russian and Soviet History*, ed. Joseph L. Wieczynsky, 54 vols. With suppl. Gulf Breeze, Florida: Academic International Press, 1976–1990.

O'Connor, Timothy E. "Tikhomirov, Lev Alexandrovich." *Modern Encyclopedia of Russian and Soviet History*, ed. Joseph L. Wieczynsky, 54 vols. With suppl. Gulf Breeze, Florida: Academic International Press, 1976–1990.

Offord, Derek. *Nineteenth Century Russia: Opposition to Autocracy*. New York: Longman, 1999.

O'Meara, Patrick J. "Ivanovich, Pestel' Pavel ." *Modern Encyclopedia of Russian and Soviet History,* ed., Joseph L. Wieczynski, 54 vols. With suppl. Gulf Breeze, Florida, 1976–1990.

_____. "Ryleev, Kondratii Fedorovich." *Modern Encyclopedia of Russian and Soviet History,* ed., Joseph L. Wieczynski, 54 vols. With suppl. Gulf Breeze, Florida: Academic International Press, 1976–1990.

Oppenheim, Samuel A. "Succession Crisis of 1630." *Modern Encyclopedia of Russian and Soviet History*, ed. Joseph L. Wieczynsky, 54 vols. With suppl. Gulf Breeze, Florida: Academic International Press, 1976–1990.

Orchard, G. Edward. "Fedorovich, Mikhail." *Modern Encyclopedia of Russian and Soviet History*, ed. Joseph L. Wieczynsky, 54 vols. With suppl. Gulf Breeze, Florida: Academic International Press, 1976–1990.

_____. "Filaret." *Modern Encyclopedia of Russian and Soviet History*, ed. Joseph L. Wieczynsky, 54 vols. With suppl. Gulf Breeze, Florida: Academic International Press, 1976–1990.

_____. "Godunov, Boris." *Modern Encyclopedia of Russian and Soviet History*, ed. Joseph L. Wieczynsky, 54 vols. With suppl. Gulf Breeze, Florida: Academic International Press, 1976–1990._____. "Ivanovich, Dmitrii." *Modern Encyclopedia of Russian and Soviet History*, ed. Joseph L. Wieczynsky, 54 vols. With suppl. Gulf Breeze, Florida: Academic International Press, 1976–1990.

_____. "Morozova, Feodosiia." *Modern Encyclopedia of Russian and Soviet History*, ed. Joseph L. Wieczynsky, 54 vols. With suppl. Gulf Breeze, Florida: Academic International Press, 1976–1990.

_____. "Solovetskii Upsrising of 1668–1676." *Modern Encyclopedia of Russian and Soviet History*, ed. Joseph L. Wieczynsky, 54 vols. With suppl. Gulf Breeze, Florida: Academic International Press, 1976–1990.

_____. "Time of Troubles." *Modern Encyclopedia of Russian and Soviet History*, ed. Joseph L. Wieczynsky, 54 vols. With suppl. Gulf Breeze, Florida: Academic International Press, 1976–1990.

_____. "Zarutskii, Ivan Martynovich." *Modern Encyclopedia of Russian and Soviet History*, ed. Joseph L. Wieczynsky, 54 vols. With suppl. Gulf Breeze, Florida: Academic International Press, 1976–1990.

Payne, Robert. *The Fortress.* New York: Simon and Schuster, 1957.

_____, and Nikita Romanoff. *Ivan the Terrible.* New York: T.Y. Crowell, 1975.

Pereira, N.G.O. "Chernyshevskii, Nikolai Gavrilovich." *Modern Encyclopedia of Russian and Soviet History*, ed. Joseph L. Wieczynsky, 54 vols. With suppl. Gulf Breeze, Florida: Academic International Press, 1976–1990.

Perrie, Maureen. "Socialist Revolutionary Party." *Modern Encyclopedia of Russian and Soviet History*, ed. Joseph L. Wieczynsky, 54 vols. With suppl. Gulf Breeze, Florida: Academic International Press, 1976–1990.

Pertzoff, Margaret H. "Plehve, Vyacheslav Konstantinovich." *Modern Encyclopedia of Russian and Soviet History*, ed. Joseph L. Wieczynsky, 54 vols. With suppl. Gulf Breeze, Florida: Academic International Press, 1976–1990.

Platonov, Sergei. *The Time of Troubles.* Trans. John T. Alexander. Lawrence: University of Kansas Press, 1970.

Plimak, E.G. "Nechaev, Sergei Gennadievich." *Modern Encyclopedia of Russian and Soviet History*, ed. Joseph L. Wieczynsky, 54 vols. With suppl. Gulf Breeze, Florida: Academic International Press, 1976–1990.

Pollard, Alan P. "Movement to the People." *Modern Encyclopedia of Russian and Soviet History*, ed. Joseph L. Wieczynsky, 54 vols. With suppl. Gulf Breeze, Florida: Academic International Press, 1976–1990.

Pomper, Philip. *Sergei Nechaev.* New Brunswick, New Jersey: Rutgers University Press, 1979.

Purishkevich, V.M. *The Murder of Rasputin.* Ed. Michael E. Shaw, trans. Bella Costello. Ann Arbor, Michigan: Ardis, 1985.

Ragsdale, Hugh. "Paul I (Pavel Petrovich)." *Modern Encyclopedia of Russian and Soviet History*, ed. Joseph L. Wieczynsky, 54 vols. With suppl. Gulf Breeze, Florida: Academic International Press, 1976–1990.

Razinsky, Edvard. *The Rasputin File.* Trans. Judson Rosengrant. New York: Anchor, 2000.

Riasanovsky, Nicholas. *A History of Russia.* New York and Oxford: Oxford University Press, 1984.

Rollins, Patrick J. "Iliodor." *Modern Encyclopedia of Russian and Soviet History*, ed. Joseph L. Wieczynsky, 54 vols. With suppl. Gulf Breeze, Florida: Academic International Press, 1976–1990.

_____. "Rasputin, Grigorii Efimovich." *Modern Encyclopedia of Russian and Soviet History*, ed. Joseph L. Wieczynsky, 54 vols. With suppl. Gulf Breeze, Florida: Academic International Press, 1976–1990.

Roweland, Daniel B. "Mniszek, Marina." *Modern Encyclopedia of Russian and Soviet History*, ed. Joseph L. Wieczynsky, 54 vols. With suppl. Gulf Breeze, Florida: Academic International Press, 1976–1990.

_____. "Trubetskoi, Dmitrii Timofeevich." *Modern Encyclopedia of Russian and Soviet History*, ed. Joseph L. Wieczynsky, 54 vols. With suppl. Gulf Breeze, Florida: Academic International Press, 1976–1990.

Rudnitskaia, E.L. "Ogarev, Nikolai Platonovich." *Modern Encyclopedia of Russian and Soviet History*, ed. Joseph L. Wieczynsky, 54 vols. With suppl. Gulf Breeze,

Florida: Academic International Press, 1976–1990.

Sablinsky, Walter, "Police Socialism." *Modern Encyclopedia of Russian and Soviet History*, ed. Joseph L. Wieczynsky, 54 vols. With suppl. Gulf Breeze, Florida: Academic International Press, 1976–1990.

Schlafly, Daniel L. "Military Colonies." *Modern Encyclopedia of Russian and Soviet History*, ed. Joseph L. Wieczynsky, 54 vols. With suppl. Gulf Breeze, Florida: Academic International Press, 1976–1990.

Schweizer, Karl W. "Arakcheev, Aleksei Andreevich," *Modern Encyclopedia of Russian and Soviet History*, ed. Joseph L. Wieczynsky, 54 vols. With suppl. Gulf Breeze, Florida: Academic International Press, 1976–1990.

_____. "Ivan IV (Ivan Antonovich)." *Modern Encyclopedia of Russian and Soviet History*, ed. Joseph L. Wieczynsky, 54 vols. With suppl. Gulf Breeze, Florida: Academic International Press, 1976–1990.

_____. "Kurbsky, Andrei Mikhailovich." *Modern Encyclopedia of Russian and Soviet History*, ed. Joseph L. Wieczynsky, 54 vols. With suppl. Gulf Breeze, Florida: Academic International Press, 1976–1990.

Service, Robert. *Lenin*. Cambridge, Massachusetts: Harvard University Press, 2000.

Shul'gin, V.S. "Schism in Russian Orthodox Church." *Modern Encyclopedia of Russian and Soviet History*, ed. Joseph L. Wieczynsky, 54 vols. With suppl. Gulf Breeze, Florida: Academic International Press, 1976–1990.

Skrynnikov, Ruslan G. *Boris Godunov*. The Russian Series, v. 35. Moscow: Nauka, 1978.

_____. *Ivan Groznyi. Moscow:* Nauka, 1980.

_____. *Samozvantsev v Rossii, v Nachale XVII veka-Grigorii Otrep'ev*. Novosibirsk: Nauka, 1987.

_____. *The Time of Troubles: Russia in Crisis*. Ed. and trans. Hugh Graham. Gulf Breeze, Florida: Academic International Press, 1988.

Sokol, Edward D. "Cossacks." *Modern Encyclopedia of Russian and Soviet History*, ed. Joseph L. Wieczynsky, 54 vols. With suppl. Gulf Breeze, Florida: Academic International Press, 1976–1990.

Stites, Richard. "Figner, Vera Nikolaevna." *Modern Encyclopedia of Russian and Soviet History*, ed. Joseph L. Wieczynsky, 54 vols. With suppl. Gulf Breeze, Florida: Academic International Press, 1976–1990.

Timberlake, Charles E. "Alexander III." *Modern Encyclopedia of Russian and Soviet History*, ed. Joseph L. Wieczynsky, 54 vols. With suppl. Gulf Breeze, Florida: Academic International Press, 1976–1990.

Tobias, Henry J. "Azev, Evno Fishelevich." *Modern Encyclopedia of Russian and Soviet History*, ed. Joseph L. Wieczynsky, 54 vols. With suppl. Gulf Breeze, Florida: Academic International Press, 1976–1990.

Troyat, Henri. *Ivan the Terrible*. Trans. Joan Pinkham. New York: E.P. Dutton, 1984.

Ulam, Adam. *Alexander of Russia-Napoleon's Conqueror*. Trans. by Joan Pinkham. New York: E.P. Dutton, 1980.

_____. *In the Name of the People*. New York: Viking Press, 1970.

Venturi, Franco. *Roots of Revolution*. London: Phoenix Press, 1972.

Vernadsky, George. *A History of Russia. Vol. 5*. New Haven: Yale University Press, 1963.

Warnes, David. *Chronicle of the Russian Tsars*. London: Thames and Hudson, 1999.

Warth, Robert D. "Nicholas II (Nikolai Aleksandrovich)." *Modern Encyclopedia of Russian and Soviet History*, ed. Joseph L. Wieczynsky, 54 vols. With suppl. Gulf Breeze, Florida: Academic International Press, 1976–1990.

_____. "Pobedonostsev, Konstantin Petrovich." *Modern Encyclopedia of Russian and Soviet History*, ed. Joseph L. Wieczynsky, 54 vols. With suppl. Gulf Breeze, Florida: Academic International Press, 1976–1990.

_____. "Potemkin Mutiny of 1905." *Modern Encyclopedia of Russian and Soviet History*, ed. Joseph L. Wieczynsky, 54 vols. With suppl. Gulf Breeze, Florida: Academic International Press, 1976–1990.

_____. "Sipiagin, Dmitrii Sergeevich." *Modern Encyclopedia of Russian and Soviet History*, ed. Joseph L. Wieczynsky, 54 vols. With suppl. Gulf Breeze, Florida: Academic International Press, 1976–1990.

_____. "Stolypin, Petr Arkad'evich." *Modern Encyclopedia of Russian and Soviet History*, ed. Joseph L. Wieczynsky, 54 vols. With suppl. Gulf Breeze, Florida: Academic International Press, 1976–1990.

Weeks, Albert L. "Tkachev, Petr Nikitich." *Modern Encyclopedia of Russian and Soviet History*, ed. Joseph L. Wieczynsky, 54 vols. With suppl. Gulf Breeze, Florida: Academic International Press, 1976–1990.

Weider, George. "Butashevich-Petrashevskii, Mikhail Vasil'evich." *Modern Encyclopedia of Russian and Soviet History*, ed. Joseph L. Wieczynsky, 54 vols. With suppl. Gulf Breeze, Florida: Academic International Press, 1976–1990.

Weissman, Neil B. "Witte, Sergei Yul'evich." *Modern Encyclopedia of Russian and Soviet History*, ed. Joseph L. Wieczynsky, 54 vols. With suppl. Gulf Breeze, Florida: Academic International Press, 1976–1990.

Wieczynski, Joseph L. "Semenovskii Regiment, Mutiny of." *Modern Encyclopedia of Russian and Soviet History*, ed. Joseph L. Wieczynsky, 54 vols. With suppl. Gulf Breeze, Florida: Academic International Press, 1976–1990.

_____. "Uglich Affair." *Modern Encyclopedia of Russian and Soviet History*, ed. Joseph L. Wieczynsky, 54 vols. With suppl. Gulf Breeze, Florida: Academic International Press, 1976–1990.

Wiita, John. "Bolotnikov, Ivan Isaevich." *Modern Encyclopedia of Russian and Soviet History*, ed. Joseph L. Wieczynsky, 54 vols. With suppl. Gulf Breeze, Florida: Academic International Press, 1976–1990.

Yarmolinsky, Avrahm. *Road to Revolution*. Princeton: Princeton University Press, 1977.

Zenkovsky, Serge. "Ivan IV (Ivan Vasil'evich)." *Modern Encyclopedia of Russian and Soviet History*, ed. Joseph L. Wieczynsky, 54 vols. With suppl. Gulf Breeze, Florida: Academic International Press, 1976–1990.

_____. *Medieval Russia's Epics, Chronicles and Tales*. New York: E.P. Dutton, 1974.

INDEX

293